美しい情景イラストレーション
ノスタルジー編
情緒的な風景を描くクリエイターズファイル

Retrospective Scenes from a Sentimental World:
Background Illustrations and Scenes by an Up-and-Coming Creators

Retrospective Scenes from a Sentimental World:
Background Illustrations and Scenes by an Up-and-Coming Creators

PIE International Inc.
2-32-4 Minami-Otsuka, Toshima-ku, Tokyo 170-0005 JAPAN
international@pie.co.jp
www.pie.co.jp/english

ISBN978-4-7562-5149-7 (Outside Japan)
Printed in Japan

はじめに

いつまでも色褪せることなく、心に残っているあの日の風景。
思い出せばあの頃の気持ちにかえれる、
大切な人や場所を思い出させてくれる、
誰しもそんな心に残っている風景があるのではないでしょうか。
『美しい情景イラストレーション』第3弾となる本書では
「ノスタルジー」をテーマに、感情を揺さぶられるような
情緒的な風景を描くクリエイターの方々とその作品を紹介します。
目で見たままの、ただの美しい風景であれば
スマートフォンで画像検索すれば済むこともあるかもしれません。
本書でご紹介している作品は、ただの風景に止まらない、
クリエイター自身がさまざまな感情に丁寧に向き合い、
ニュアンスを汲み取り、描かれているキャラクターの心情や
切り取った場面の空気感、伝えたい状況を
印象的に描写したイラスト作品ならではの美しさがあります。
イラストだからこそ味わえる美しい情景の数々を
作品を通してお楽しみいただけたら幸いです。
最後になりましたが本書を制作するにあたり、
ご協力いただいたクリエイターの皆様、
その他すべての方々に心よりお礼申し上げます。

パイ インターナショナル編集部

Preface

An unforgettable scene that remains in your memory without fading.
Perhaps each one of us has one or more scenes in our minds
that upon remembering, take us back to that very moment,
calling to mind some special person or place.
Following *Everyday Scenes from a Parallel World* and *Beautiful Scenes from a Fantasy World*,
this third title presents illustrators and their nostalgic illustration,
showing emotional scenes that inspire our emotions.
Scenes that you have witnesses yourself or simply beautiful scenes
may be found with a quick search on the internet.
But the illustrations in this book are not simply "scenes".
Instead, they have a unique beauty to them, as the illustrators
thoughtfully approach a variety of emotions, understand the nuances,
and express the feelings of a drawn character, the mood of a removed location,
and a certain situation that the illustrator wanted to show, all in an impactful way.
Through the works in this book, I hope that you can enjoy the many beautiful scenes
that can only be experienced through illustrations.
We want to thank all those who helped with this book,
including all the illustrators and everyone else involved.
Thank you for making this book possible.

PIE International Inc. Editorial Department

目 次　|　Contents

本書の見方　|　Book Layout

作品掲載ページ
Works Page

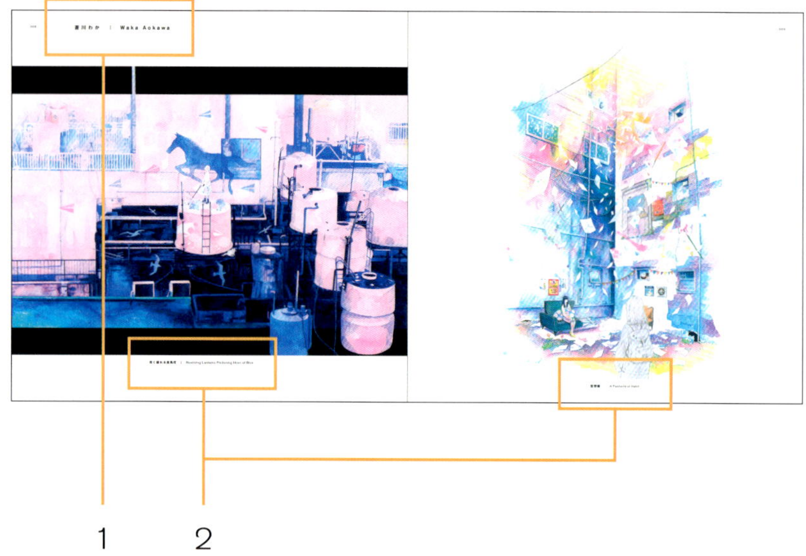

プロフィール掲載ページ
Profile Page

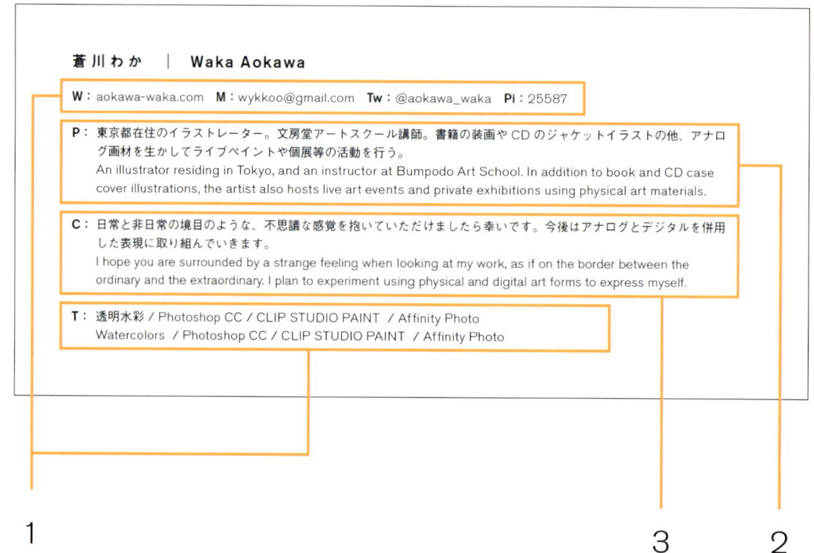

1: 作家名
Artist's name

2: 作品タイトル
Work title

1: ホームページや SNS 等のアドレス、または ID、メールアドレス、
使用している制作ツール
Website or social media website address, as well as usernames,
email addresses, and tools used.

2: 作家のプロフィール
Artist's profile

3: 創作についてのコメントやメッセージ
Comments and messages regarding the creation process.

これからご紹介する作品は、33 名のクリエイターの方々による
美しい情景イラストの世界です。
夕焼けに染まる街並み、一緒に歩いた帰り道、放課後の教室など、
今も記憶の片隅に在り続ける風景を情感いっぱいに描いた
心に染みる作品の数々をお楽しみください。
また、クリエイターの方々と本書を手に取ってくださった方々との
架け橋になることを願い、巻末にクリエイターの方々の
プロフィール、コメント等を掲載しております。

The illustrations in this book represent

a world of beautiful scenes from the eyes of 33 illustrators.

A town draped in dusk,

that road you walked together,

or that classroom after school.

Enjoy the many touching illustrations in this book,

featuring the plethora of emotions connected to

those scenes that still remain in the back of our minds.

We've also included background information,

comments, and more at the back of the book

about each of the illustrators featured

in this book in the hopes that

we may be able to bridge the gap

between viewer and illustrator.

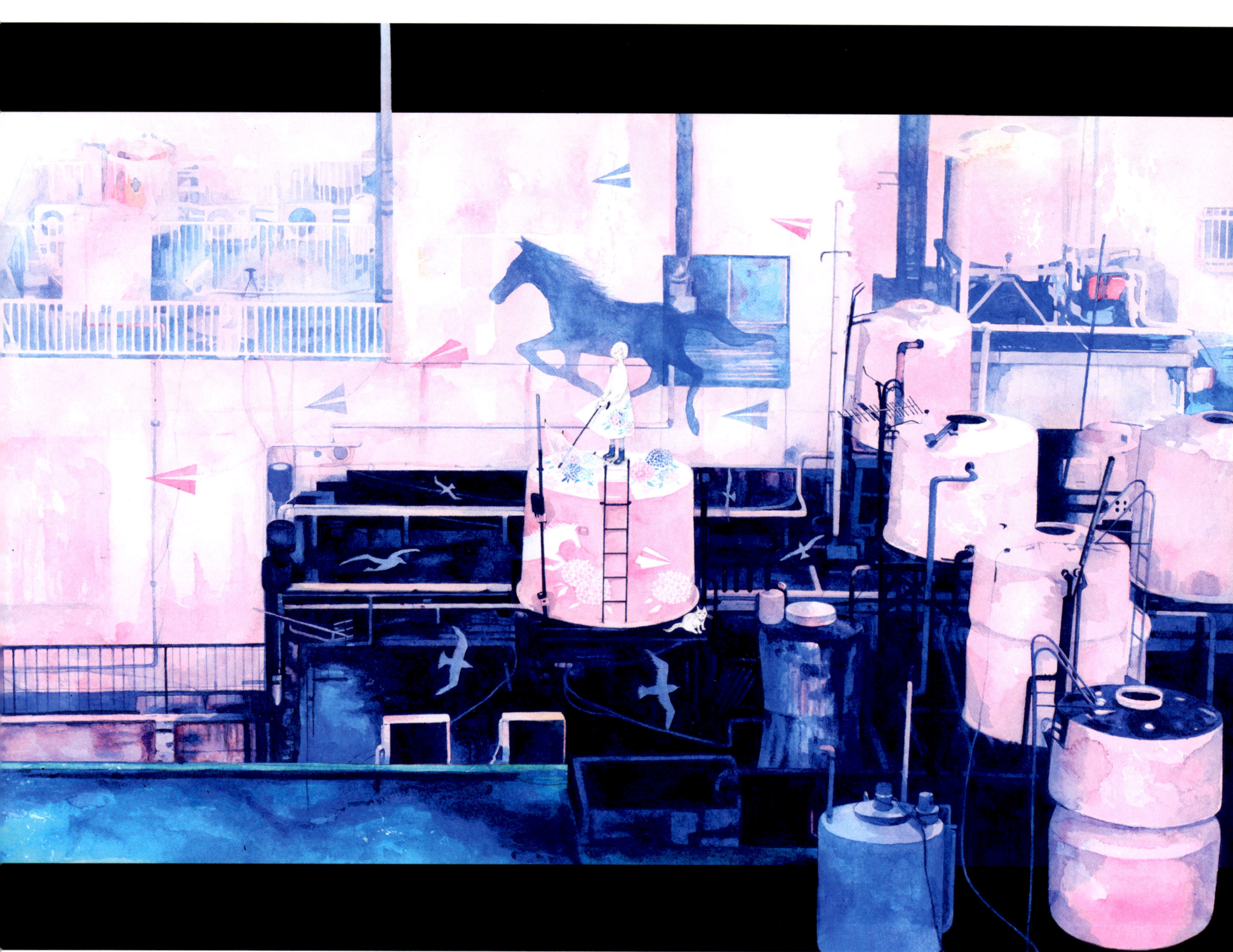

青く揺れる走馬灯　│　Revolving Lanterns Flickering Hues of Blue

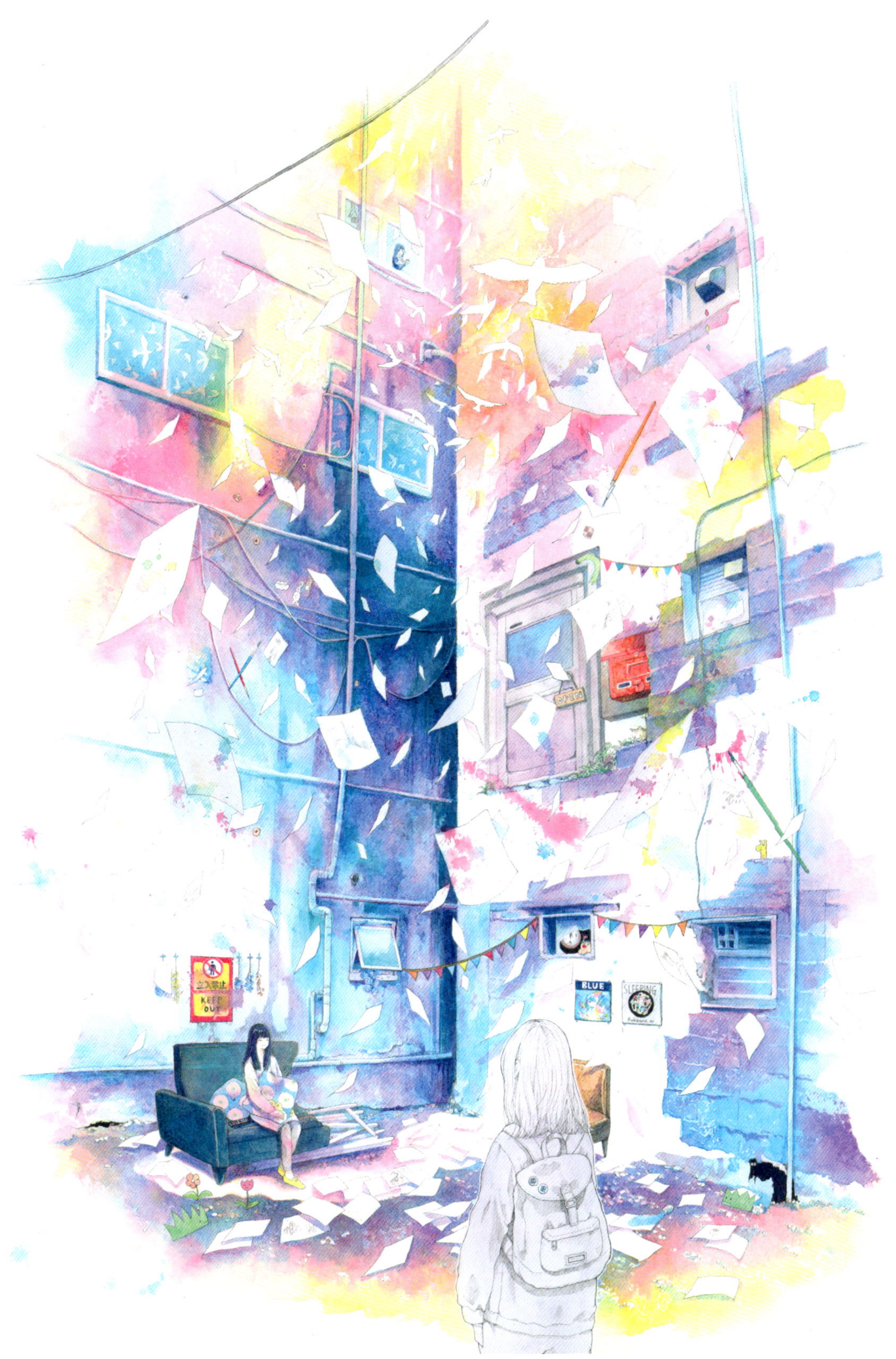

空想癖　│　A Fantastical Habit

蒼川わか ｜ Waka Aokawa

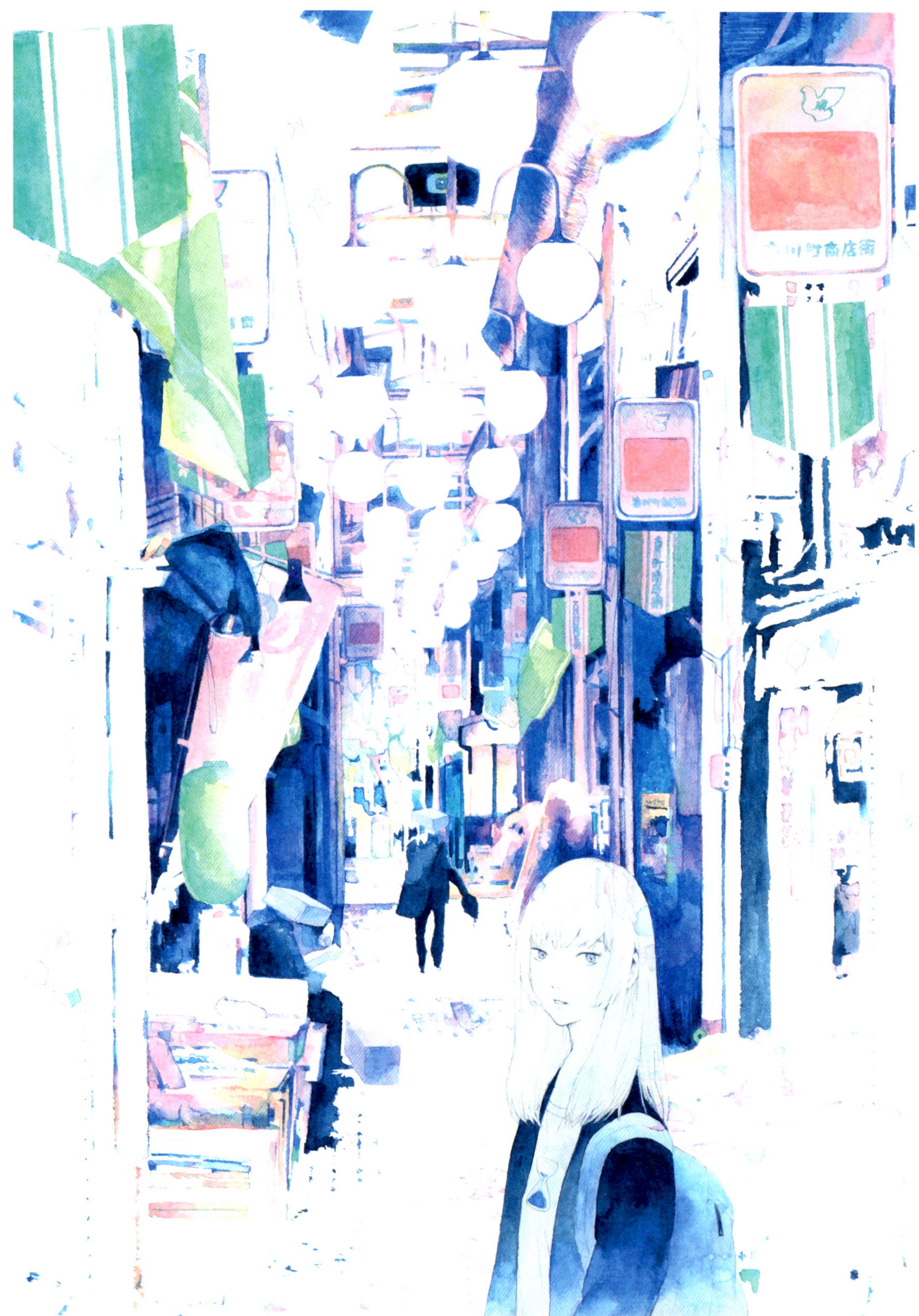

夢から醒めゆく ｜ Waking from a Dream

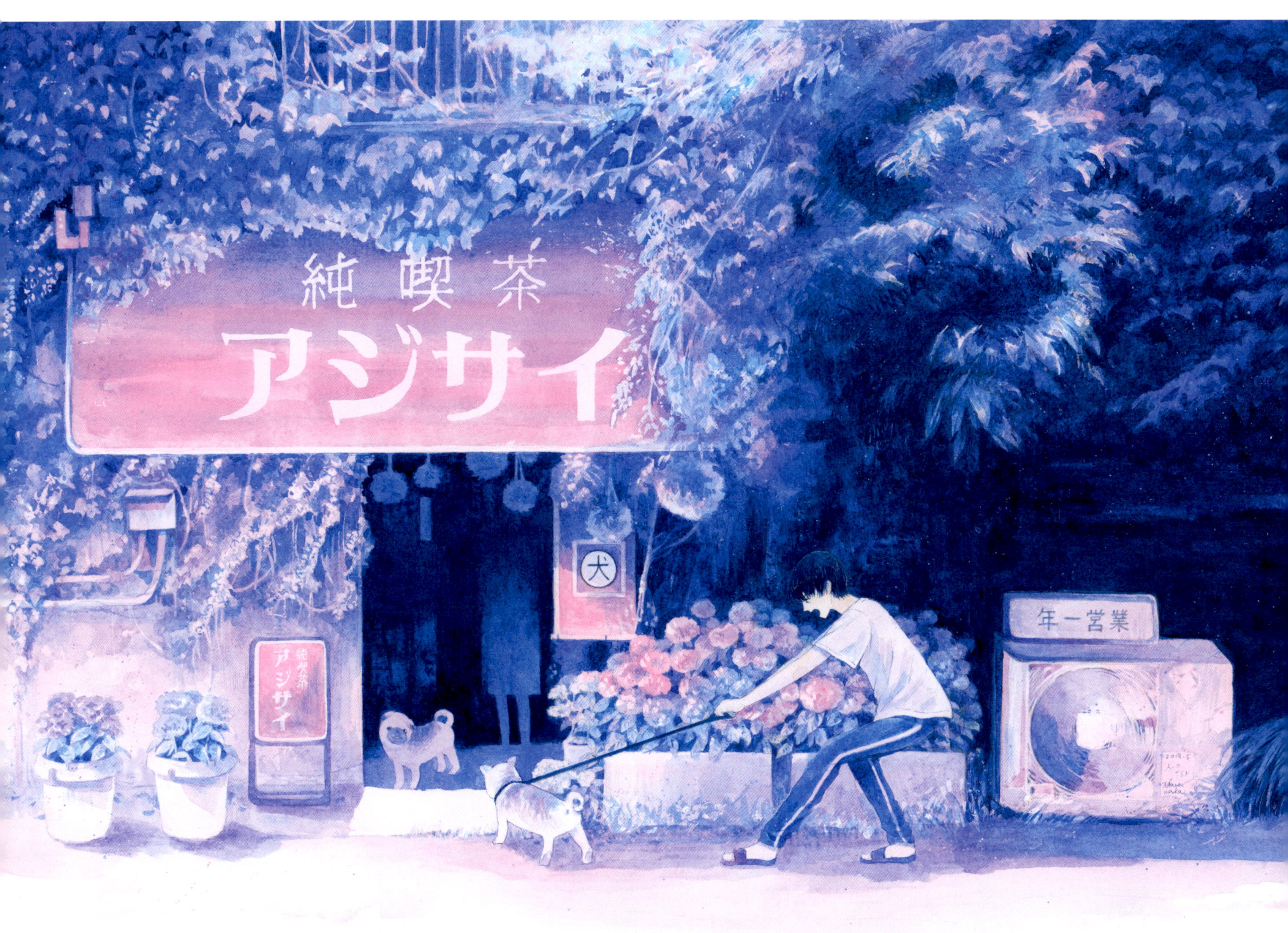

雨上がりの散歩道　│　A Walk After the Rain

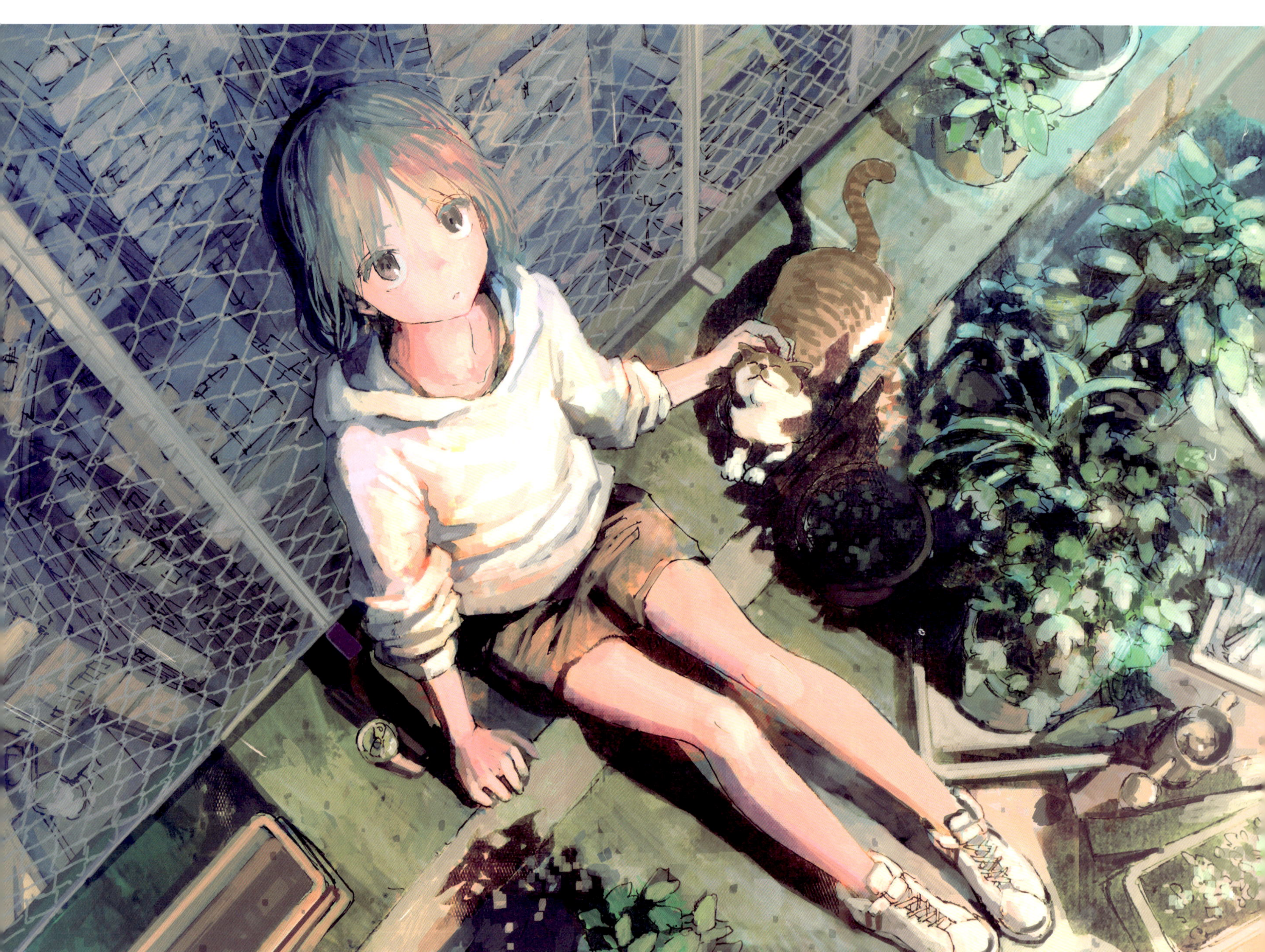

天気雨　｜　Rain in the Sun

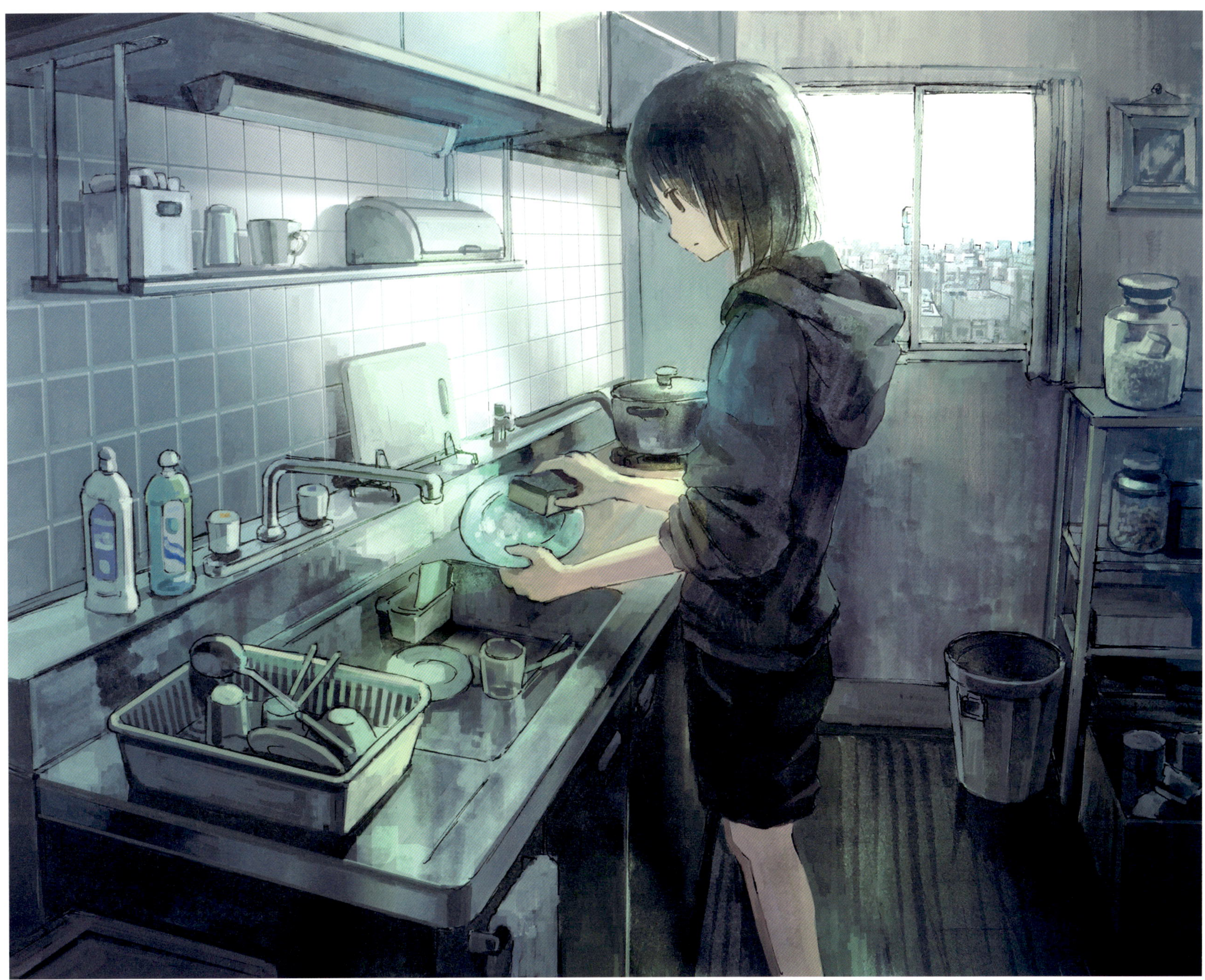

洗い物　｜　Washing Up

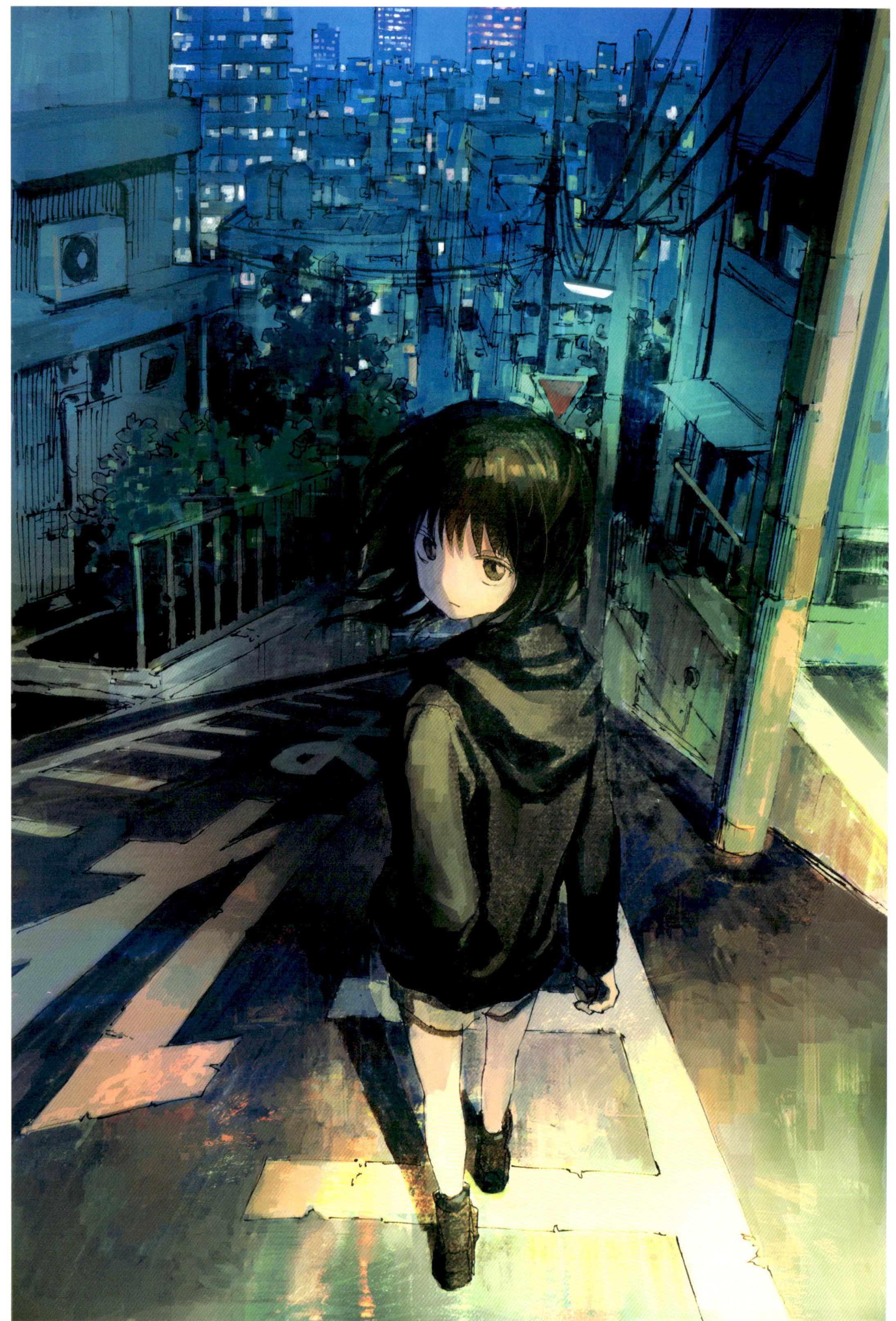

坂道　│　Hill

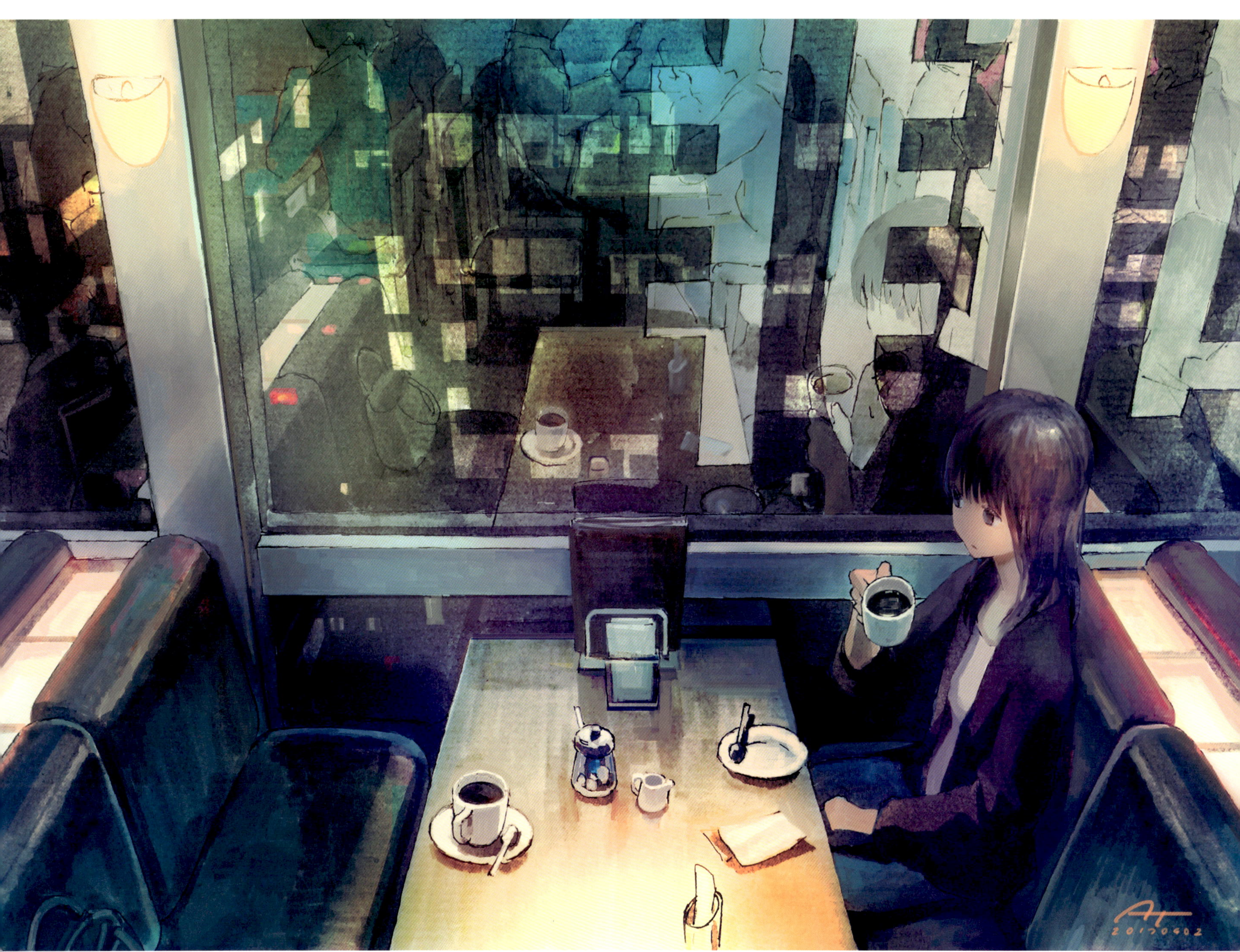

夜のカフェ　|　Evening Cafe

粟木こぽね ｜ Kobone Awaki

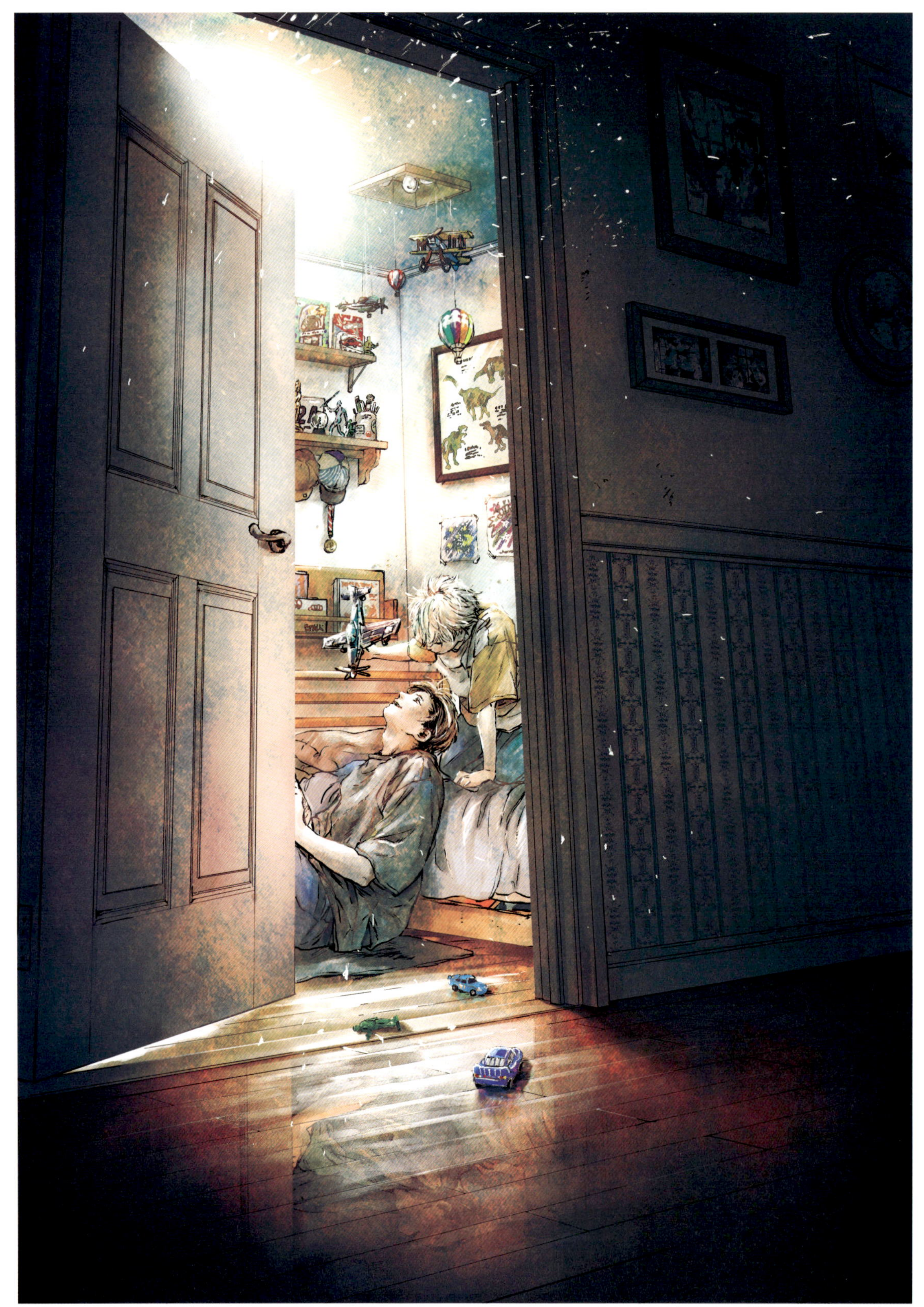

僕の世界。君の世界。 ｜ My World. Your World.

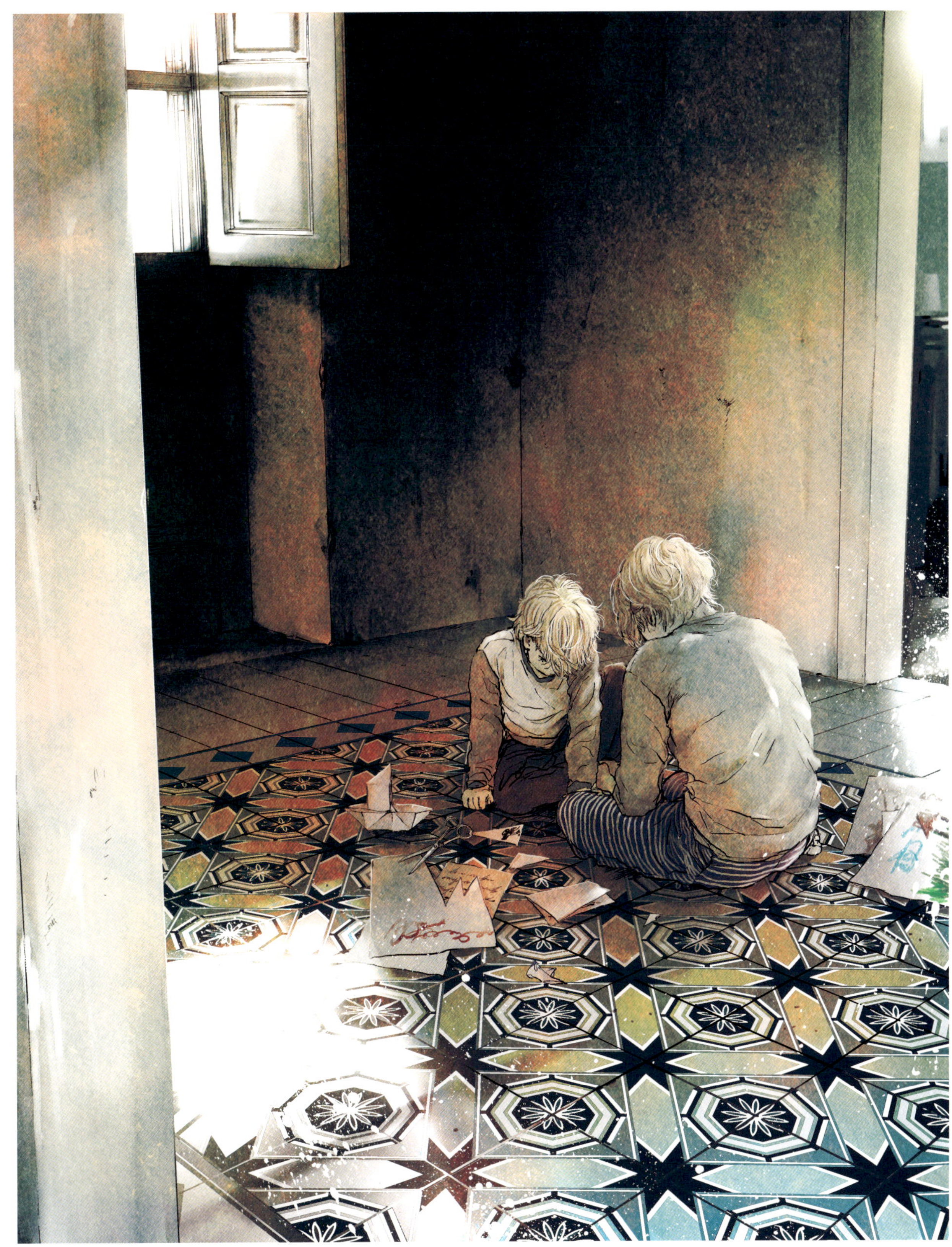

兄と弟　│　Big Brother, Little Brother

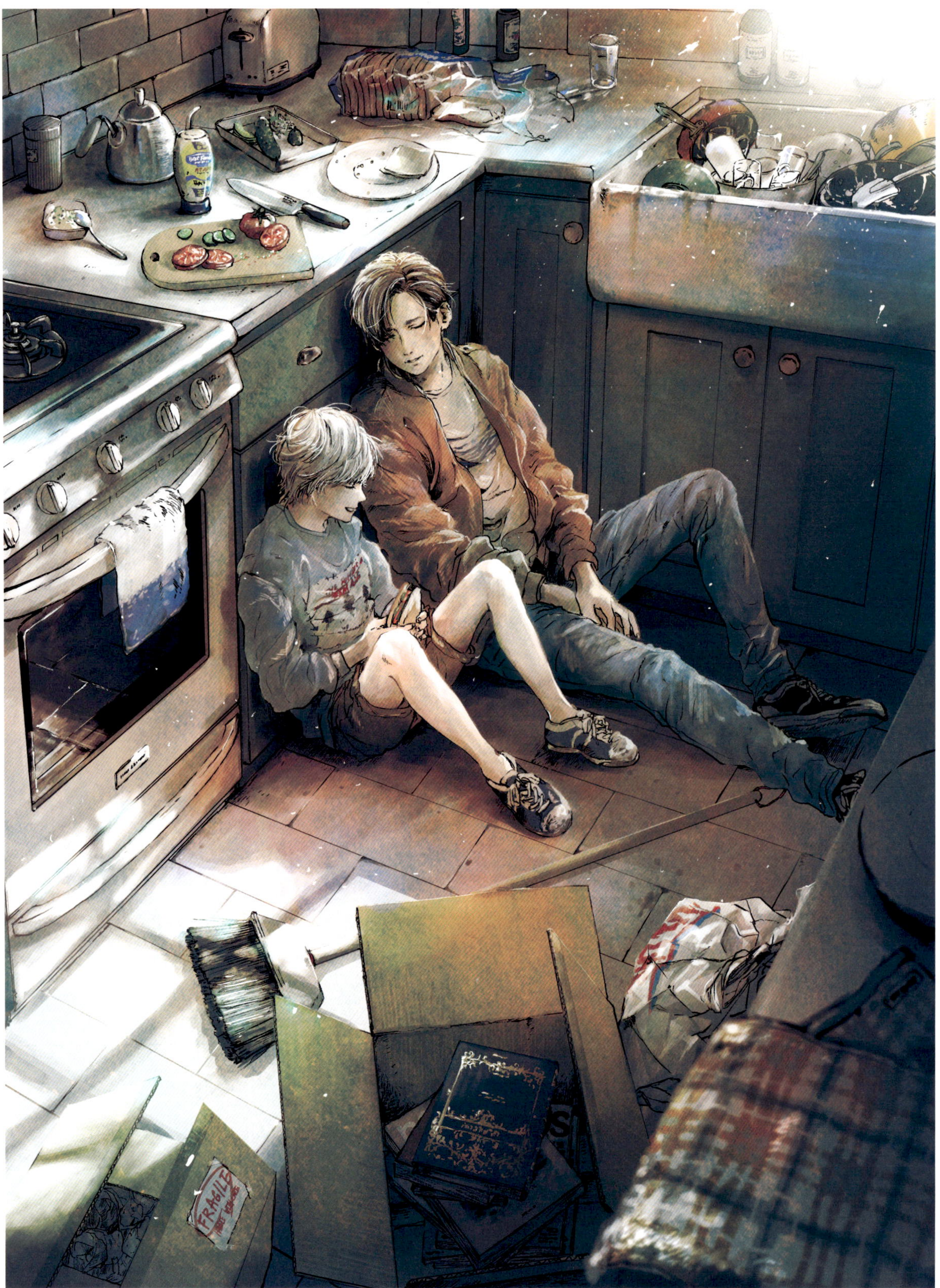

義理の弟　│　Brother-in-law

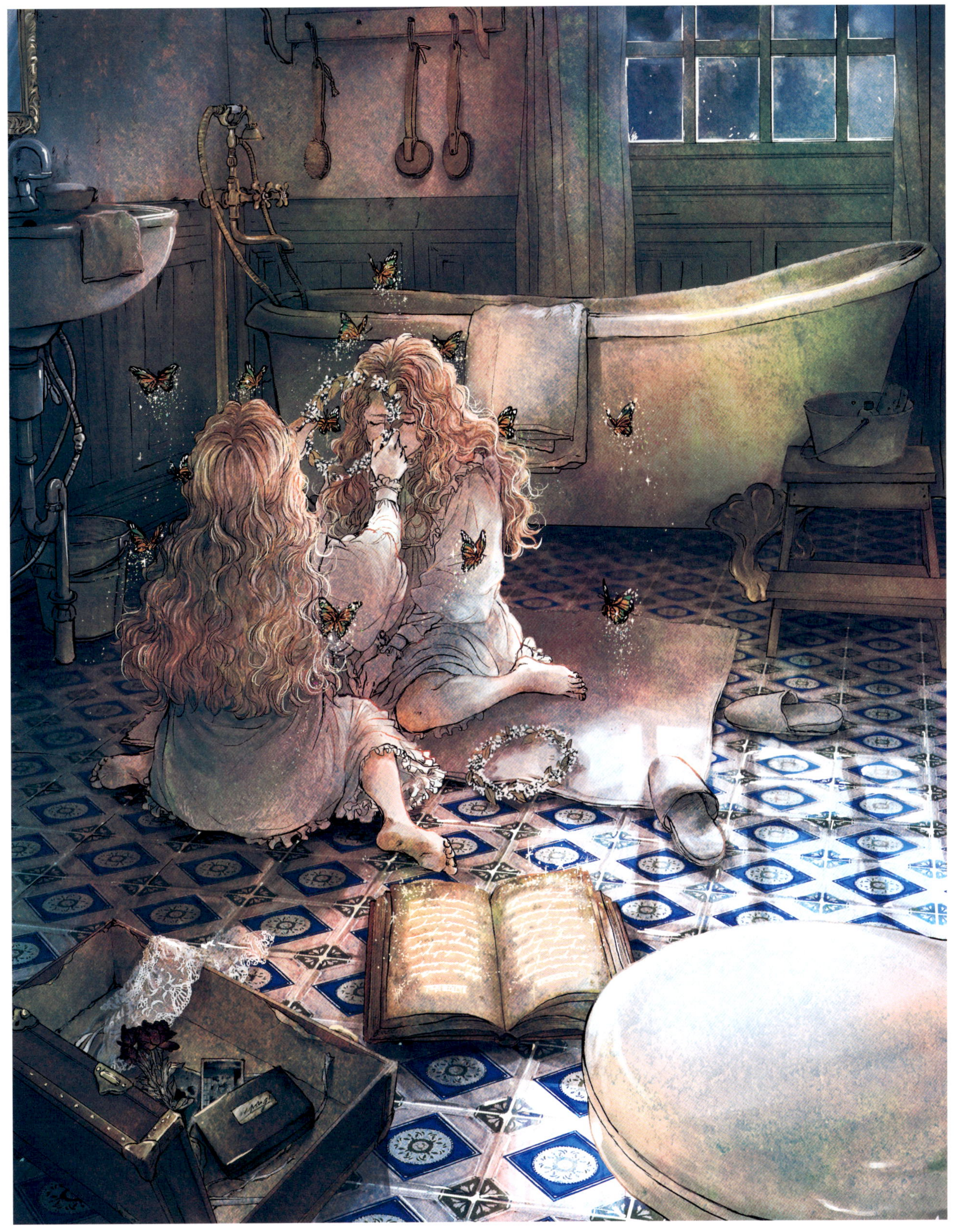

ママが遺したトランクケース　|　The Trunk Mom Left Behind

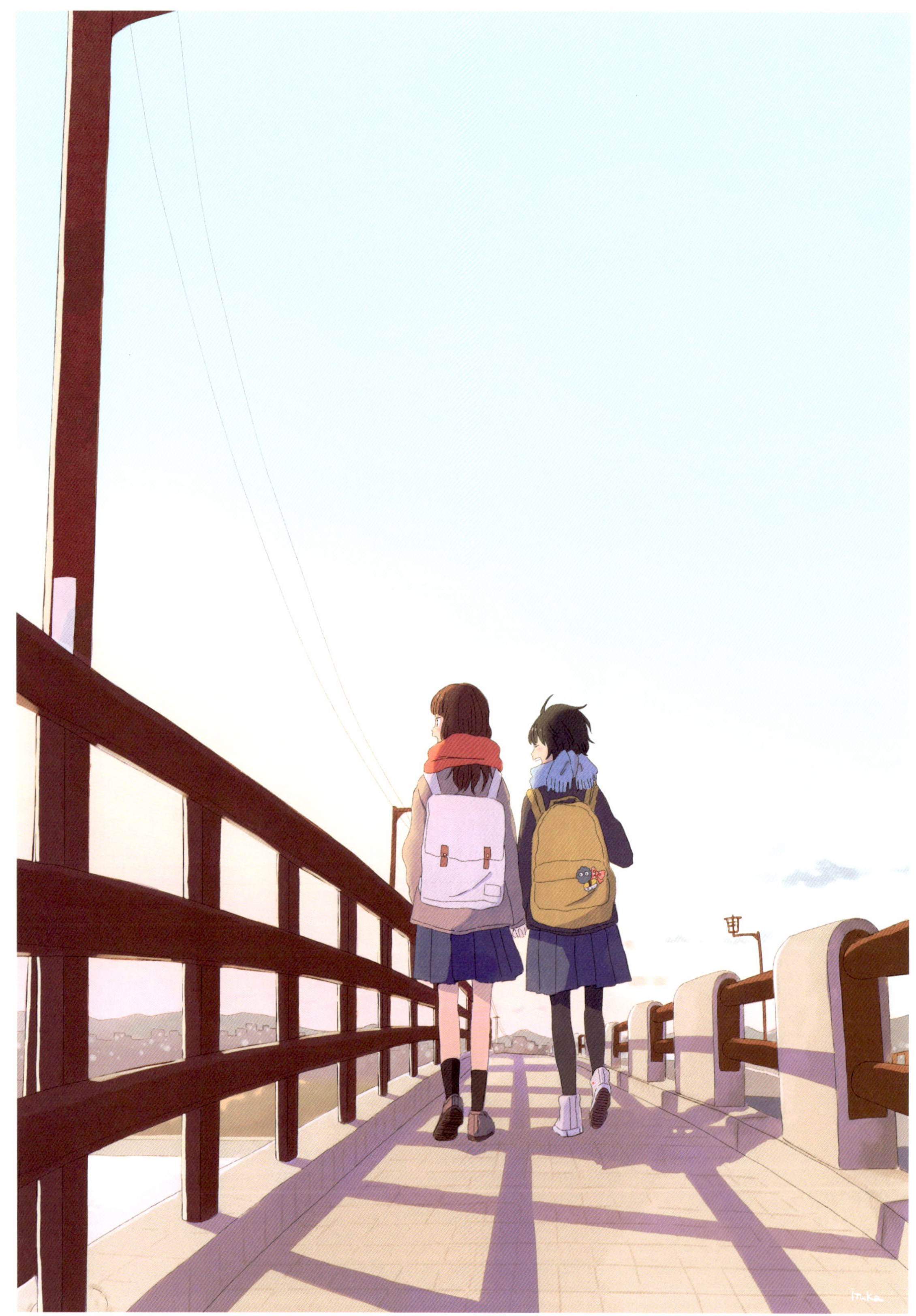

家路　|　On The Way Home

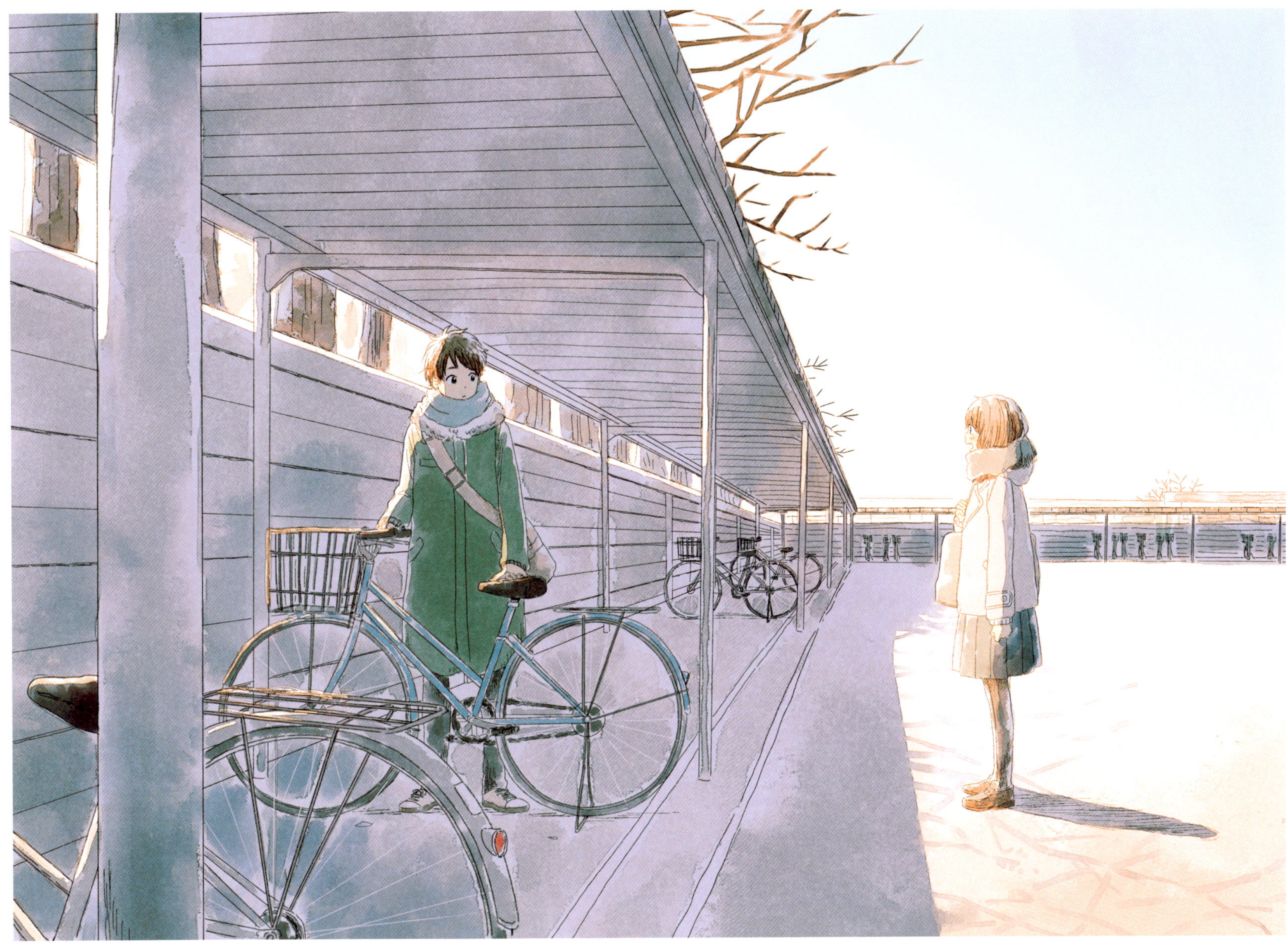

一緒に帰ろ　│　Come With Me

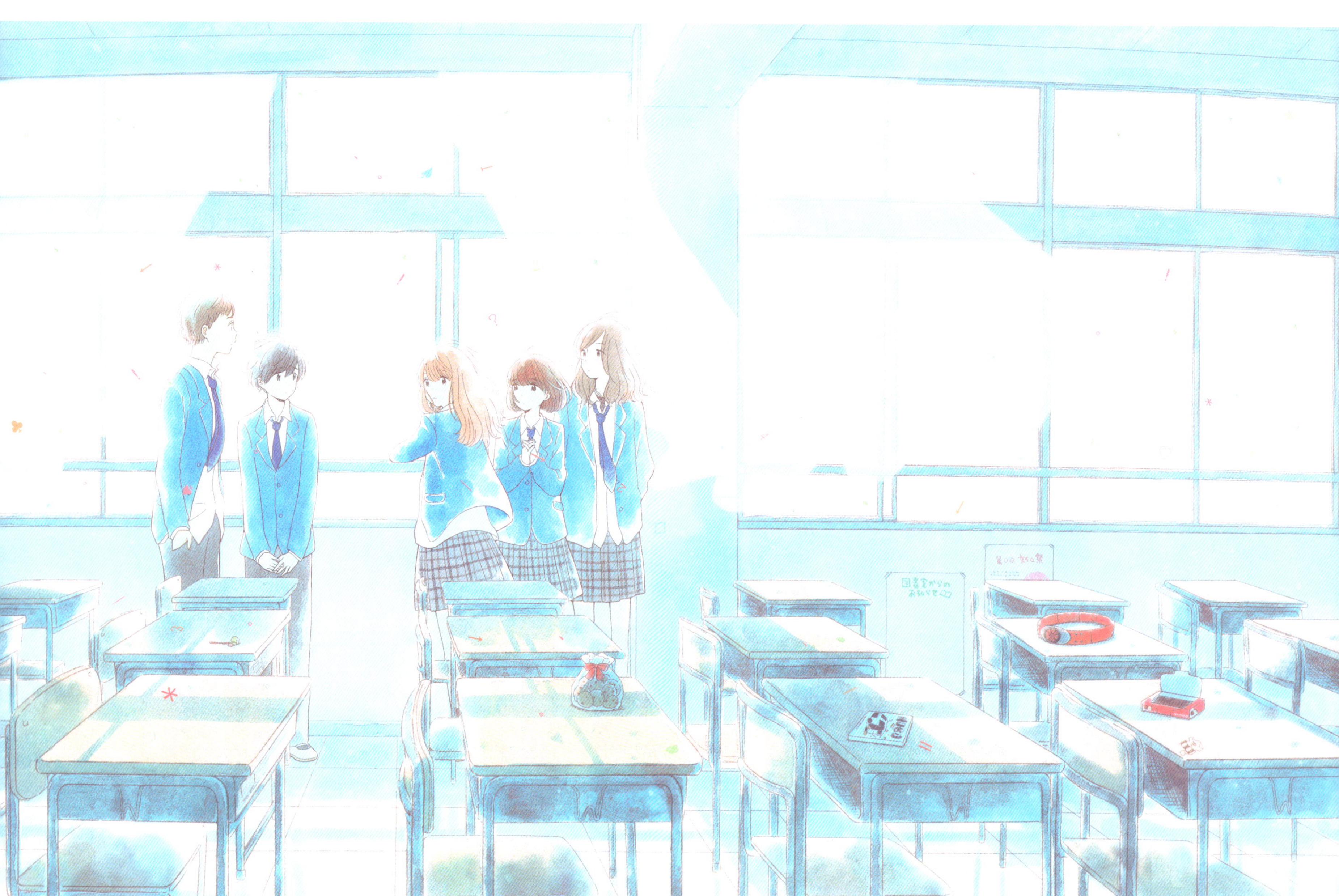

『か「」く「」し「」ご「」と「」（住野よる 著、新潮社）装画　|　Cover illustration for *Ka-Ku-Shi-Go-To-* (written by Yoru Sumino, published by SHINCHOSHA)

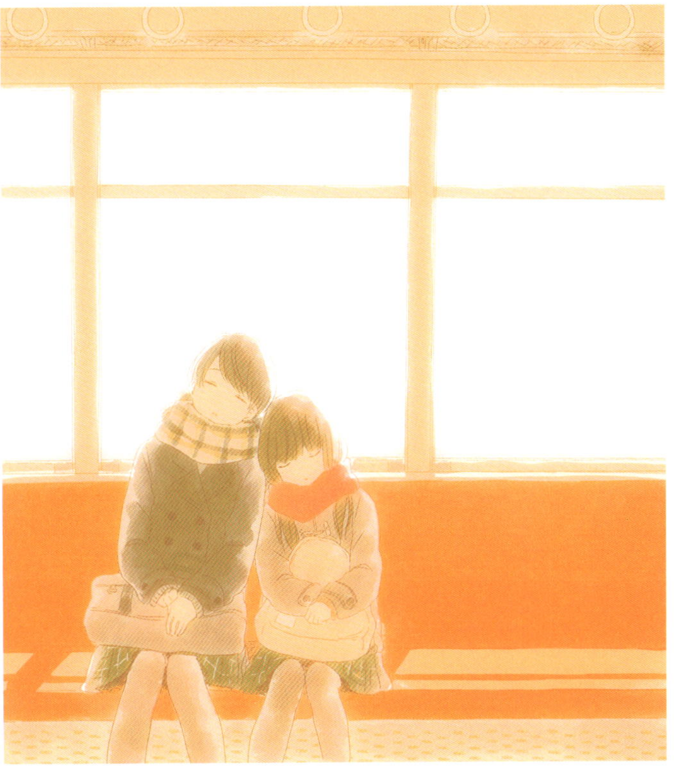

夕暮れ電車 | Evening Train

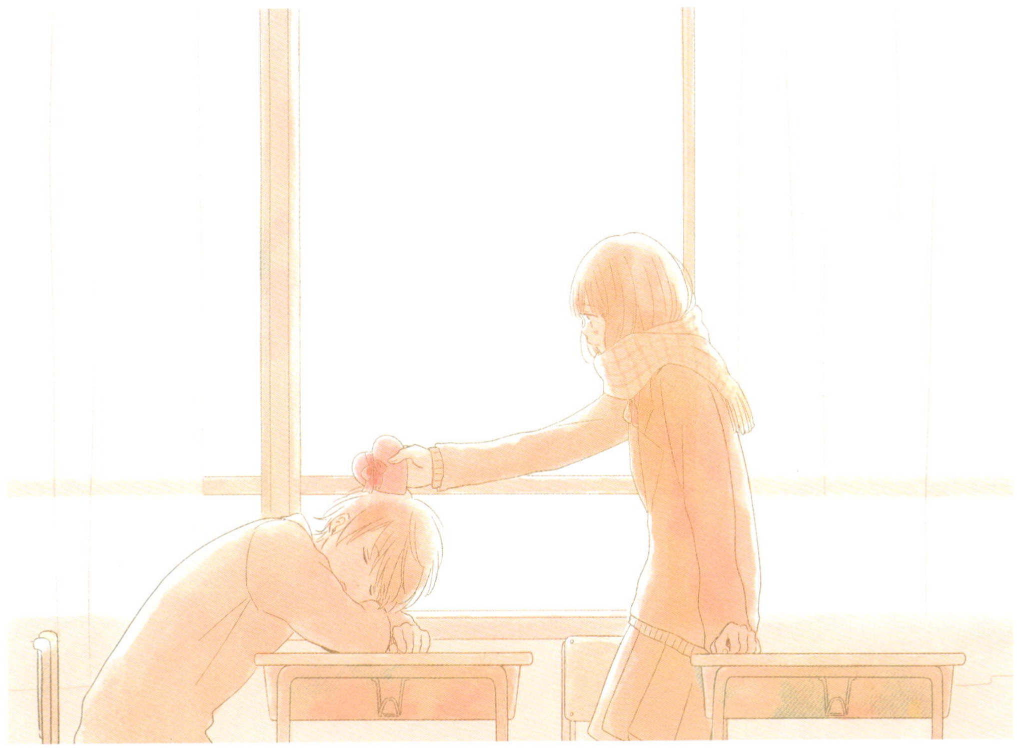

気付いてないでしょ『**いつかCALENDAR2018**』（徳間書店）掲載イラスト
You Probably Don't Even Notice, from *Itsuka CALENDAR 2018* (Tokuma Shoten)

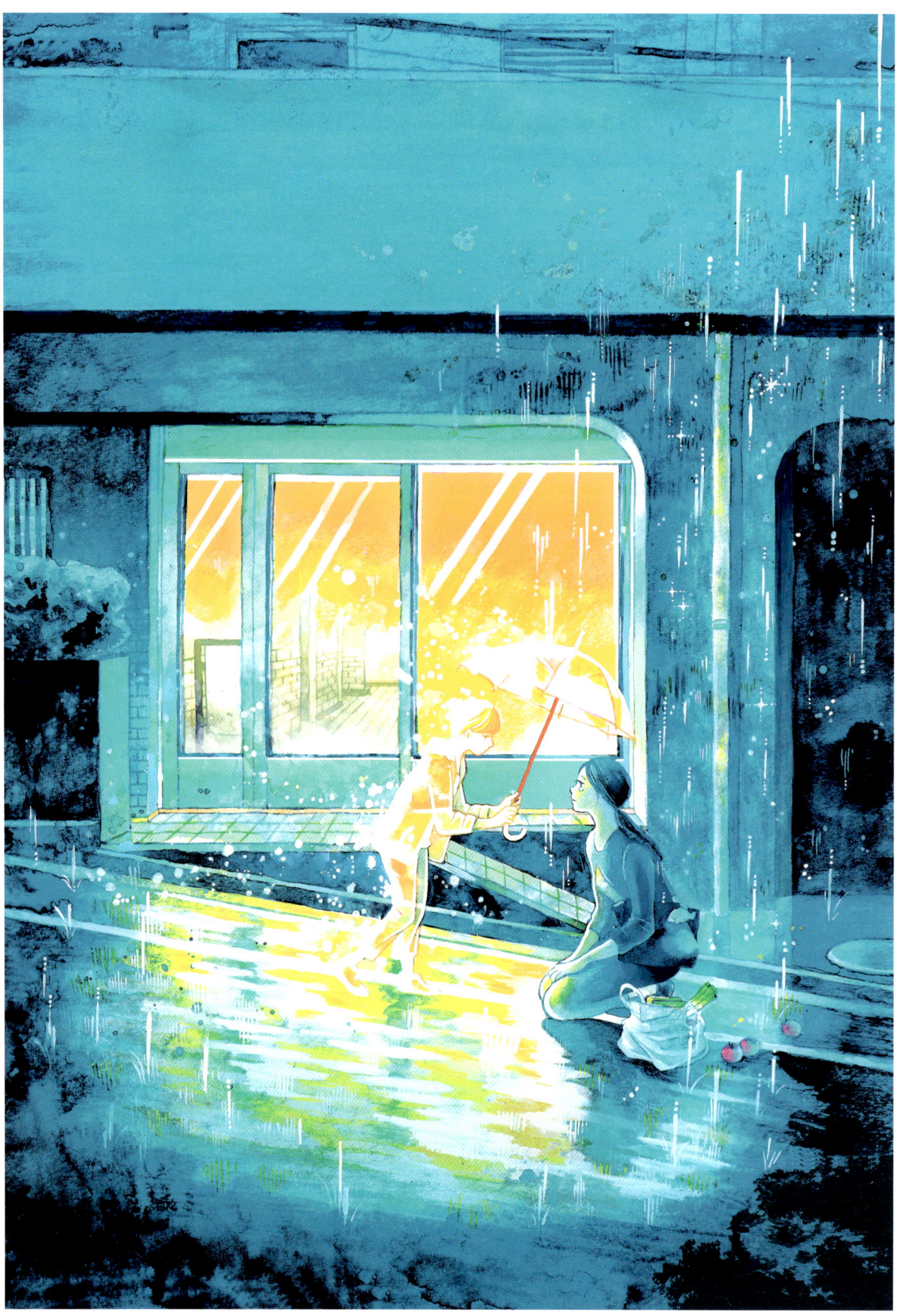

わたしのひかり　｜　My Little Light

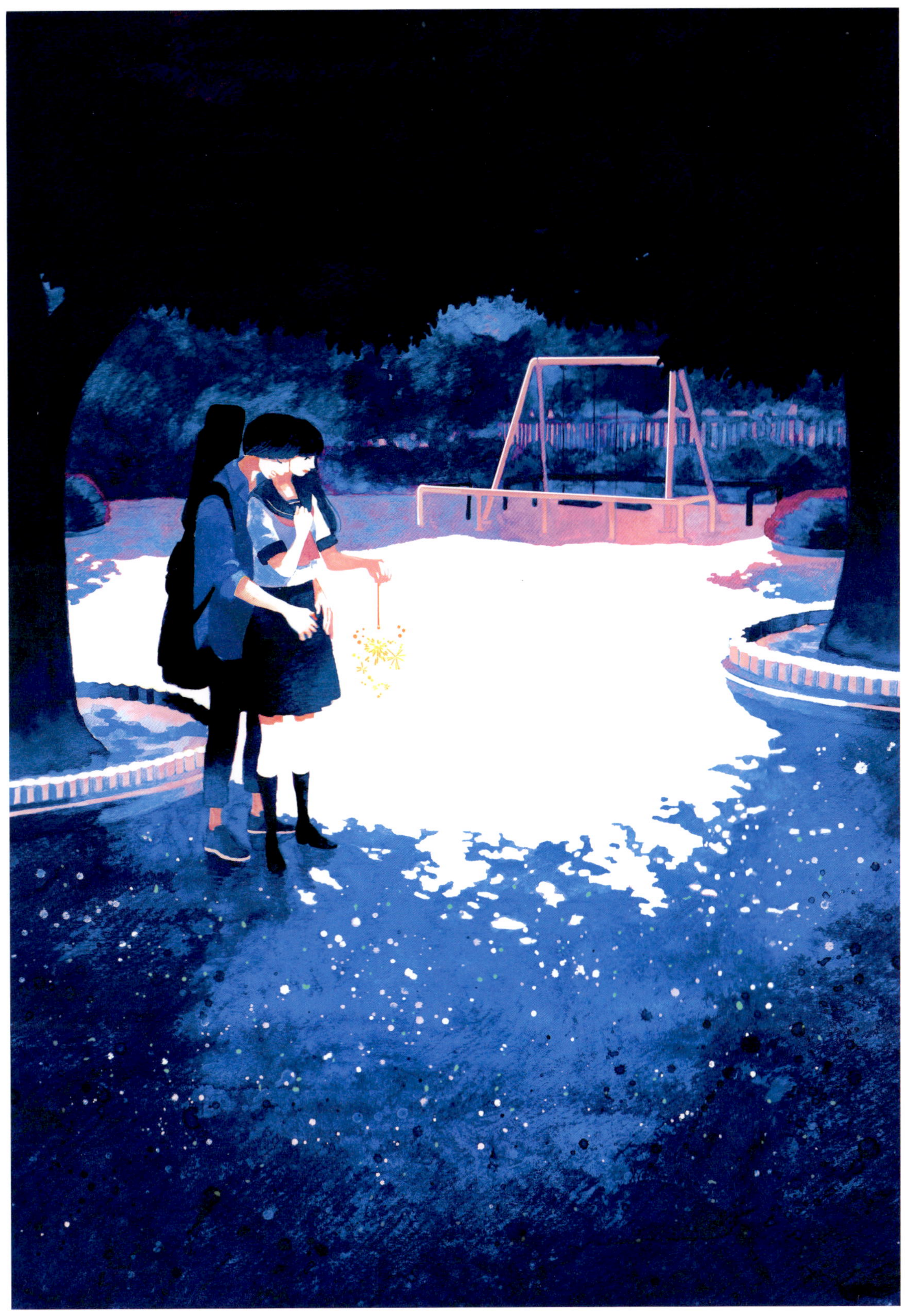

頑張れないよ　│　I Just Can't

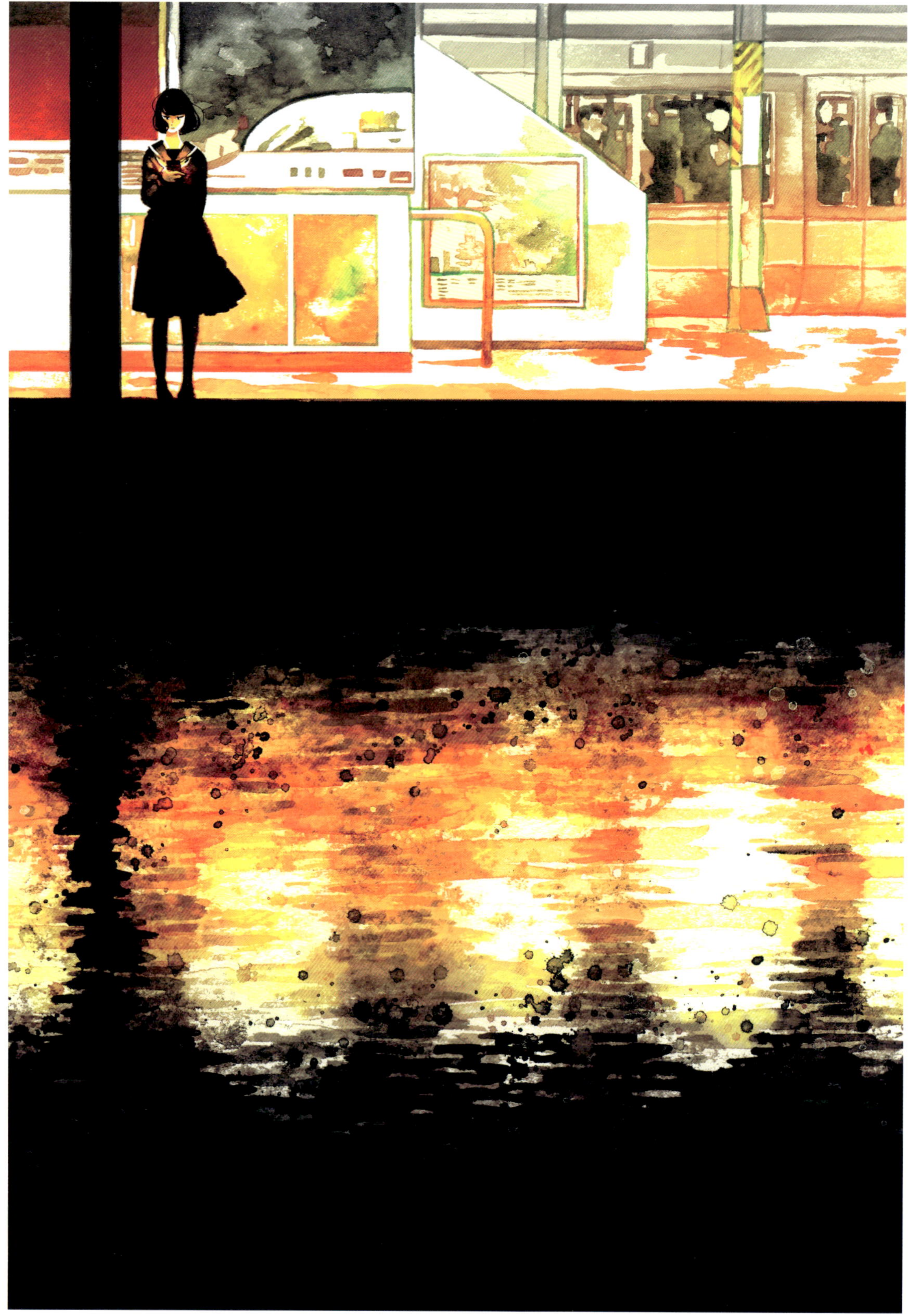

約束したのに ｜ But You Promised

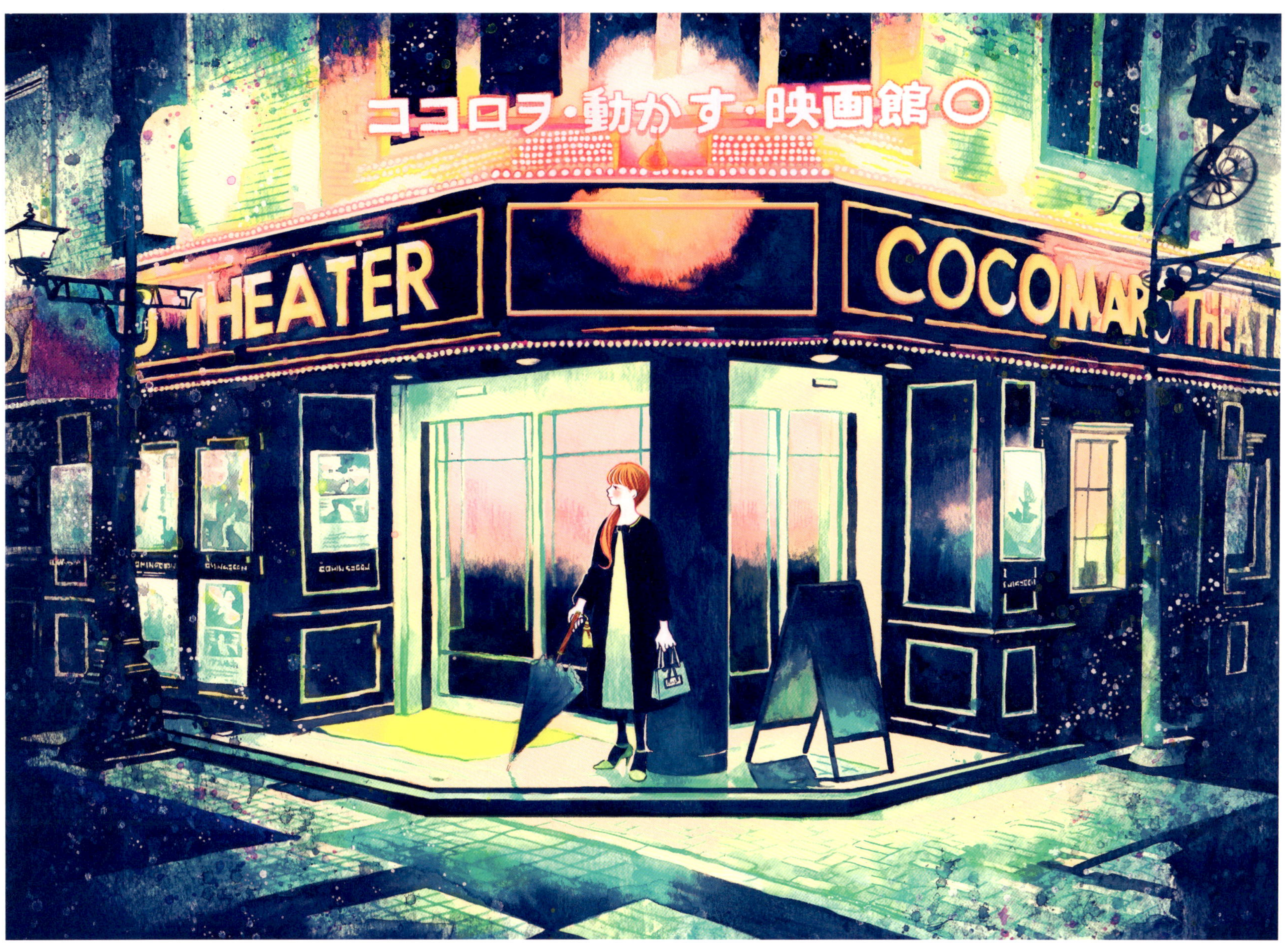

待ち合わせ（吉祥寺 ココマルシアター）　｜　Waiting (Kichijoji Cocomaru Theater)

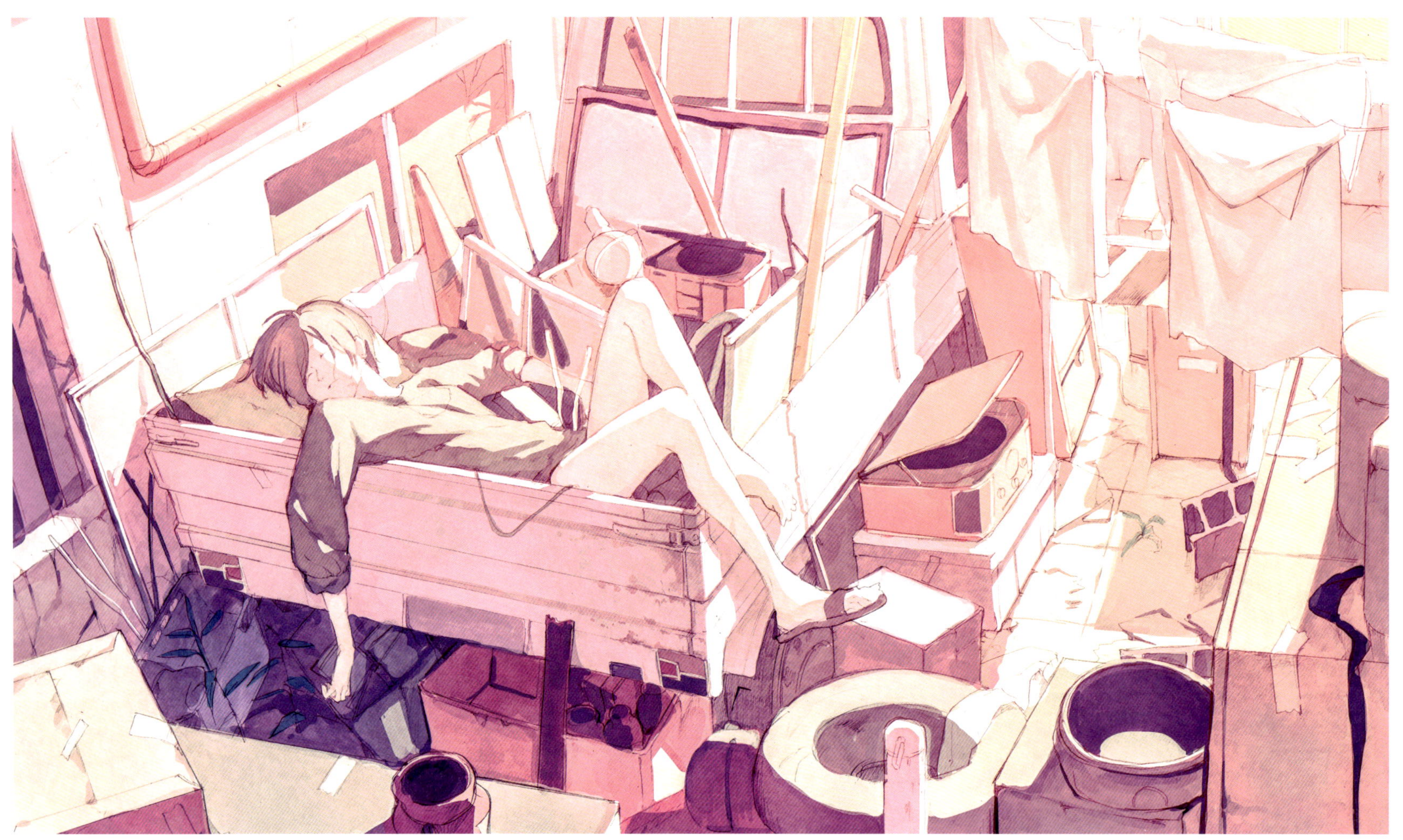

うたた寝　｜　Napping

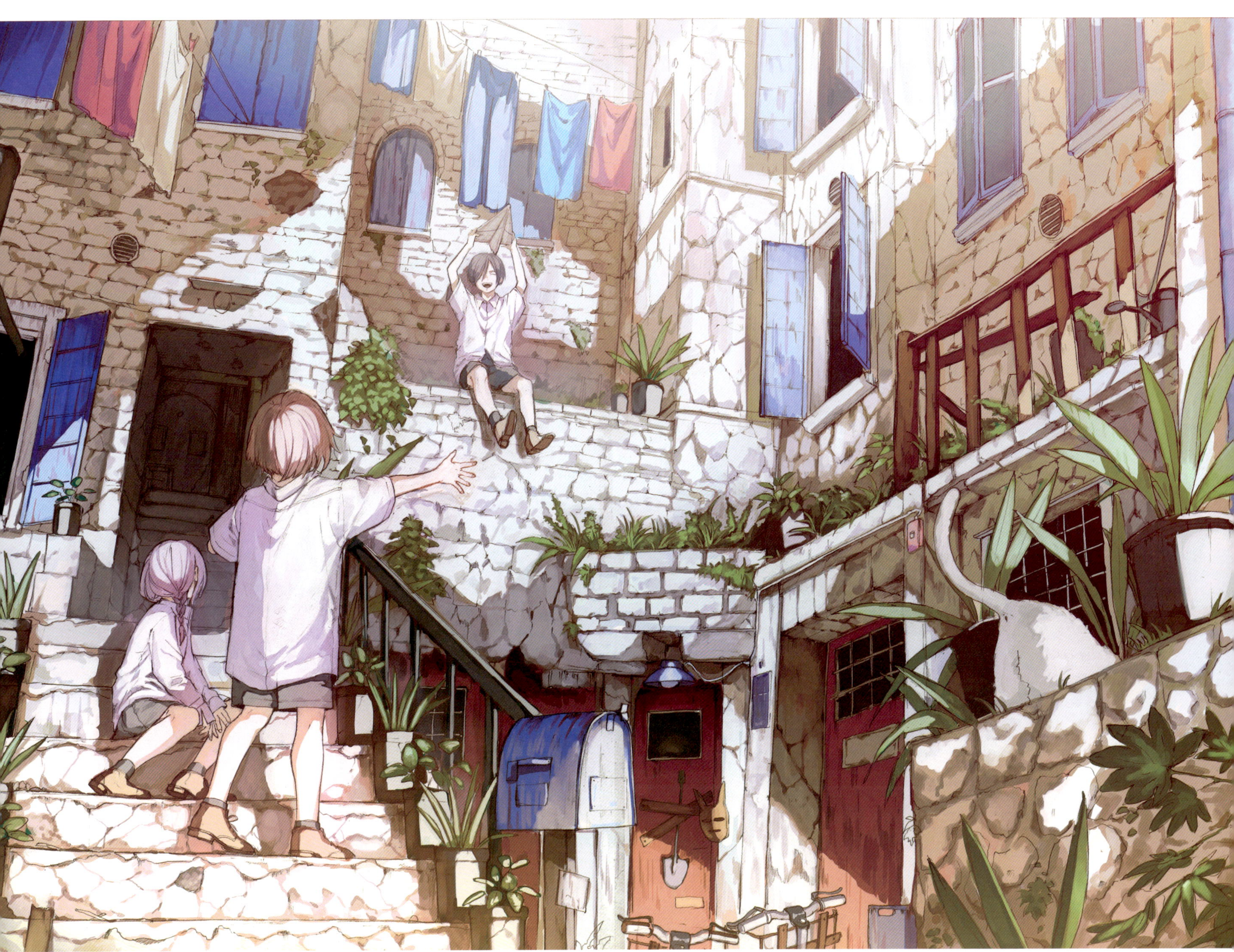

孤児たち ｜ The Orphans

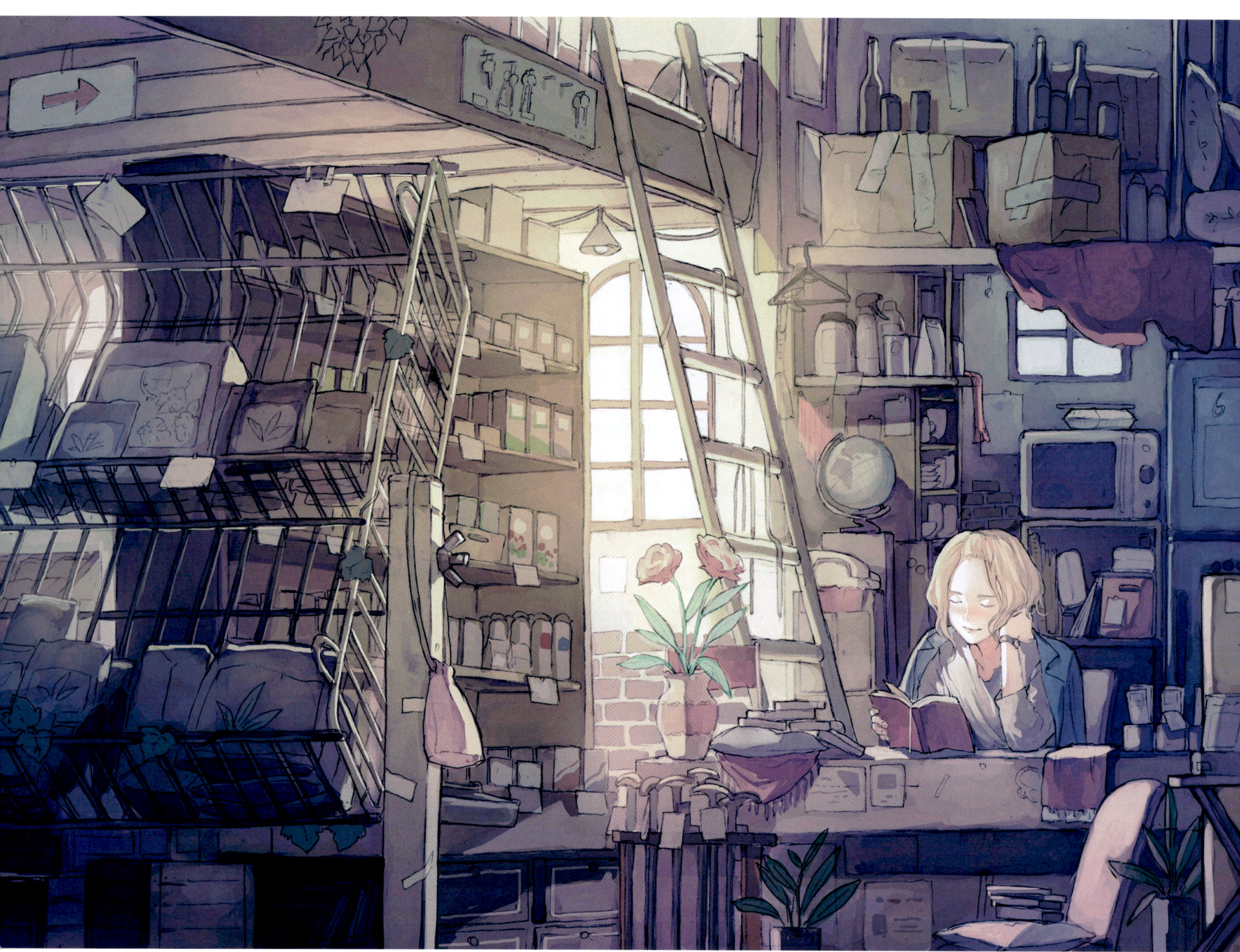

秘密基地　|　The Hideout

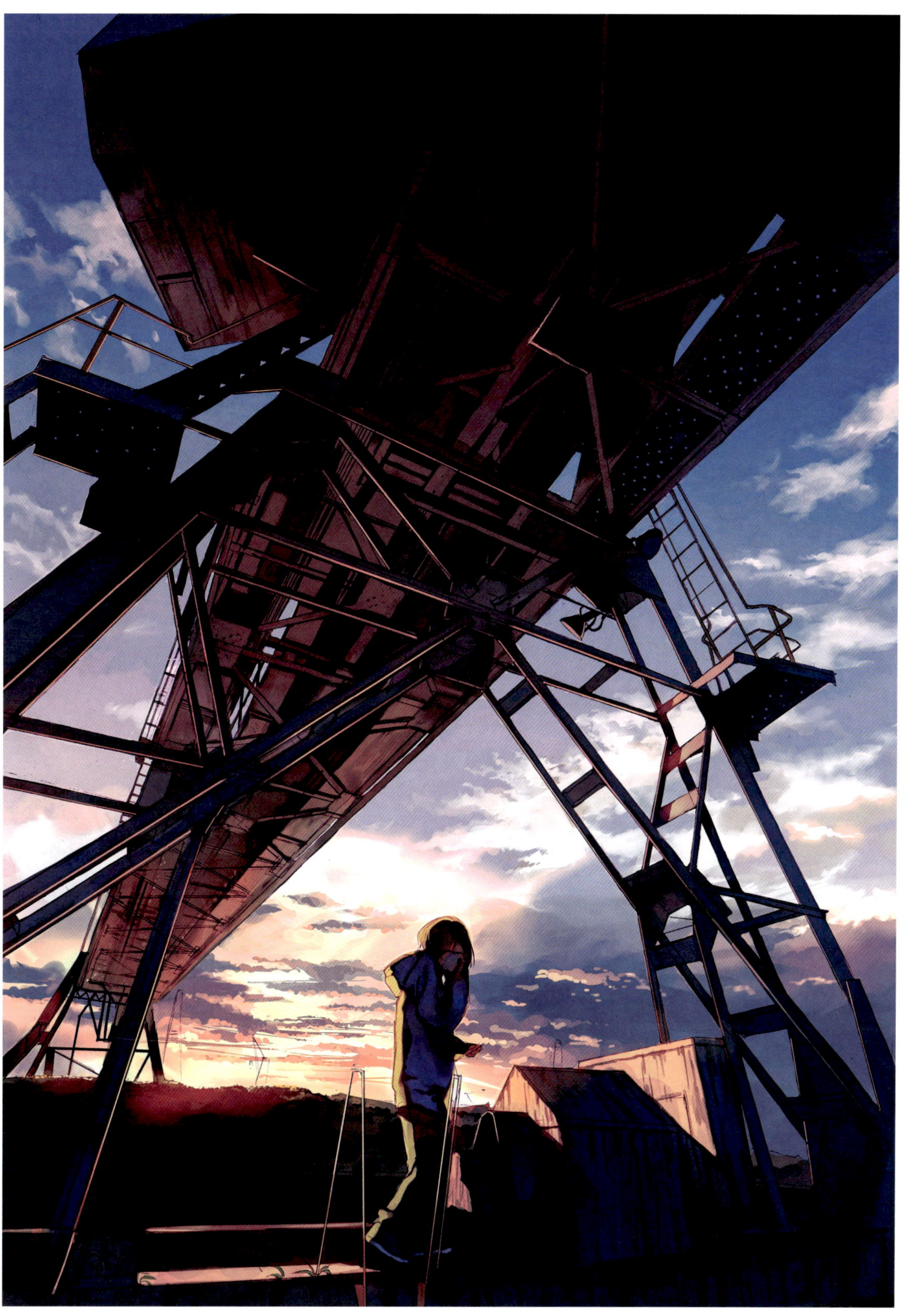

港の隙　|　The Port Interlude

イリヤ・クブシノブ ｜ Ilya Kuvshinov

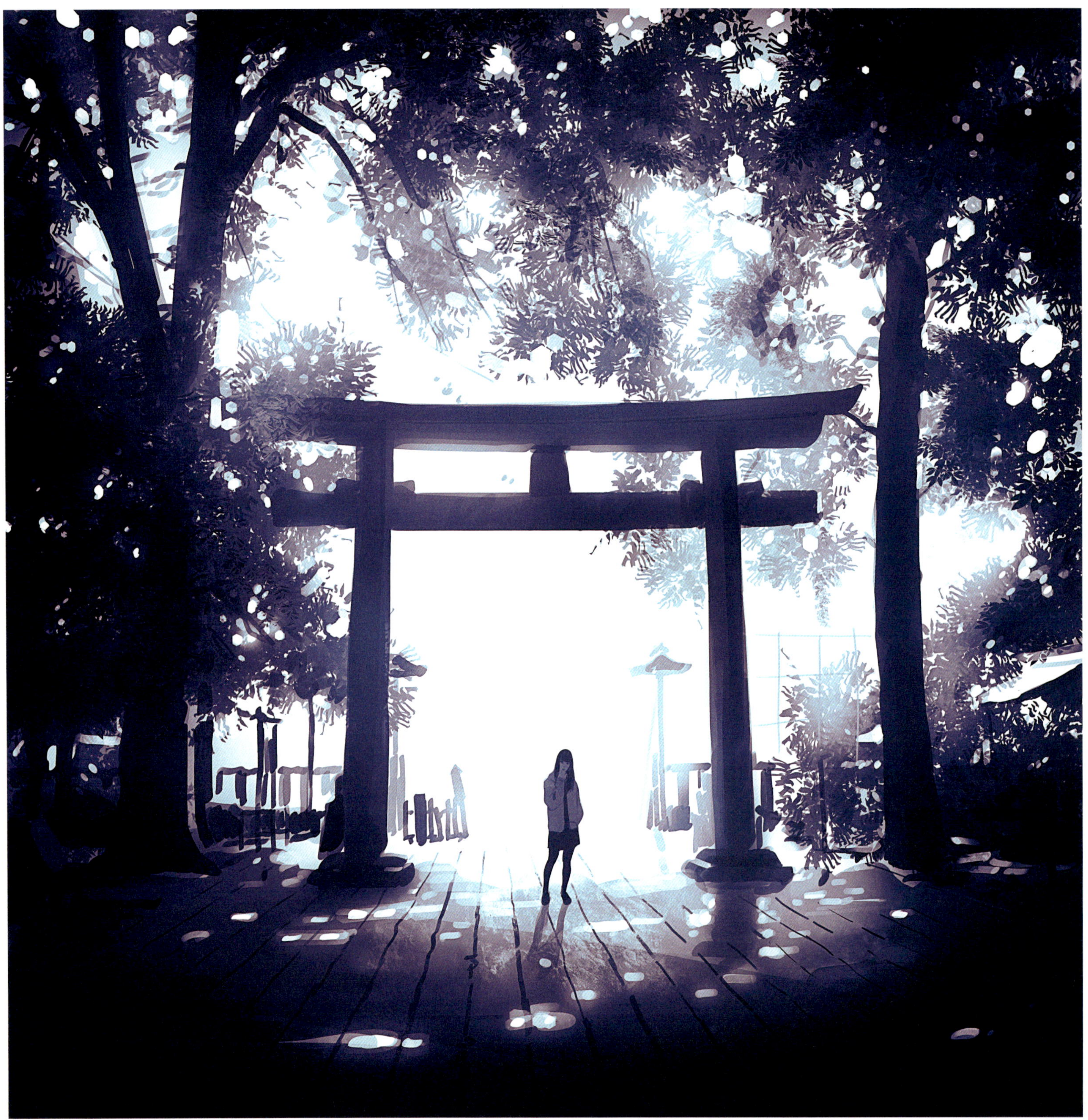

Glow

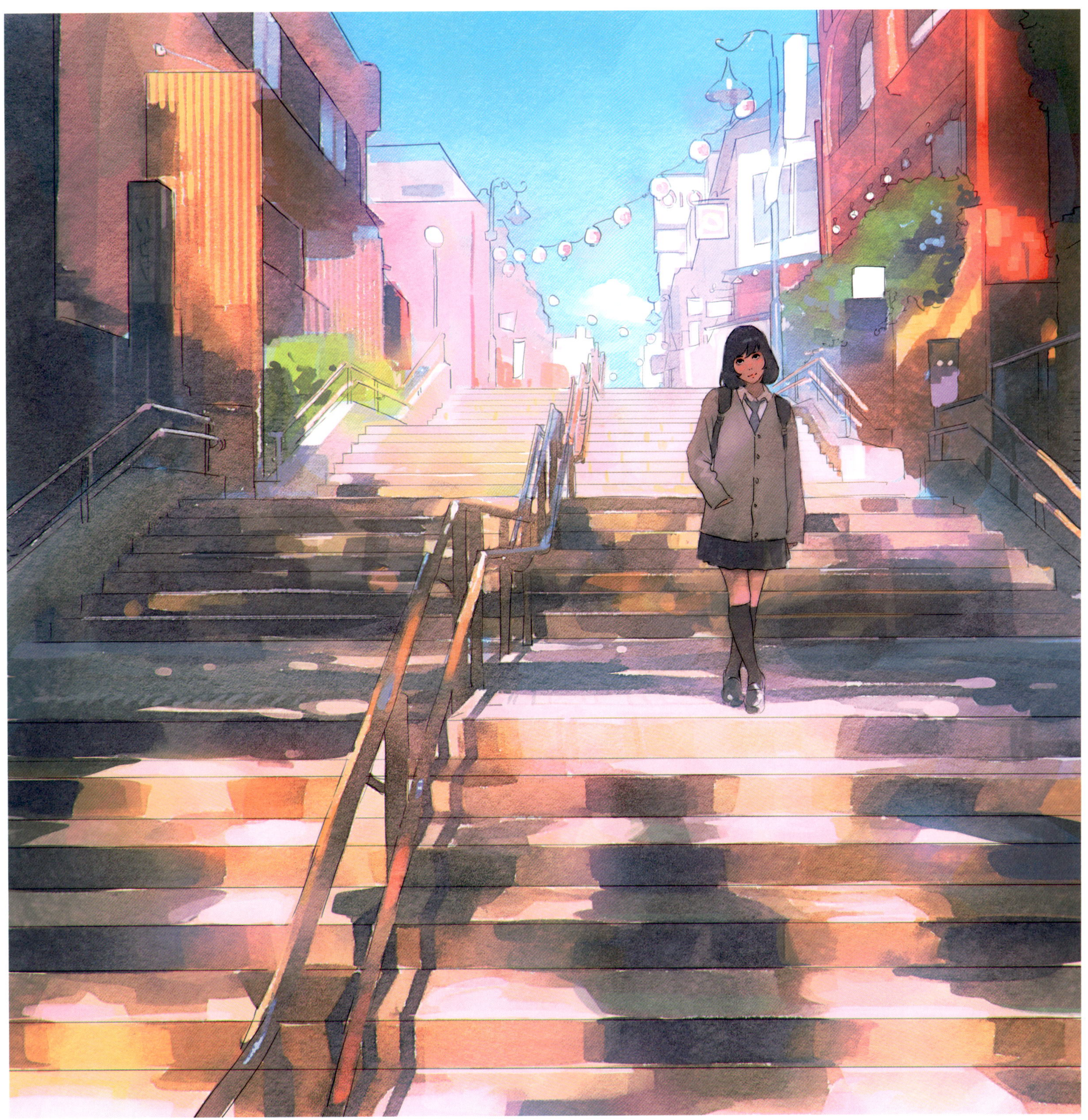

kichijoji

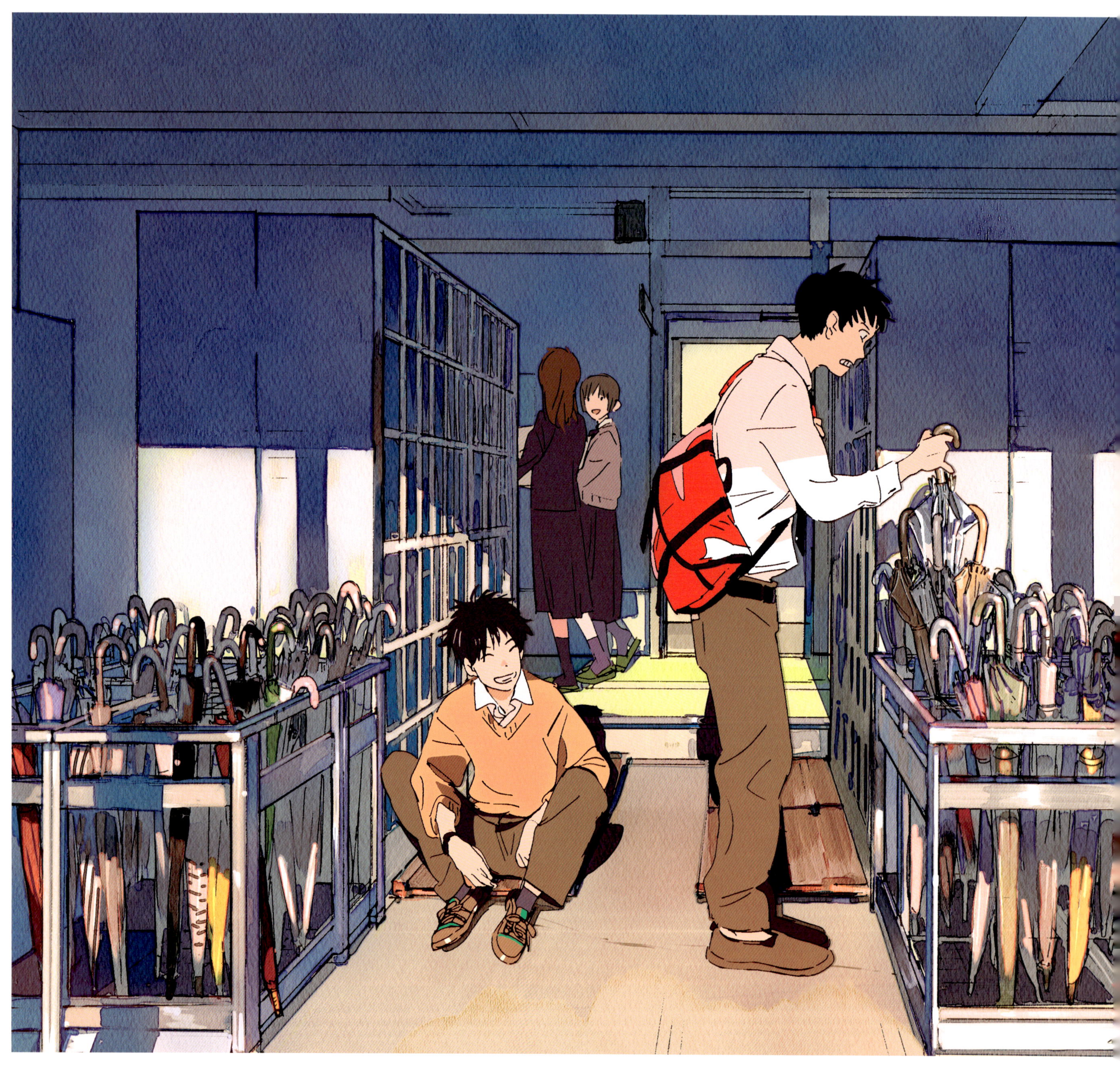

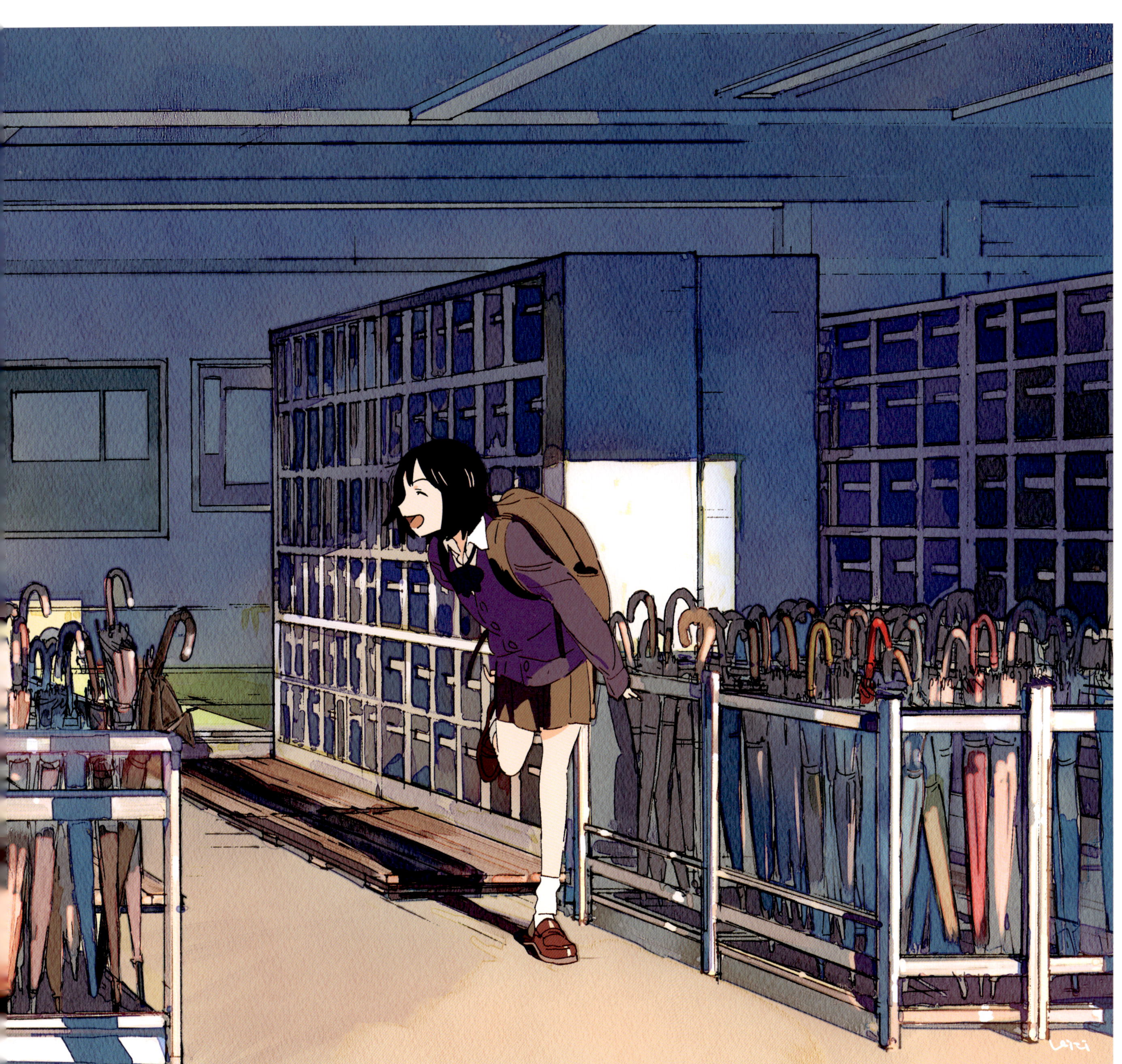

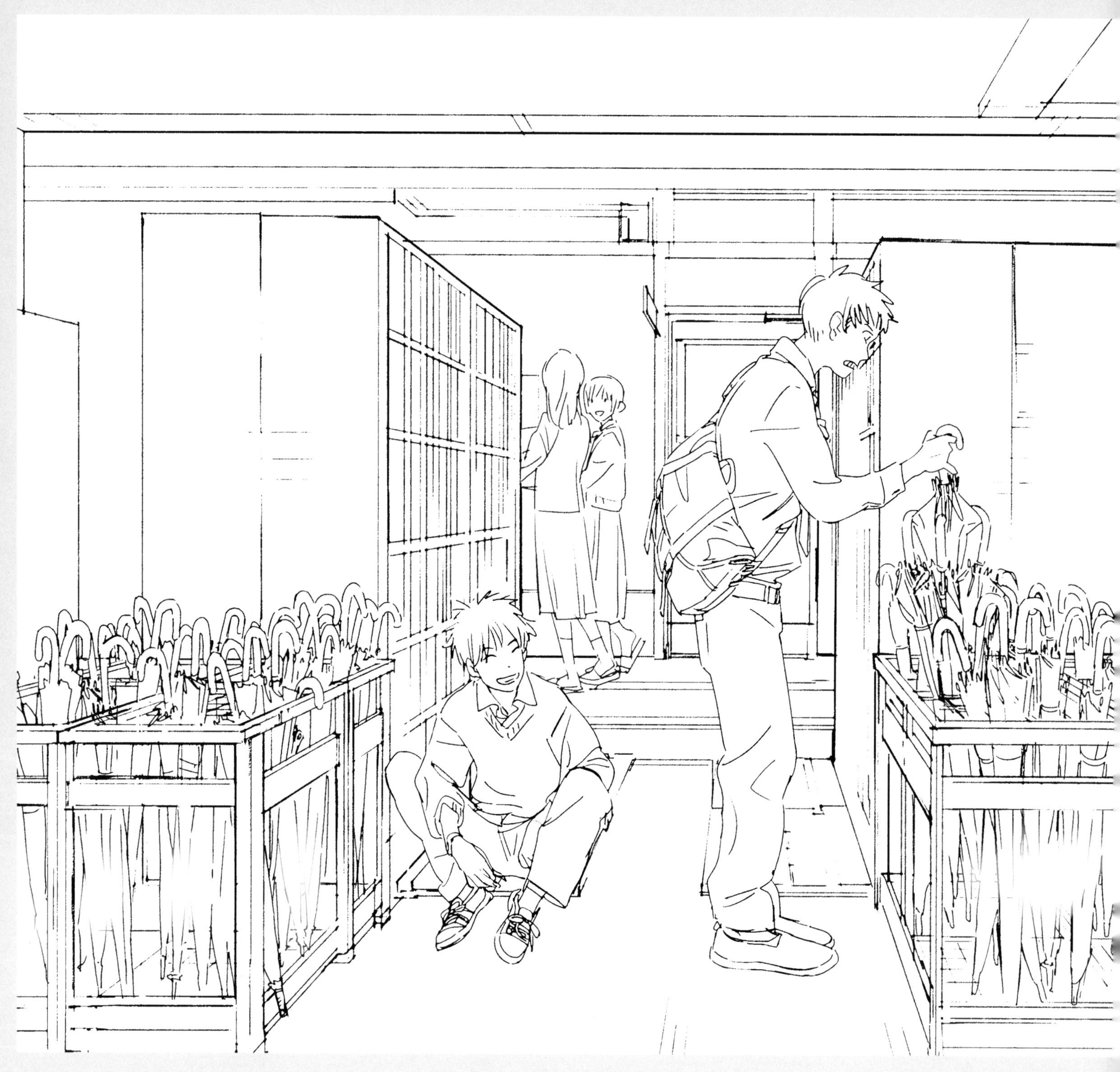

学生時代、雨の日に傘がめちゃめちゃに傘立てにつっこまれていて、よく人の傘を吊り上げました。そういう些細なことは覚えているのに、勉強したことは何も覚えていないので不思議です。

When I was a student, there were always so many umbrellas jammed into the umbrella stand, and I often pulled my umbrella up with other umbrellas attached. It's very strange to me that I remember such an unimportant thing, yet I can't really remember what I even studied in school.

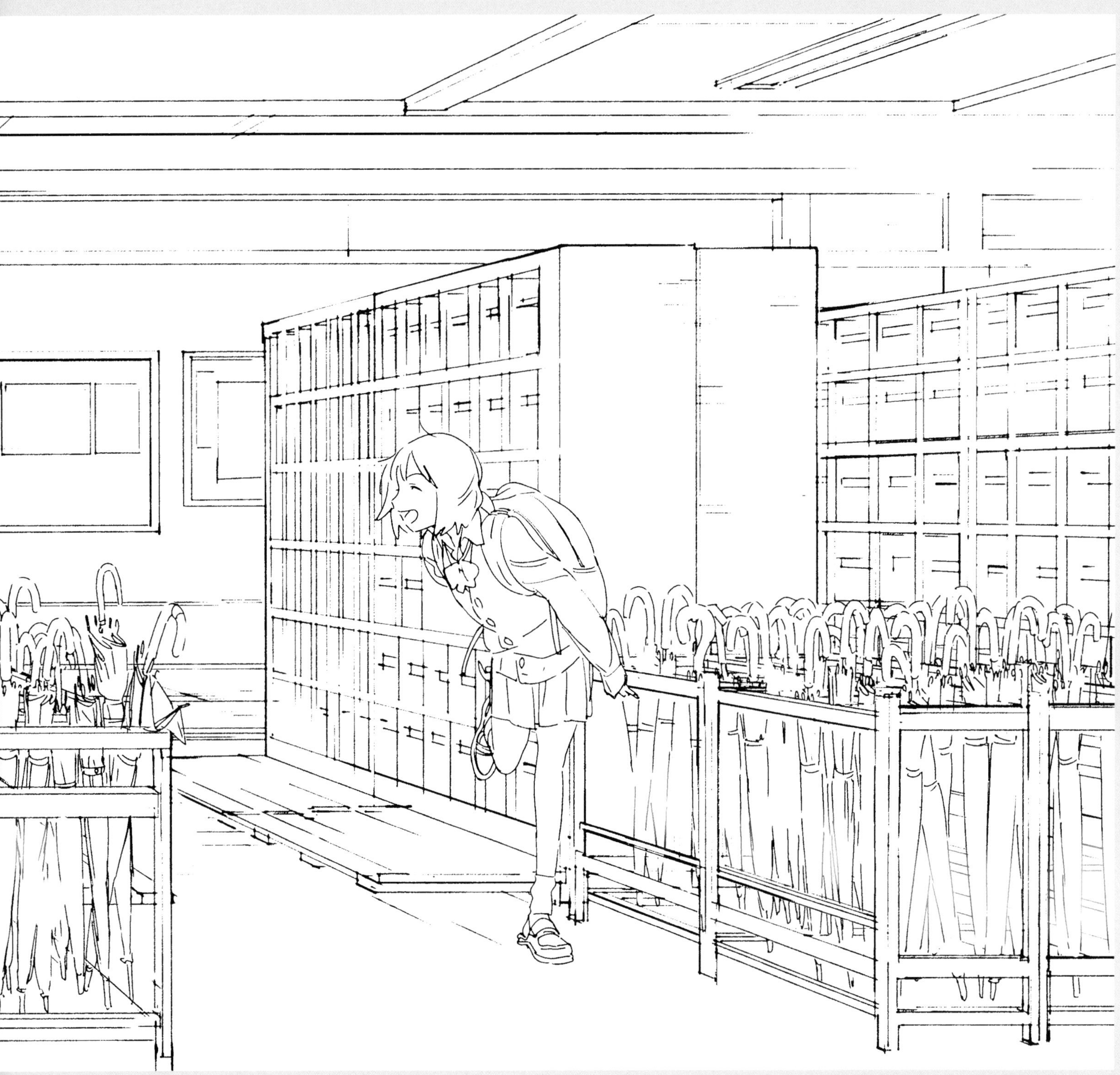

下足室（線画）　|　School Entrance (Line drawing)

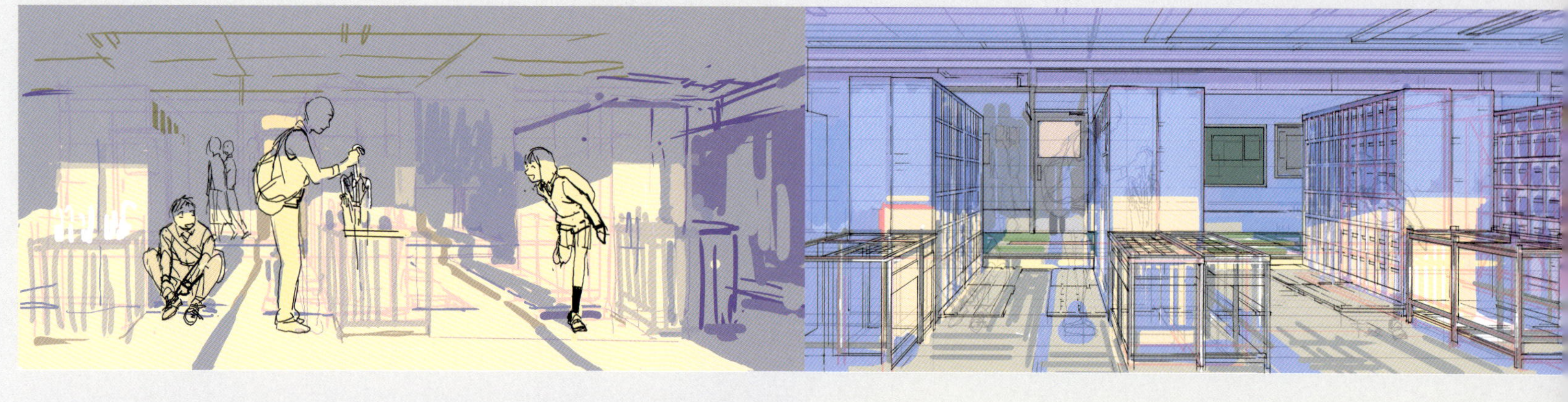

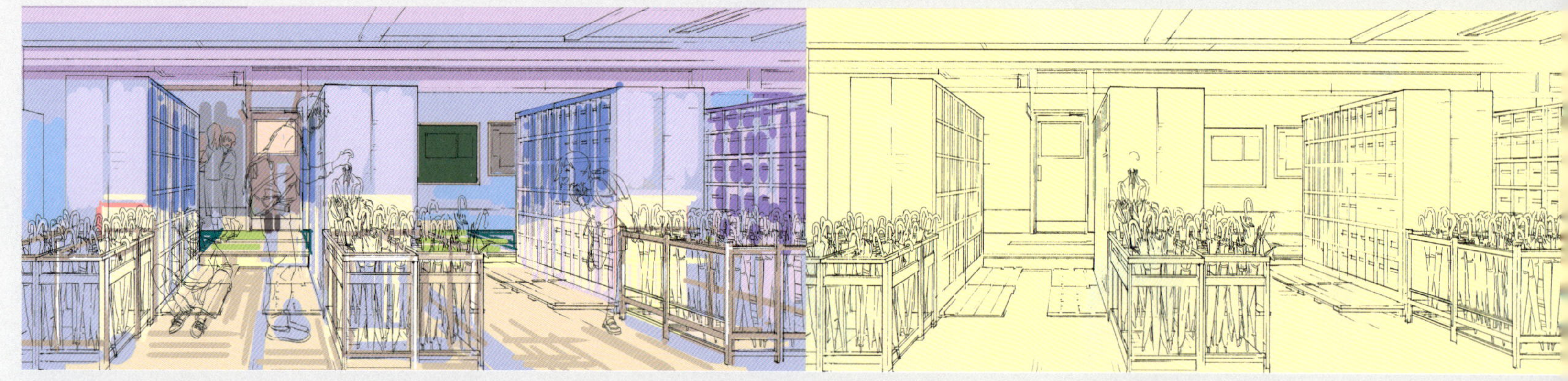

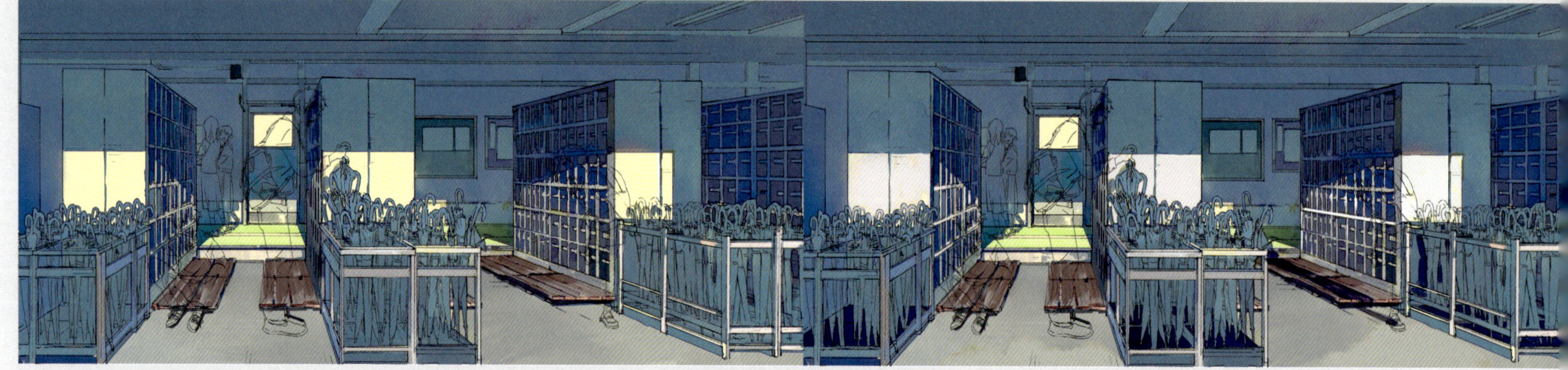

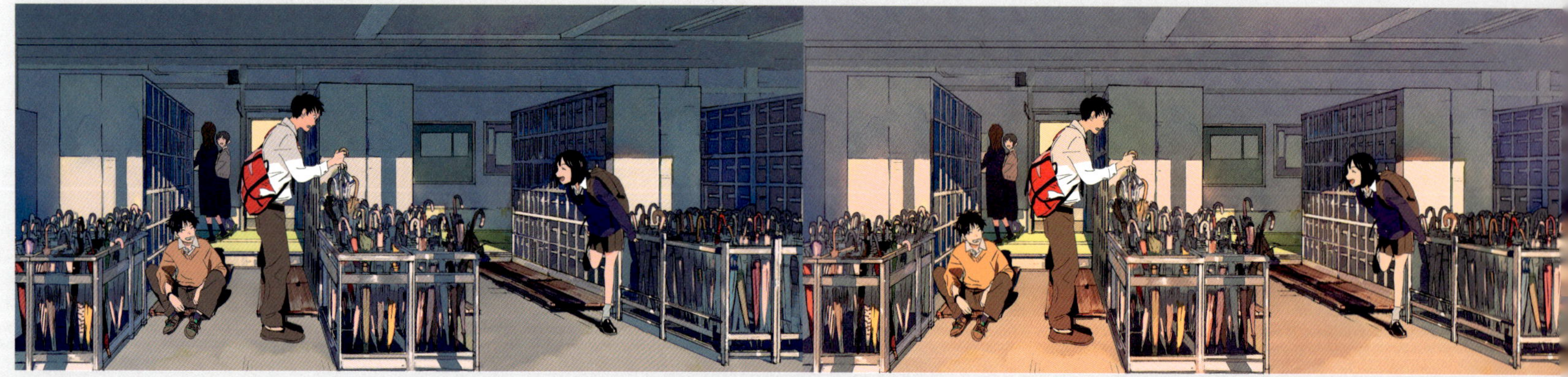

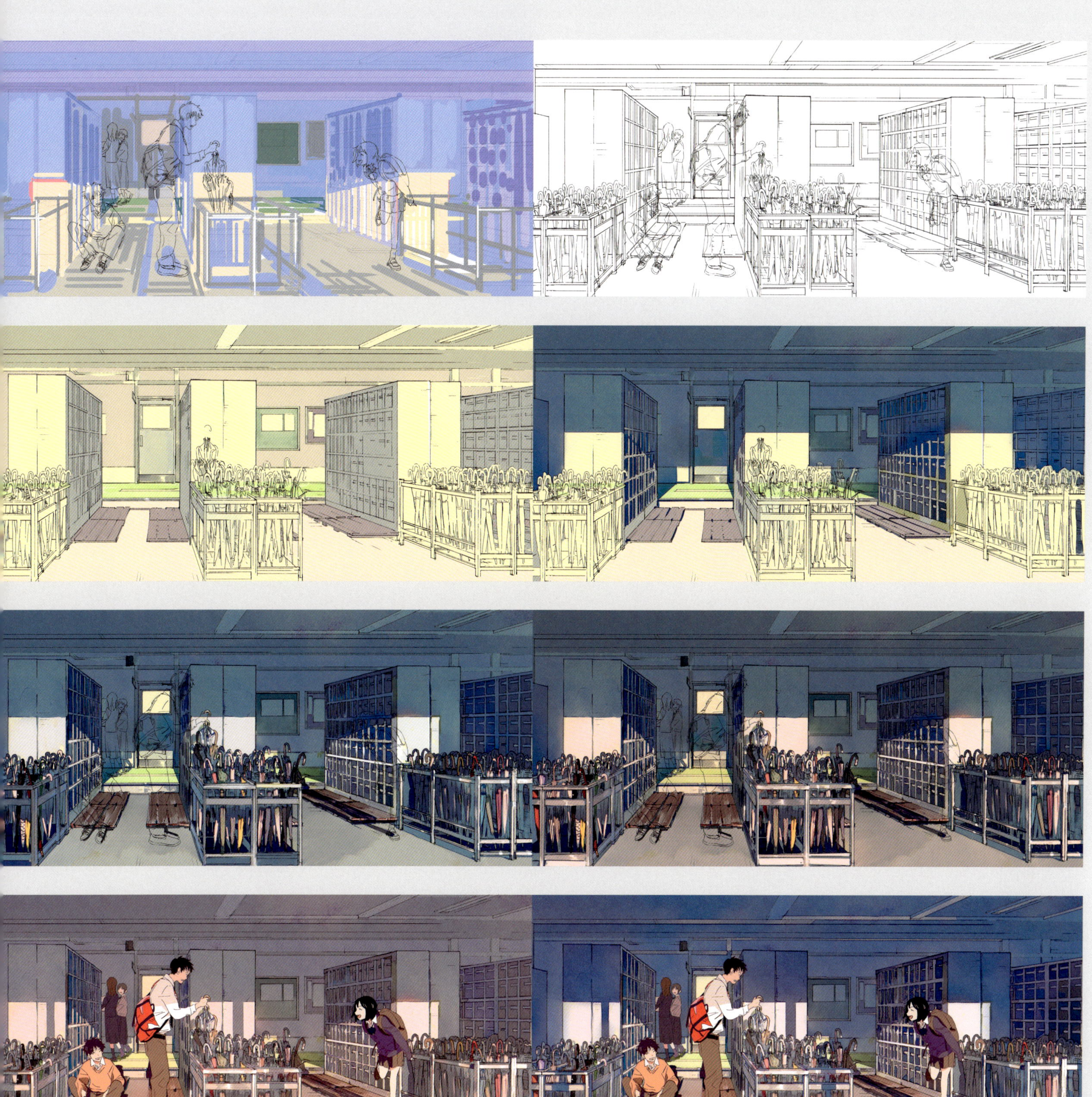

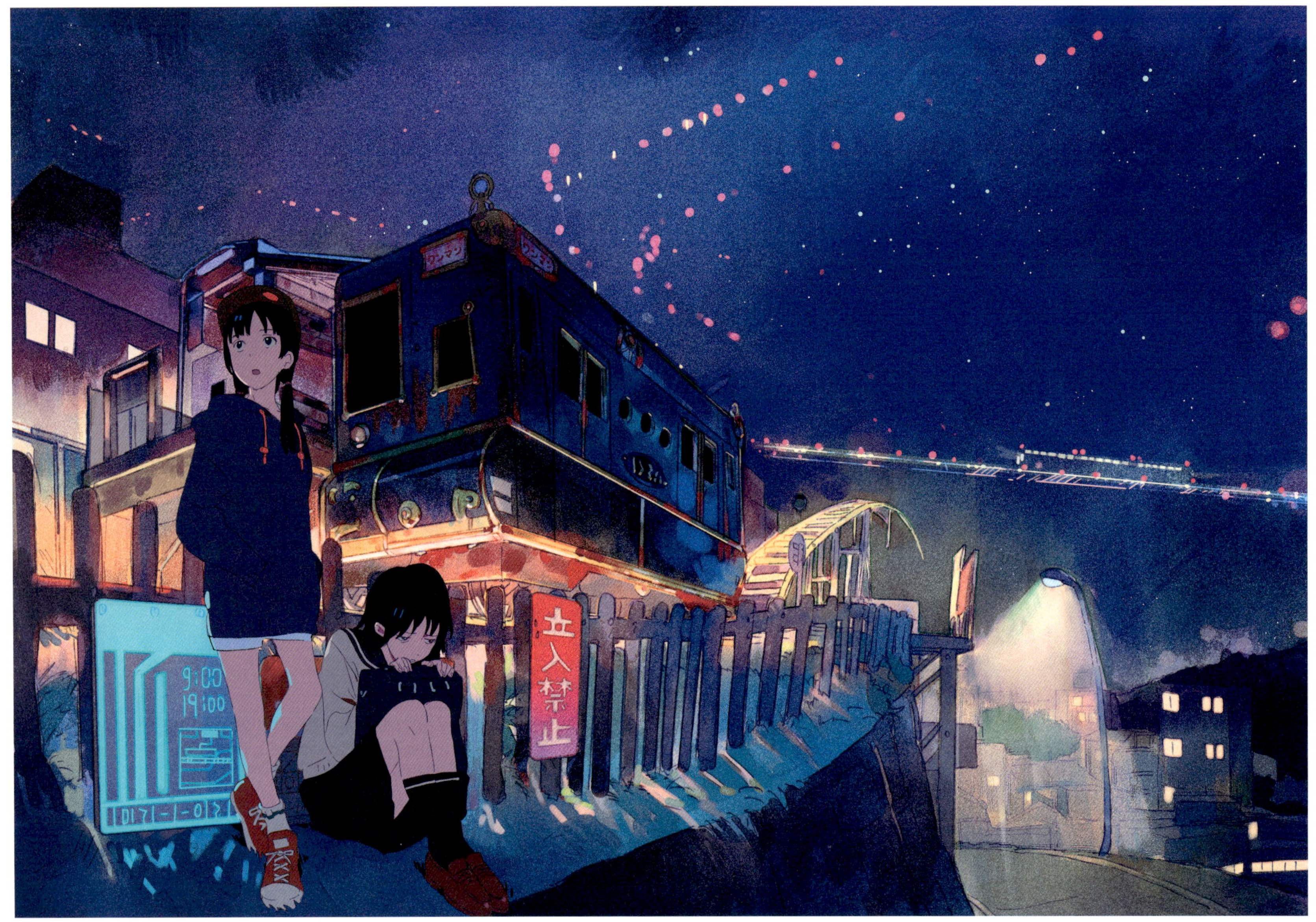

寄道 『月刊MdN2017年11月号「創る。」』（エムディエヌコーポレーション）メイキング用イラスト　｜　Detour, illustration for "Tsukuru." in the November 2017 edition of *MdN Design & Graphic* (MdN Corporation)

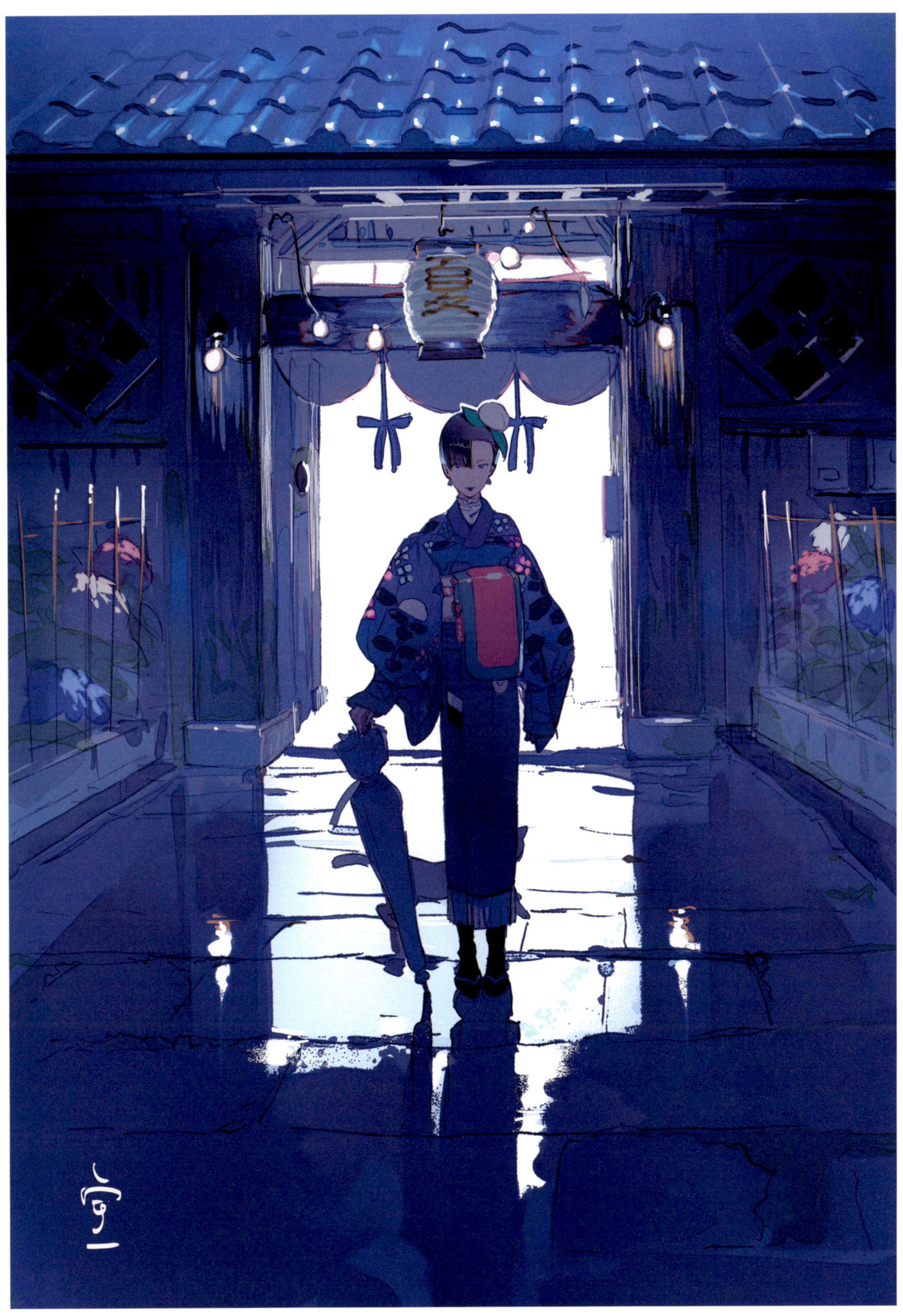
夏

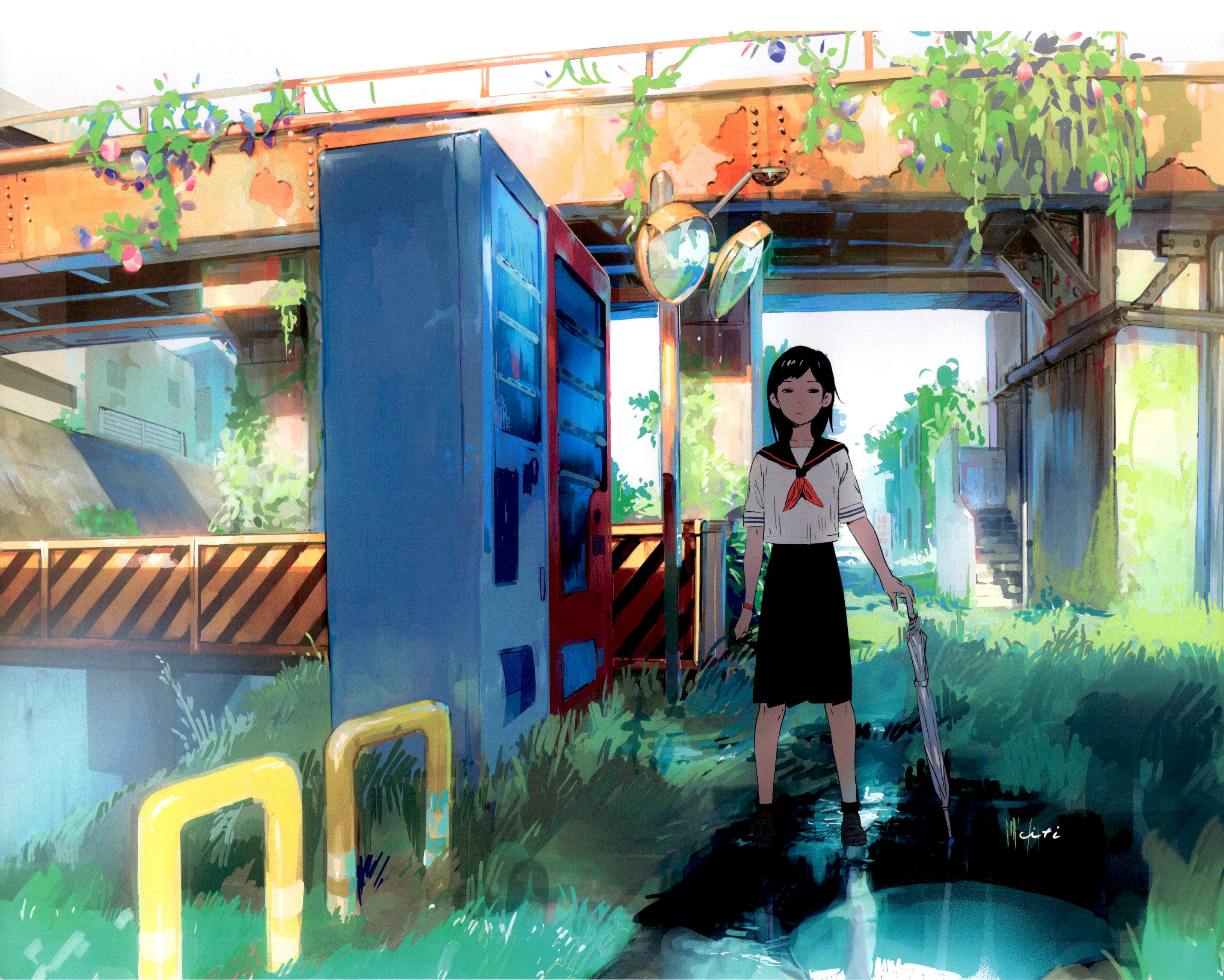

雨上がり　│　After the Rain

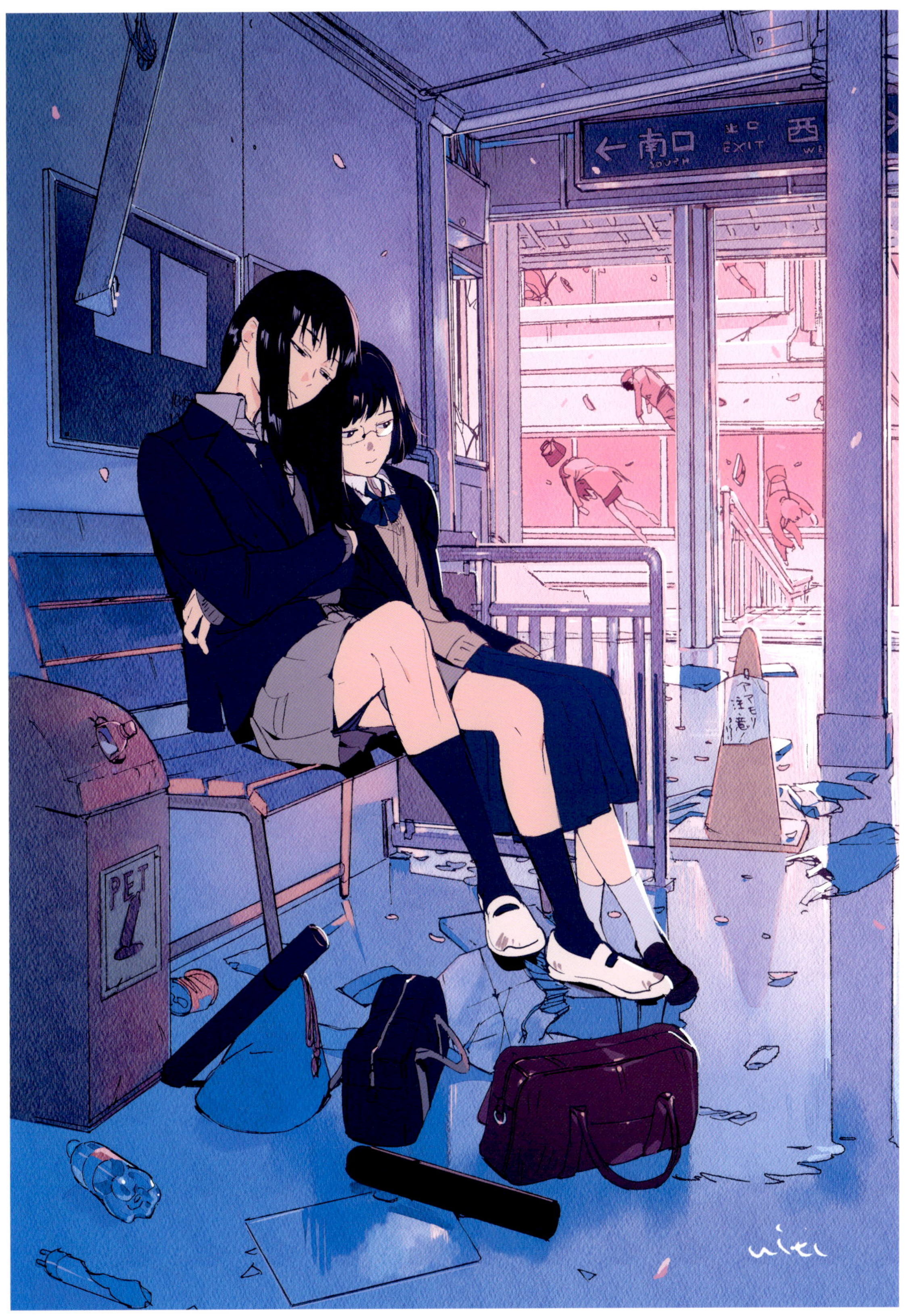

ぼくとわたし ｜ Me and Me

カタヒラシュンシ　｜　Shunshi Katahira

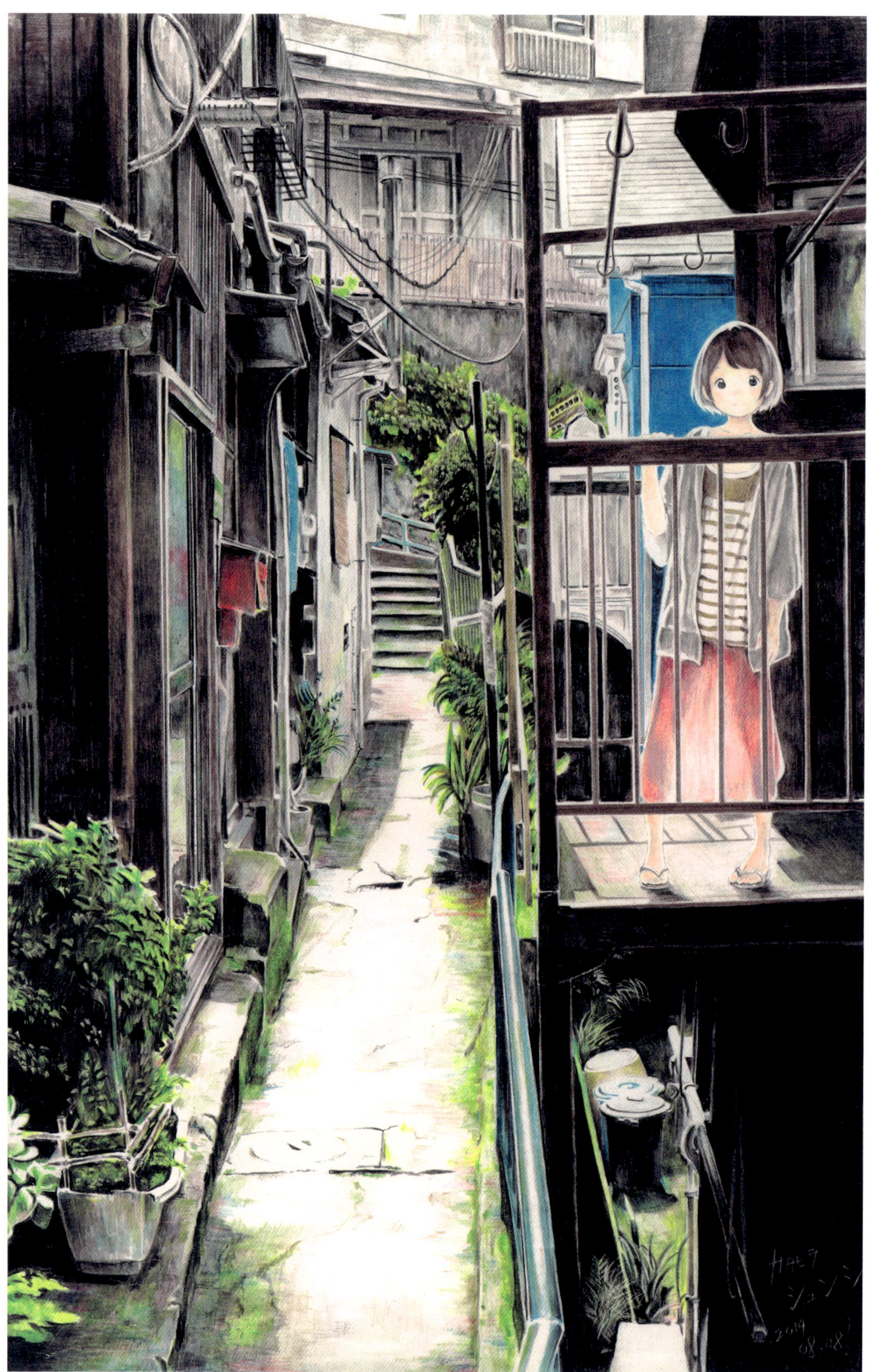

稲付谷の路地　｜　An Inatsukedani Alley

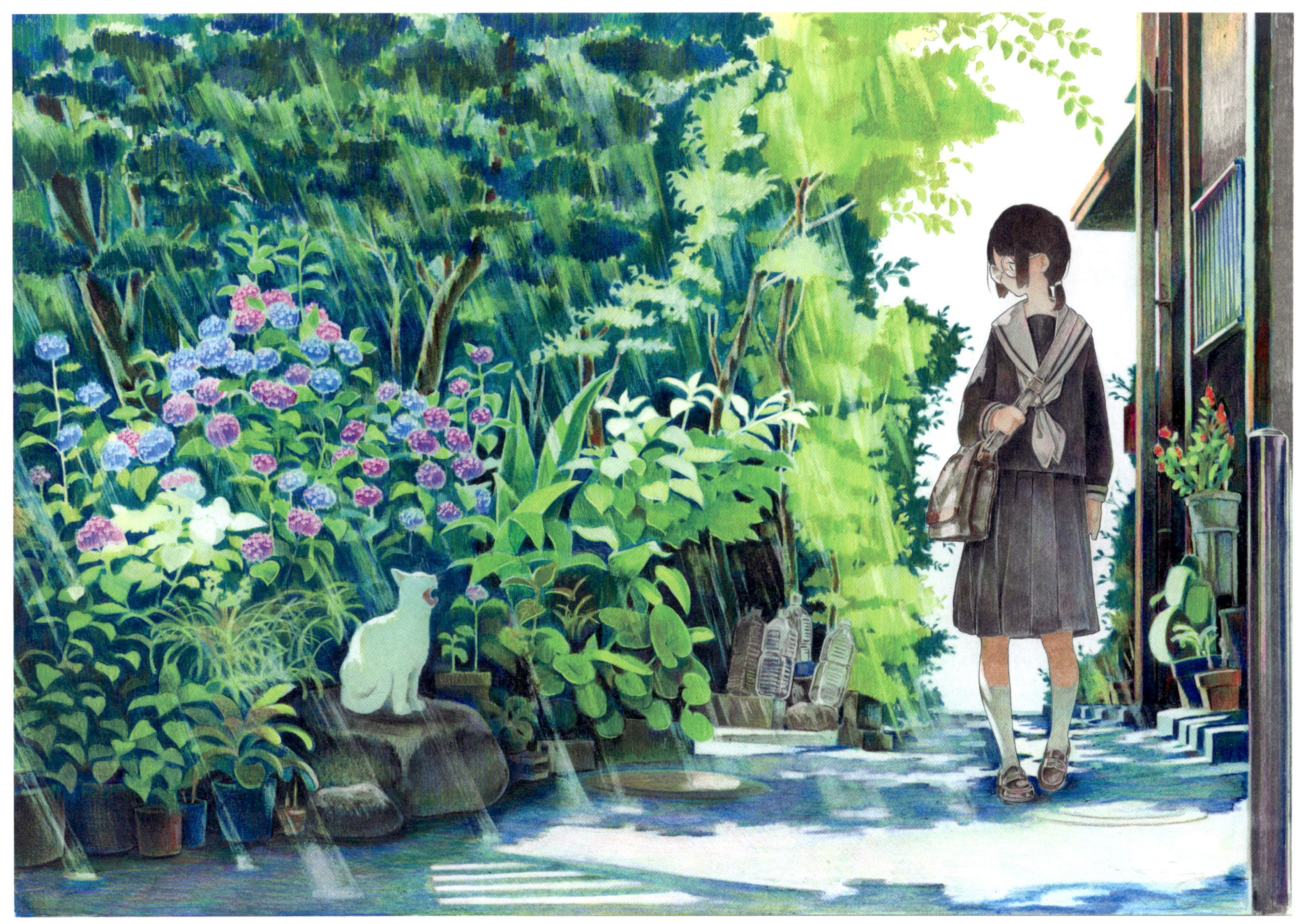

いつものみち『月刊MdN 2017年9月号』（エムディエヌコーポレーション）メイキングイラスト　|　The Same Old Path, illustration for the September 2017 edition of *MdN Design & Graphic* (MdN Corporation)

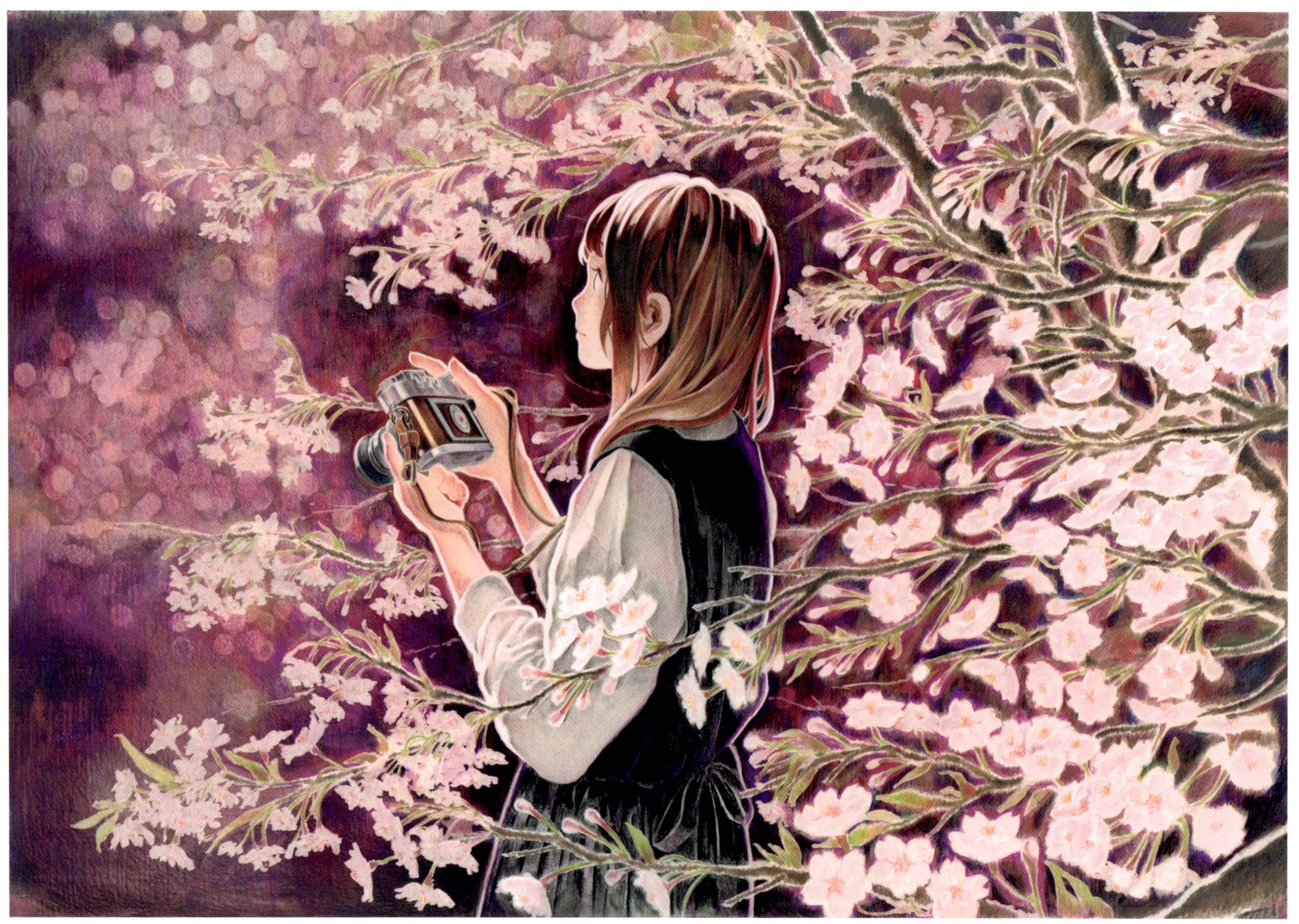

春をなぞる　|　Tracing Spring

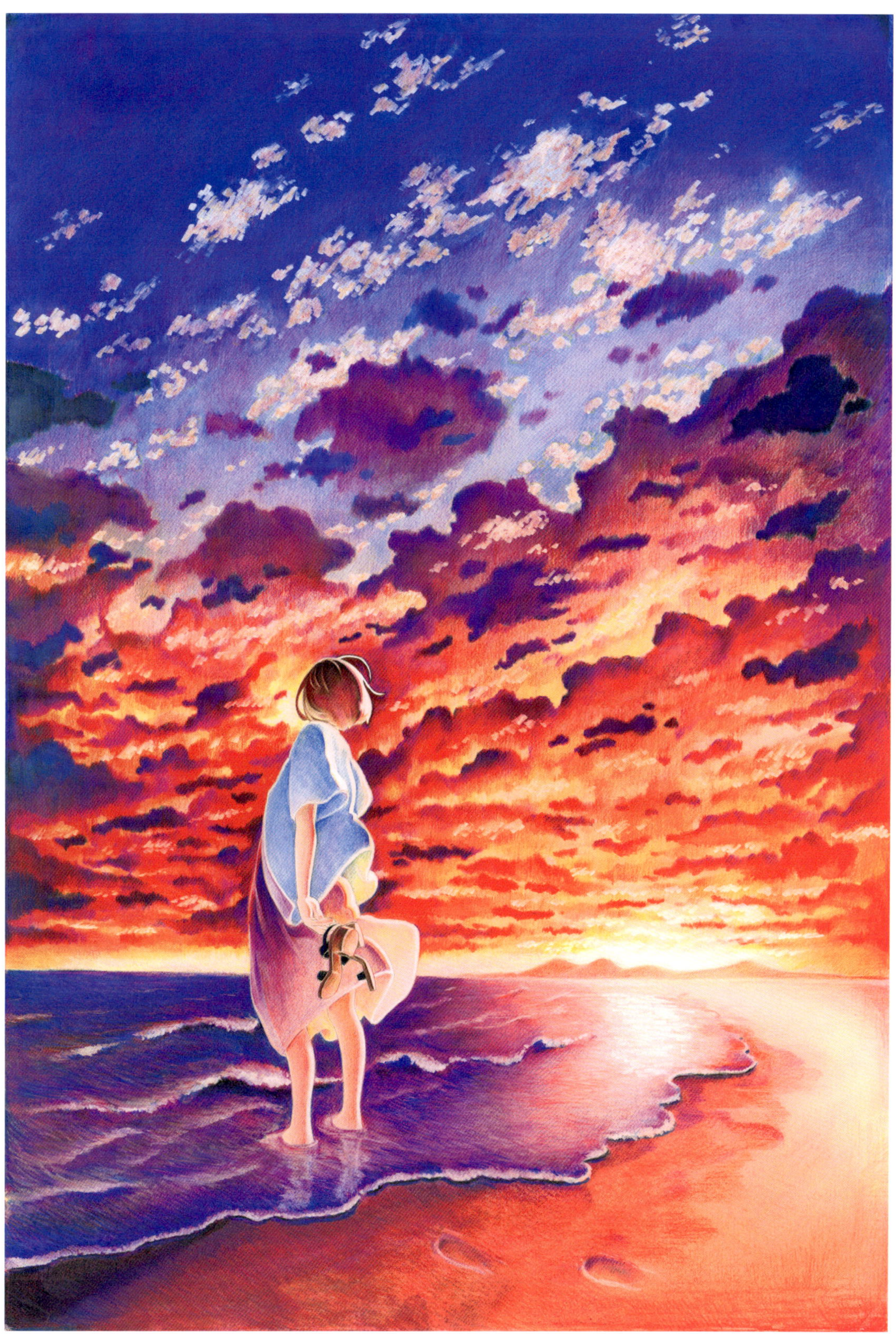

沁み込んでゆく　｜　Soaking It In

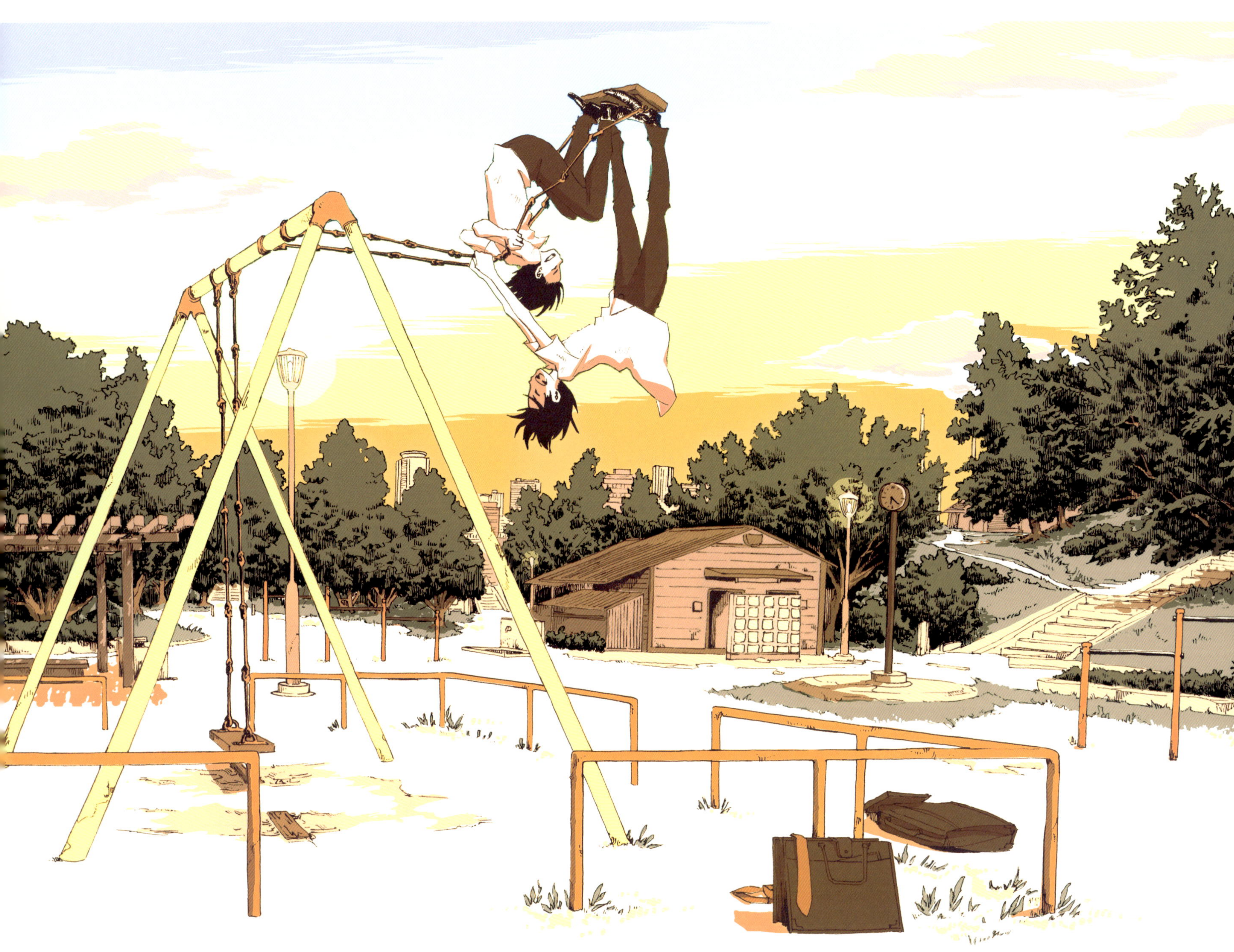

『今までも、これからも。』（oldflame）CD ジャケットイラスト　｜　*Now and Forever*, a CD cover illustration for oldflame

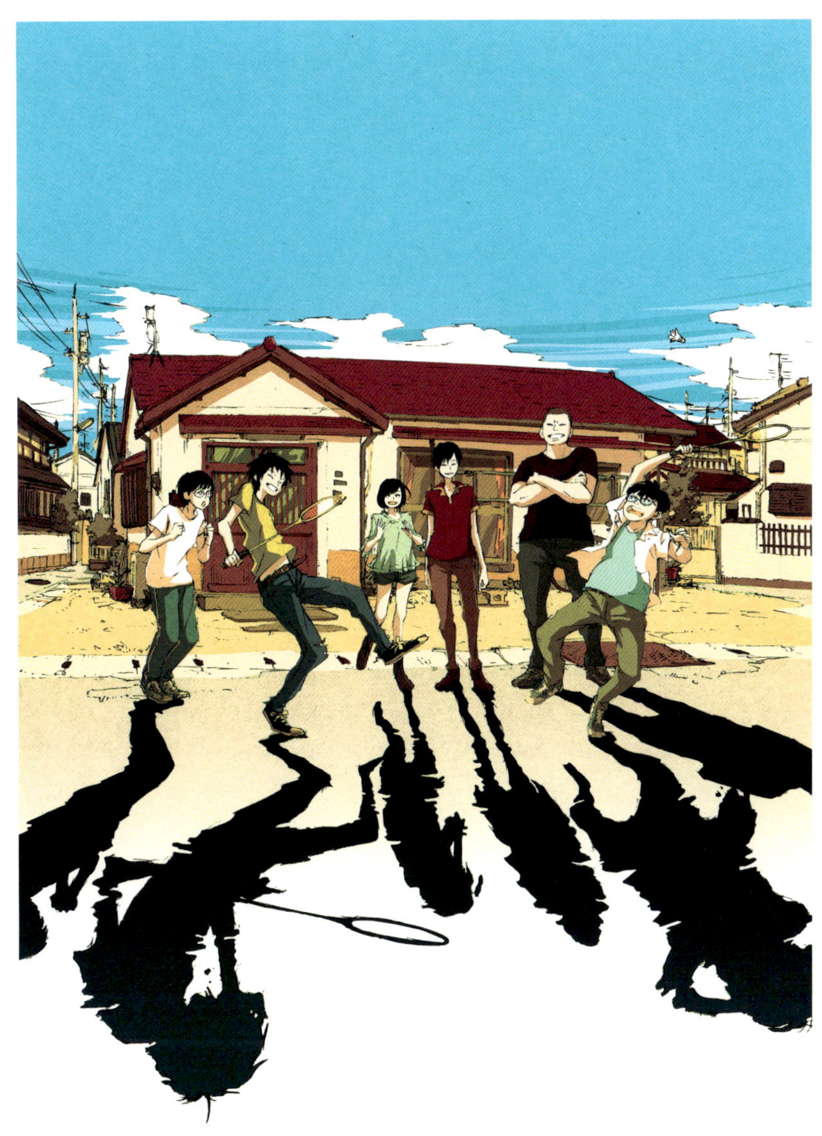

『今日からは、愛のひと』（朱川湊人 著、光文社文庫）装画
Cover illustration for *Kyo Kara wa, Ai no Hito* (a novel written by Minato Shukawa, published by Kobunsha)

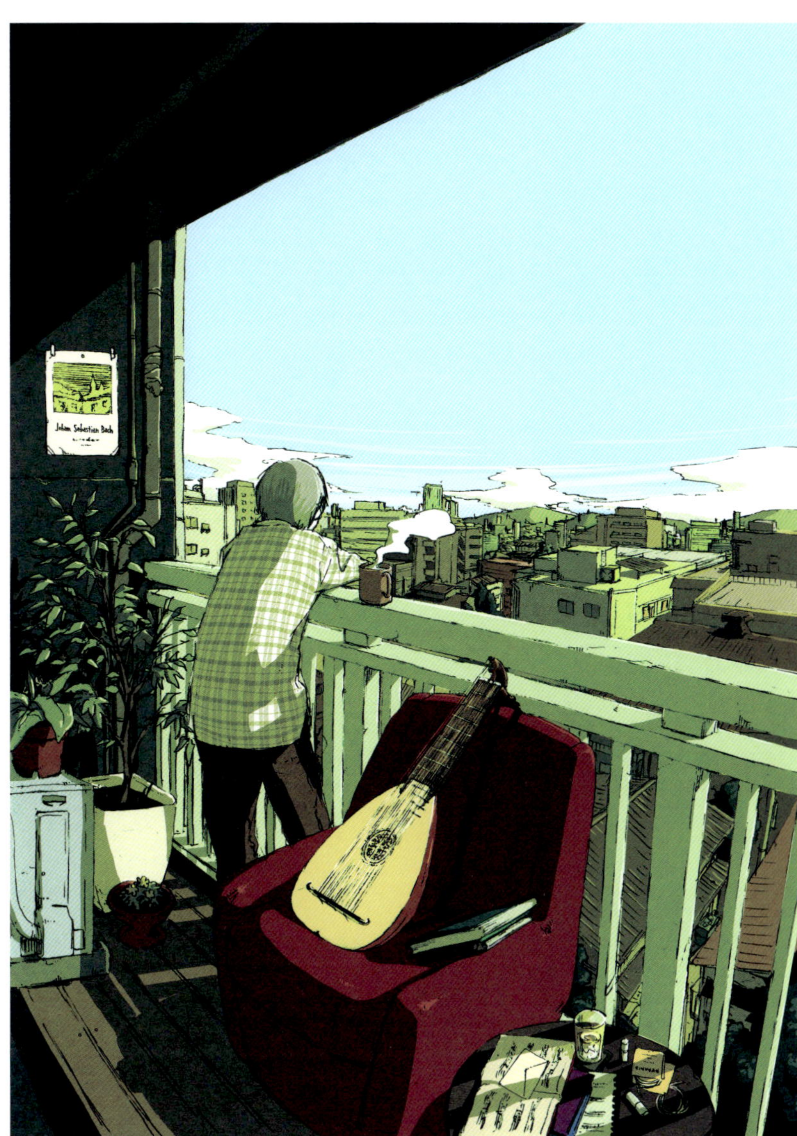

「バッハ・オン・リュート　中川祥治リュートリサイタル」（奏者 中川祥治）ポスターイラスト
Illustrated poster for *Bach on Lute – a Lute Recital by Shoji Nakagawa* (performed by Shoji Nakagawa)

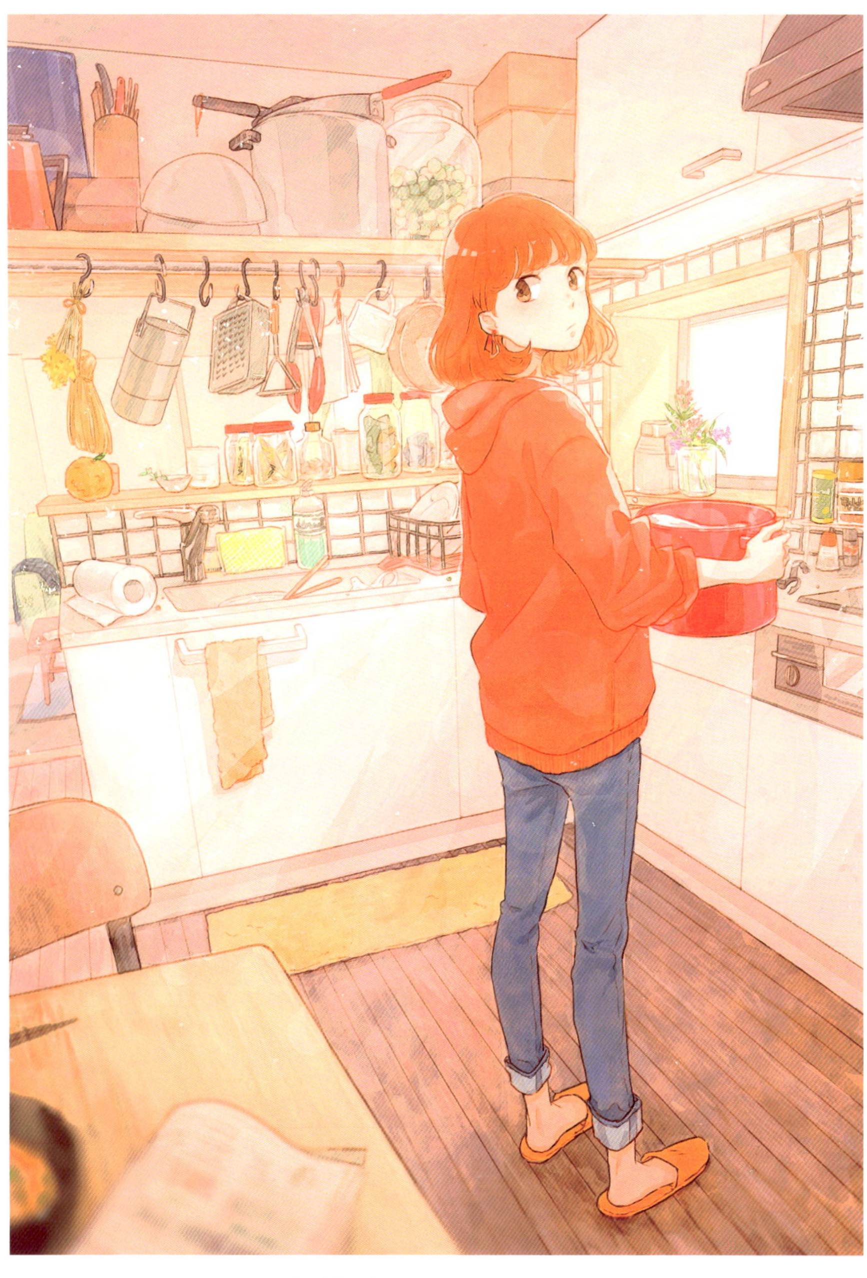

お昼は素麺　｜　Thin Cold Noodles for Lunch

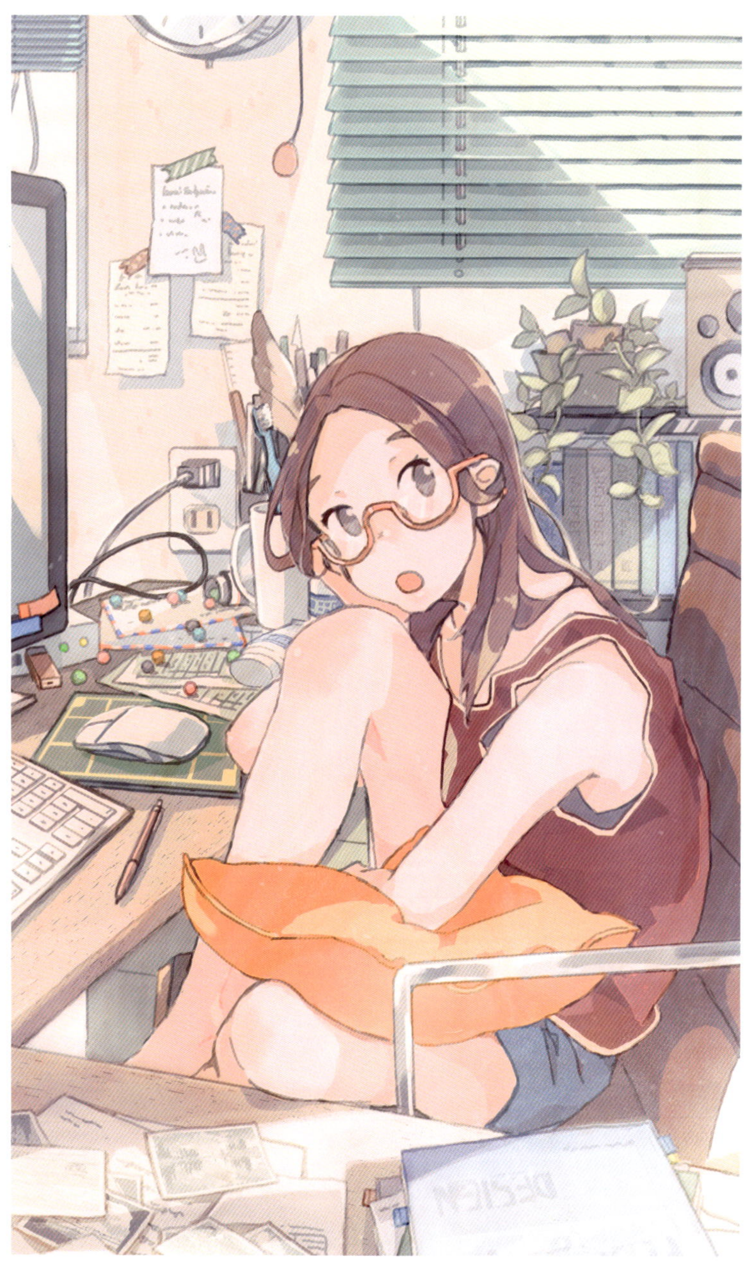

創作女子　｜　Creative Girl

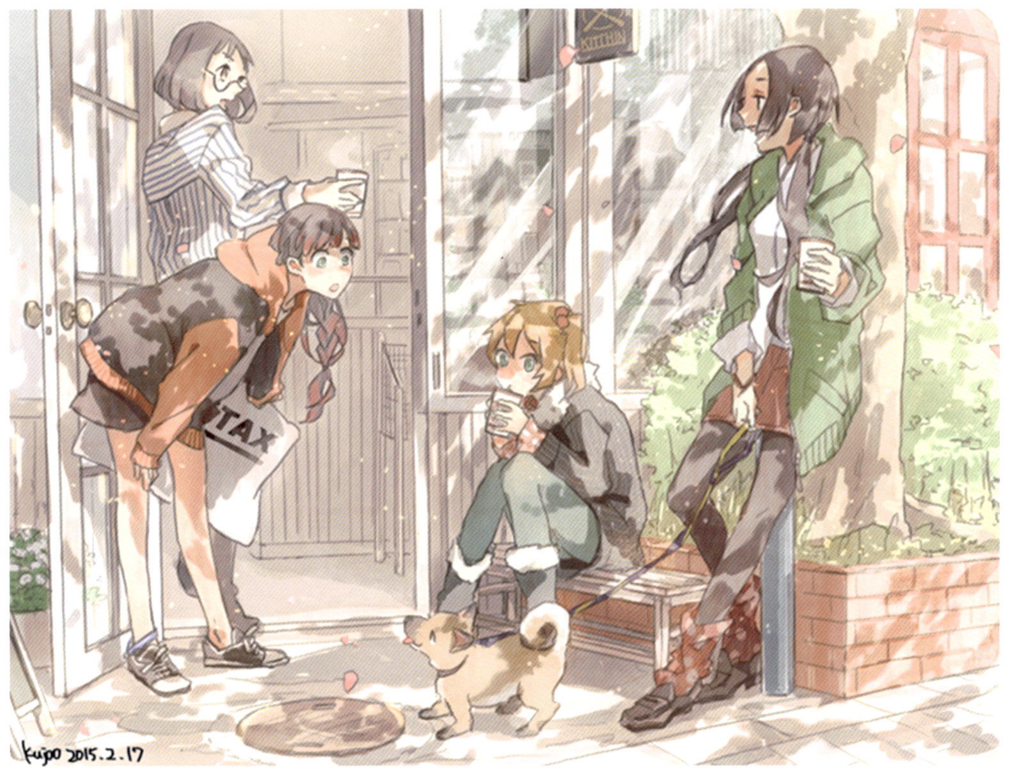

今日はどこに遊びに行こう？　│　Where Should We Go Today?

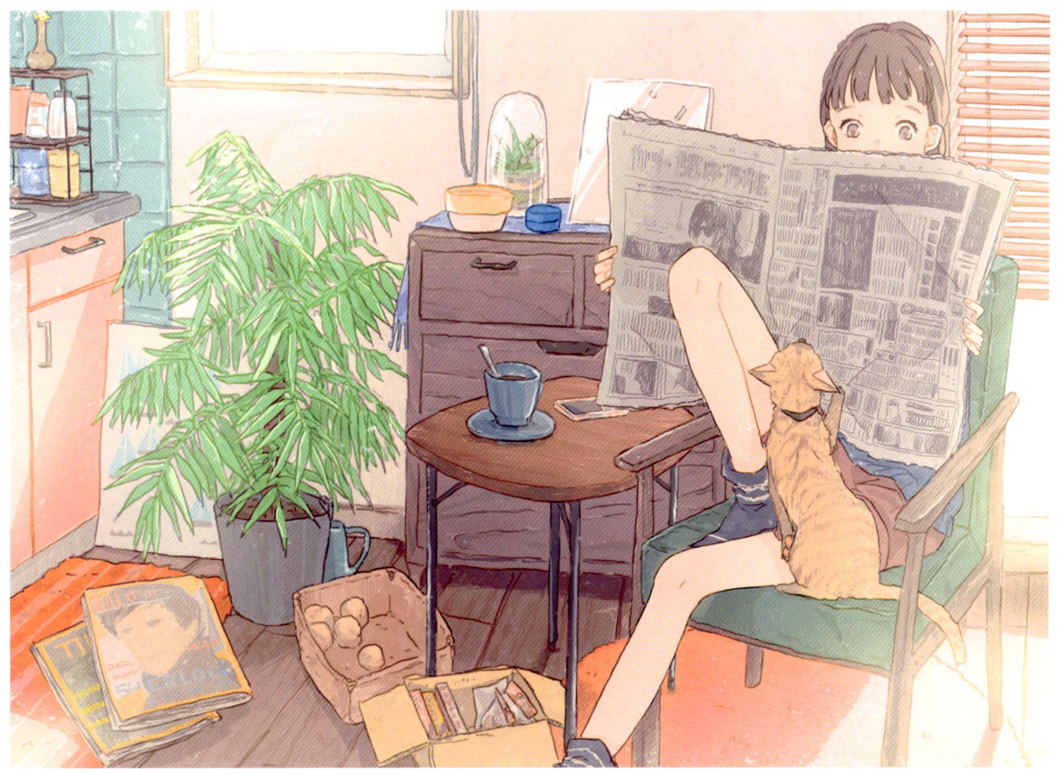

新聞とにゃー　│　Newspaper & Meow

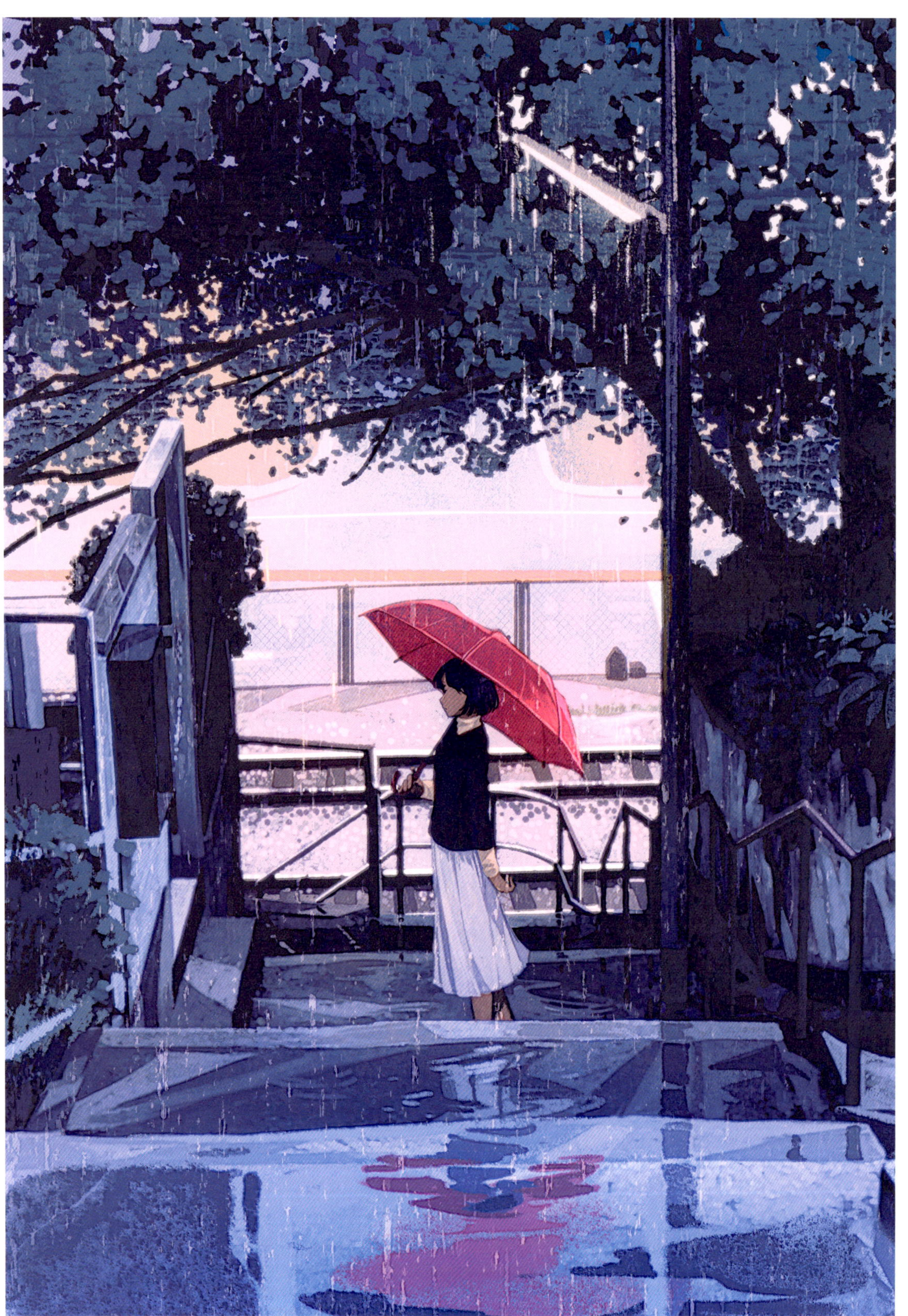

もうすぐ通る音がする　|　Should Hear the Passing Sound Soon

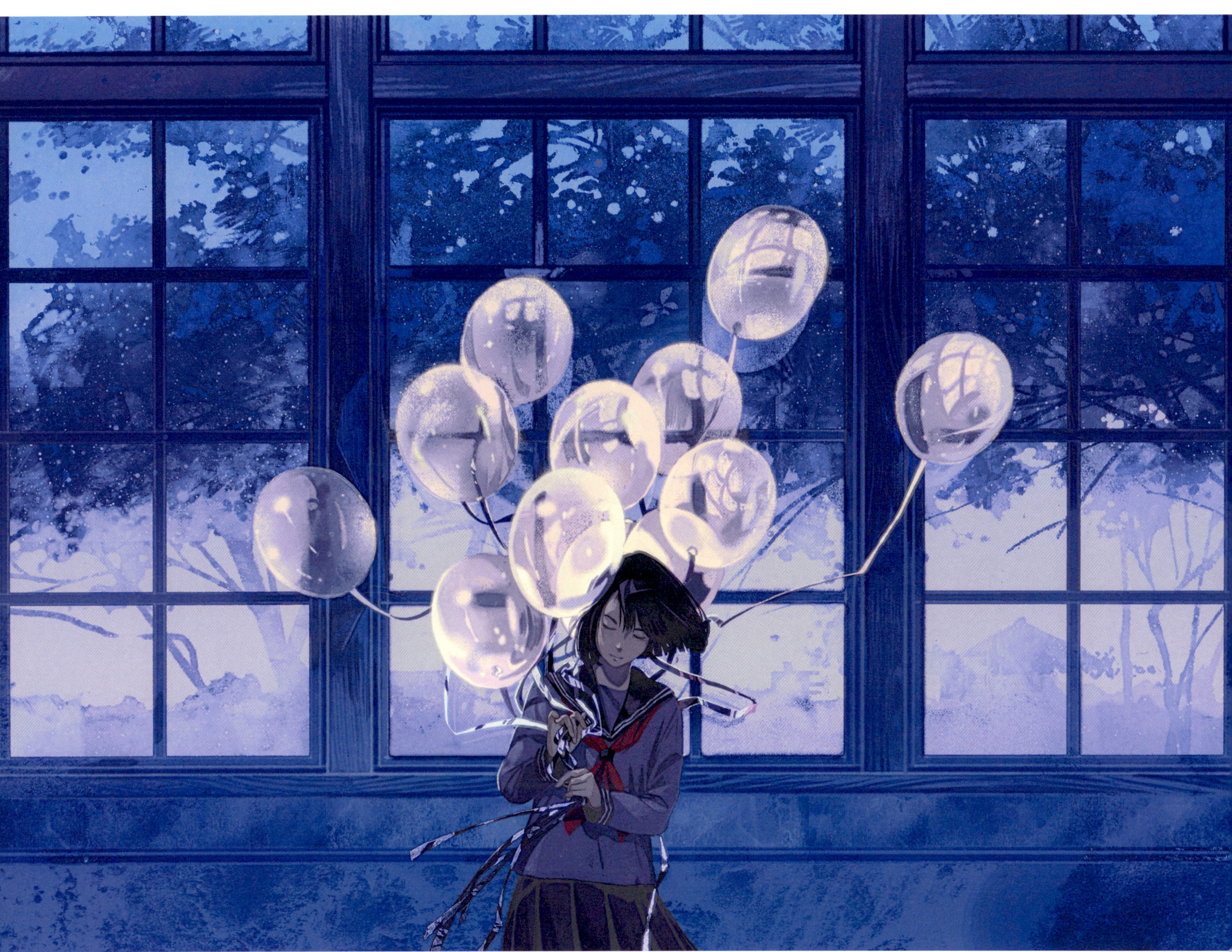

割れてしまう前に　|　Before They Broke

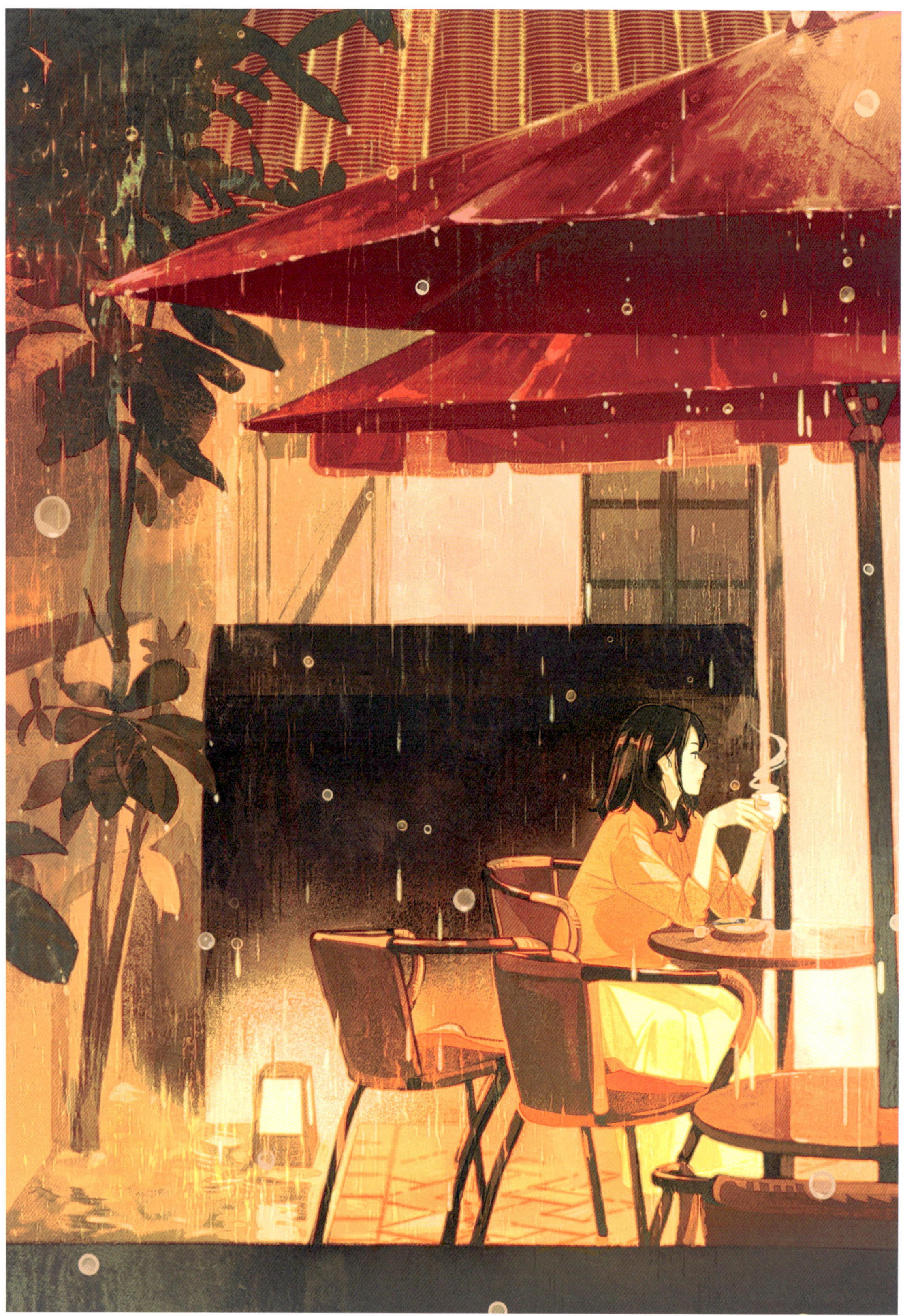

シロップ ｜ Syrup

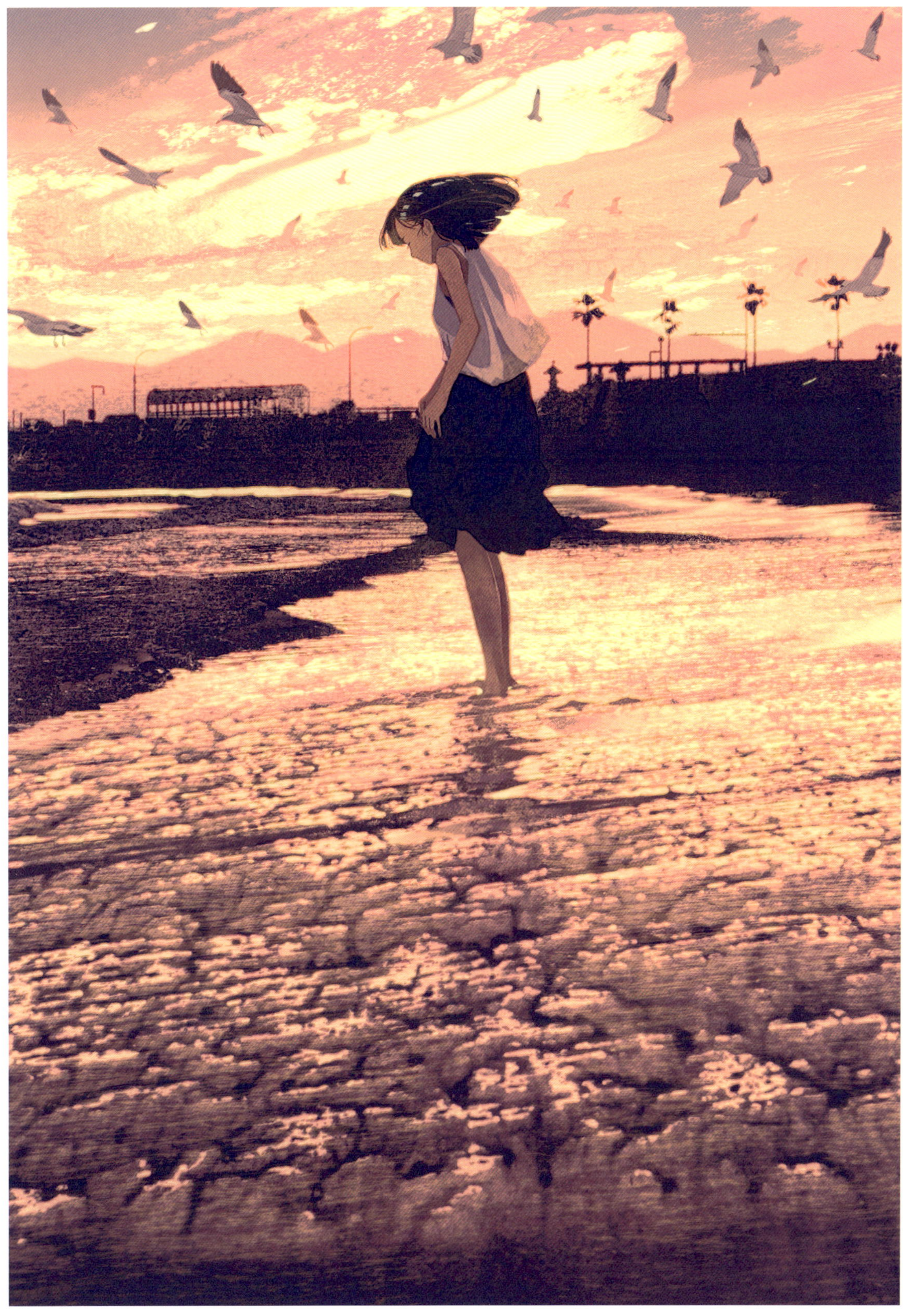

溶けゆく私　|　I'm Melting

Illustrations created for this book

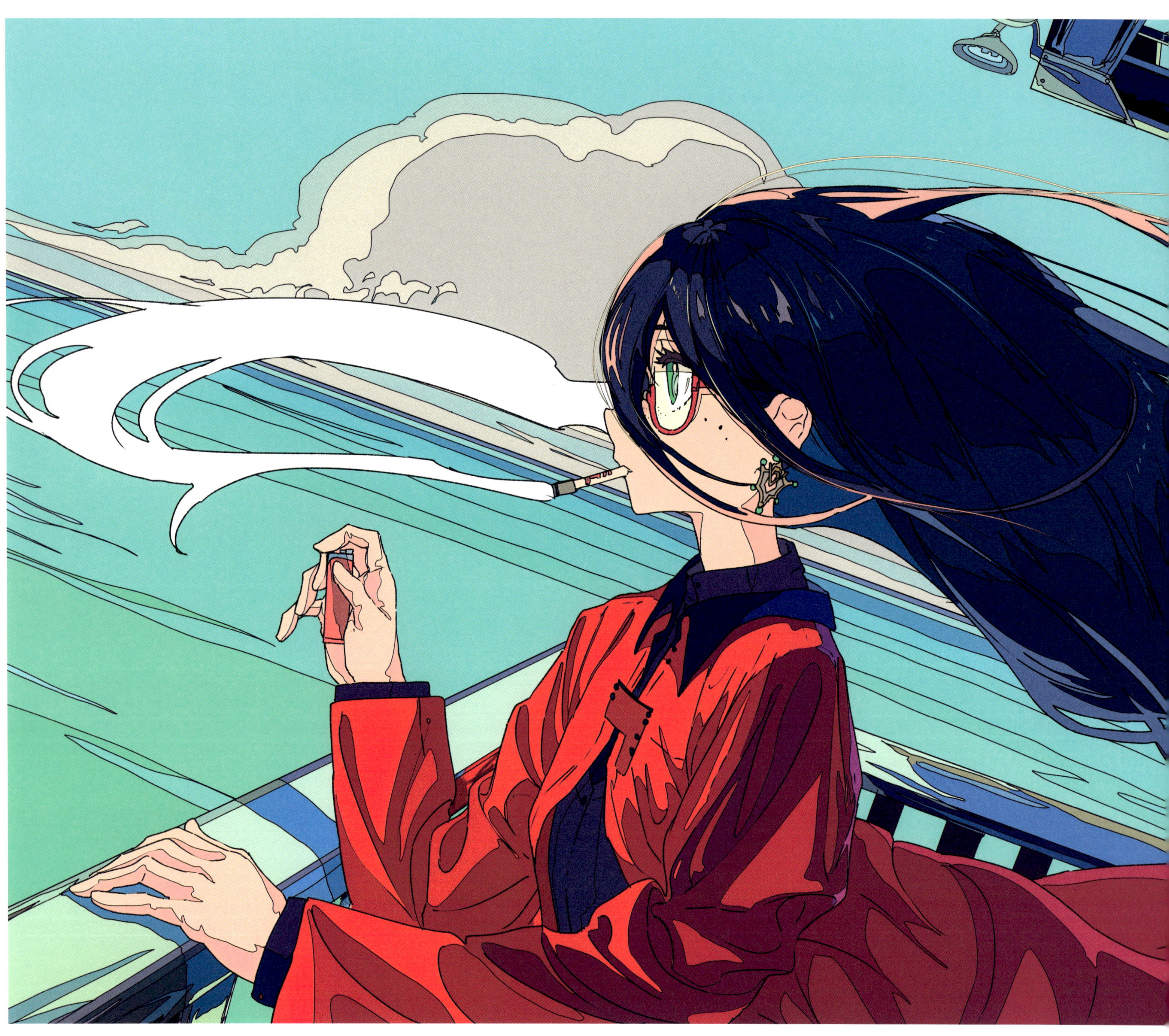

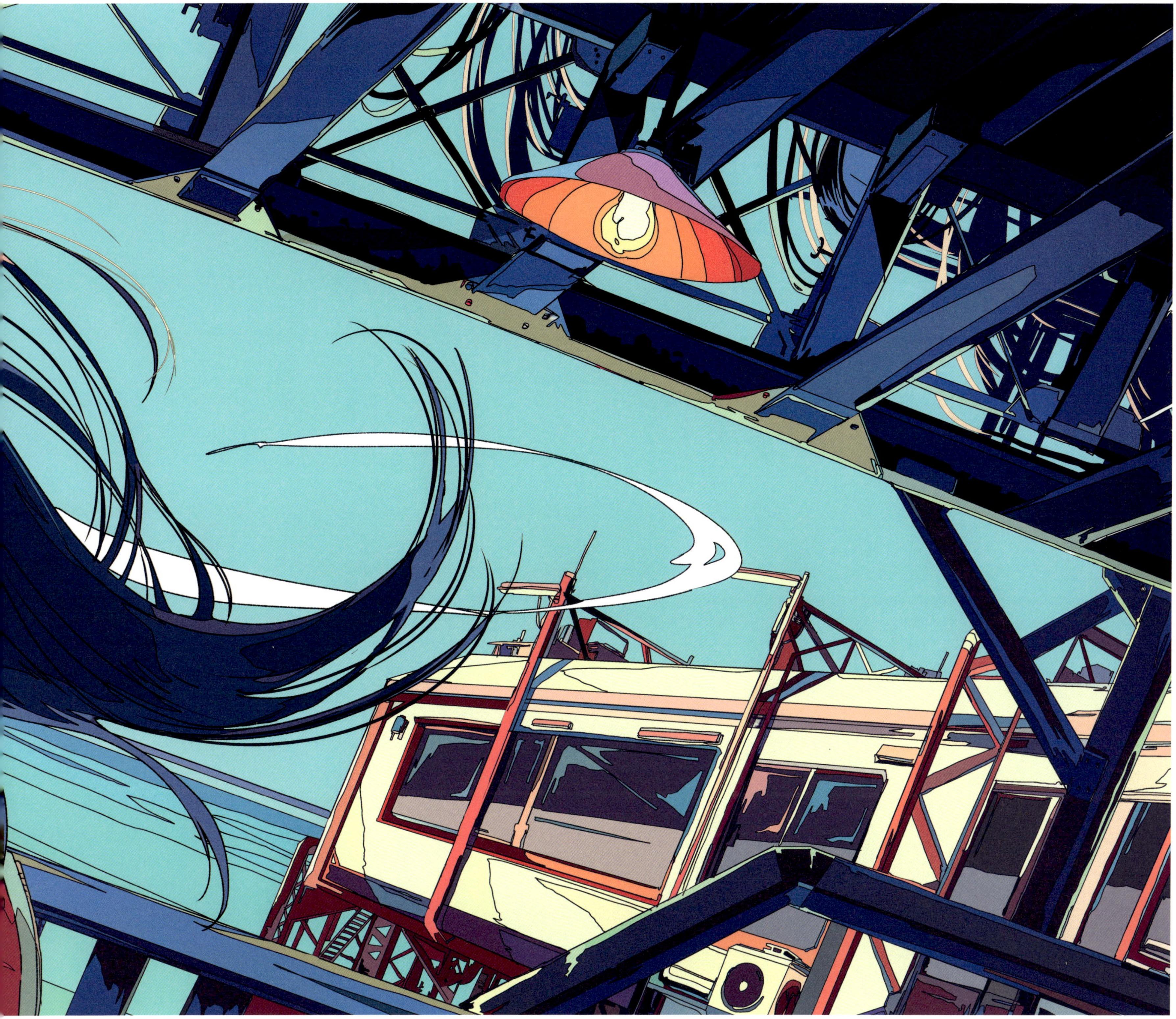

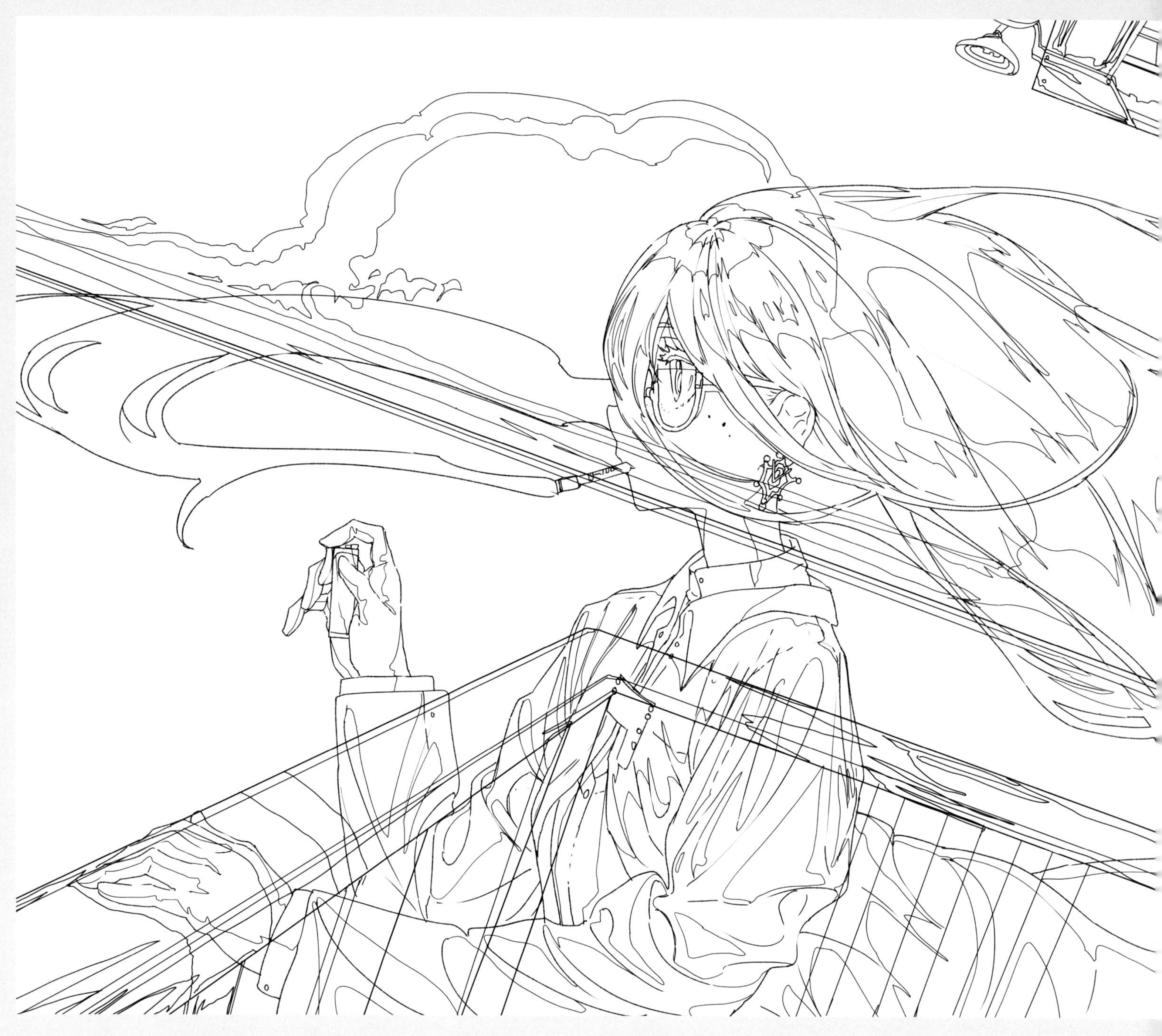

自分が一番気に入っている浅葱色と赤を組み合わせて描きました。
ほぼ僕の好きなモチーフの詰め合わせです。
最近はシネスコに近いアスペクト比で描くのにハマっています。
基本的にラフは iPad の Procreate で描いて、
仕上げは MobileStudio Pro16 で CLIP STUDIO PAINT を使っています。

I drew this by combining my favorite pale blue-green and red colors.
It's basically a mashup of my favorite motifs. I've been really into drawing illustrations with a wide aspect ratio,
similar to wide screen movies.
In general, I create rough sketches using Procreate on my iPad,
and then make the final illustrations using CLIP STUDIO PAINT on my MobileStudio Pro 16.

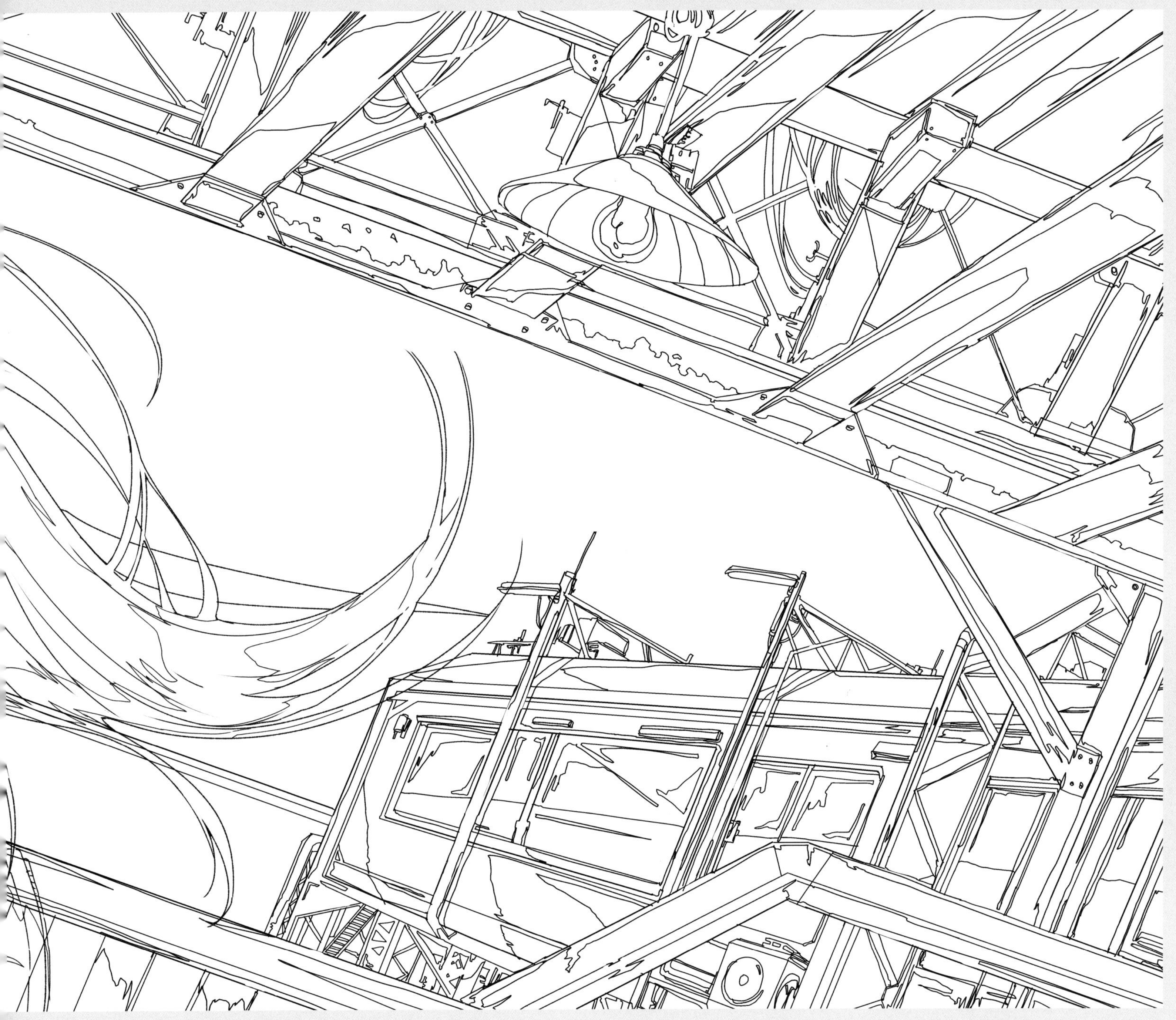

斜（線画）　|　Slope (Line drawing)

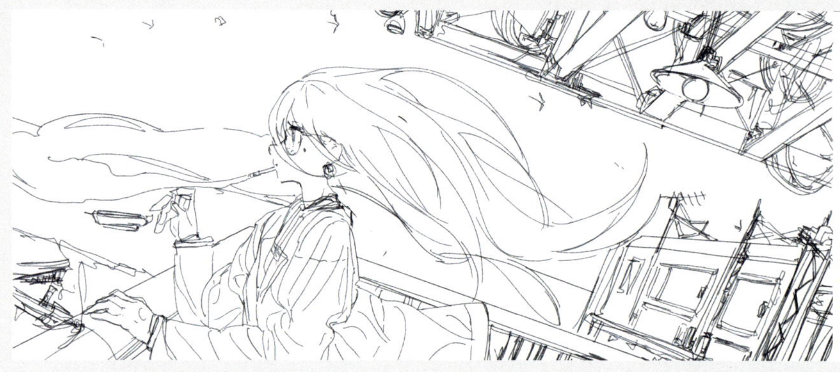

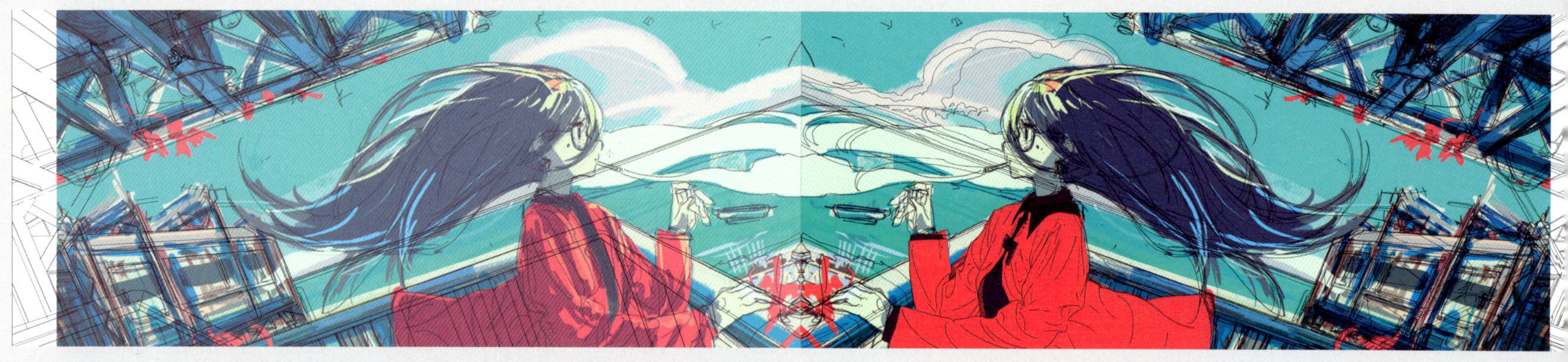

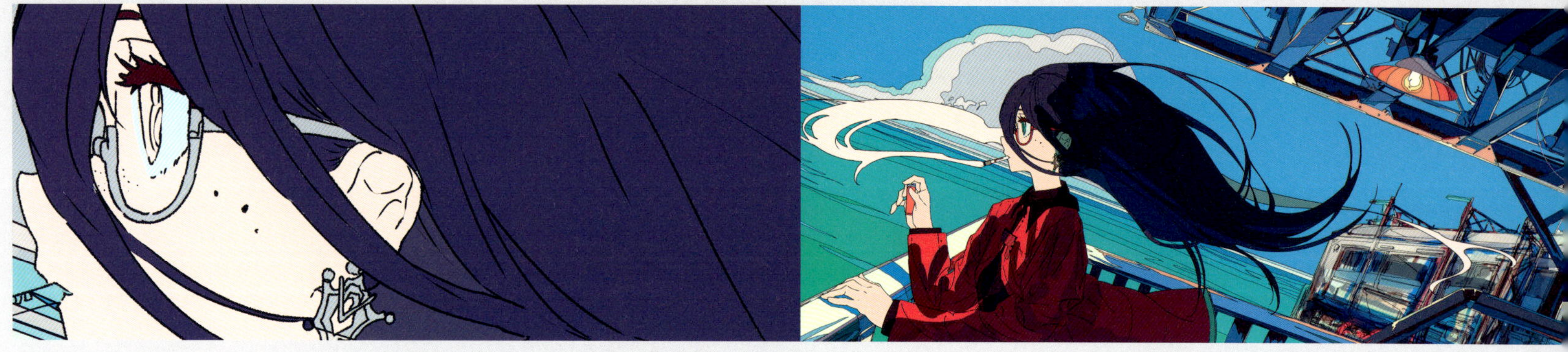

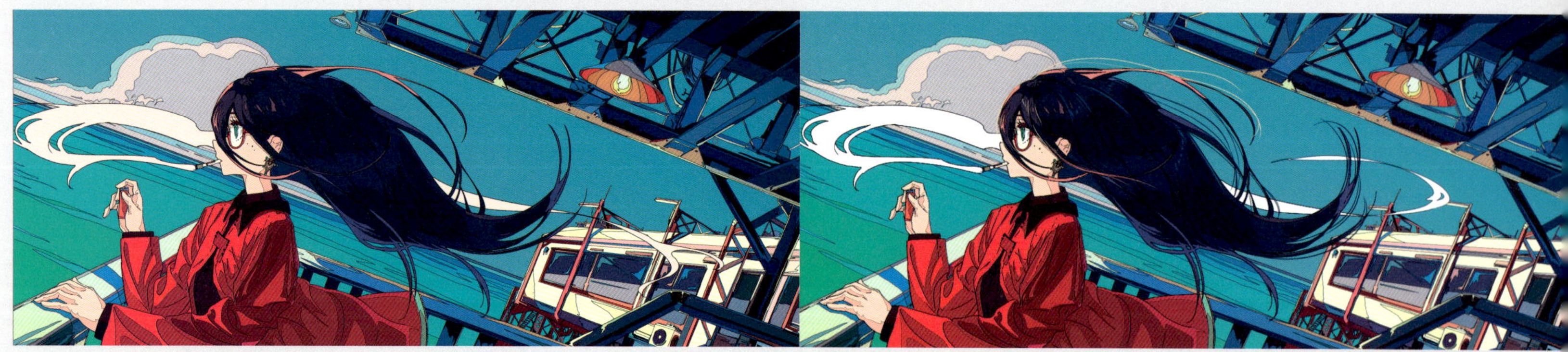

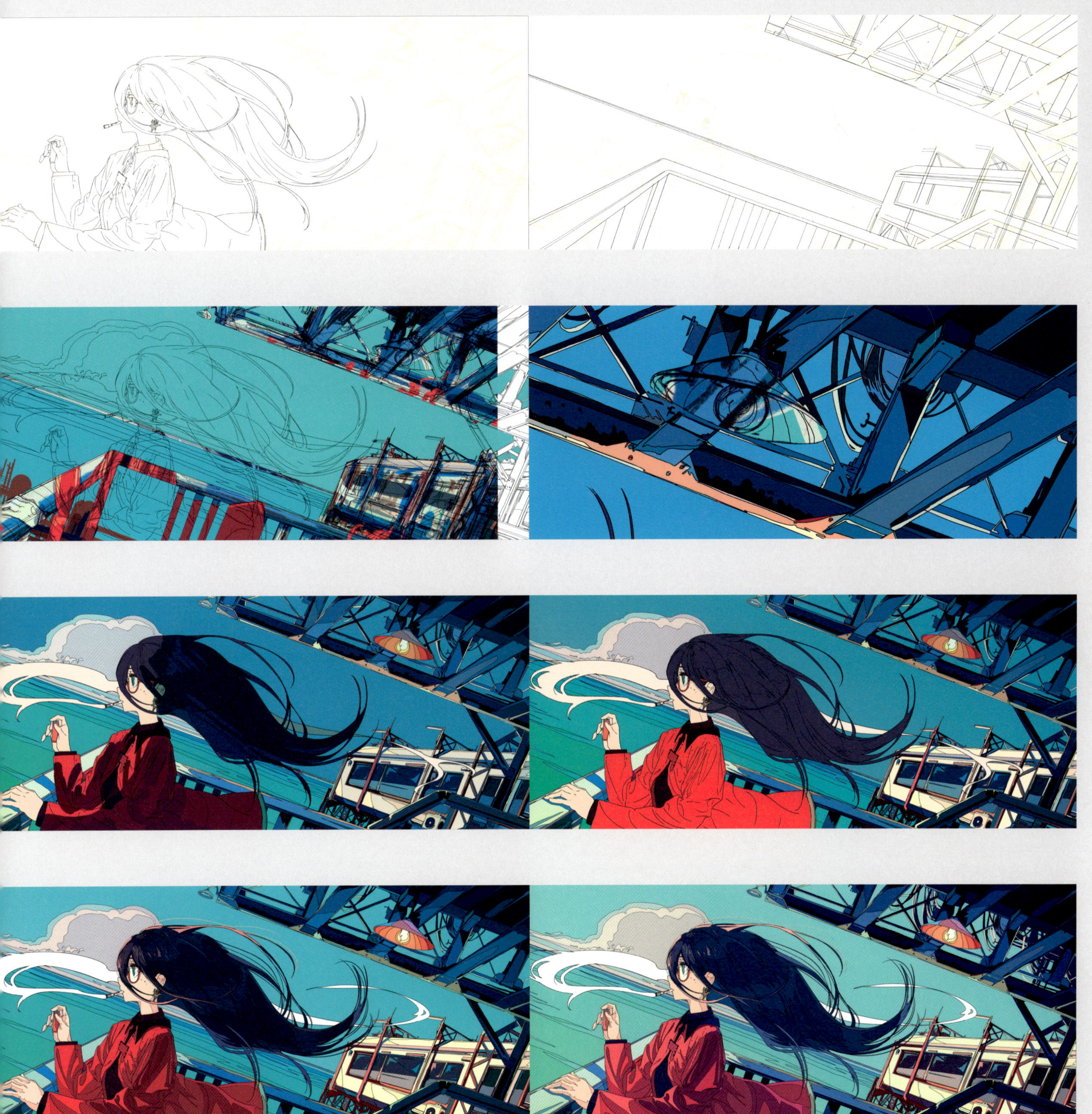

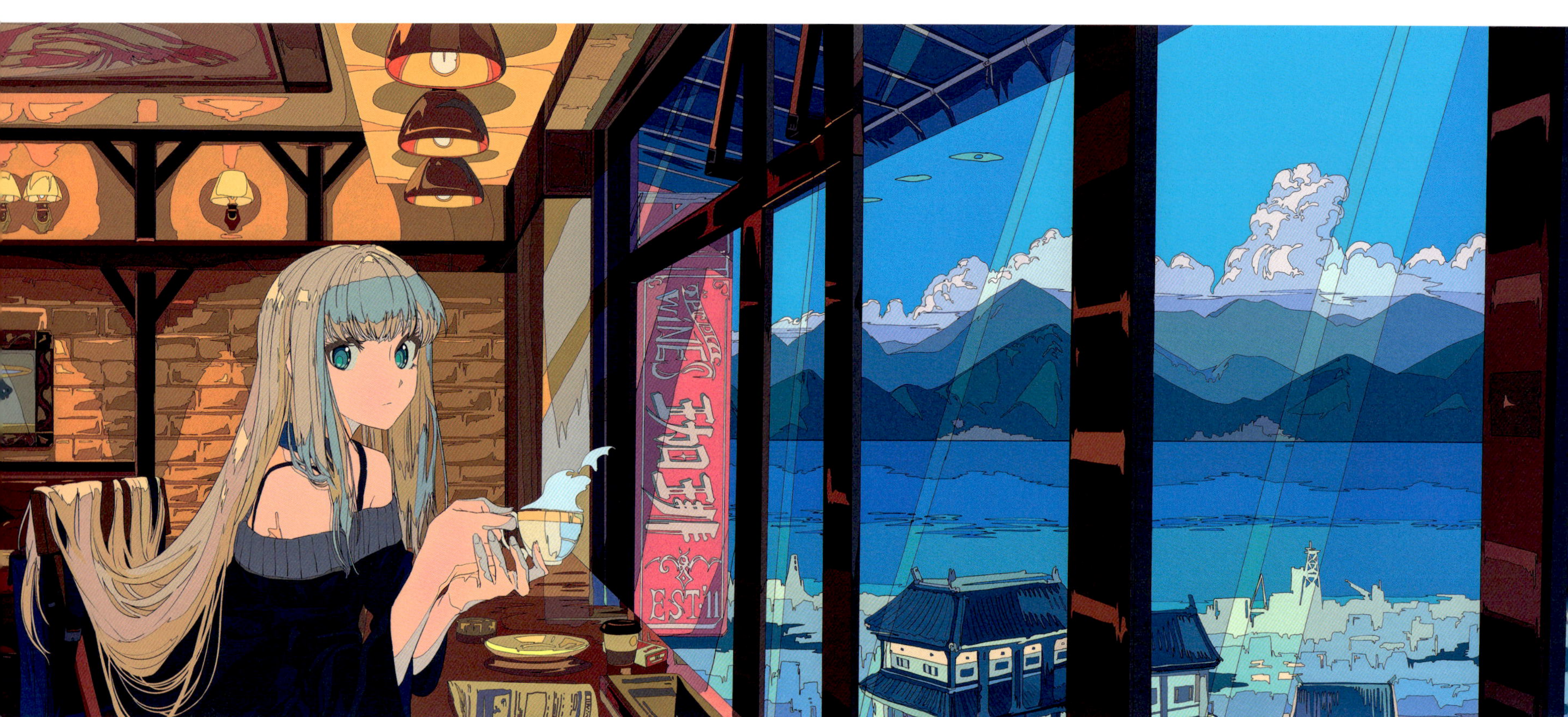

架　|　table

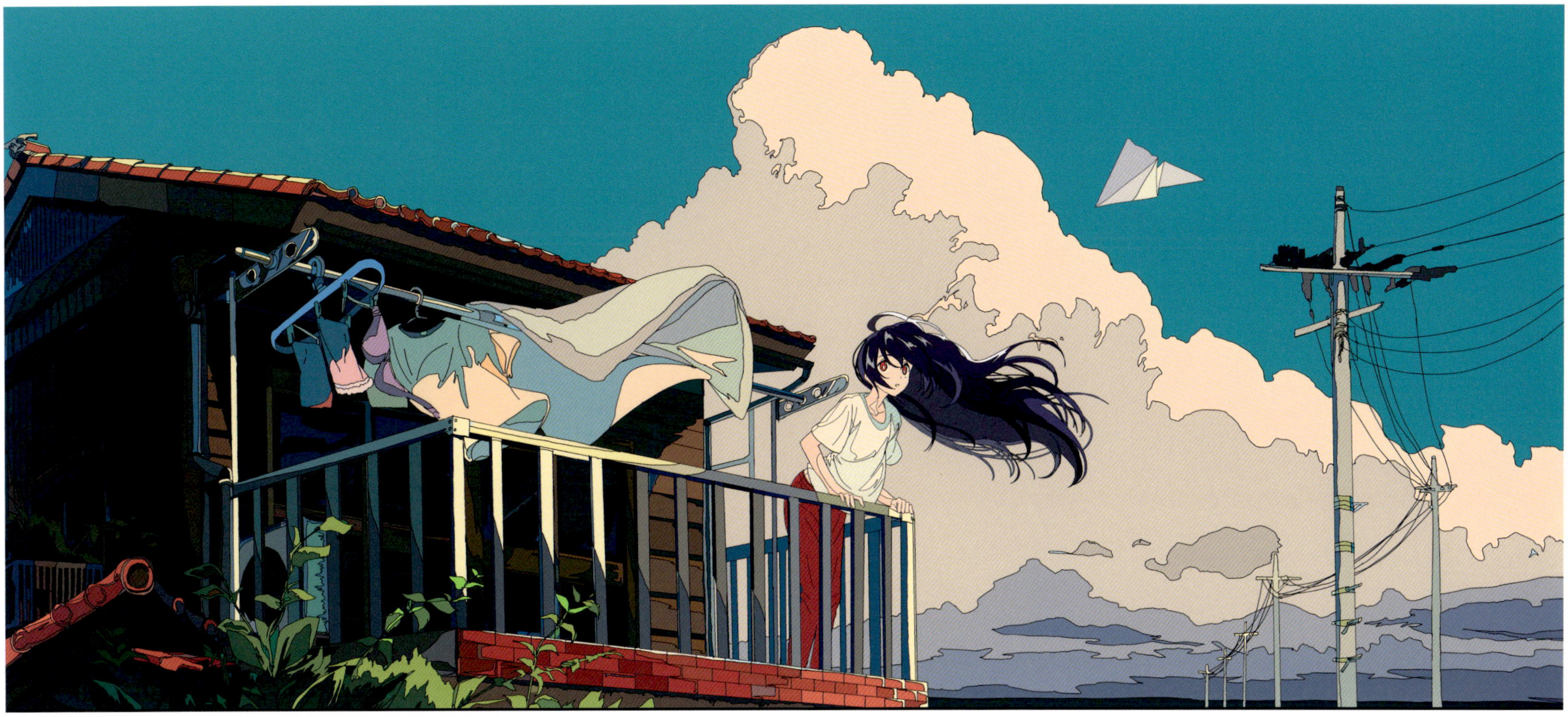

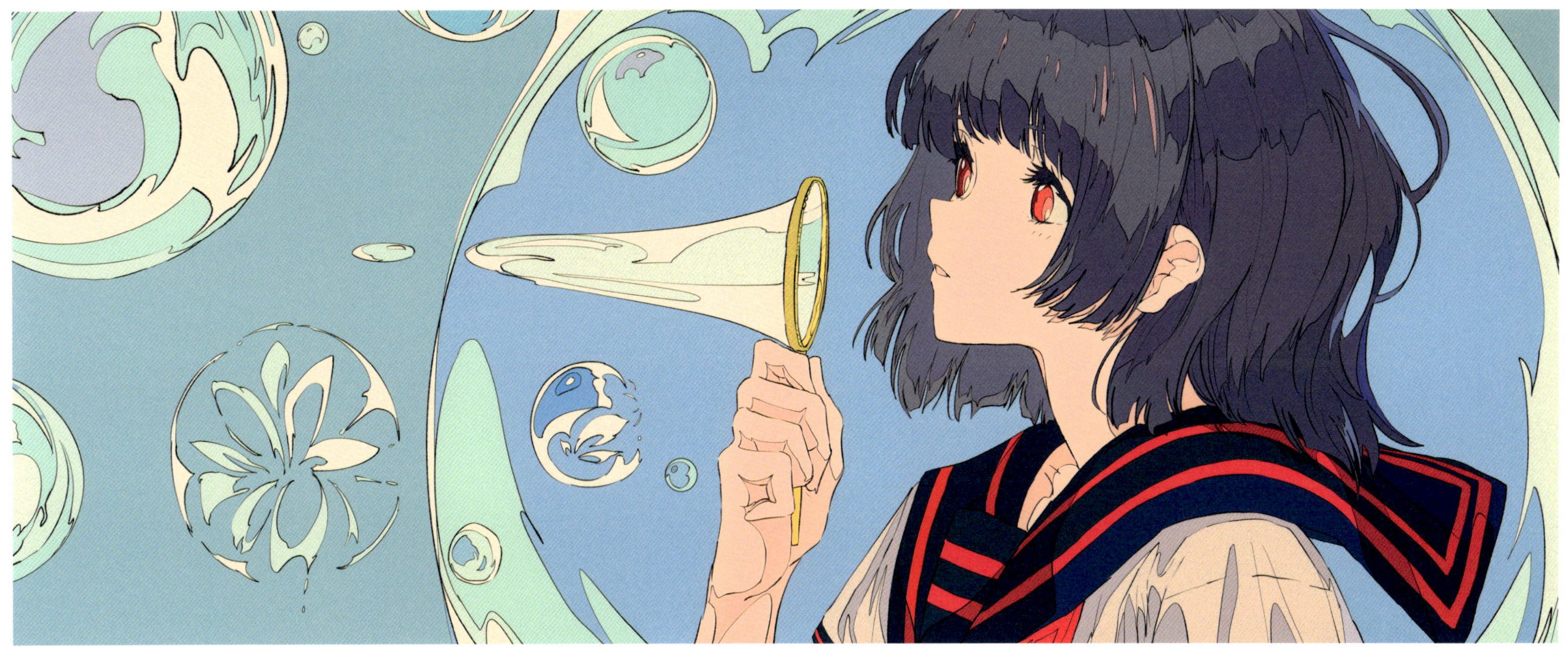

紙飛行機　|　paper airplane

隔　|　disparity

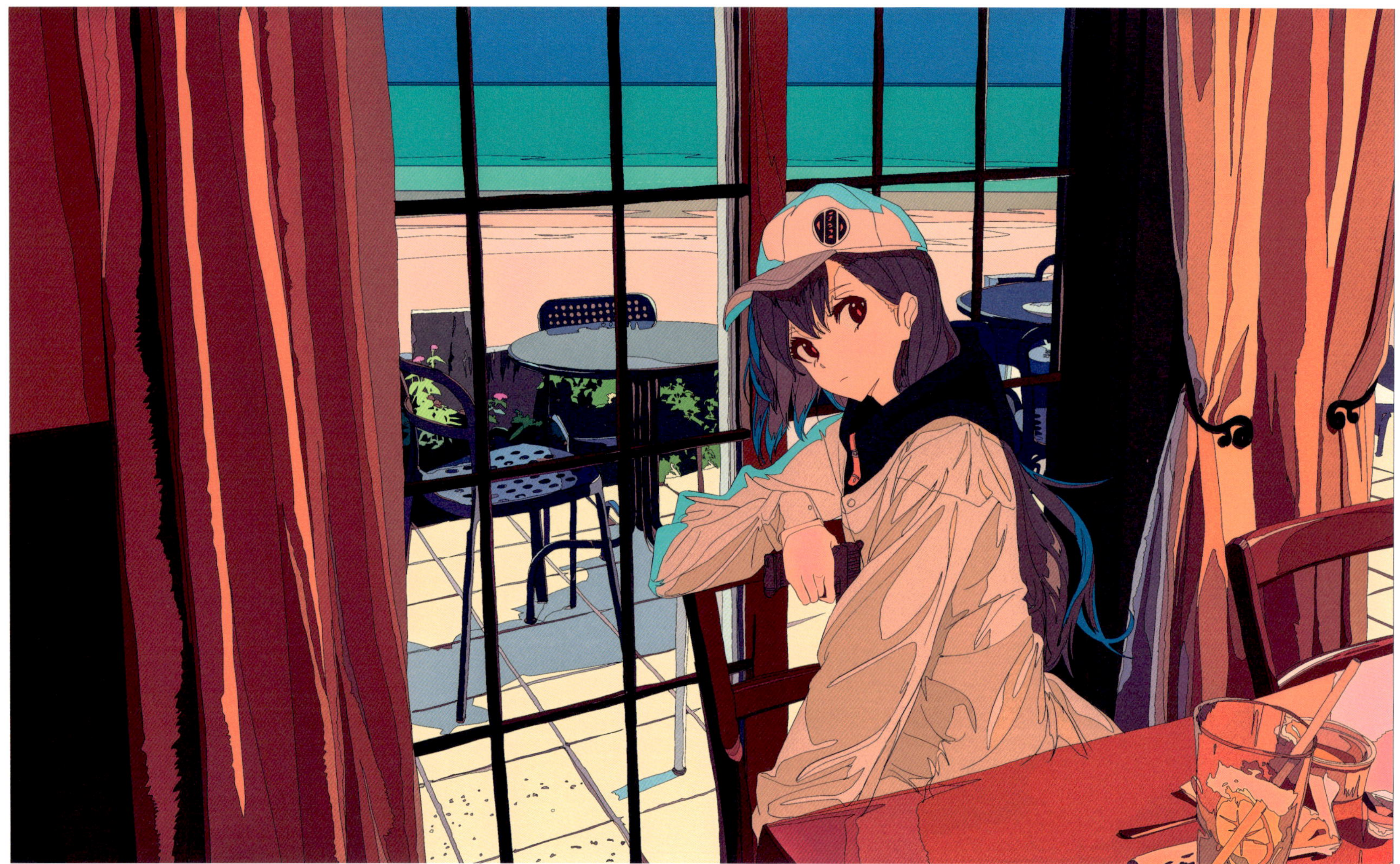

wind

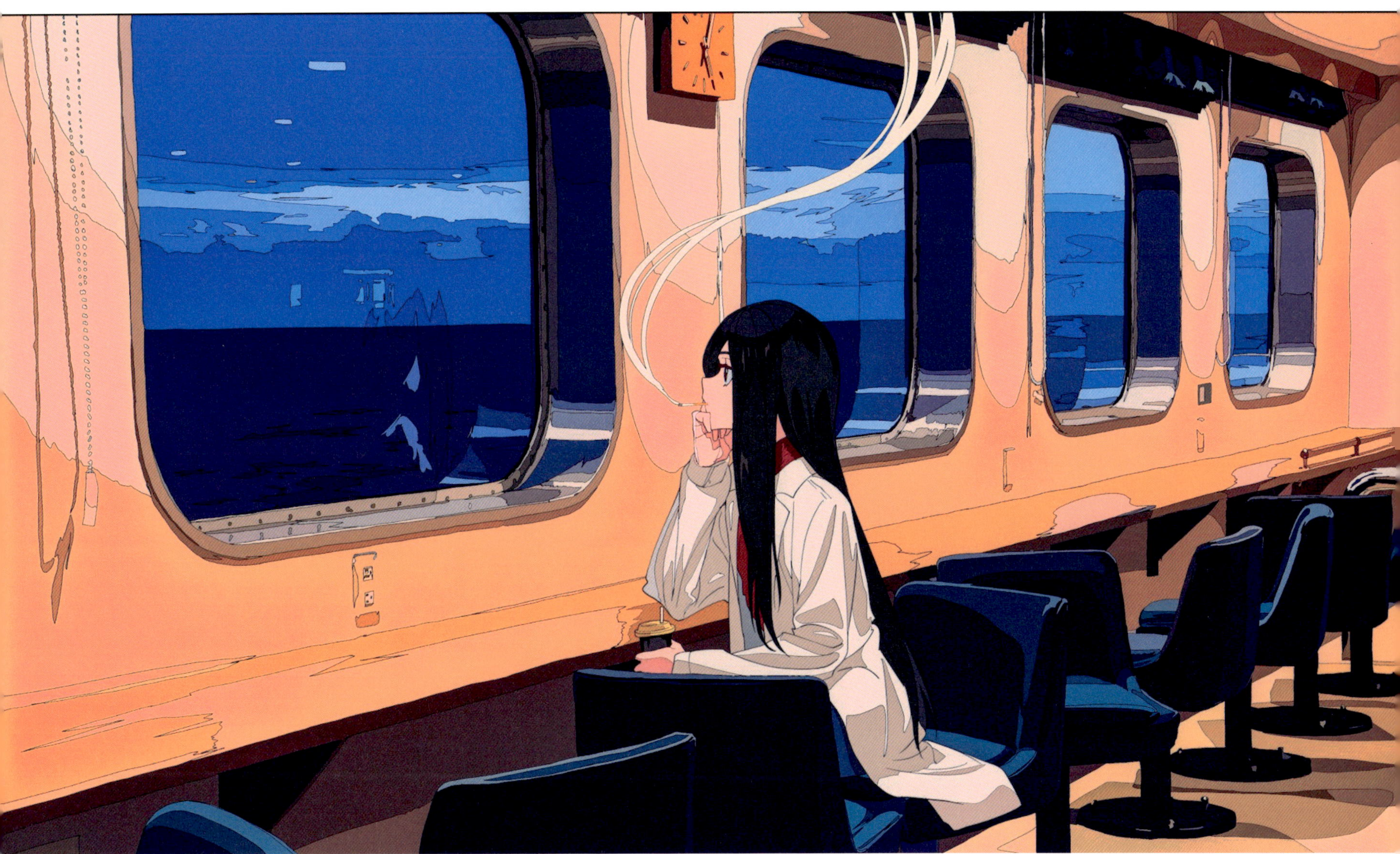

夜行 | train at night

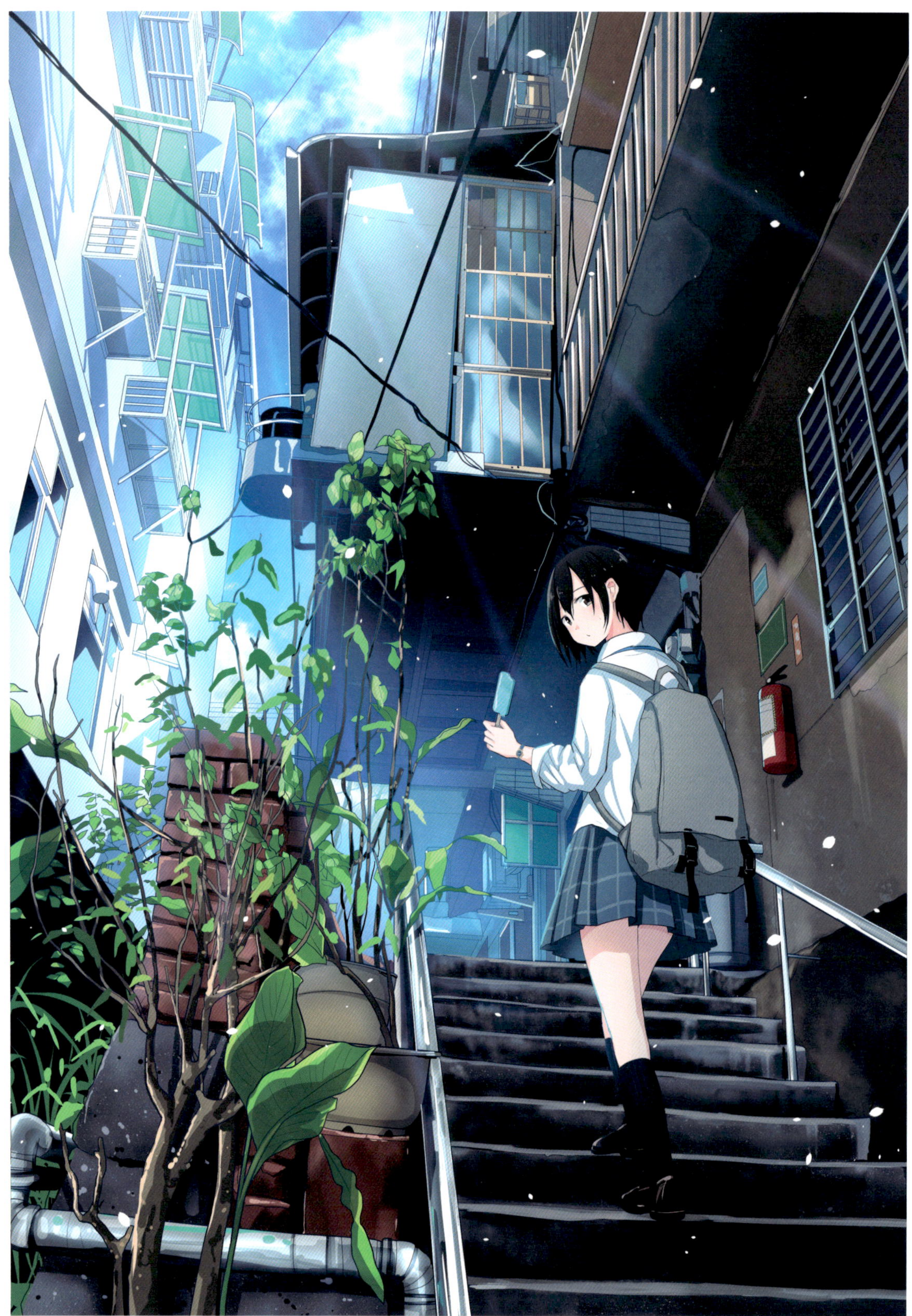

雨上がり　|　after the rain

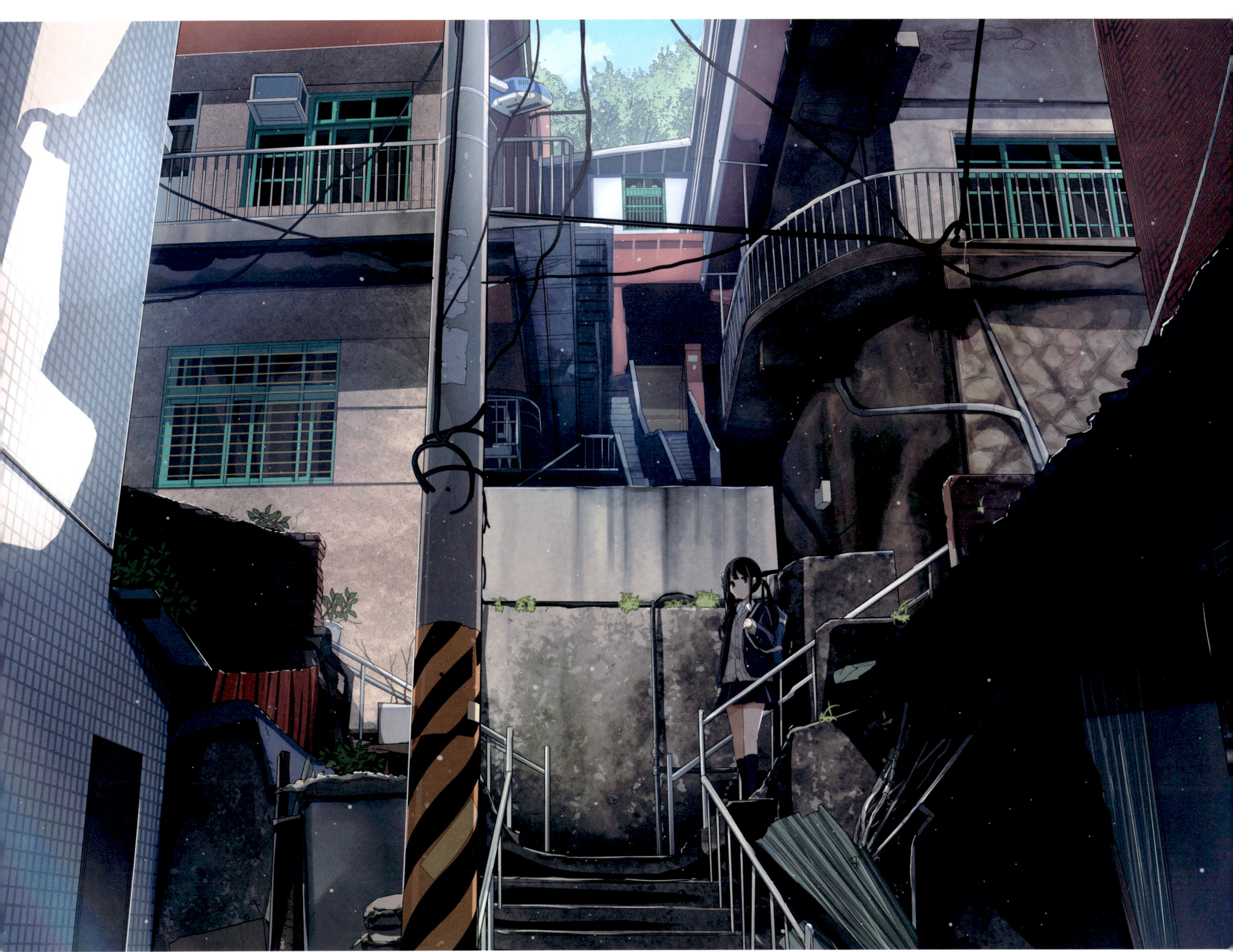

leaving school early

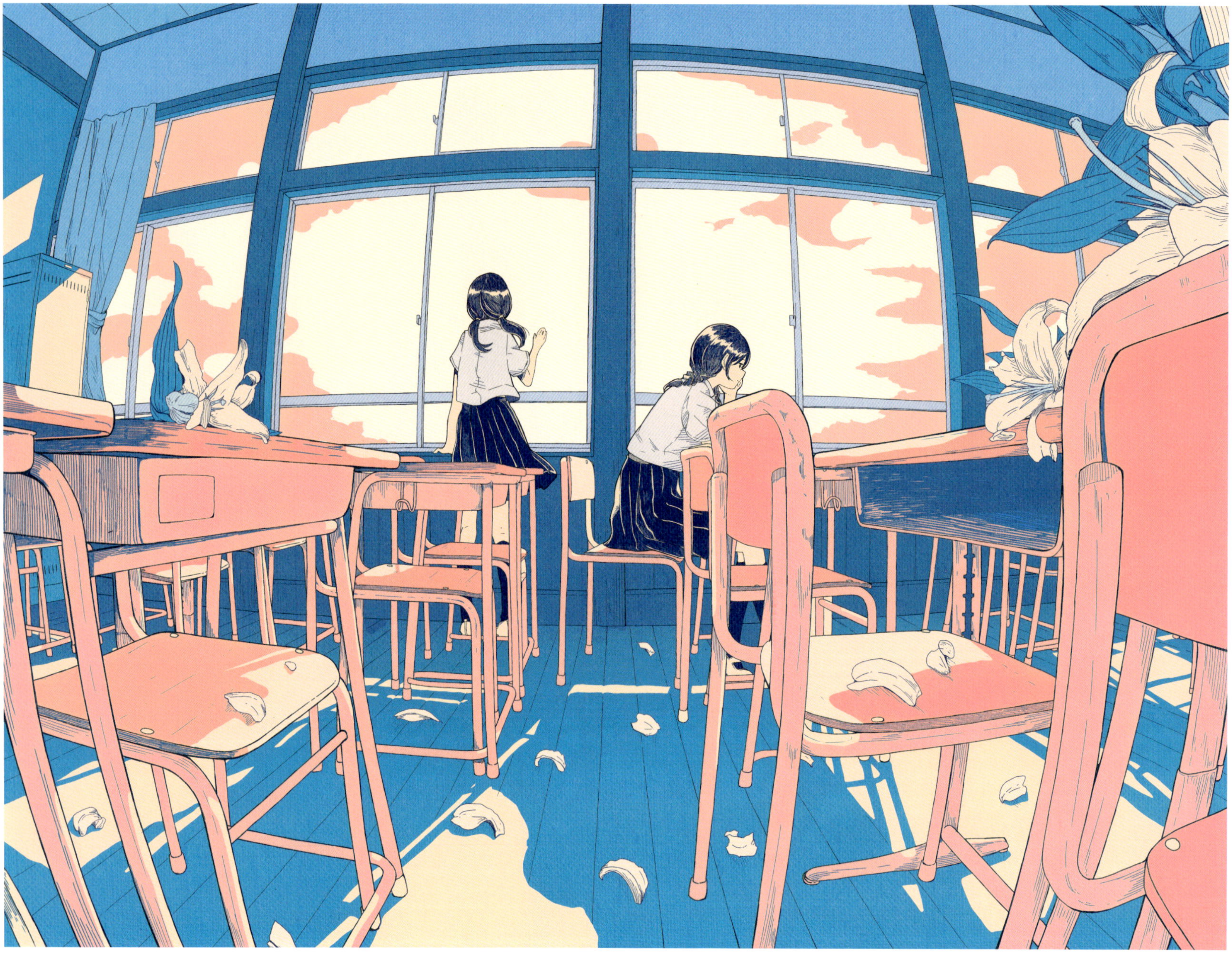

fragile

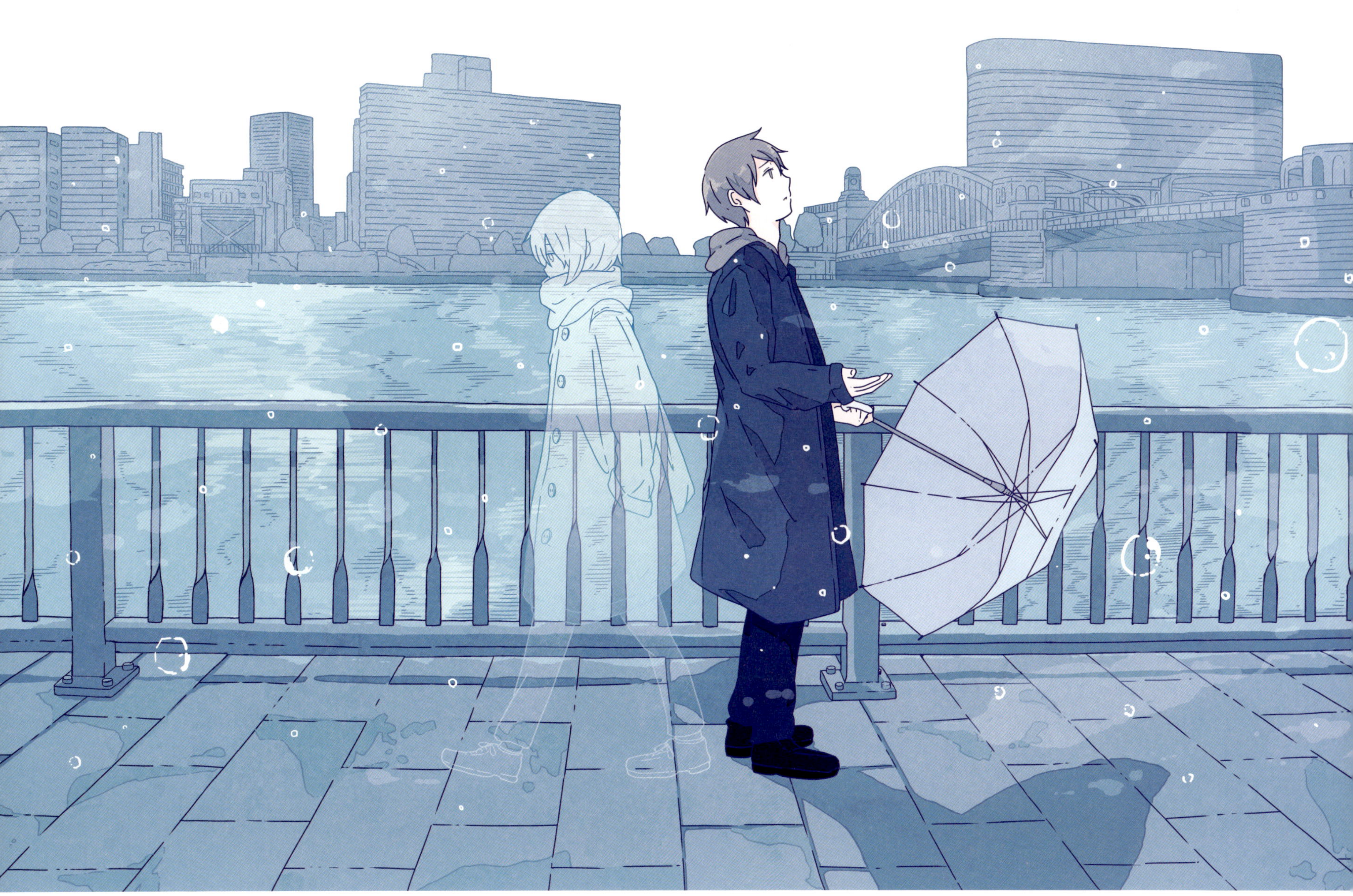

その白が　｜　That White...

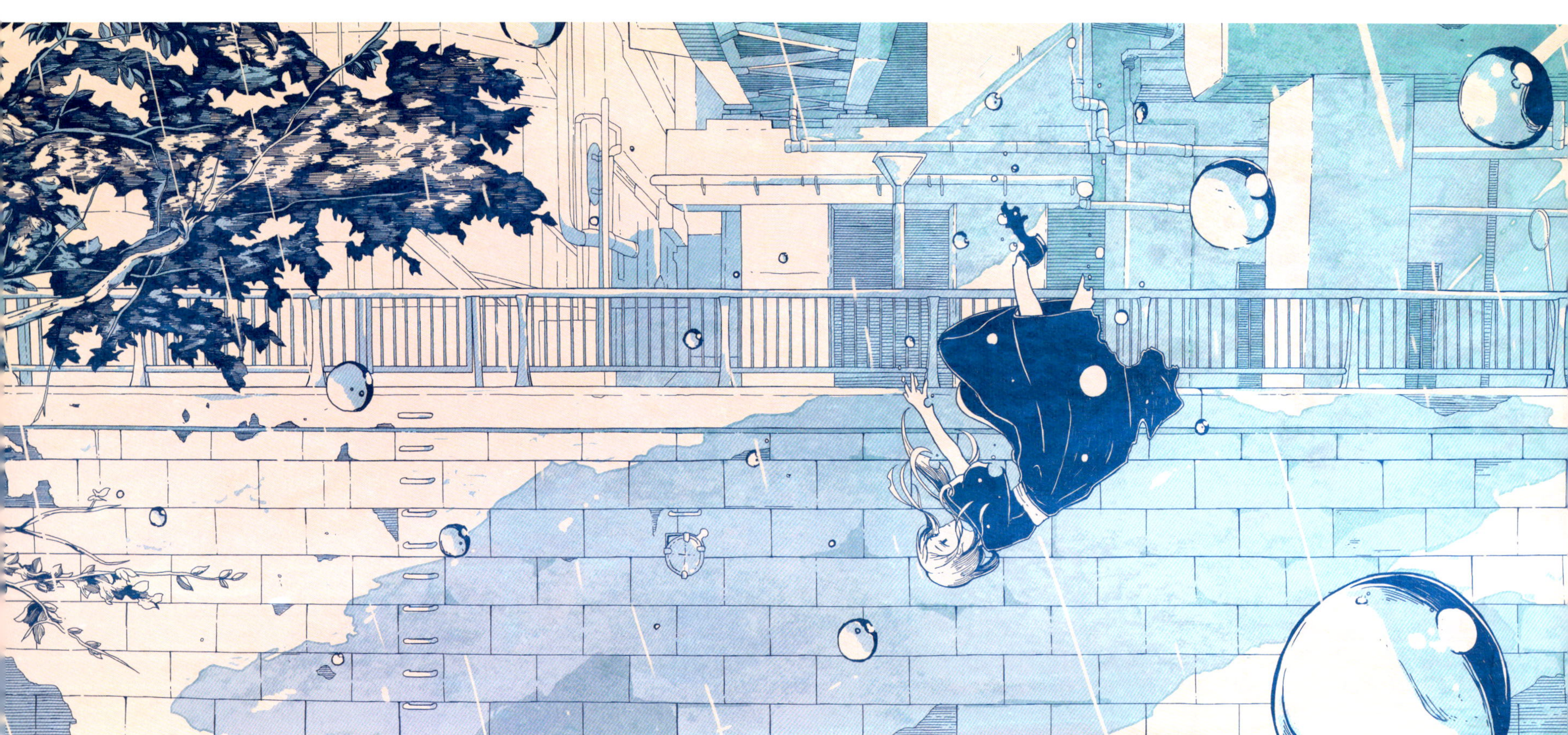

空言　|　False Words

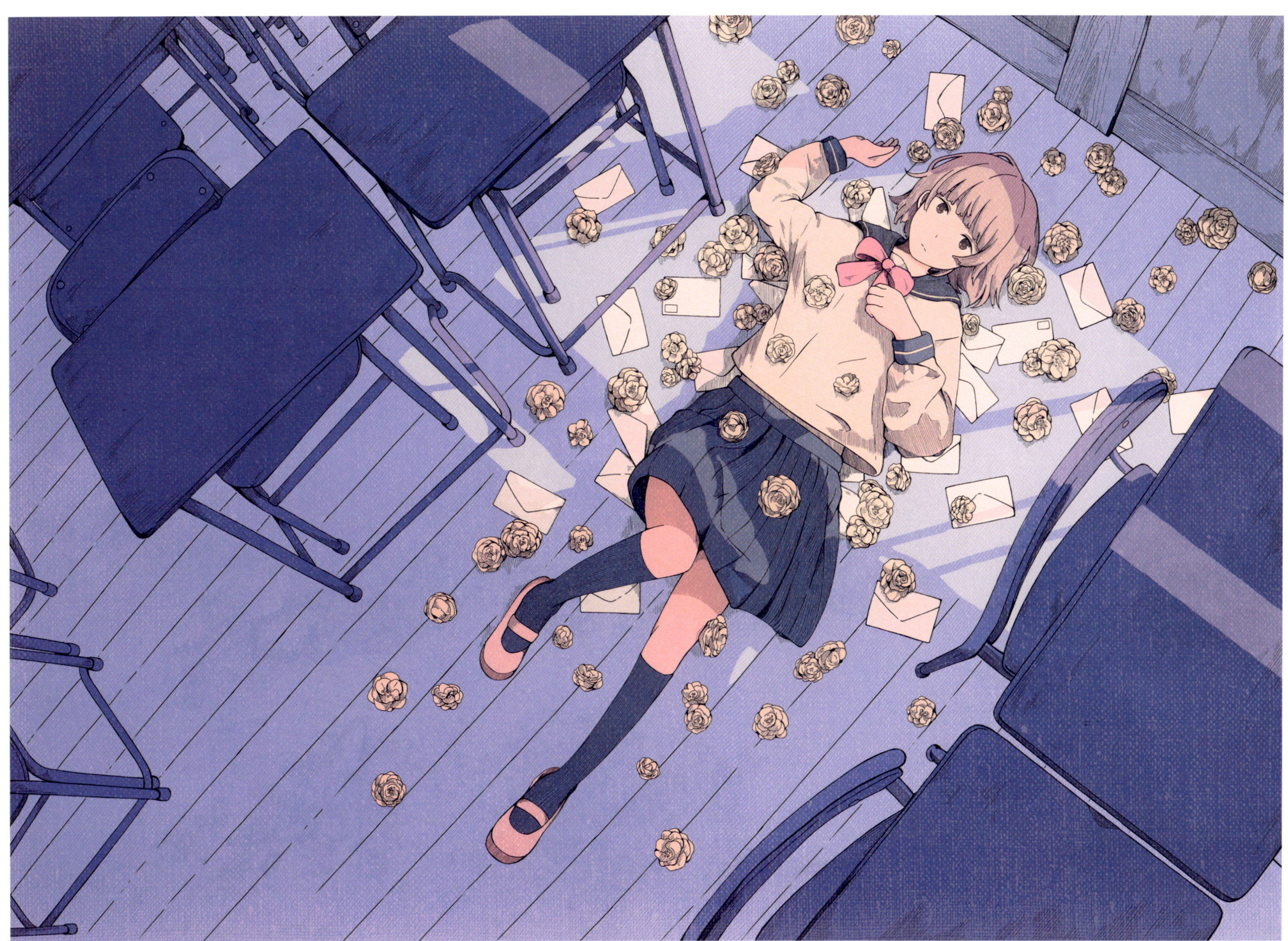

白の彼方　｜　Beyond White

しまざきジョゼ ｜ Joze Shimazaki

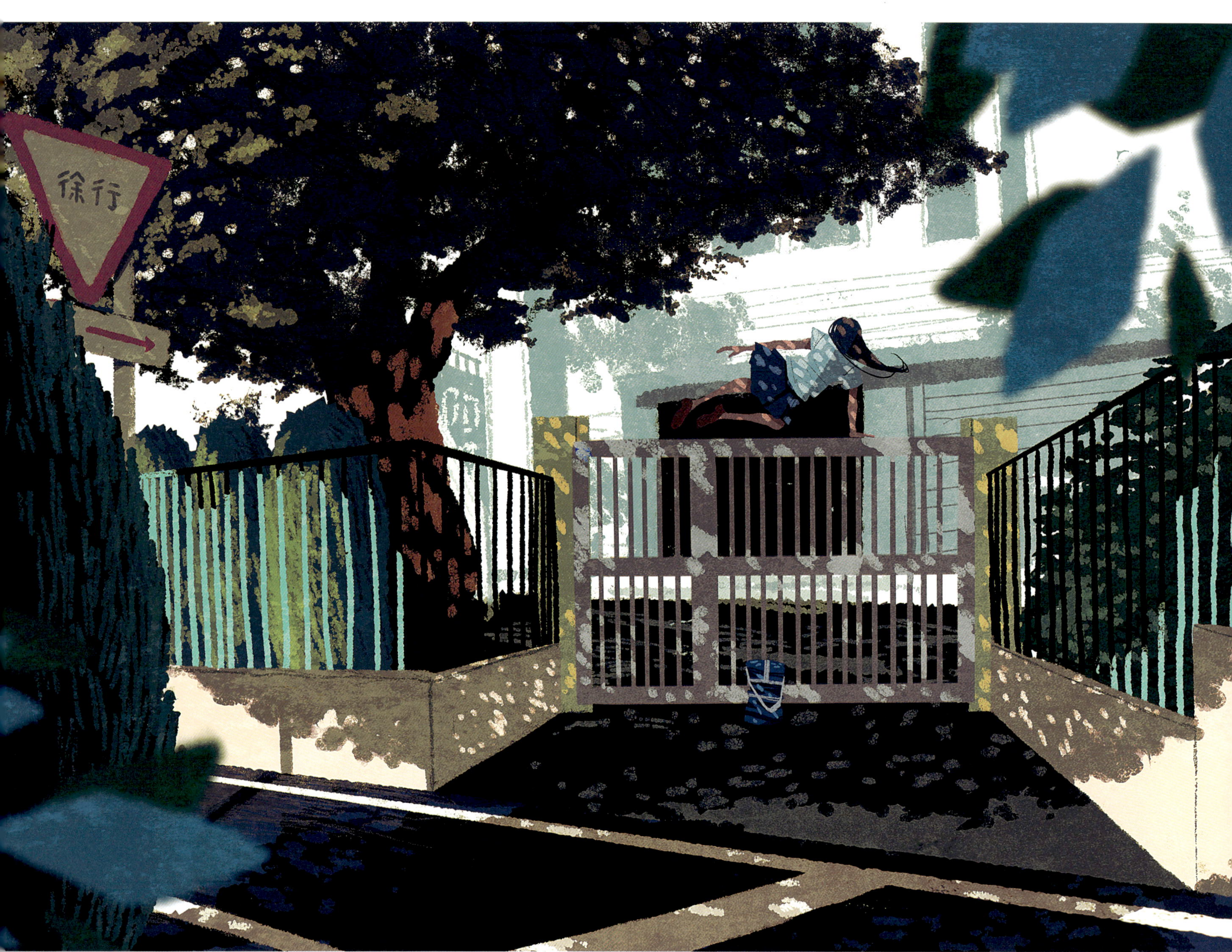

わすれもの！ ｜ Forgot Something!

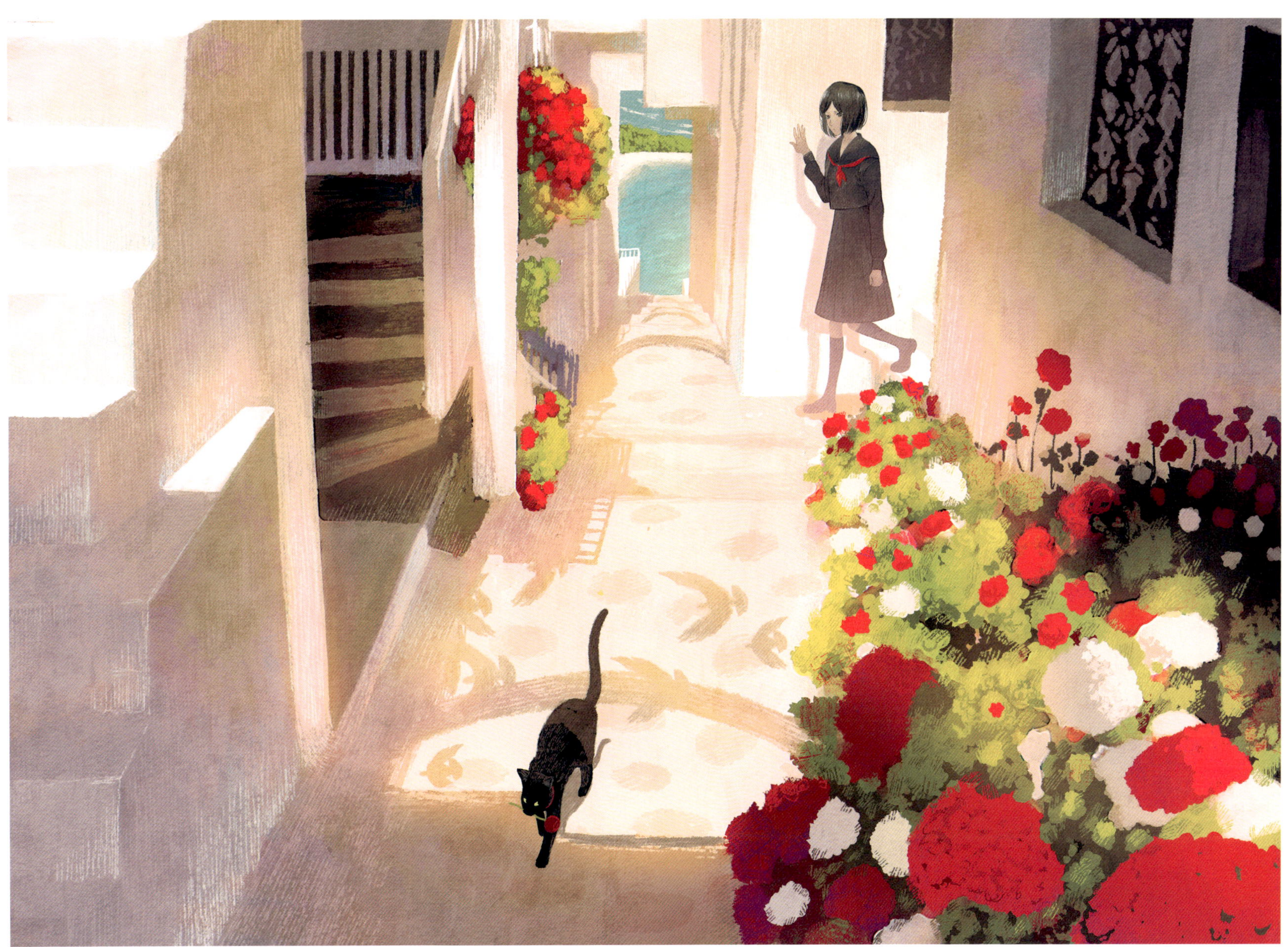

ばらのはな ｜ Rose Petals

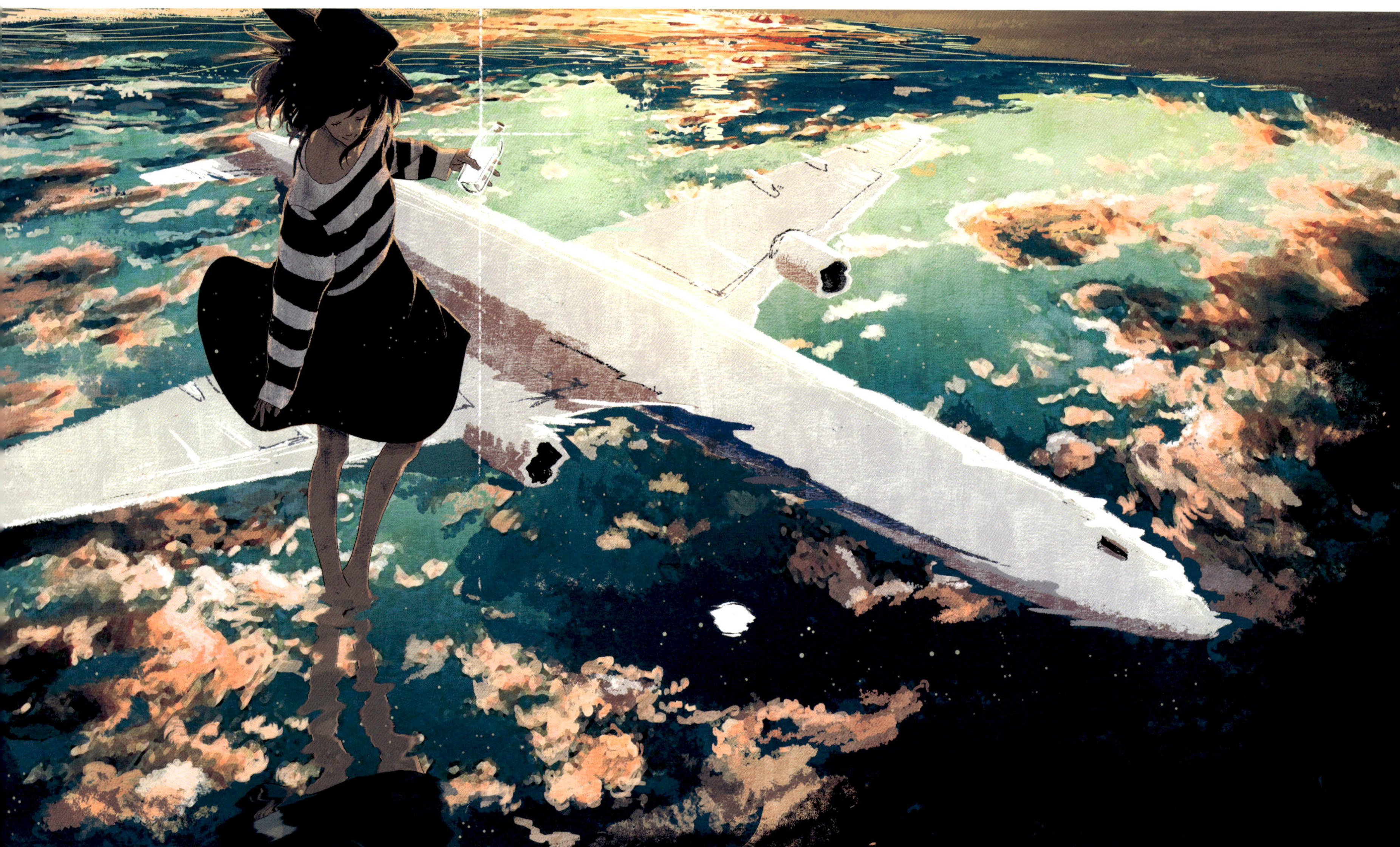

旅立つ君へ　|　As You Begin Your Journey

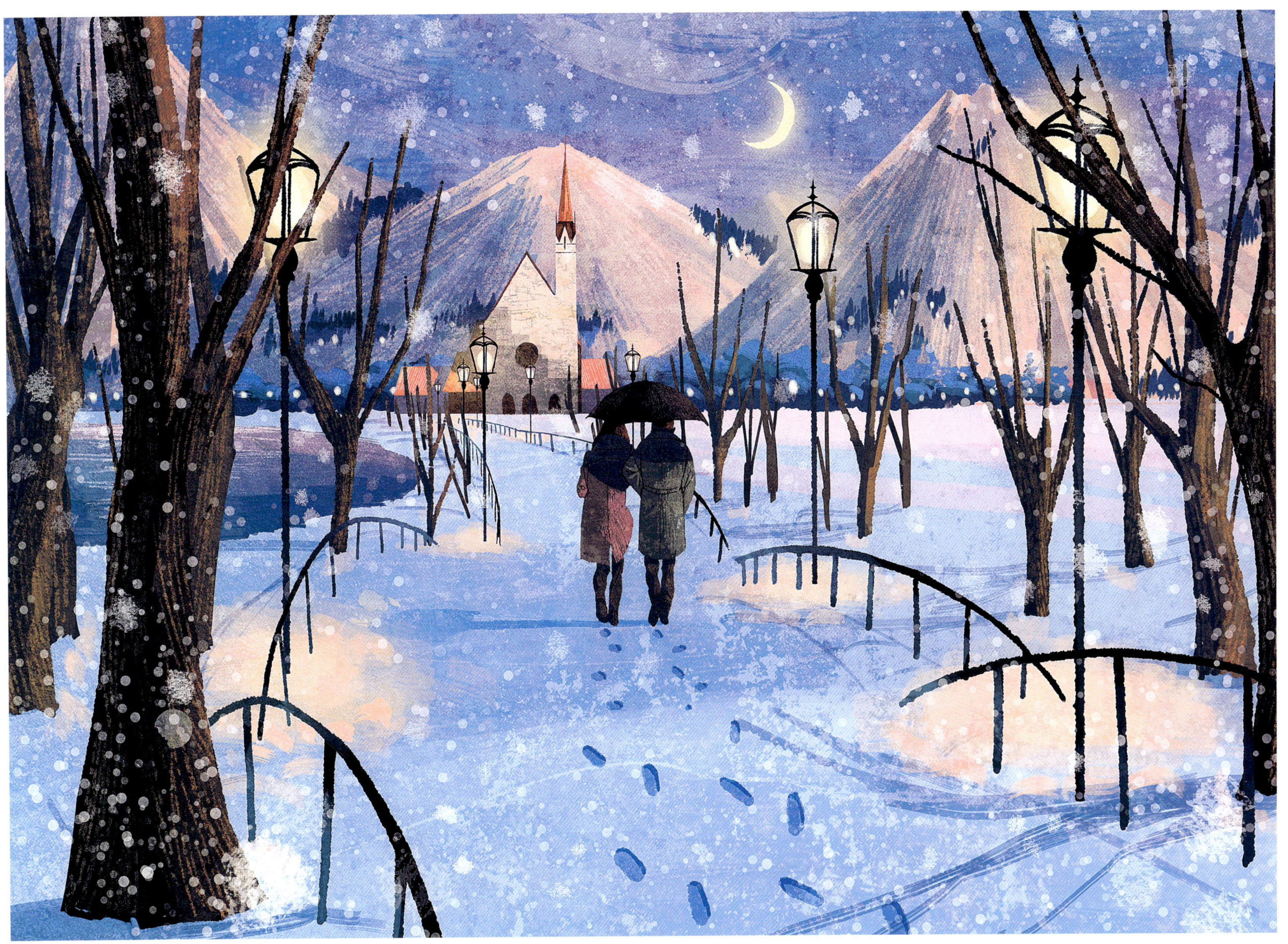

スノースマイル ｜ Snowy Smiles

杉87 | sugiyama

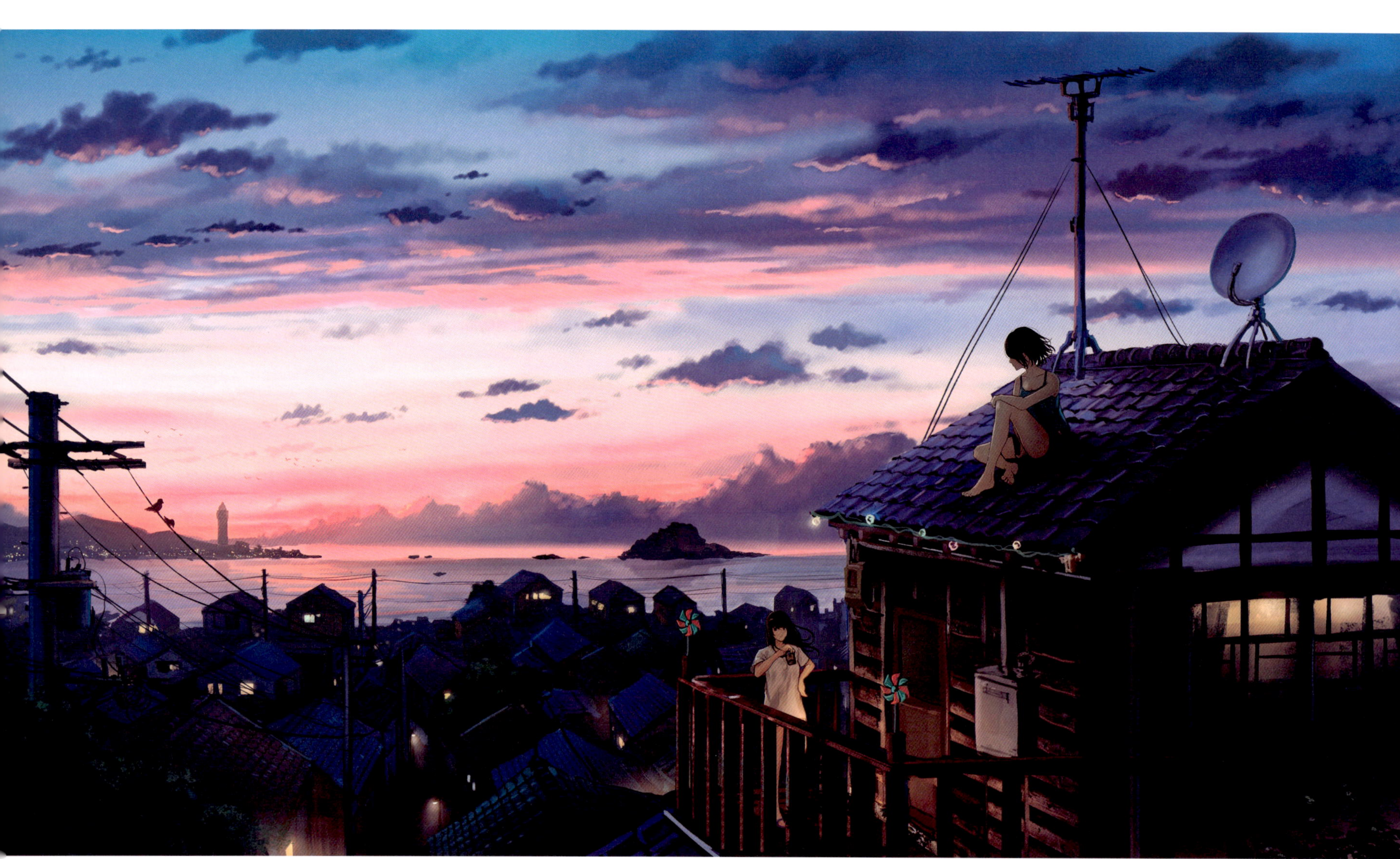

海辺の町 | Town by The Sea

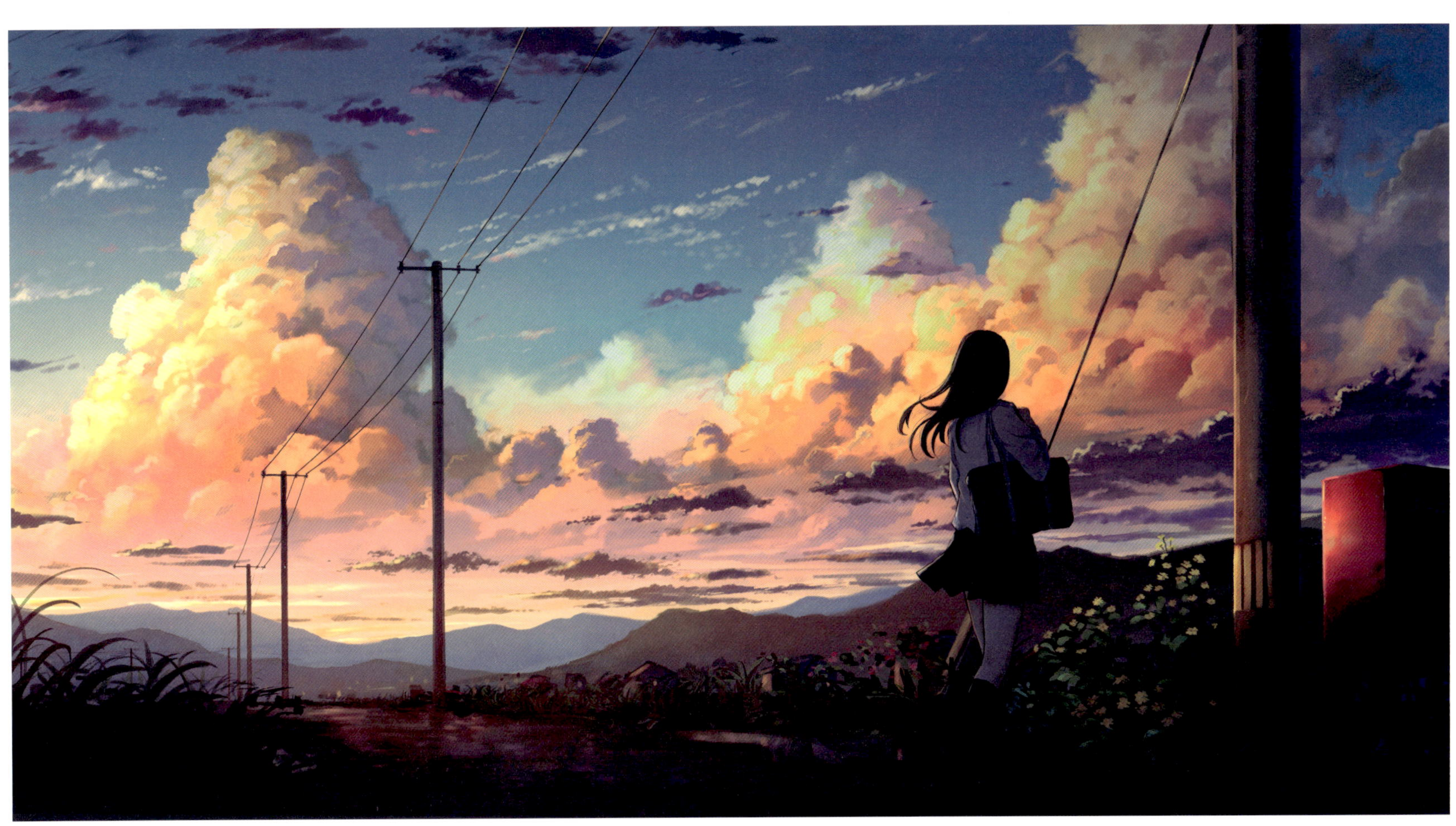

Orange

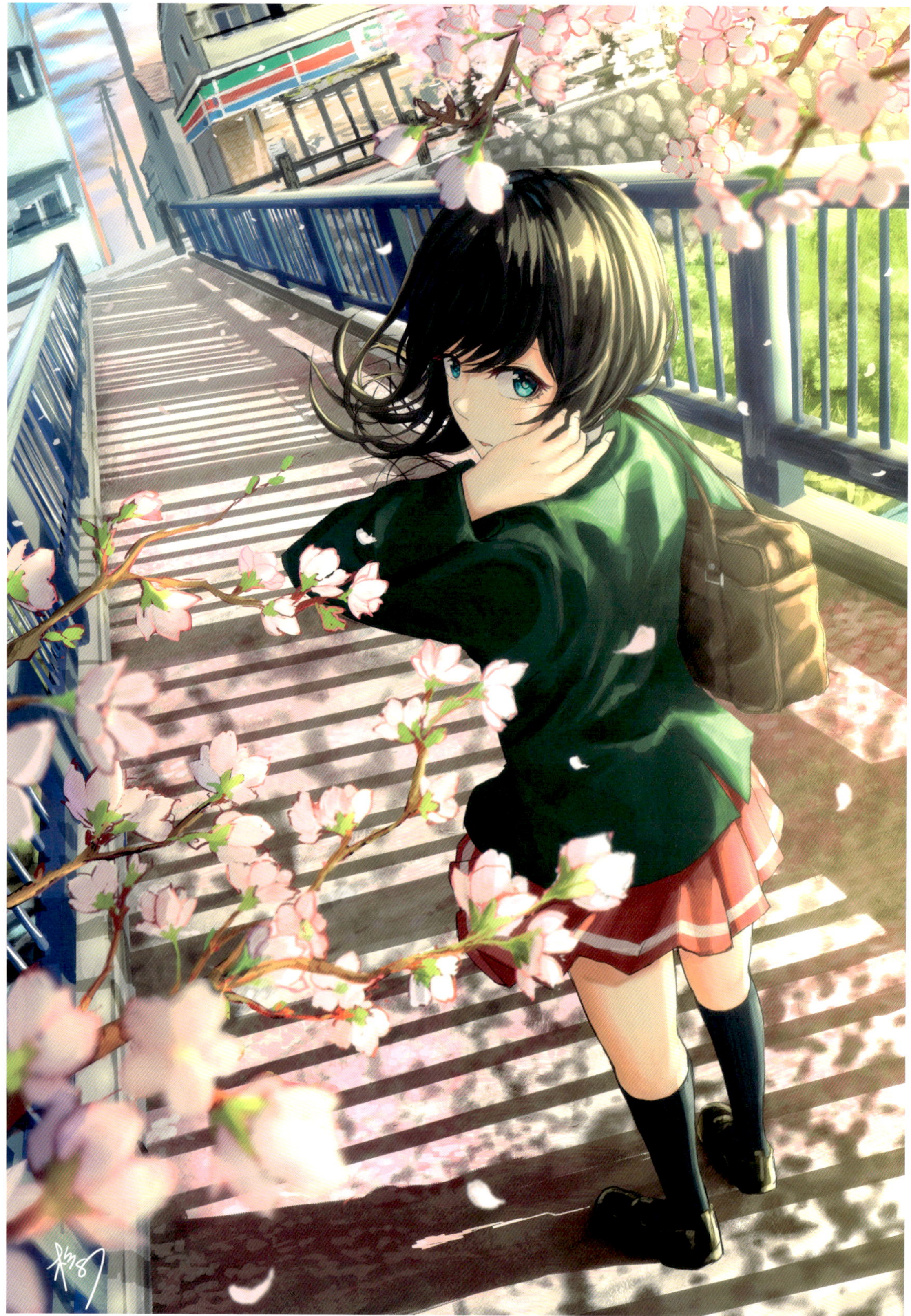

桜舞う道のり | A Path Where Cherry Blossom Petals Dance

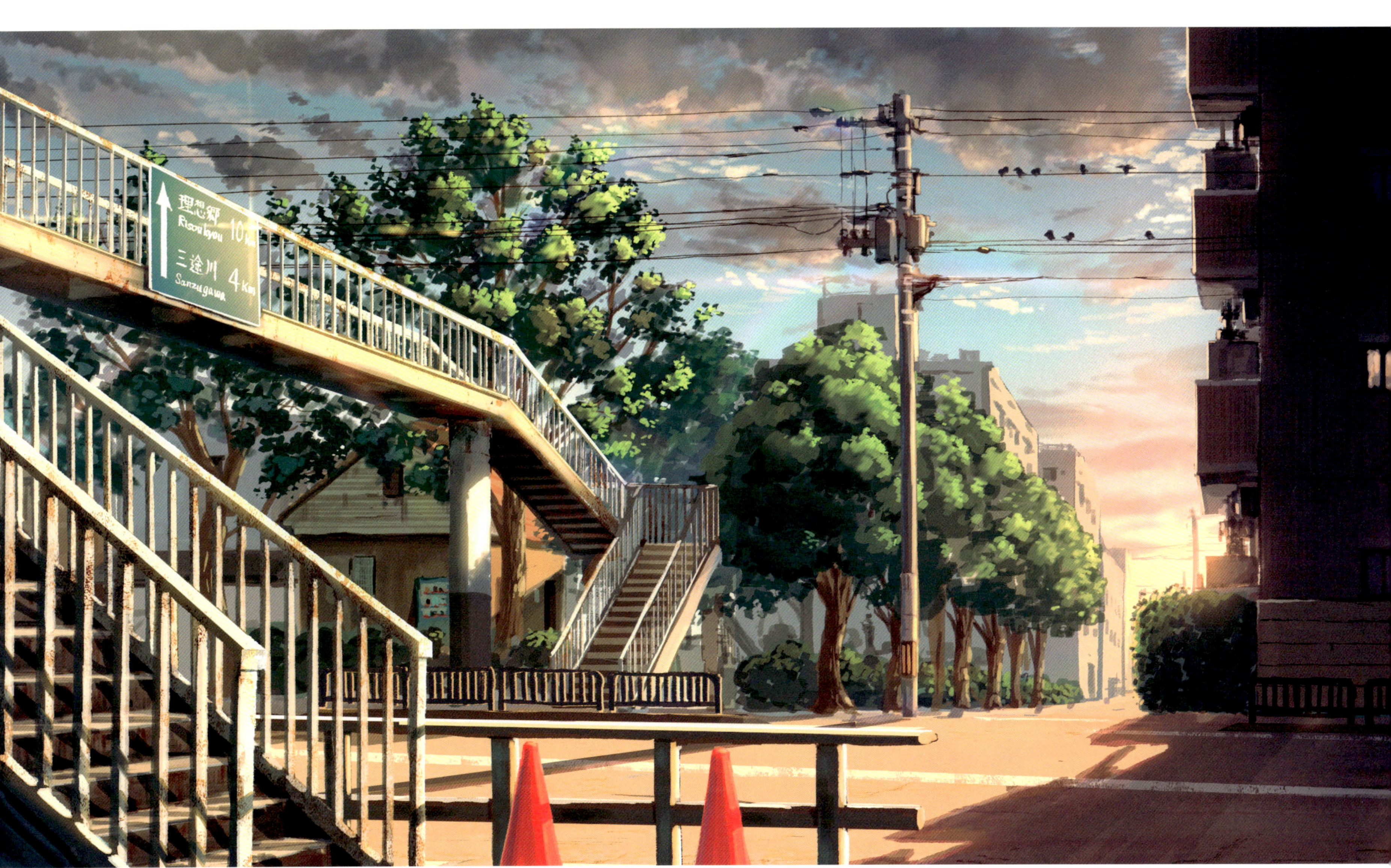

歩道橋　|　Pedestrian Bridge

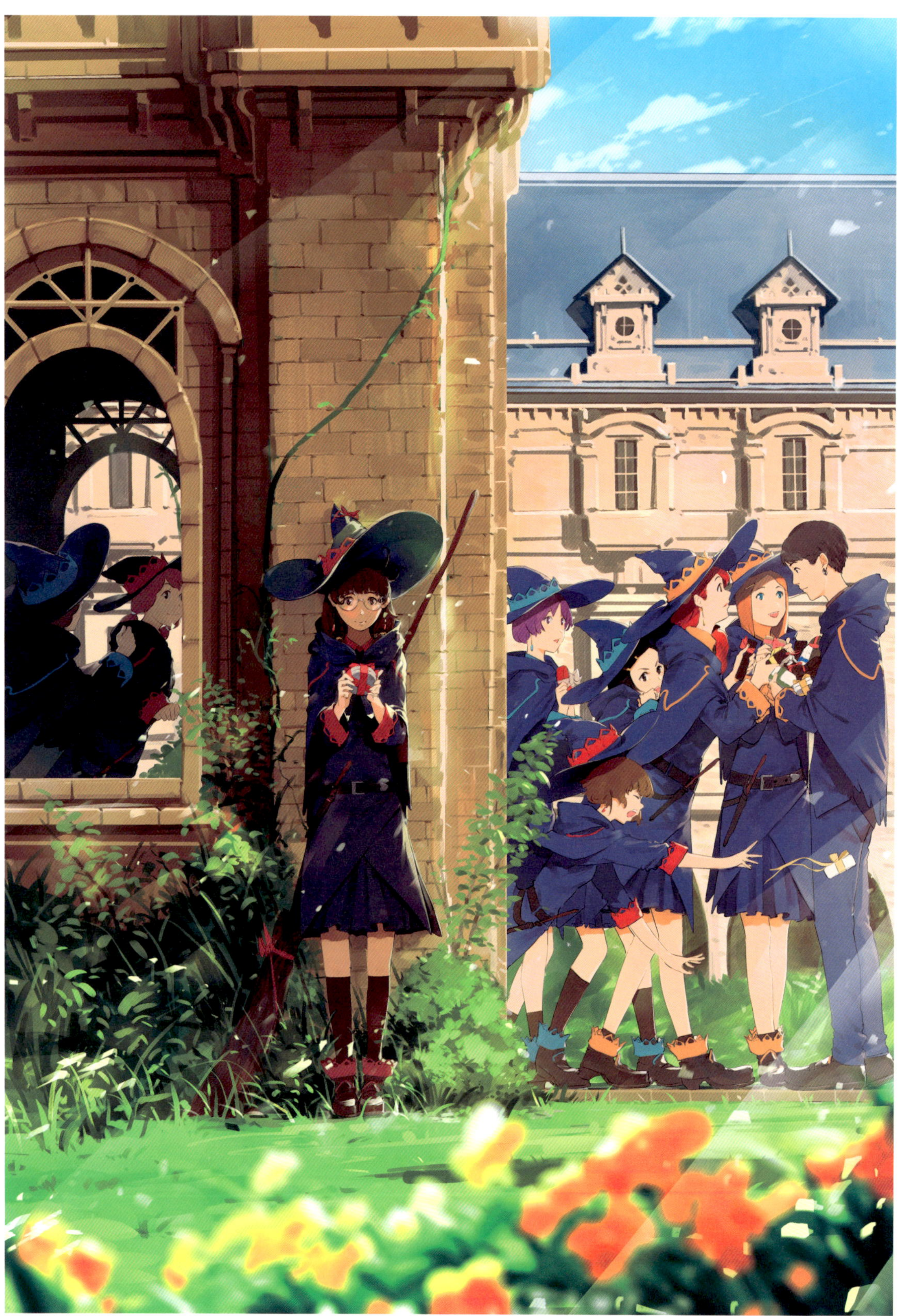

魔法のチョコレート　|　Magic Chocolate

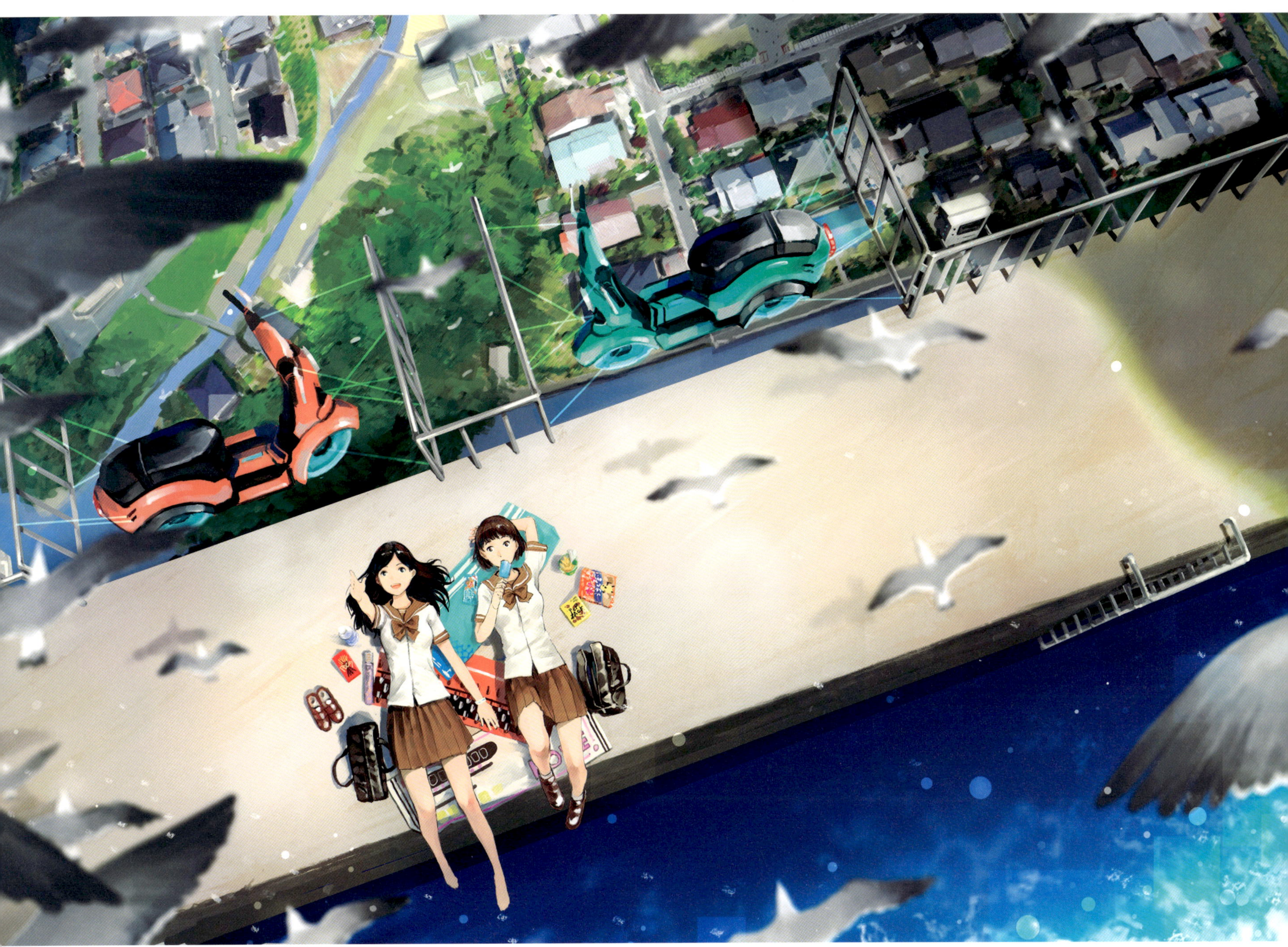

遠い、夏　│　Distant Already

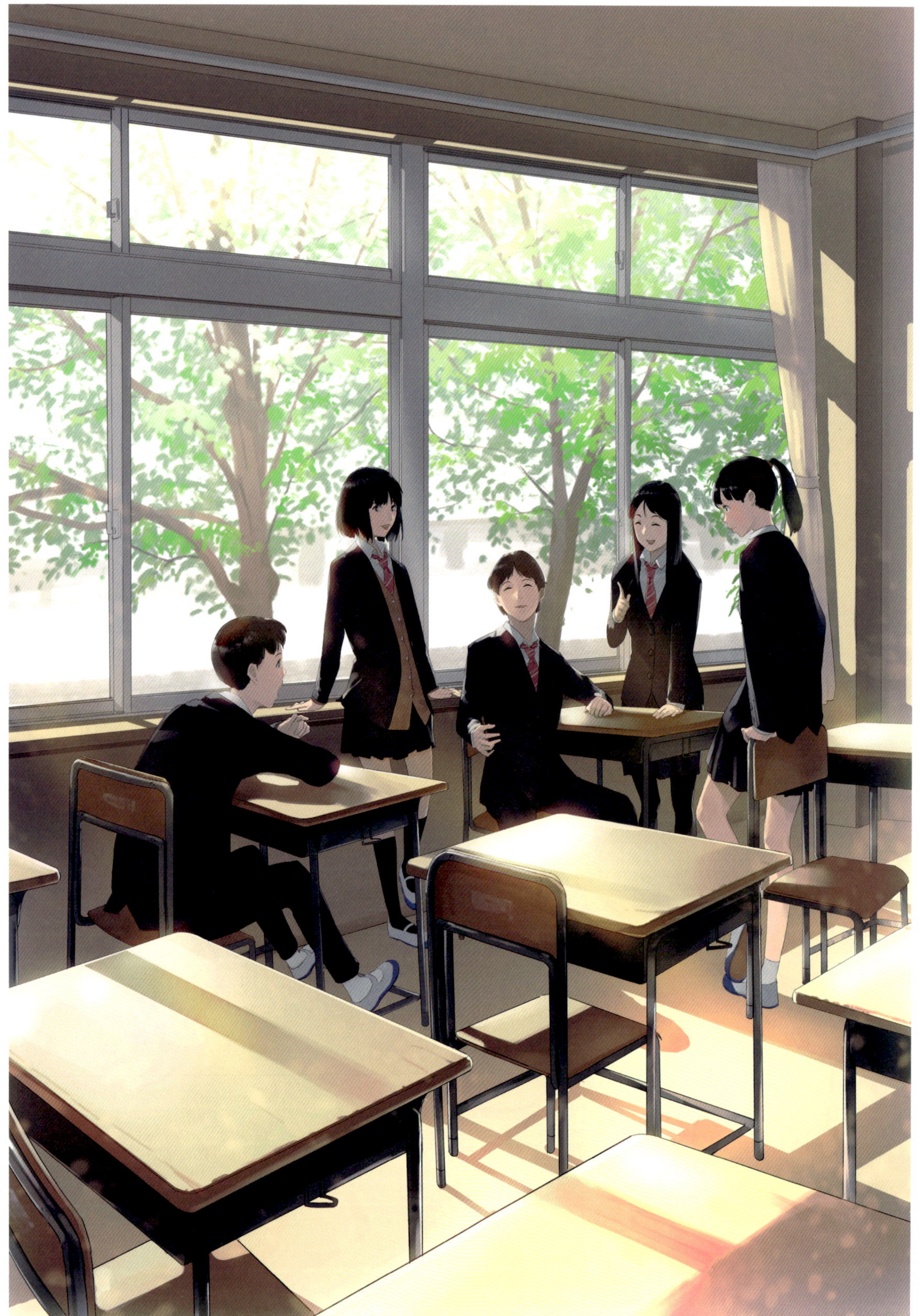

ひだまり ｜ A Sun-kissed Moment

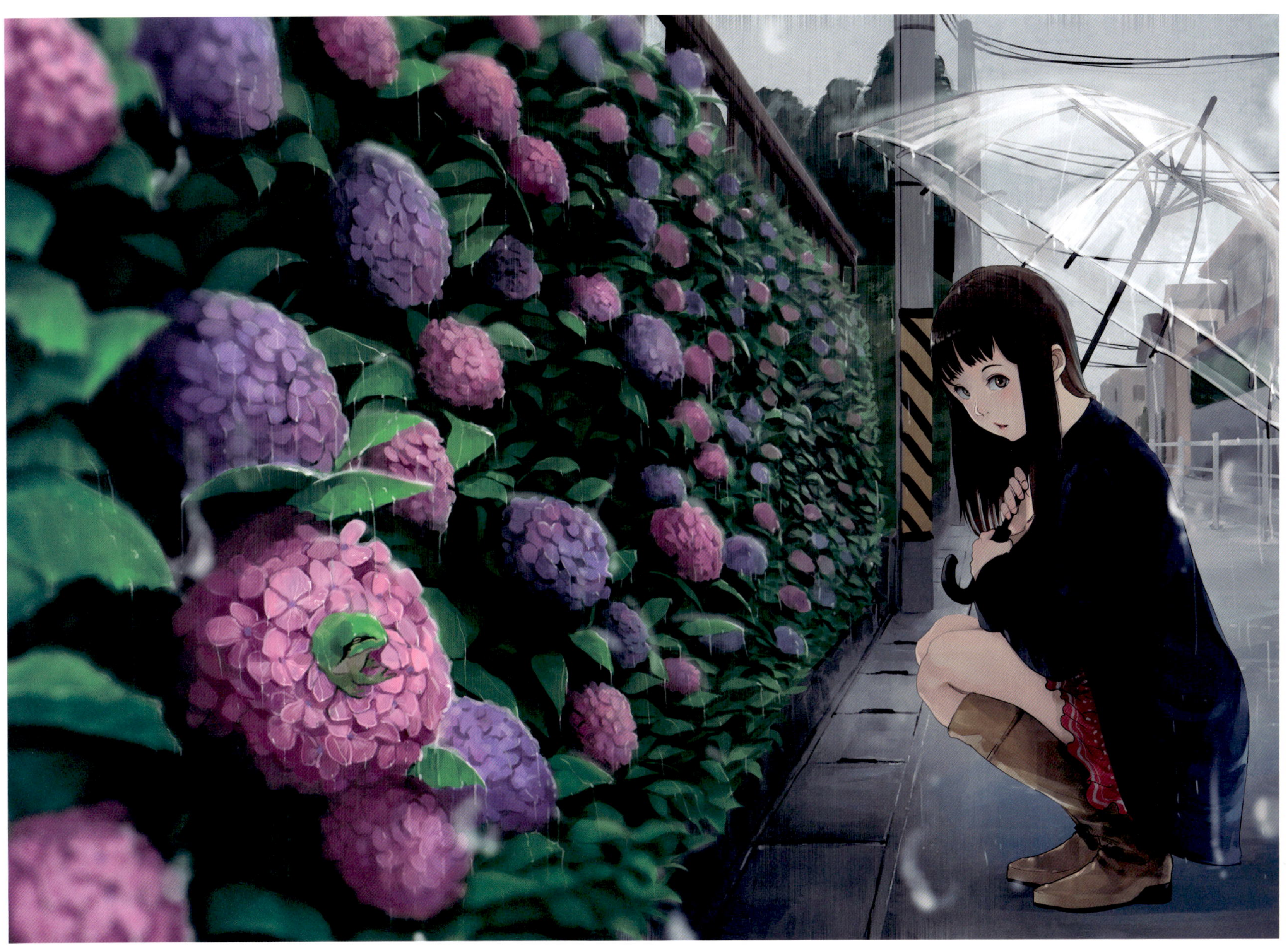

雨の匂いは紫陽花の香り | The Aroma of Hydrangeas is like the Smell of Rain

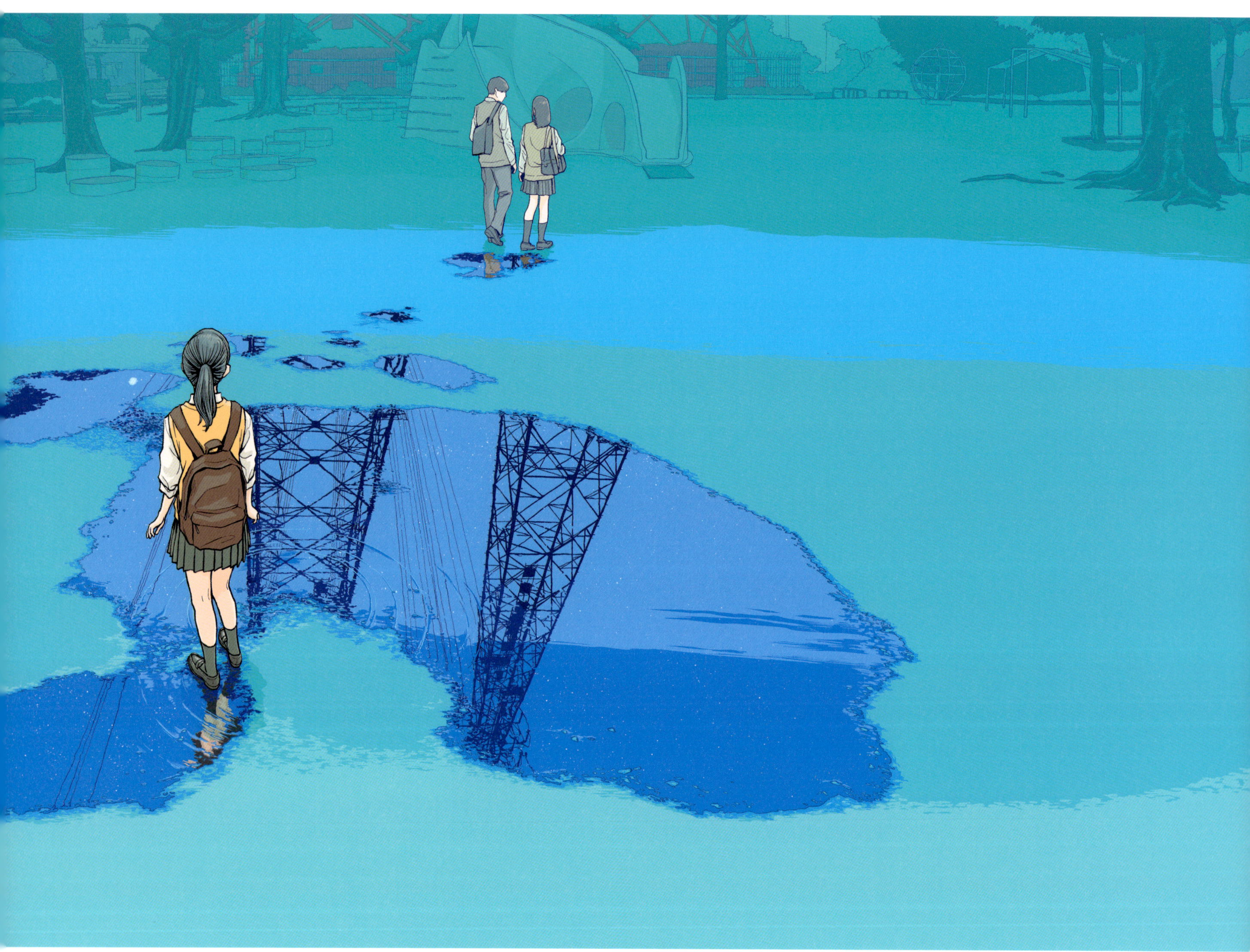

『5分後に思わず涙。青い星の小さな出来事』（桃戸ハル 編著、学研プラス）カバーイラスト
Cover illustration for *5-fungo ni Omowazu Namida. Aoi Hoshi no Chiisana Dekigoto* (written and edited by Haru Momoto, published by Gakken Plus)

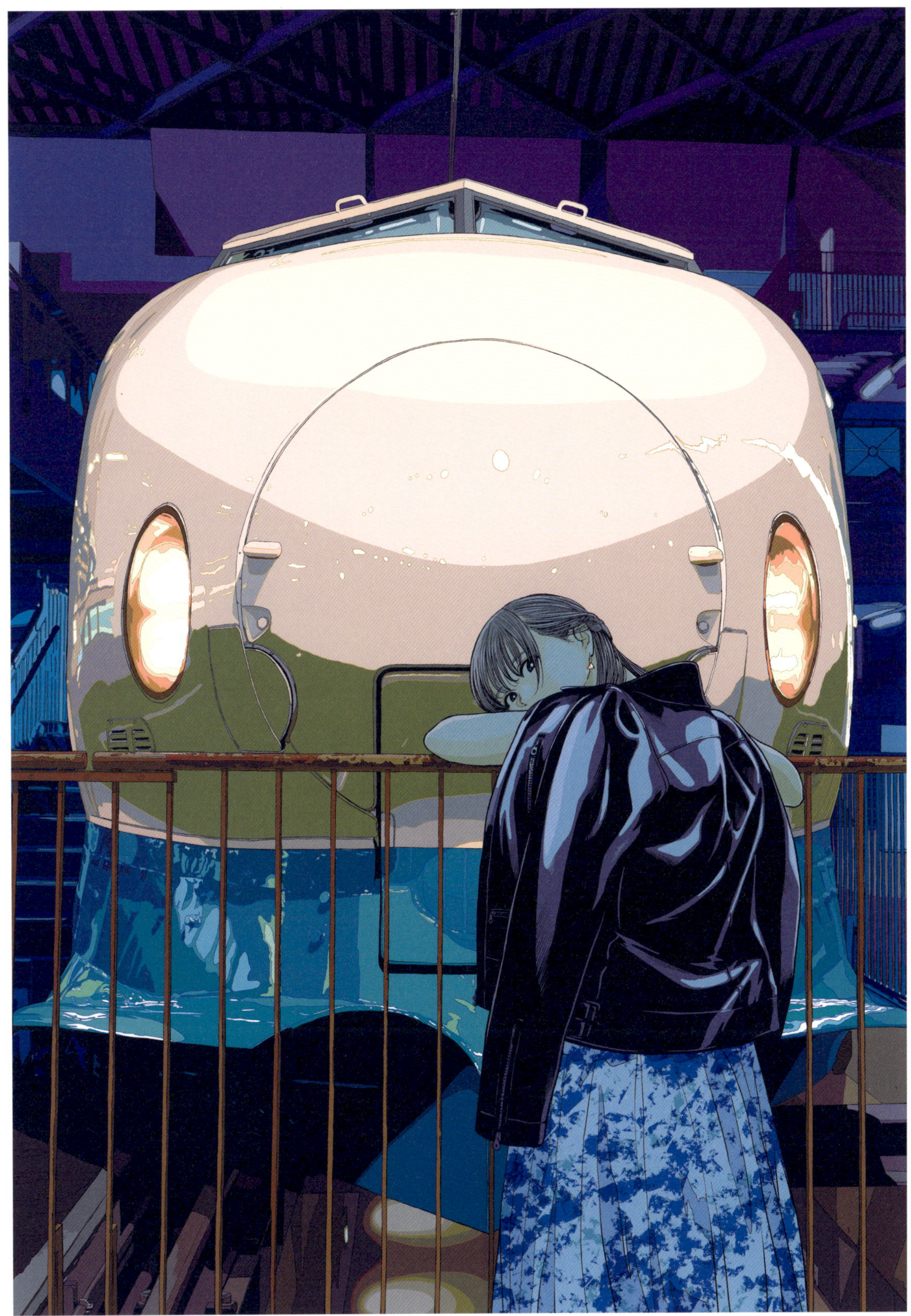

見たことない顔 | a face i've never seen

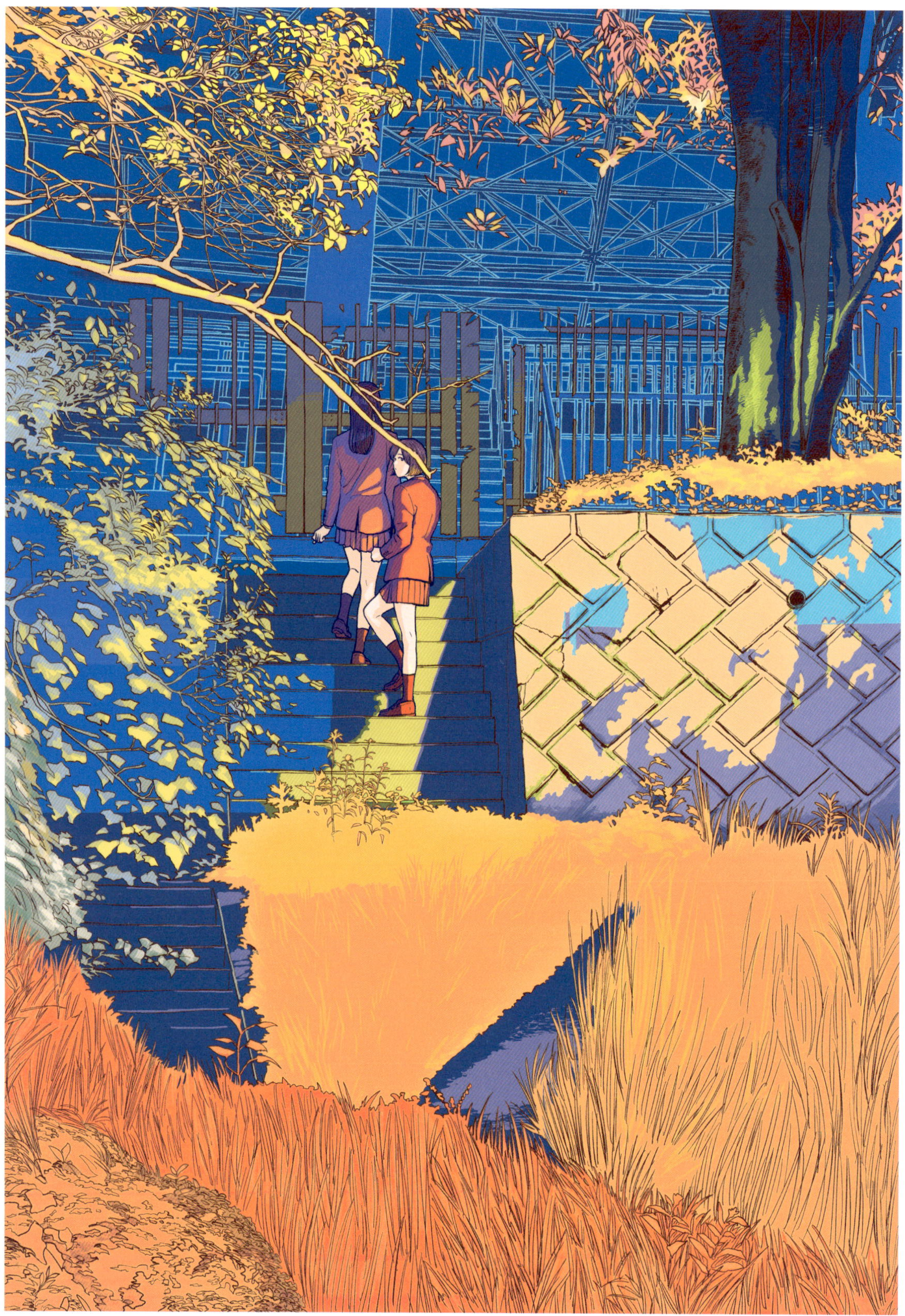

ヒミツのあそびば　|　secret playground

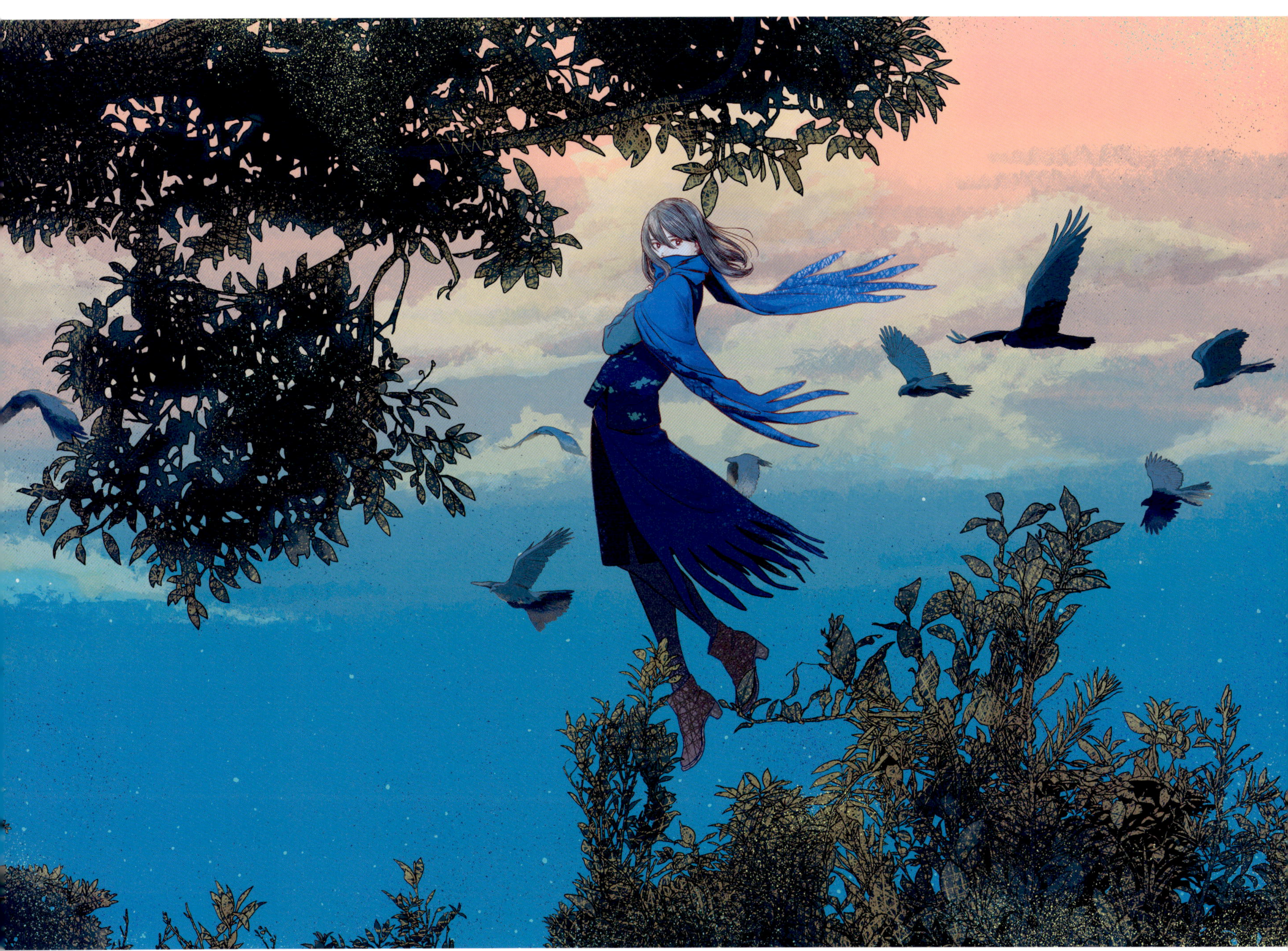

at the crack of dawn

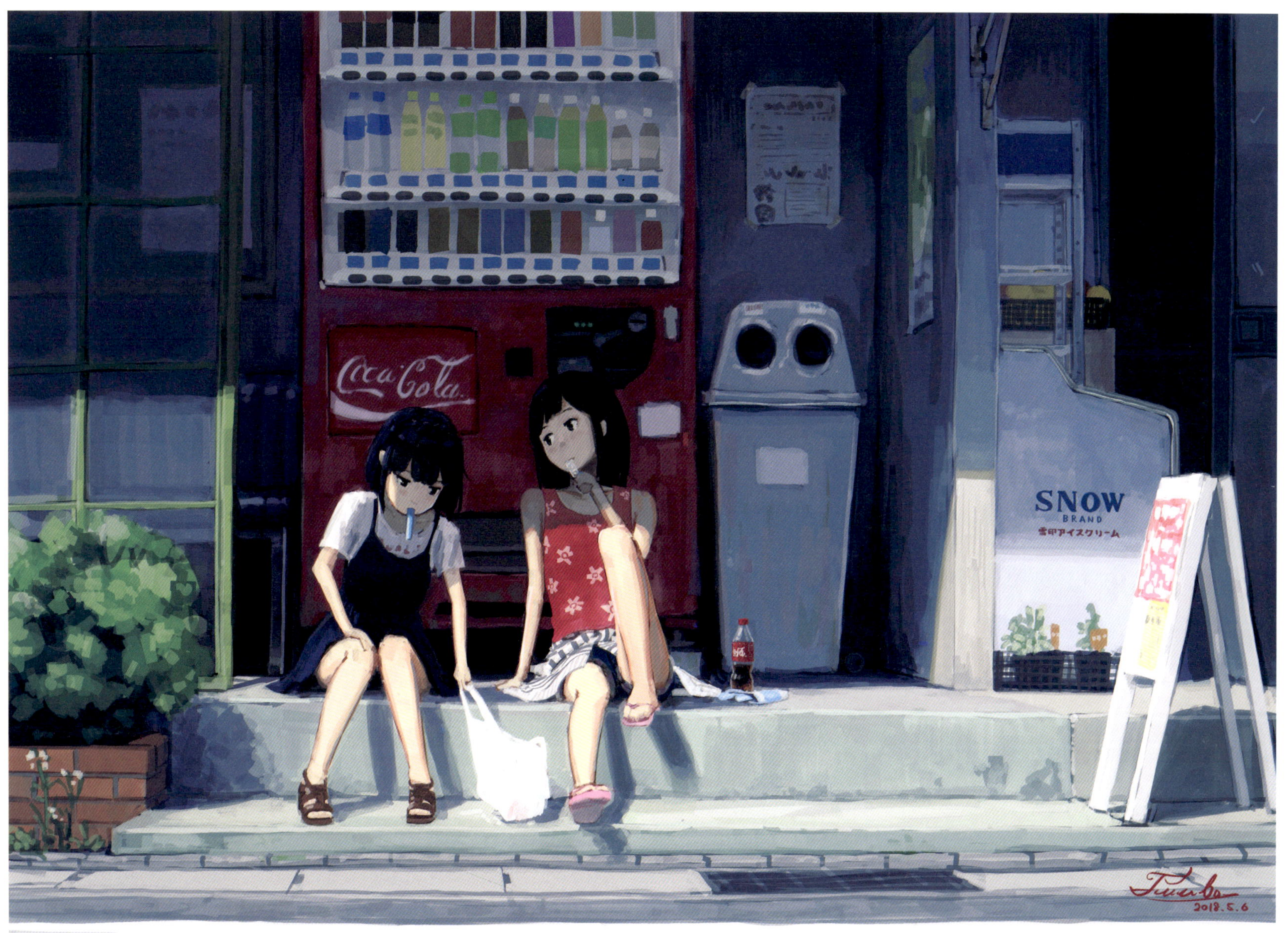

やけに暑かった春の日の話　｜　A Story on that Terribly Hot Spring Day

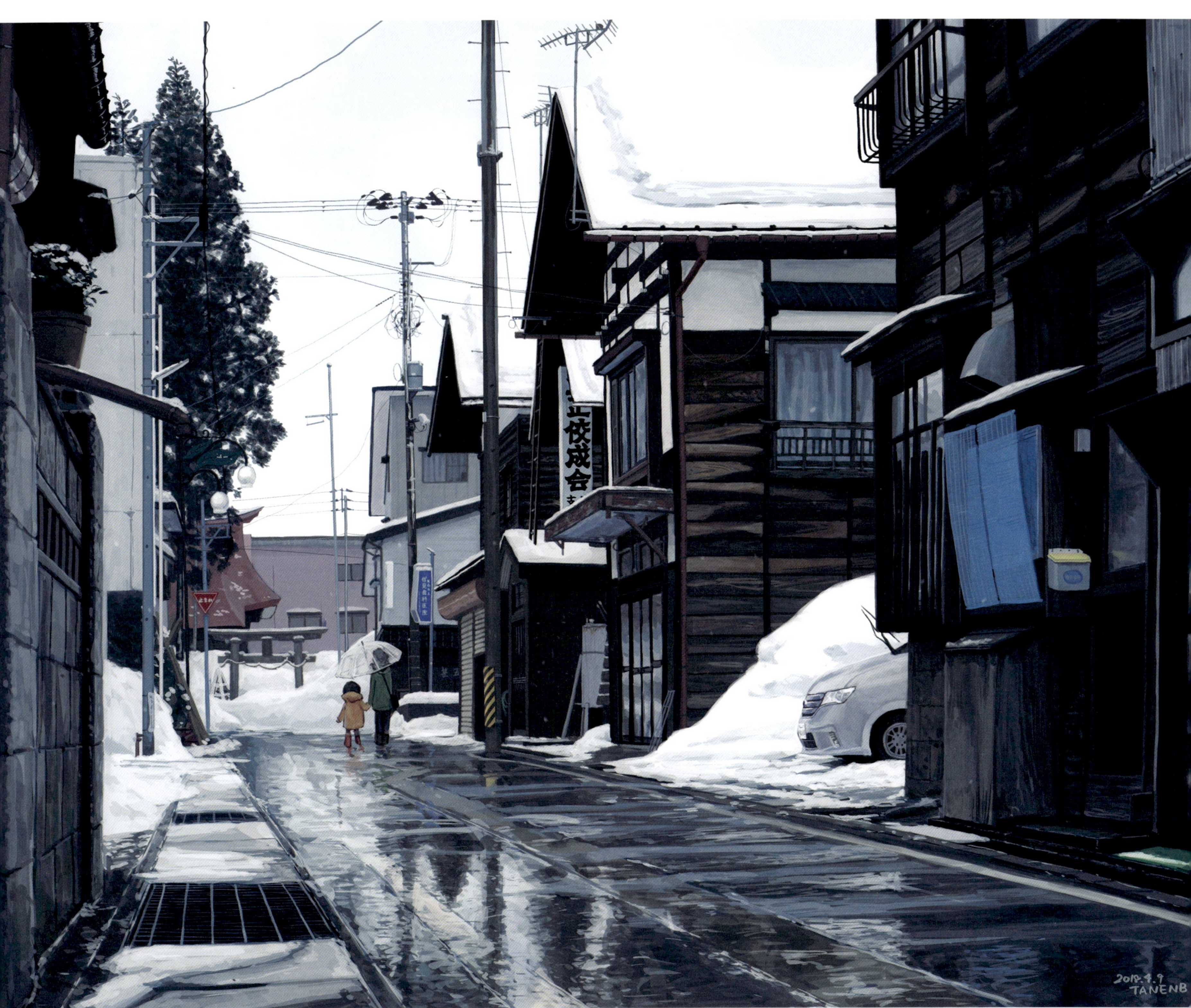

冬と春のちょうど真ん中　|　Right Between Winter and Spring

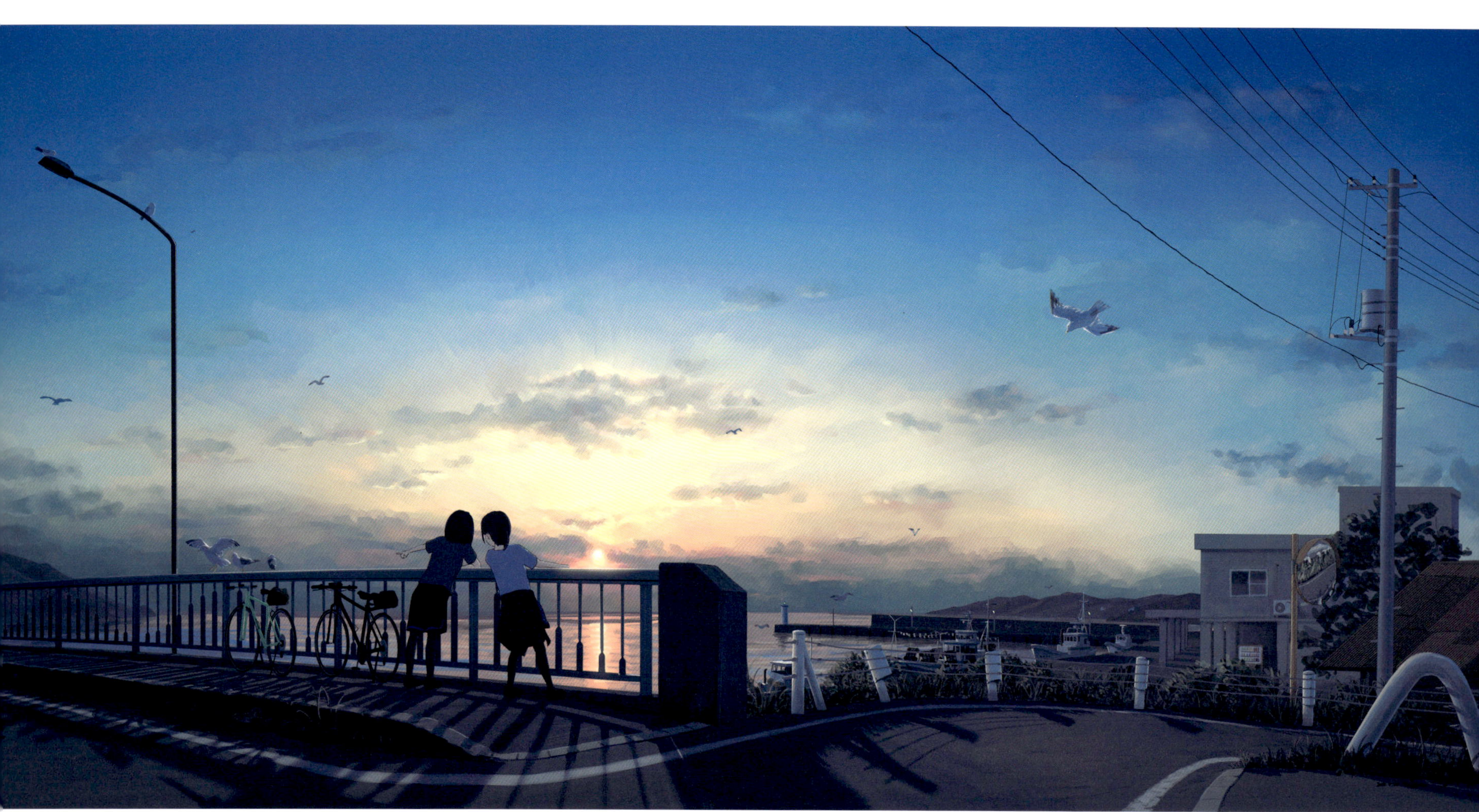

ambience

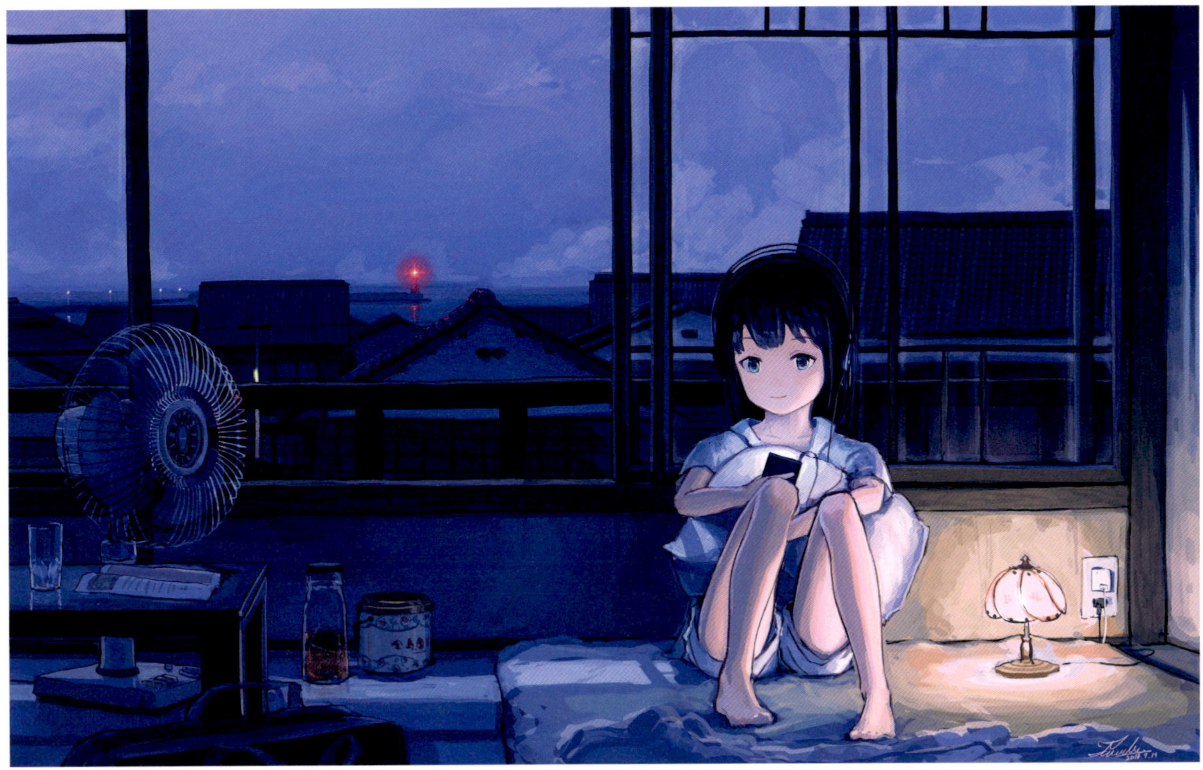

Midnight → Twilight

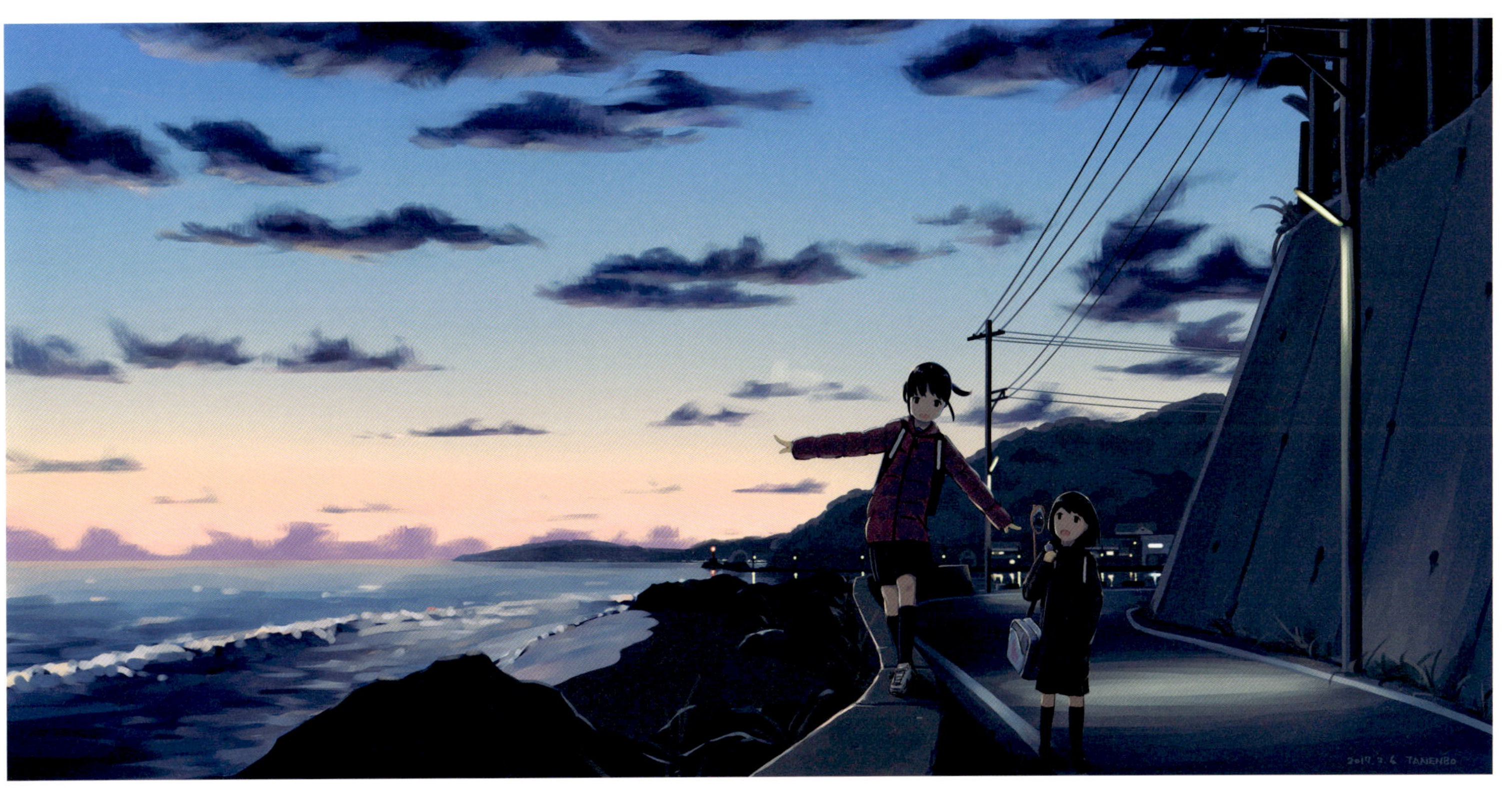

かえりみち | On the Way Home

Tamaki

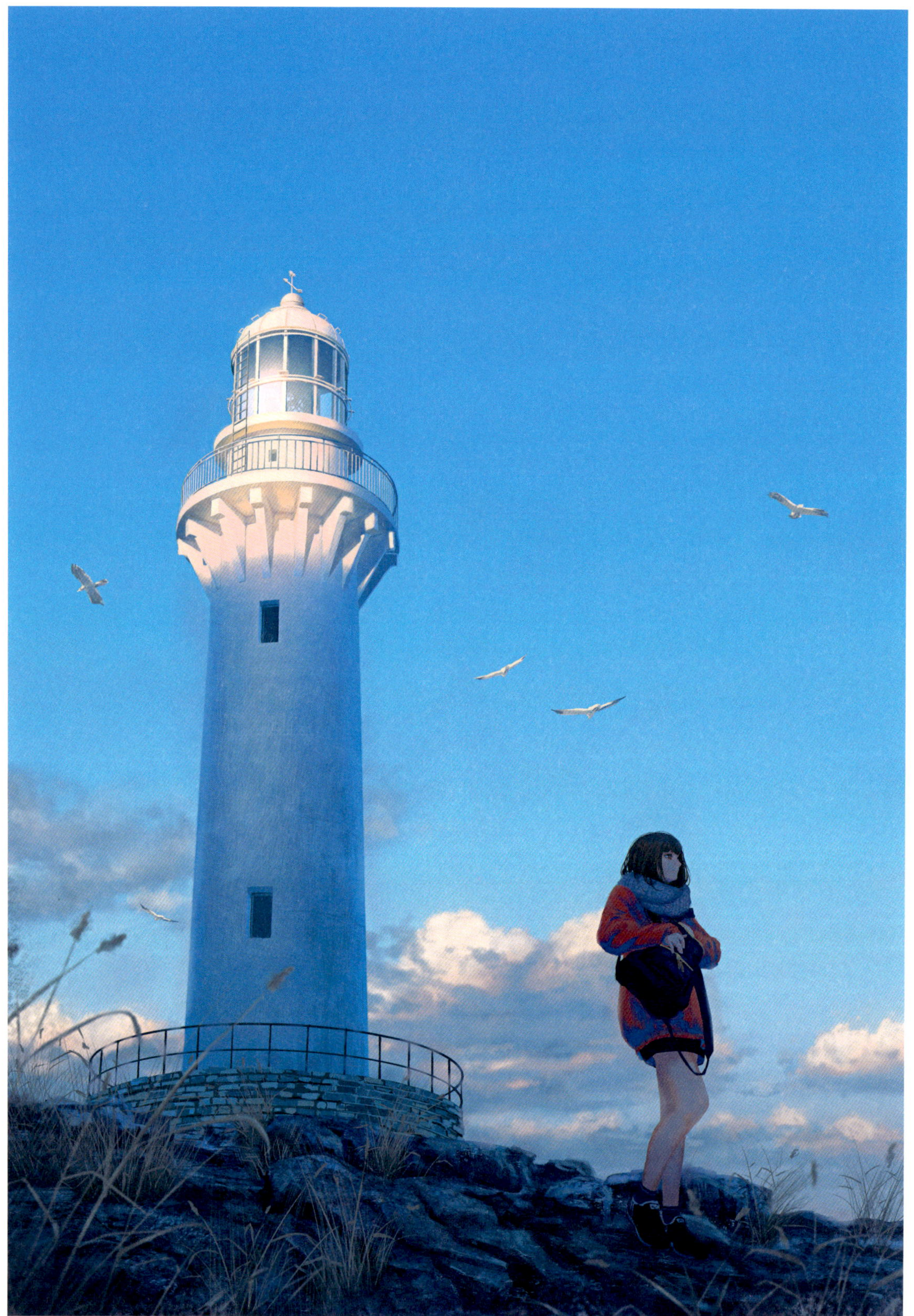

Lighthouse

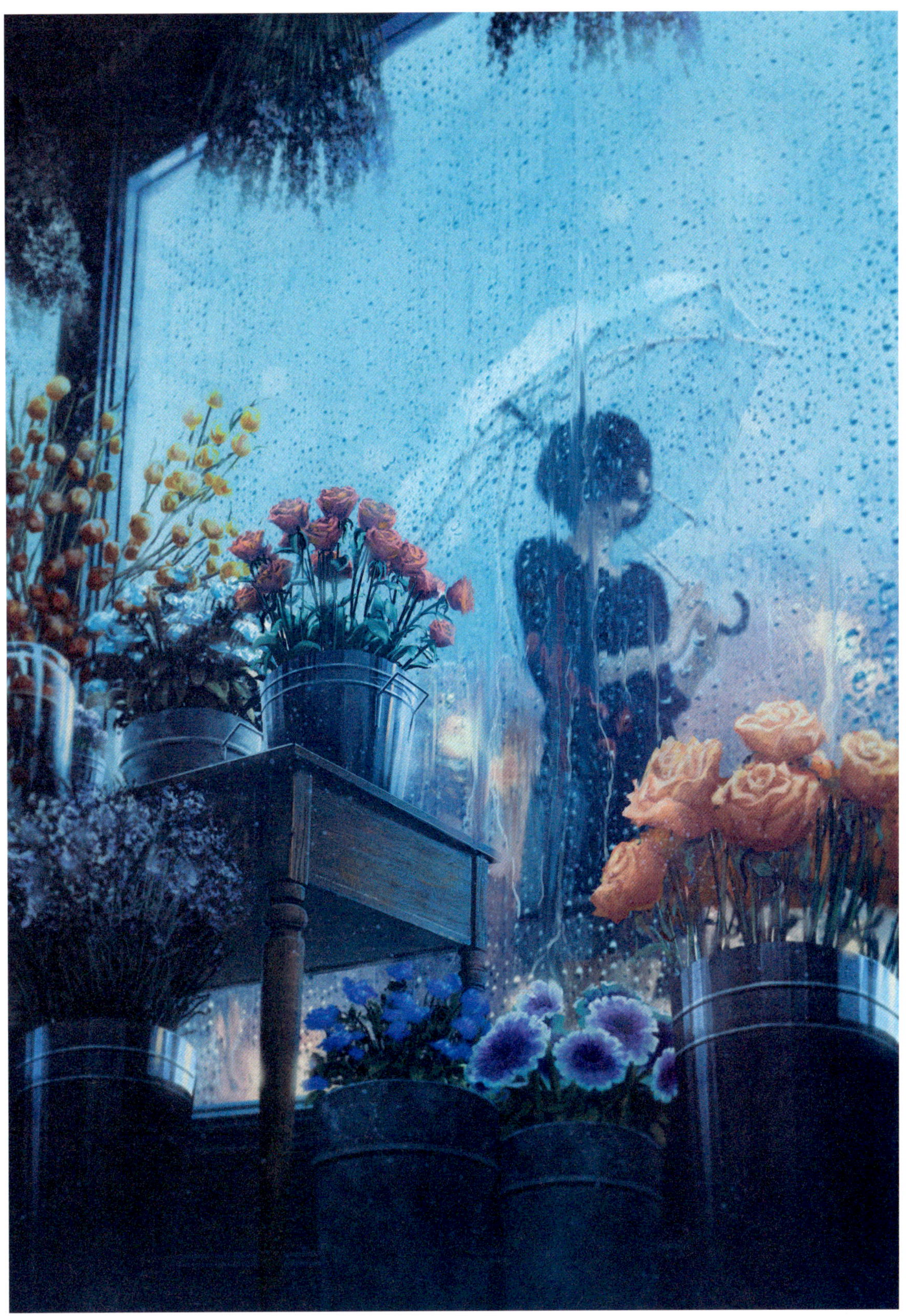

Dress

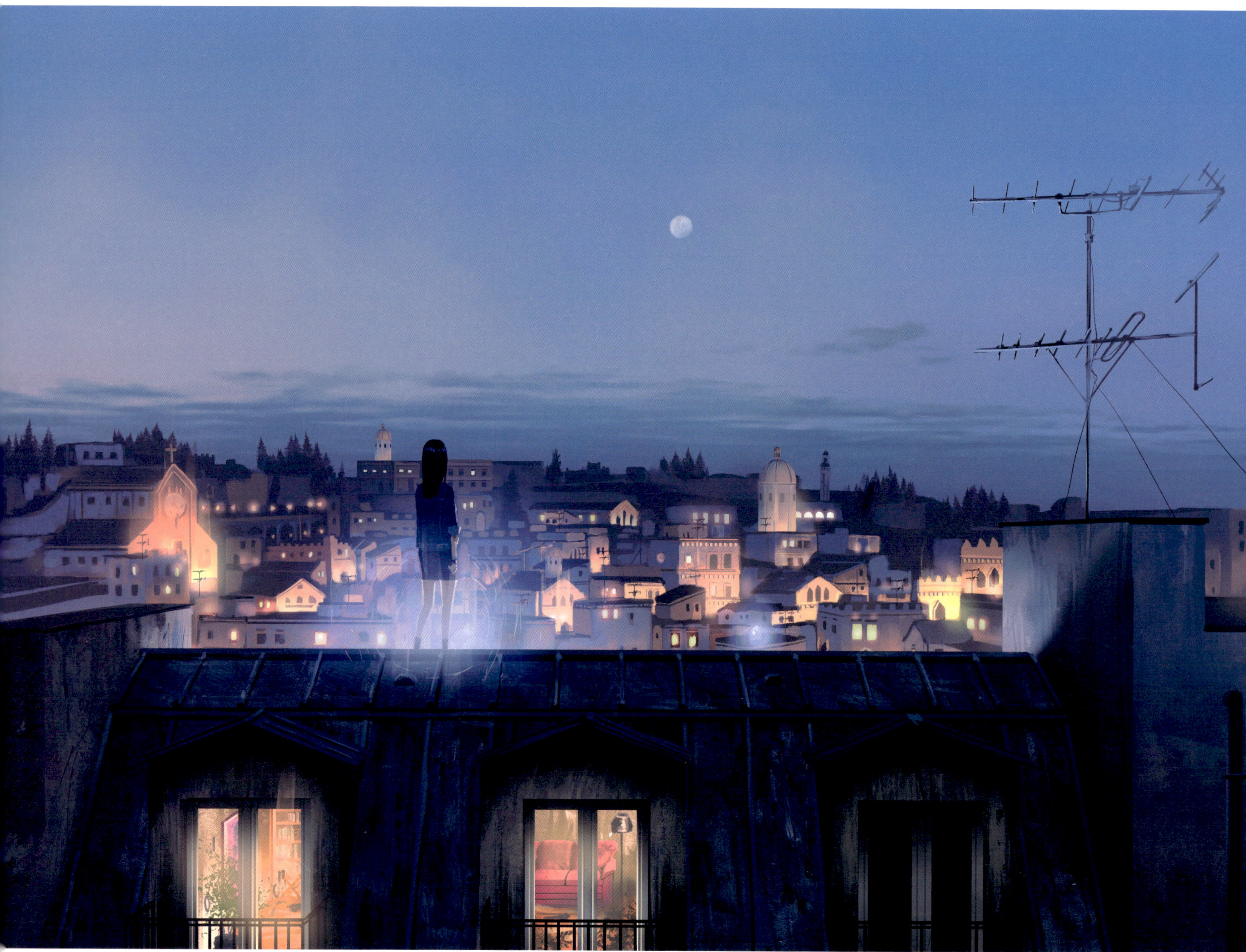

Roof

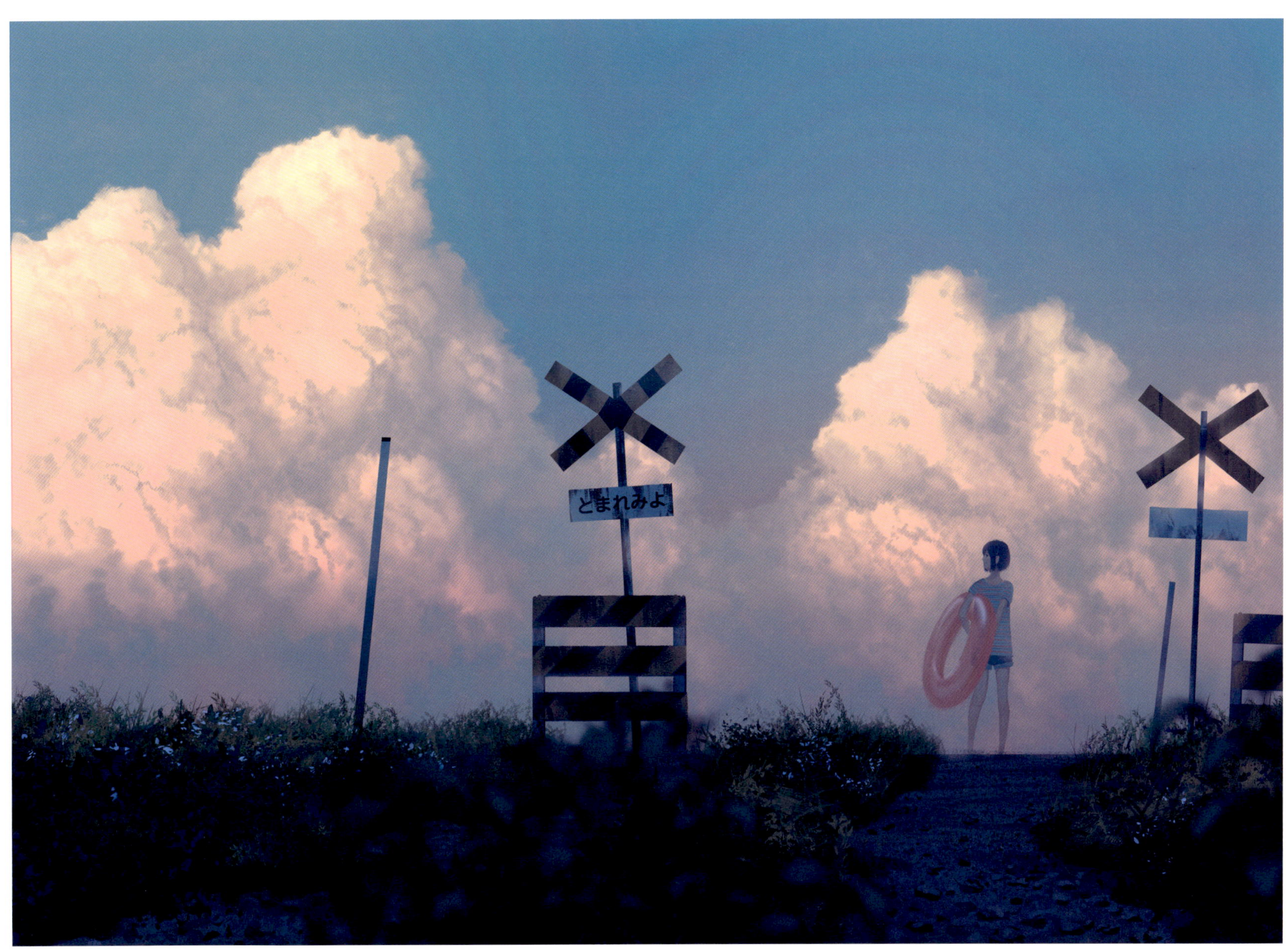

夕焼け　|　Sunset

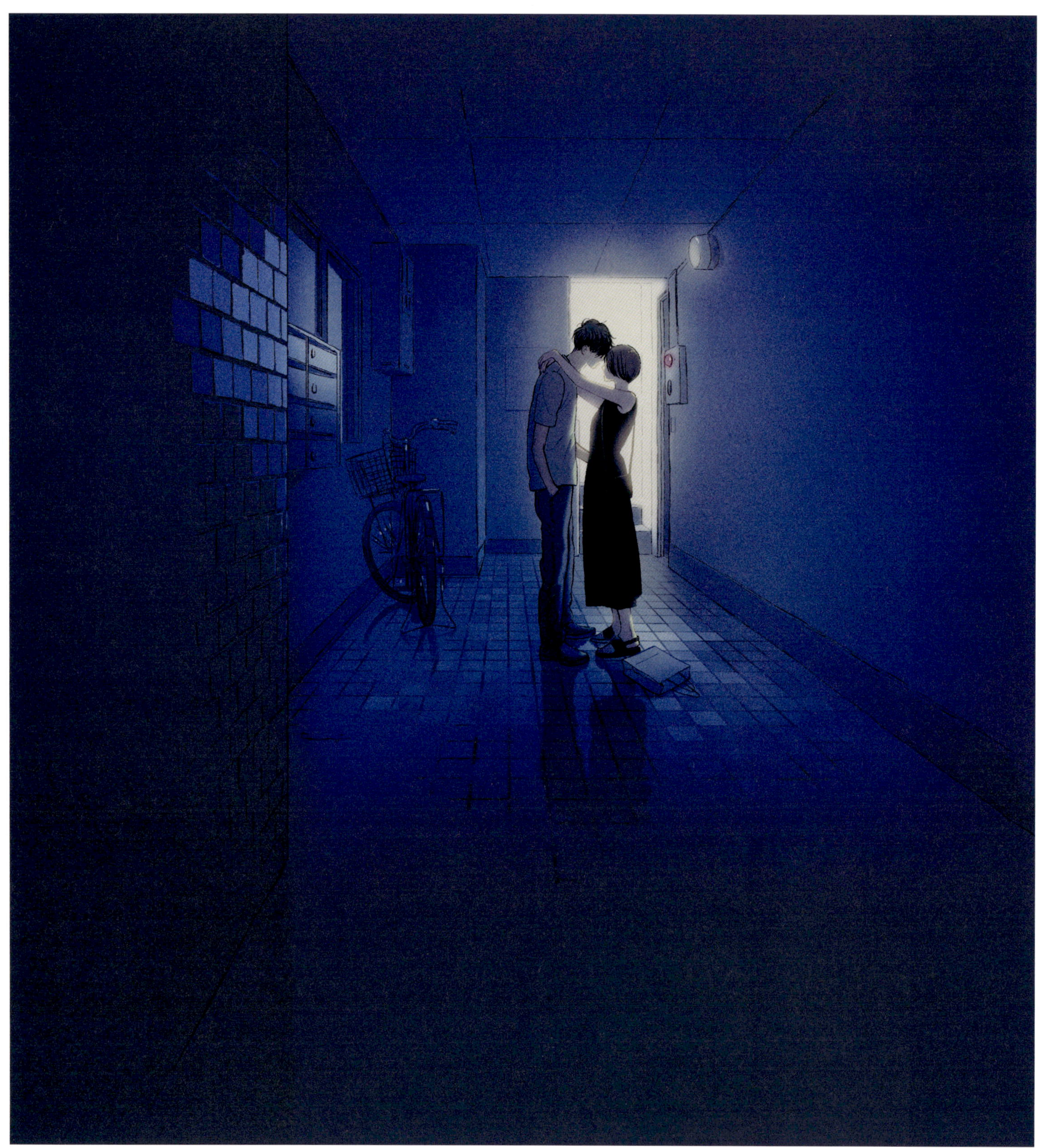

日曜の別れ　|　Parting on Sunday

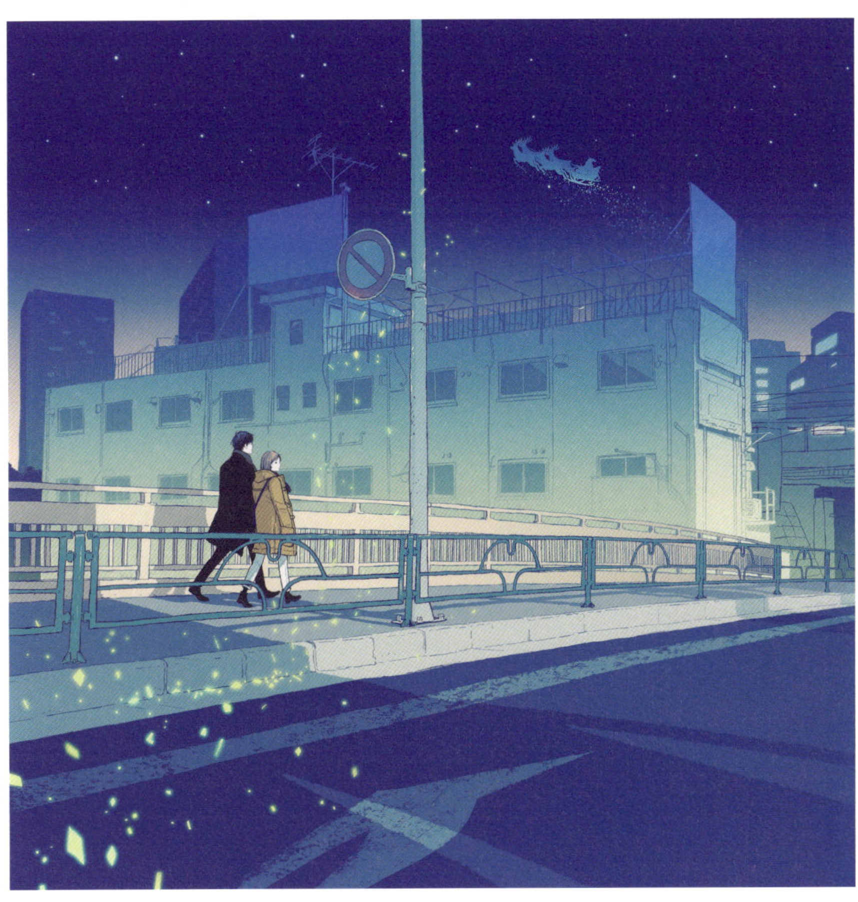

クリスマスの夜　｜　Christmas Night

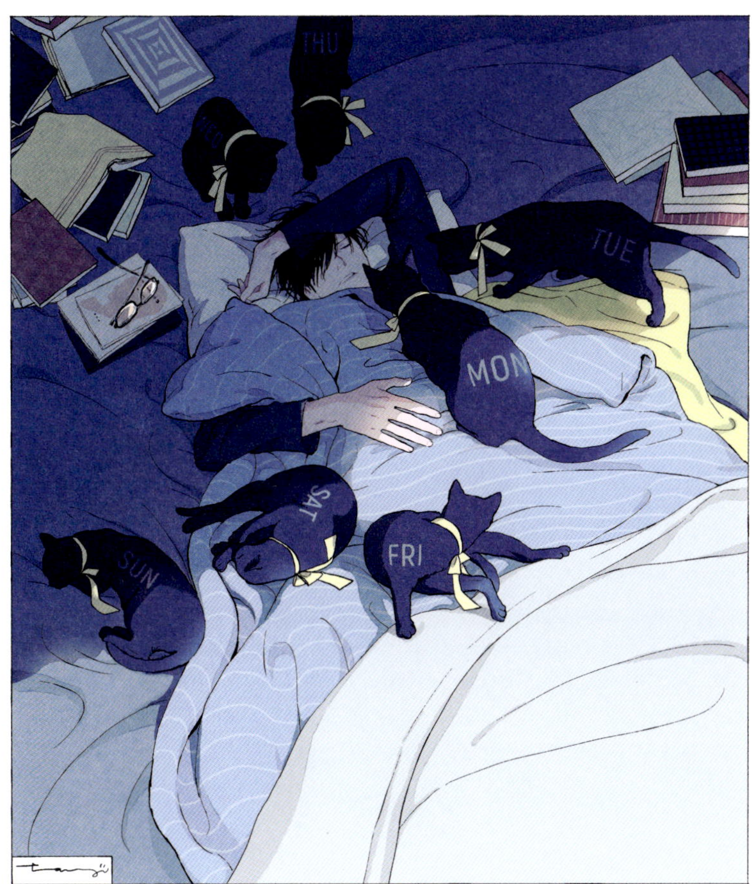

おはようございます朝です　｜　Morning It's Morning

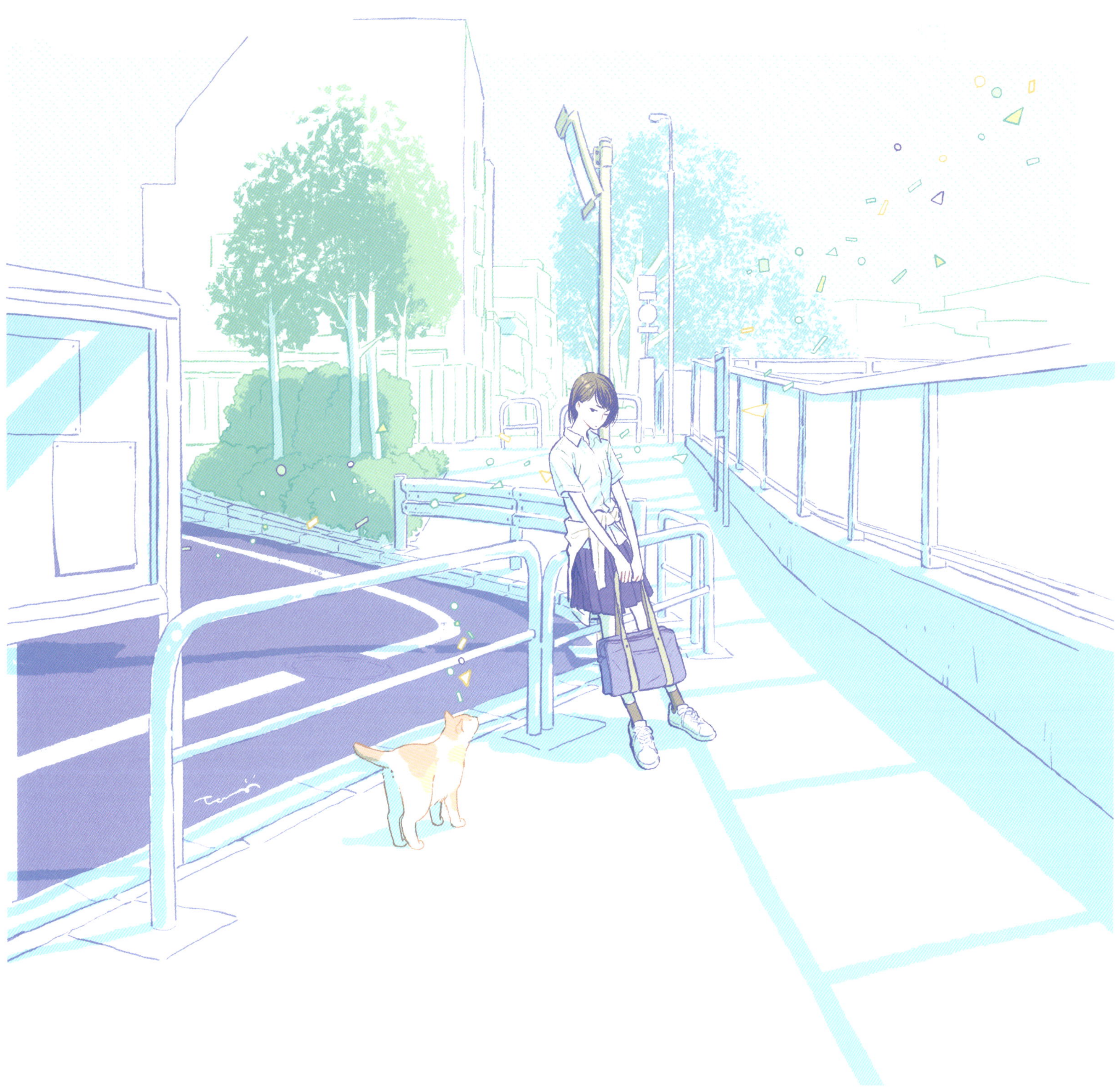

通学路 ｜ The Path to School

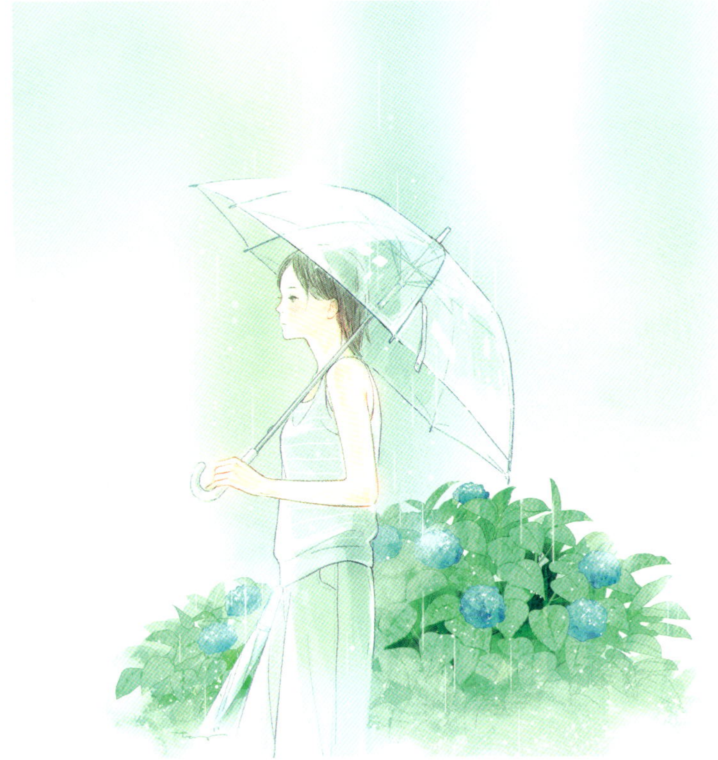

紫陽花 │ Hydrangeas

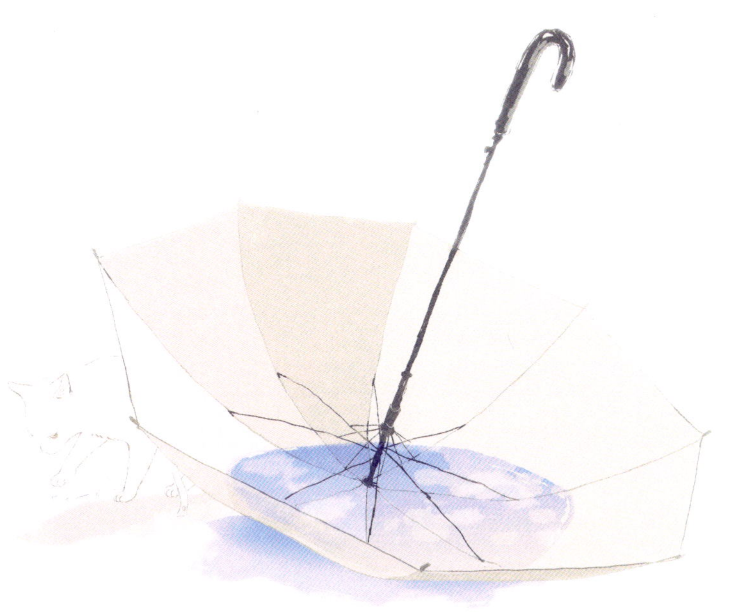

傘の青空 │ Blue Sky in an Umbrella

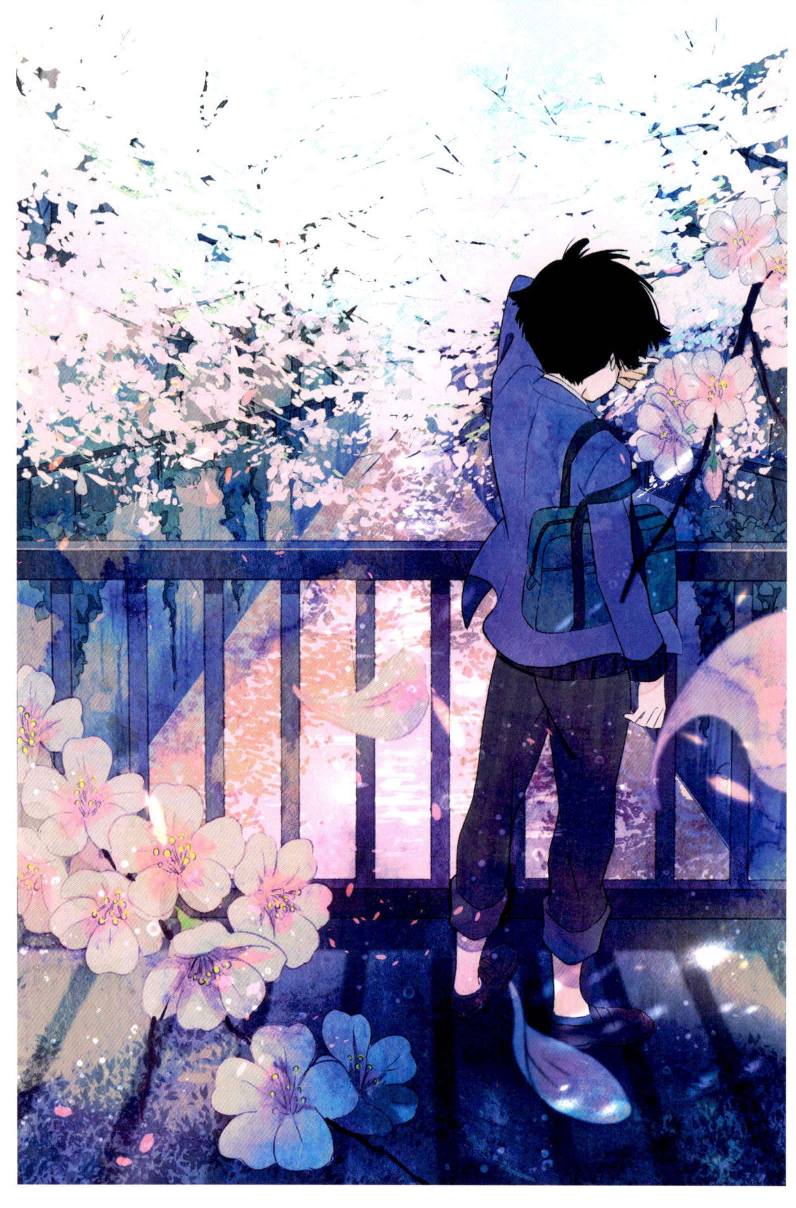

何時の間にか ｜ Before I Knew It

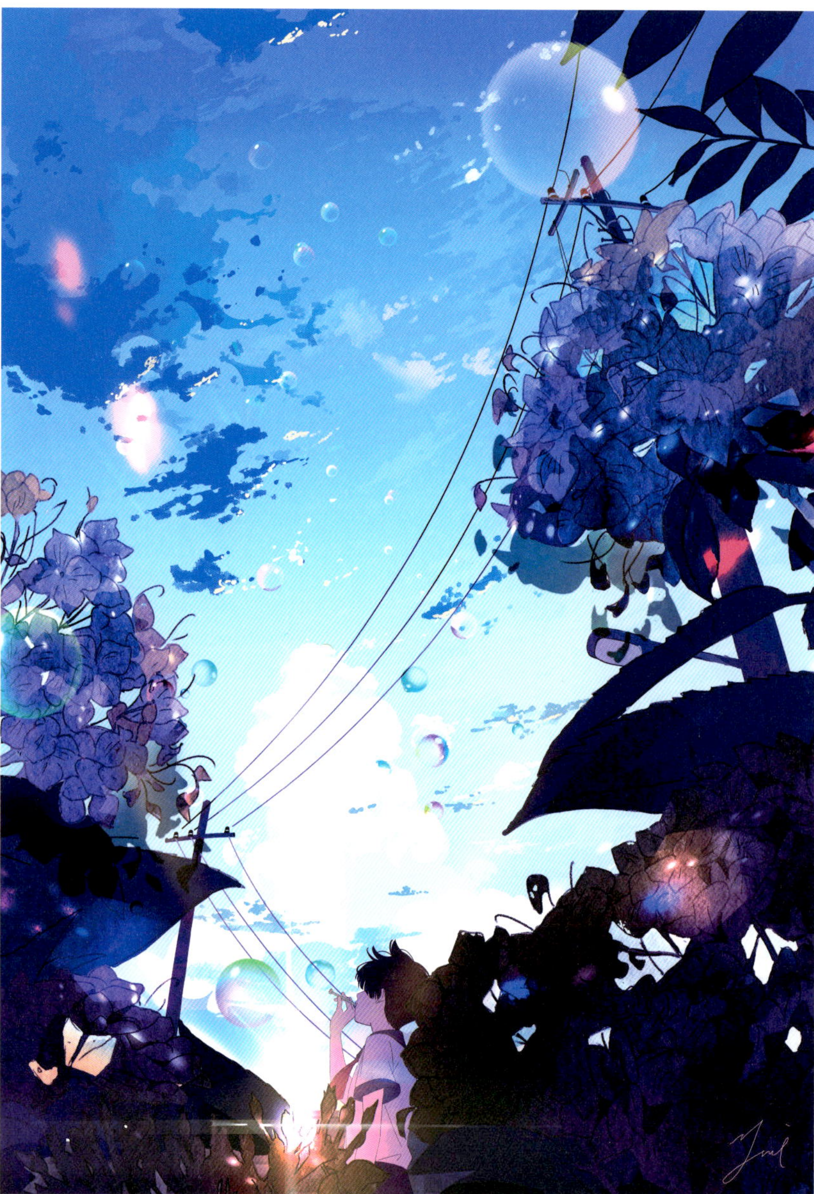

7月の陰影 ｜ July Shadows

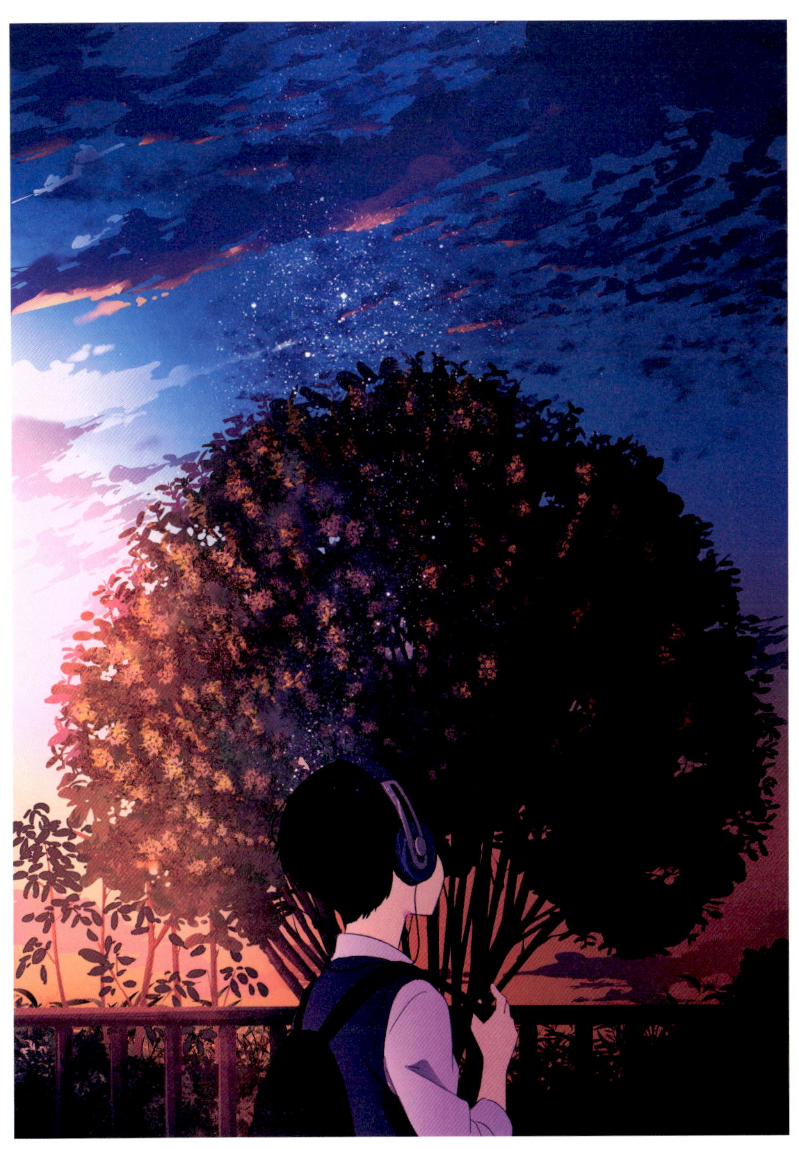

秋は夕暮れ 「ETOPICA」掲載イラスト　|　Autumn Twilight, posted online via *ETOPICA*

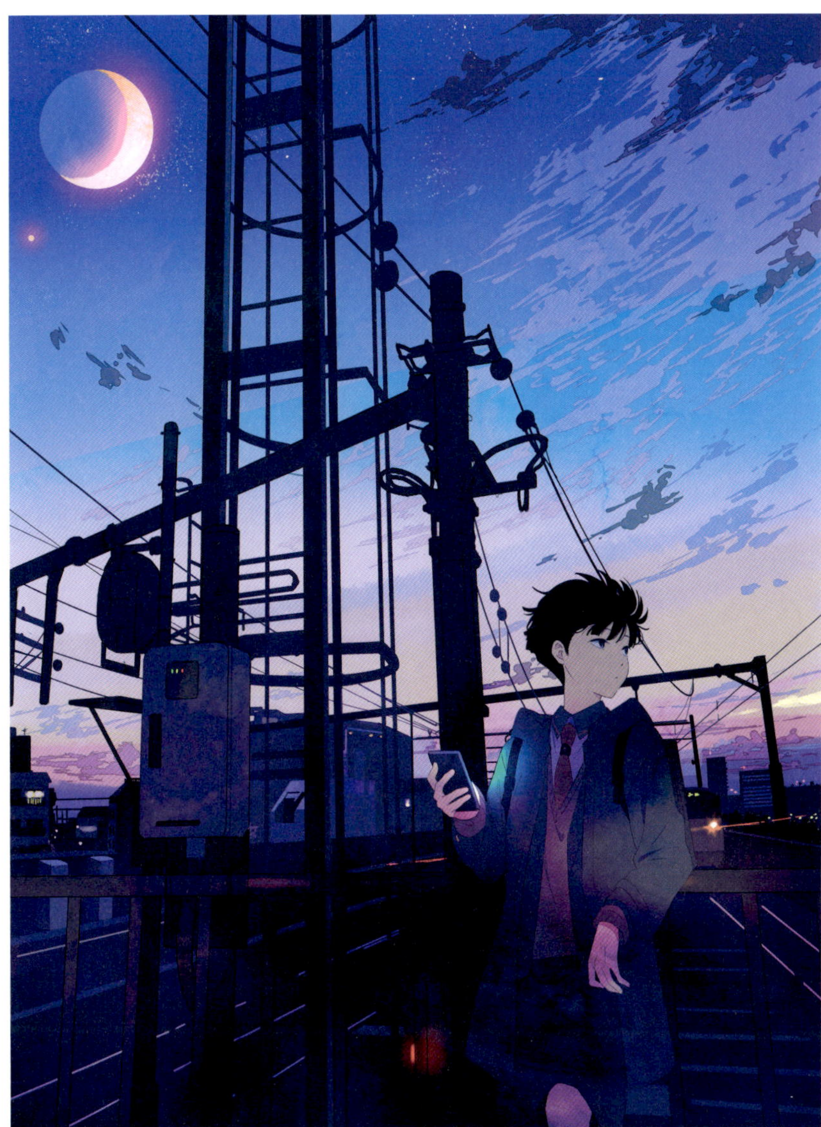

終わる魔法　|　Ending Magic

夏目ヤスム ｜ yasumu Natsume

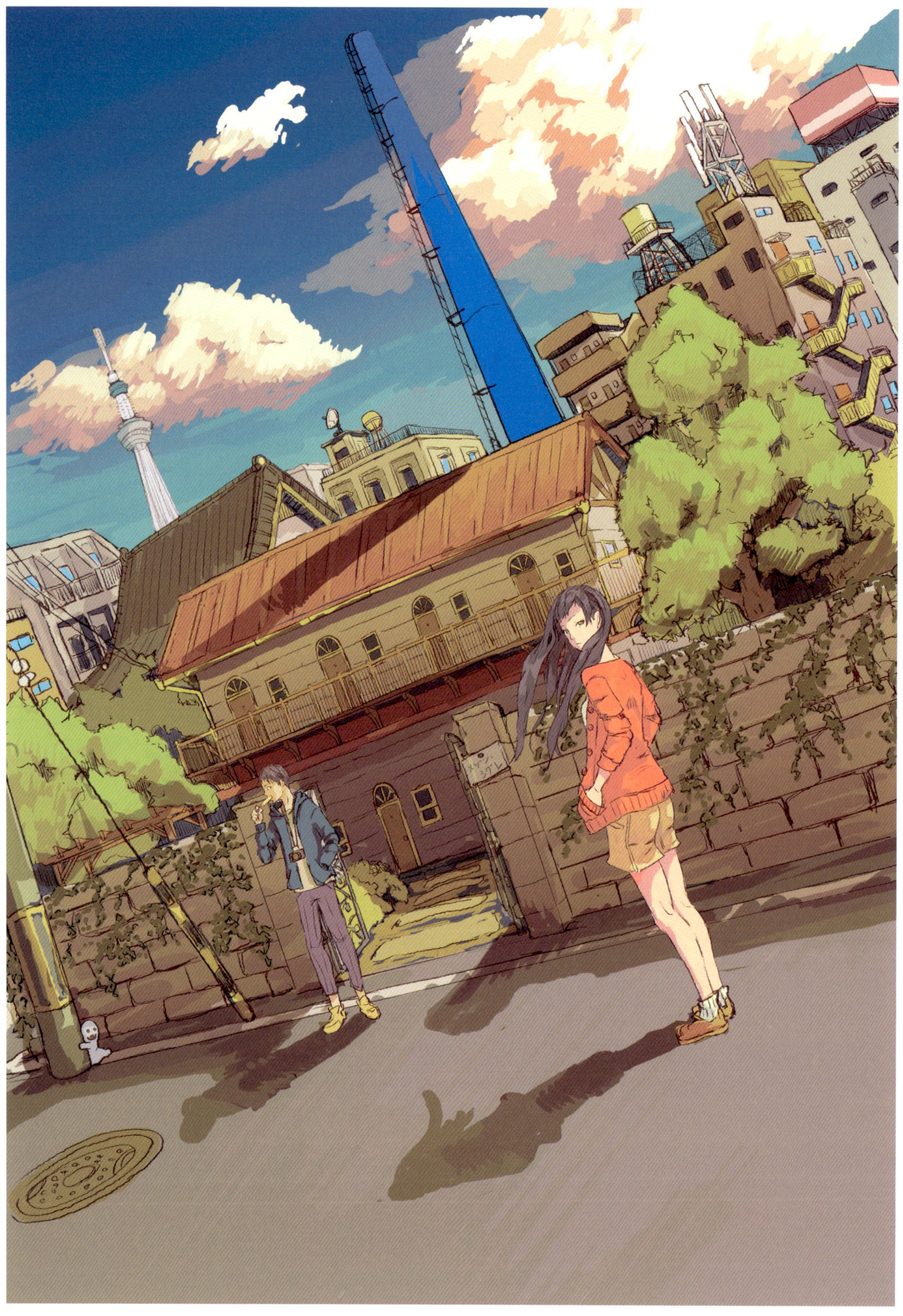

『下町アパートのふしぎ管理人』（大城密 著、角川文庫）カバーイラスト
Cover illustration for *Shitamachi Apa-to no Fushigi Kanrinin* (written by Hisoka Oshiro, published by Kadokawa Corporation)

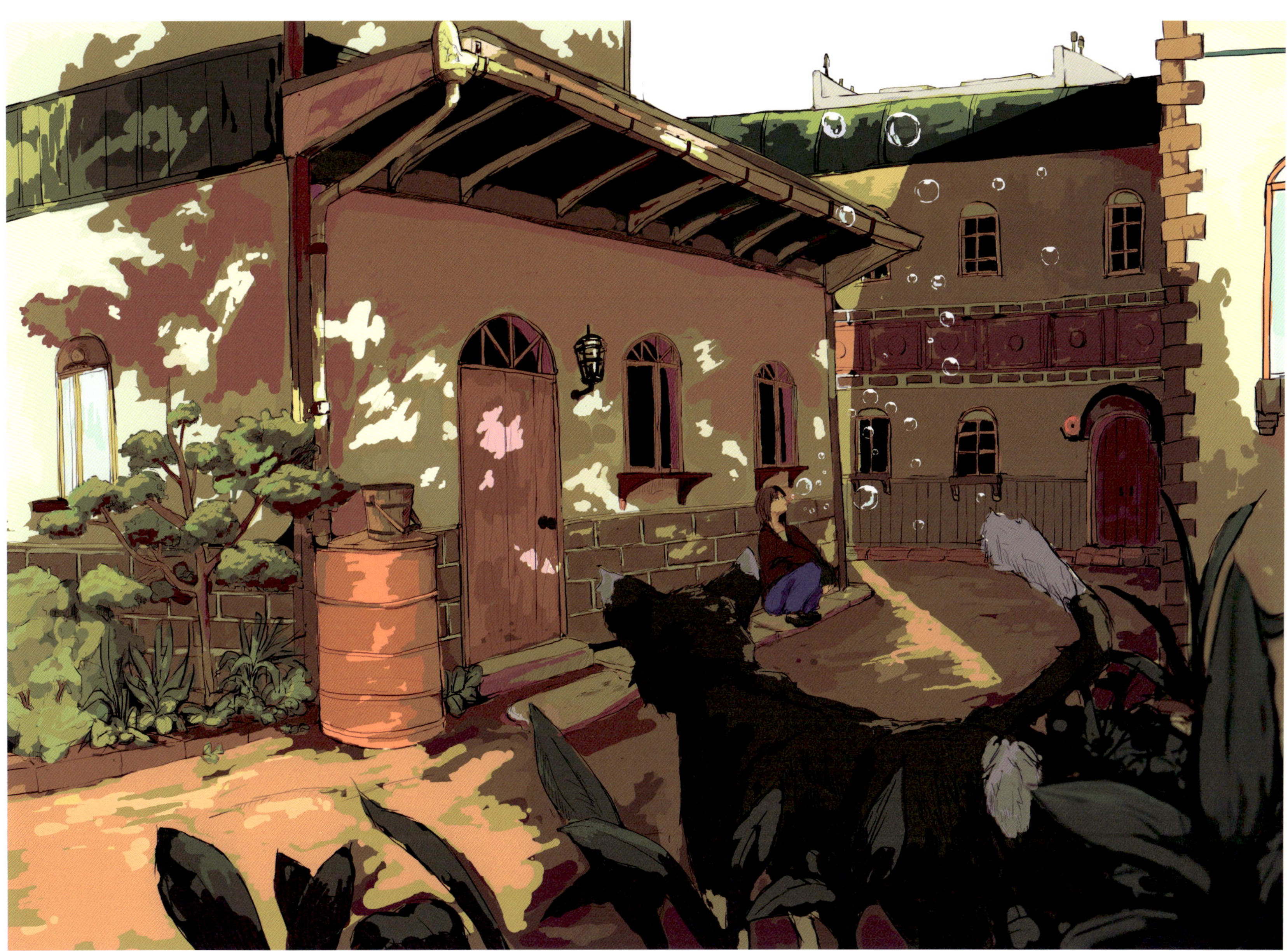

儚い願い　|　Fleeting Hope

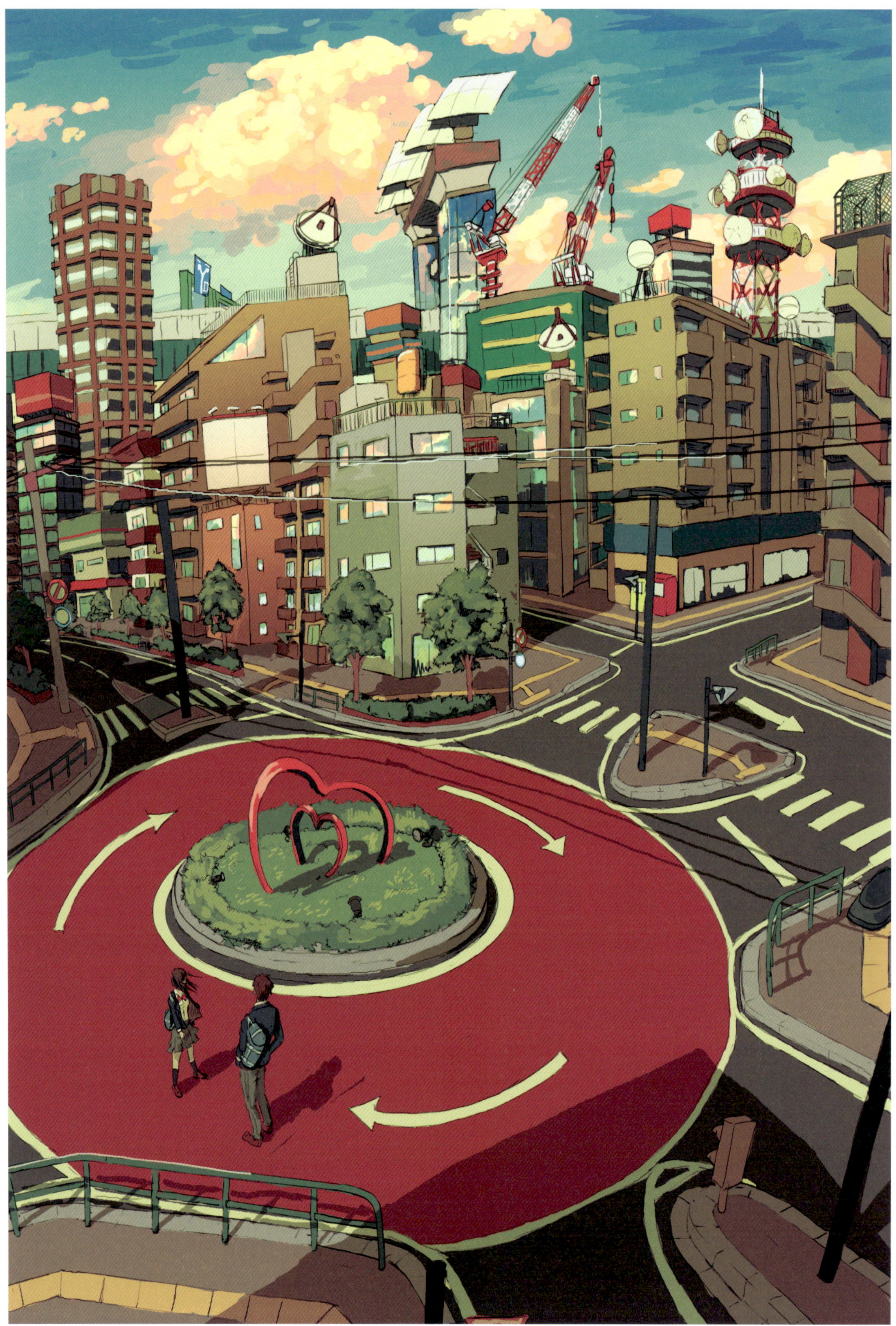

大人になったら　│　When I Grow Up

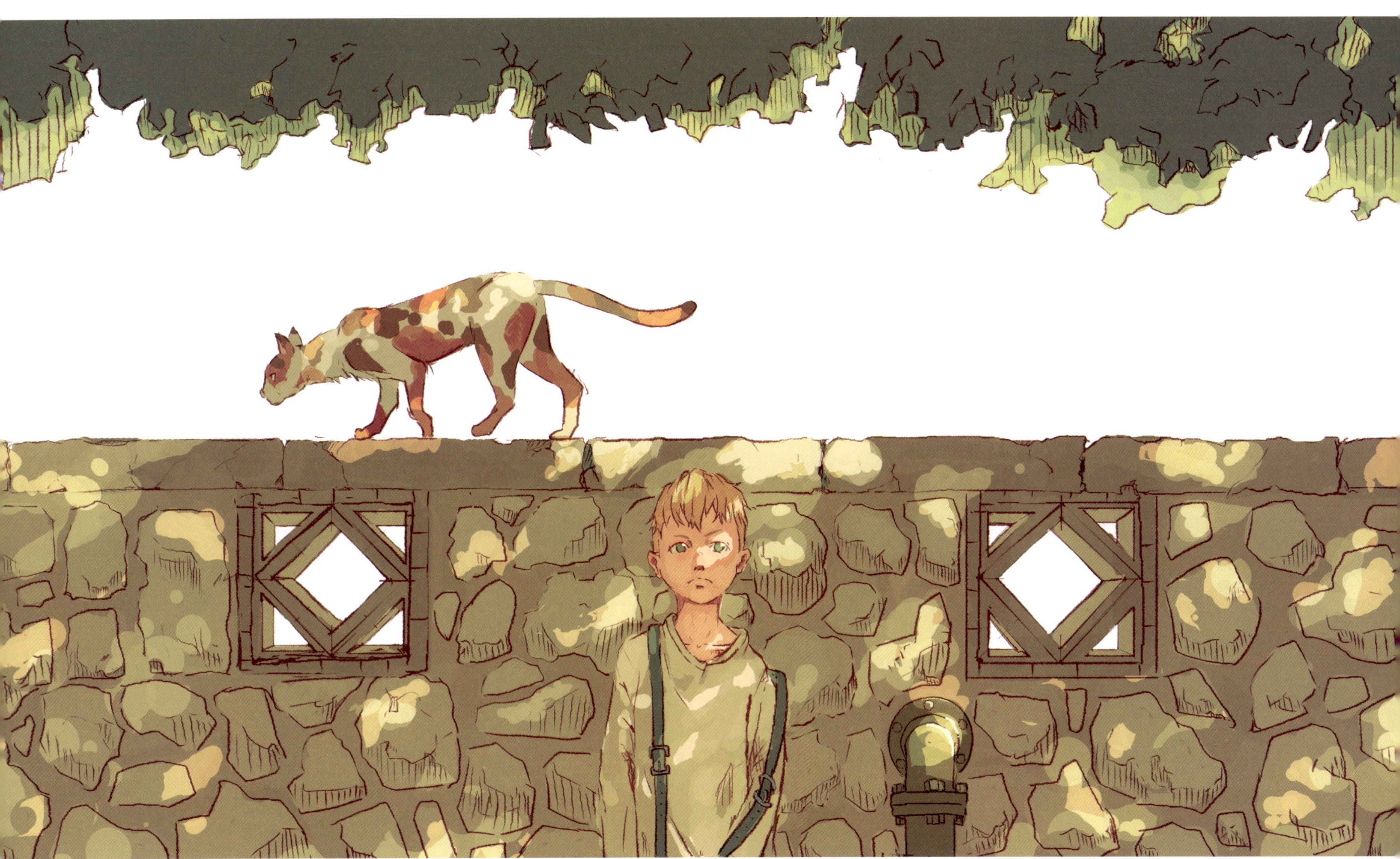

無色　│　Colorless

HAI

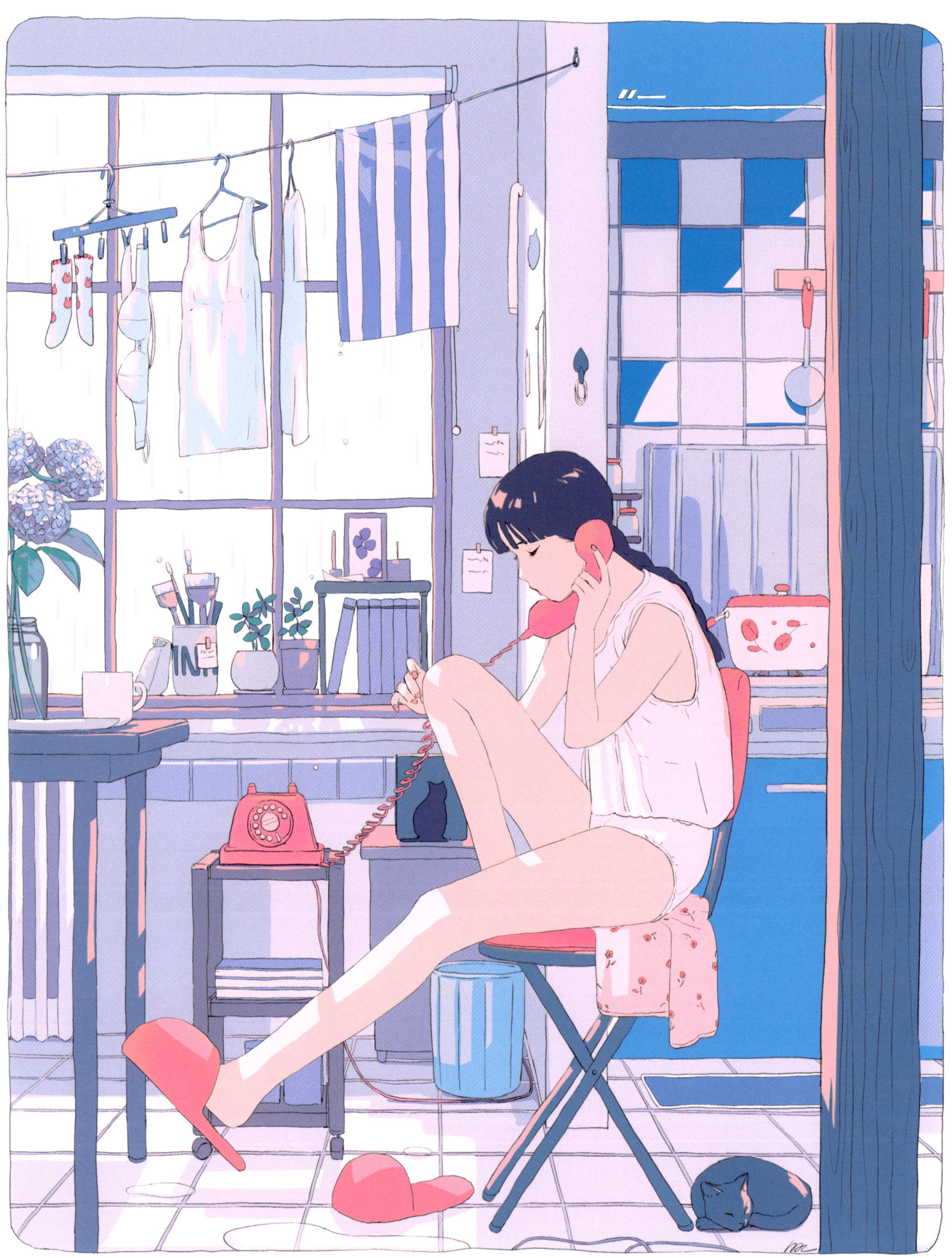

電話 | Phone

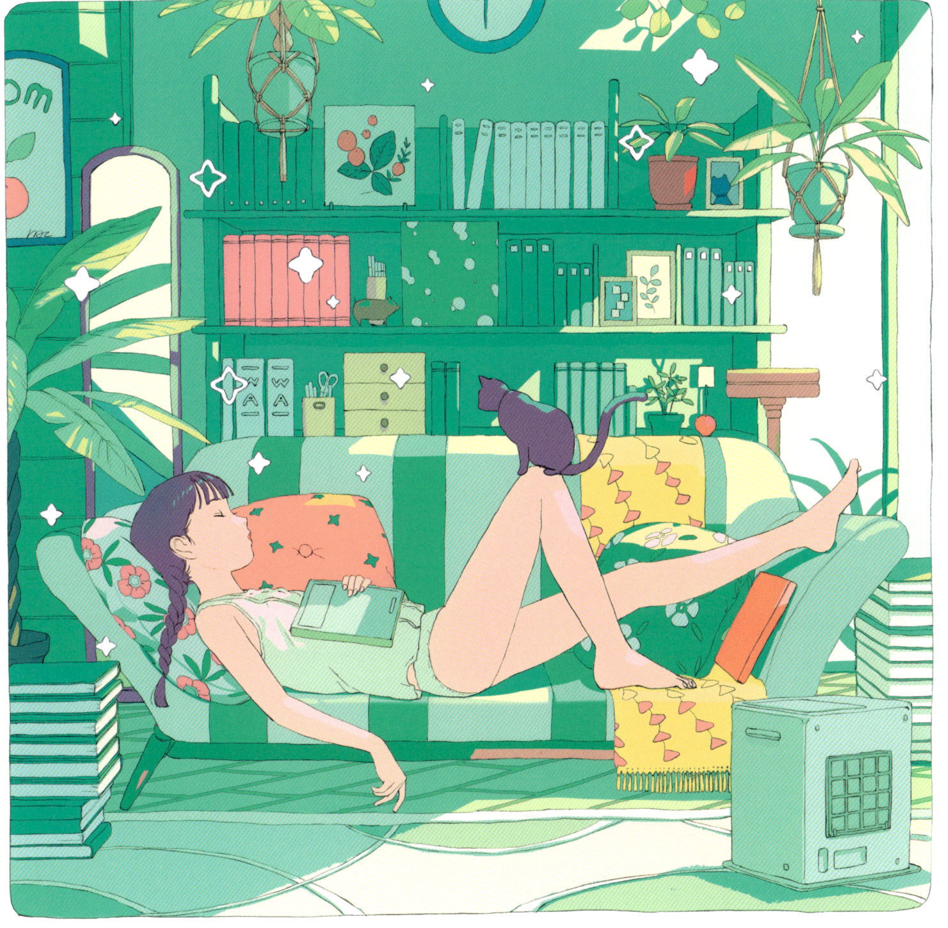

すやすや　｜　Quiet Sleep

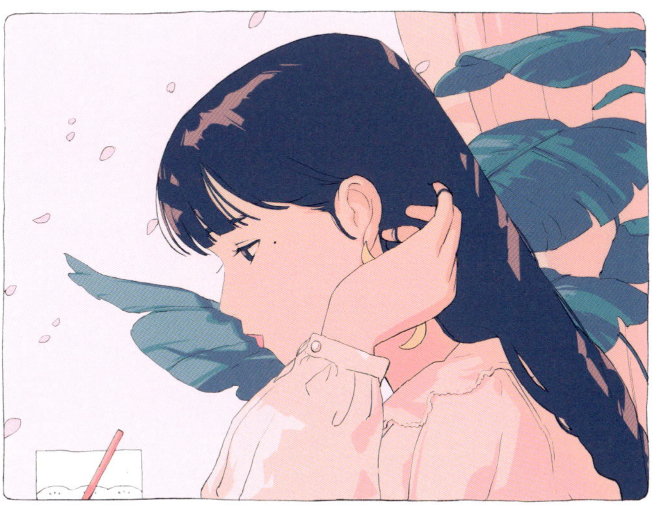

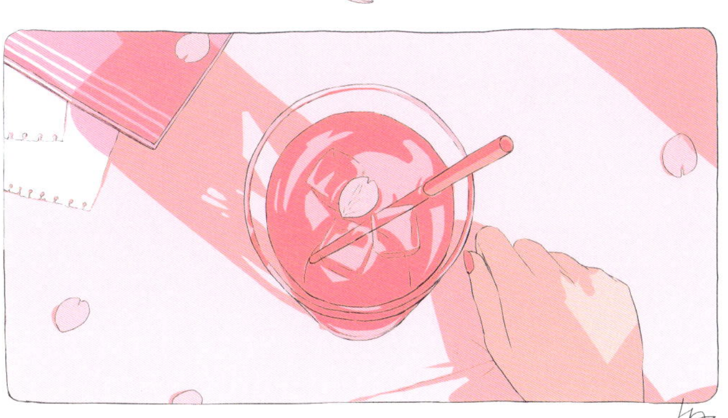

はなびら　｜　Flower Petals

前田ミック　|　**Mic Maeda**

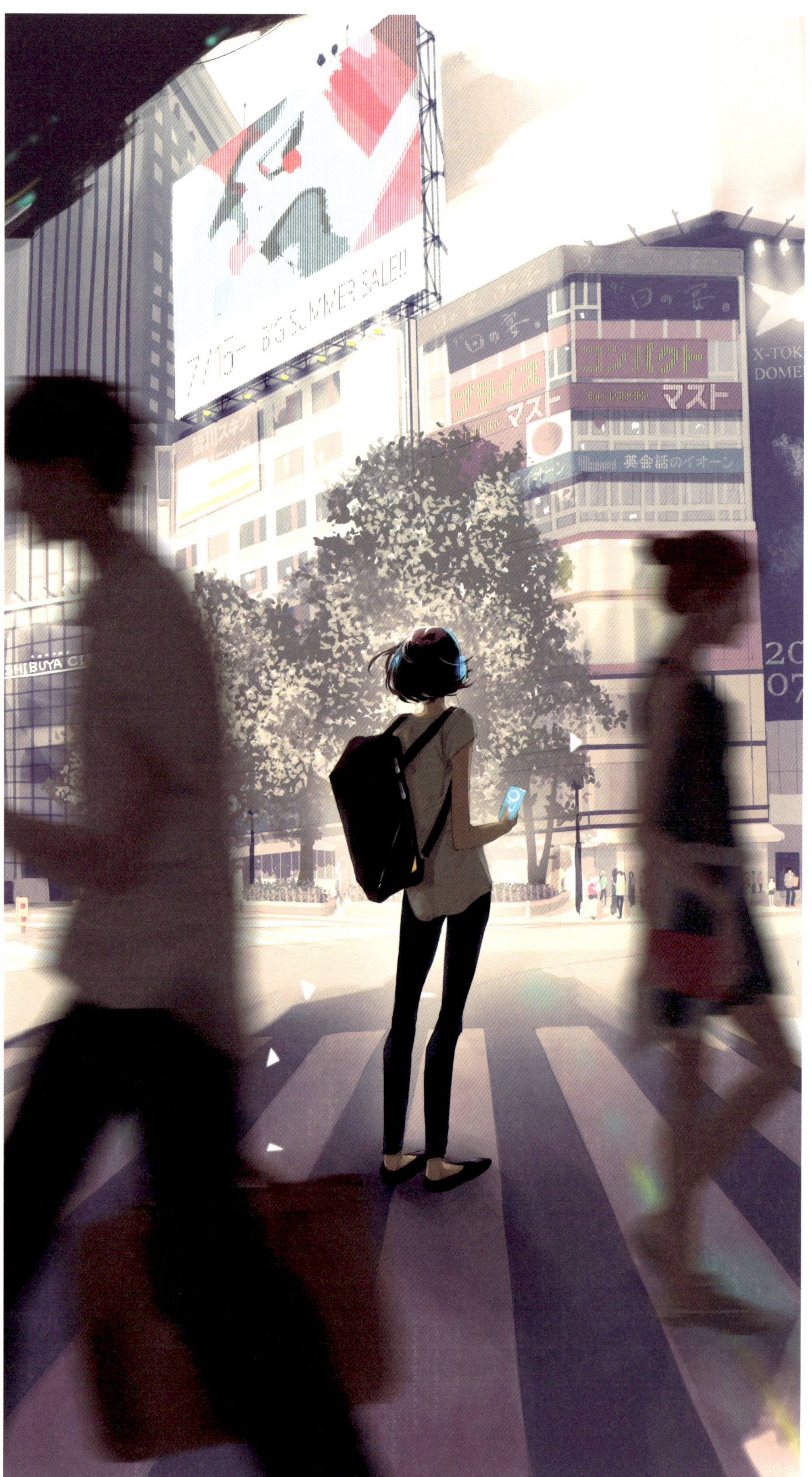

MOMo
2017 PORT zero
2017 PORT zero
twinkle twinkle
TAXI
JAPAN TAXI

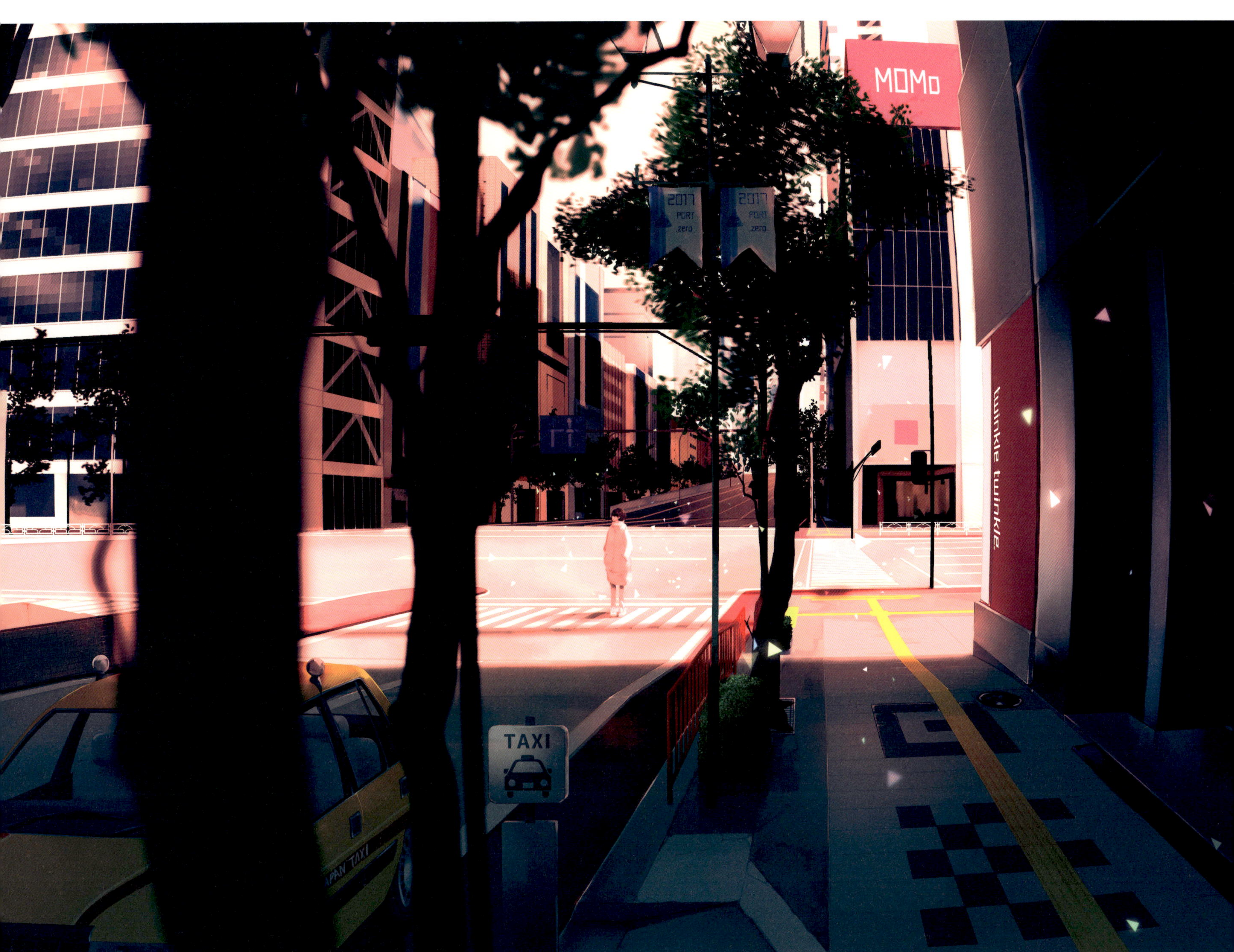

PINK

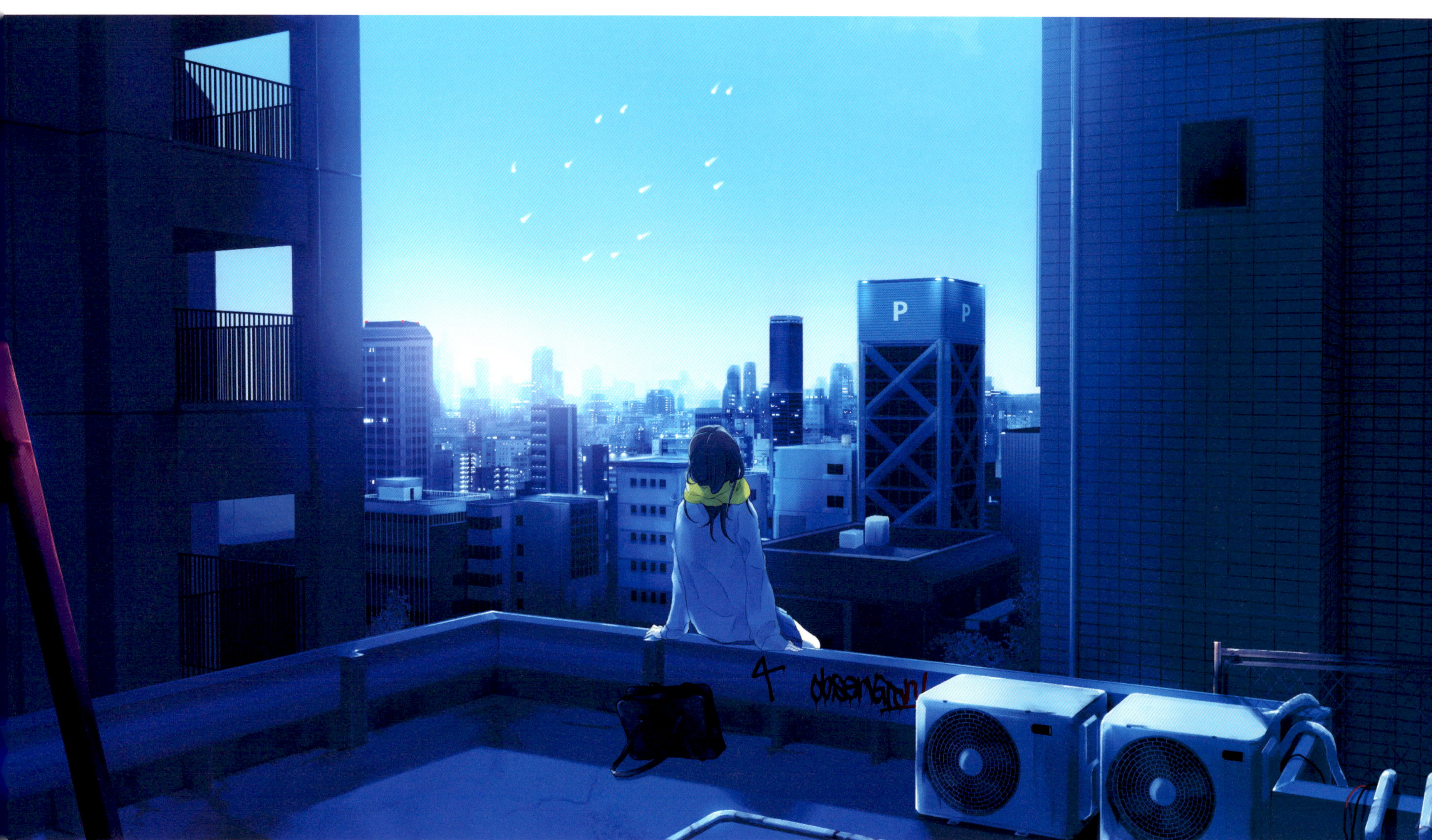

Observatory

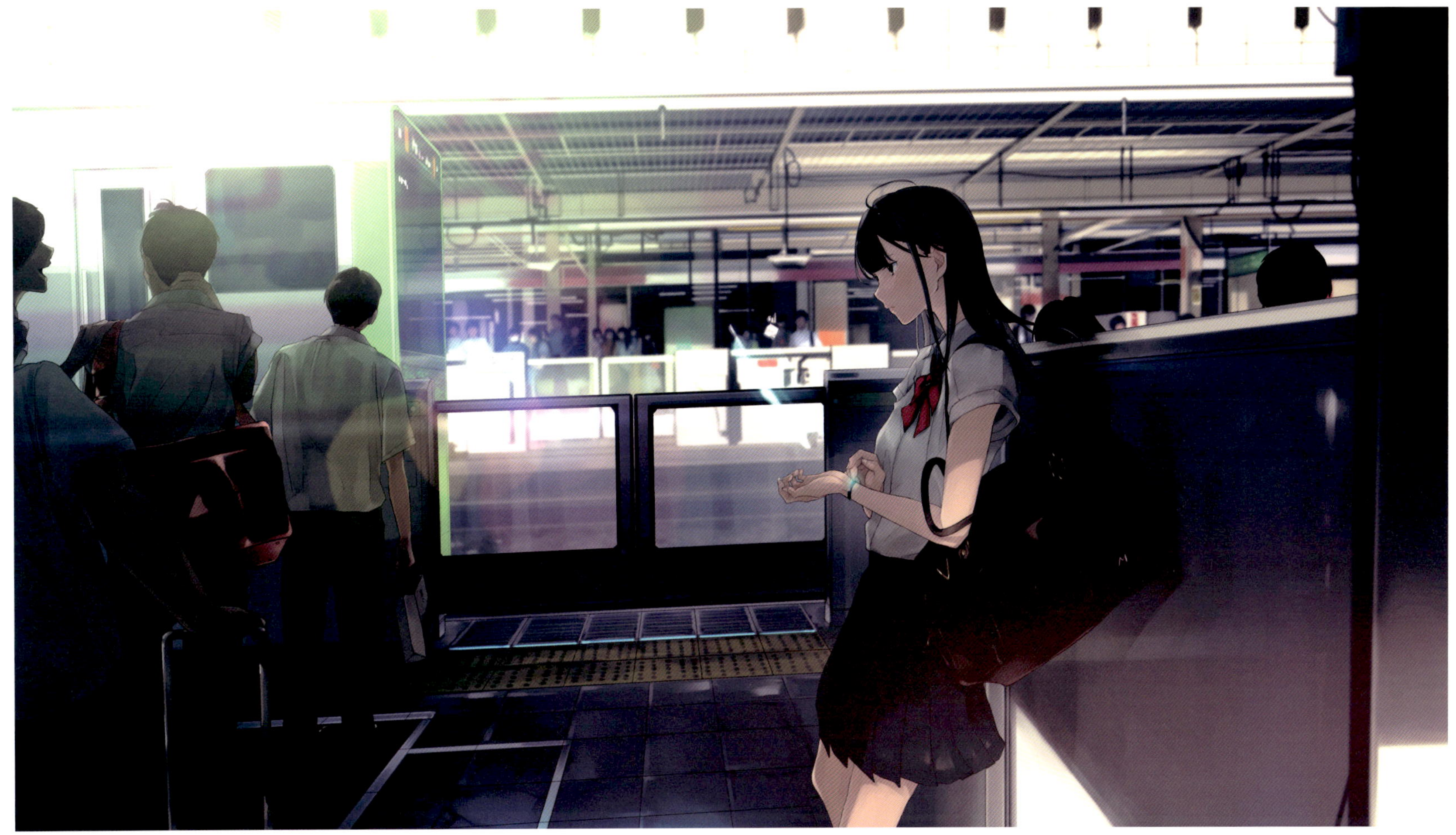

Login

Merrill Macnaut

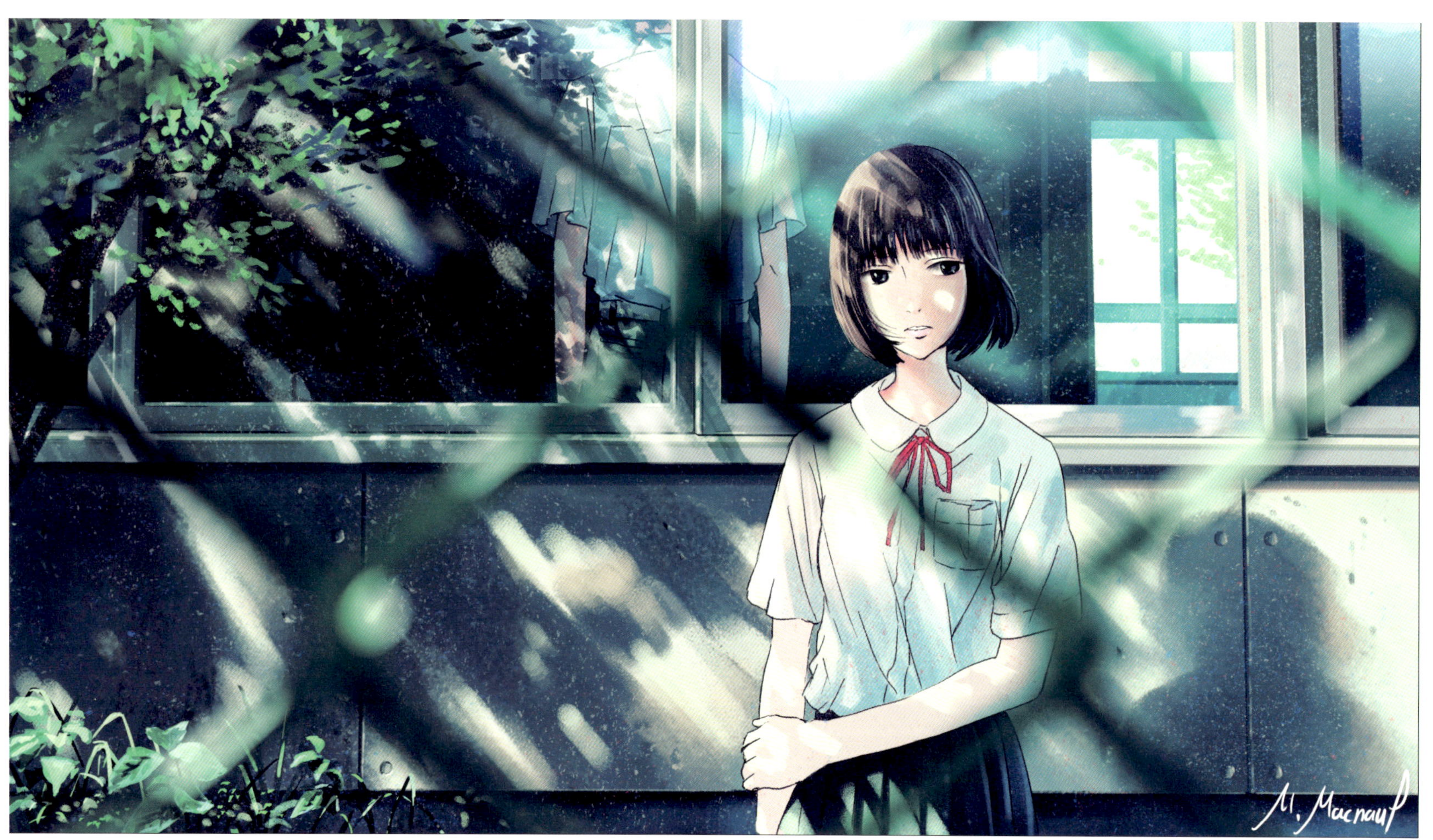

ホームルーム始まるってよ　|　Homeroom is About to Start

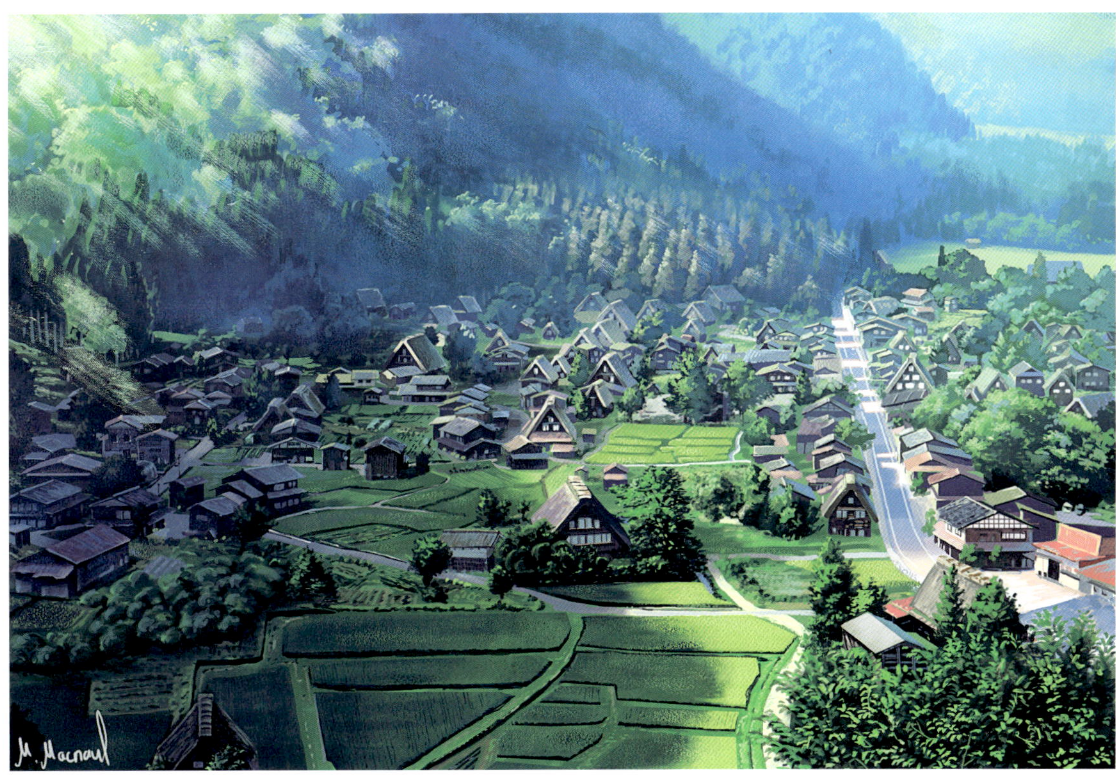

白川郷の朝 ｜ Morning at Shirakawa Village

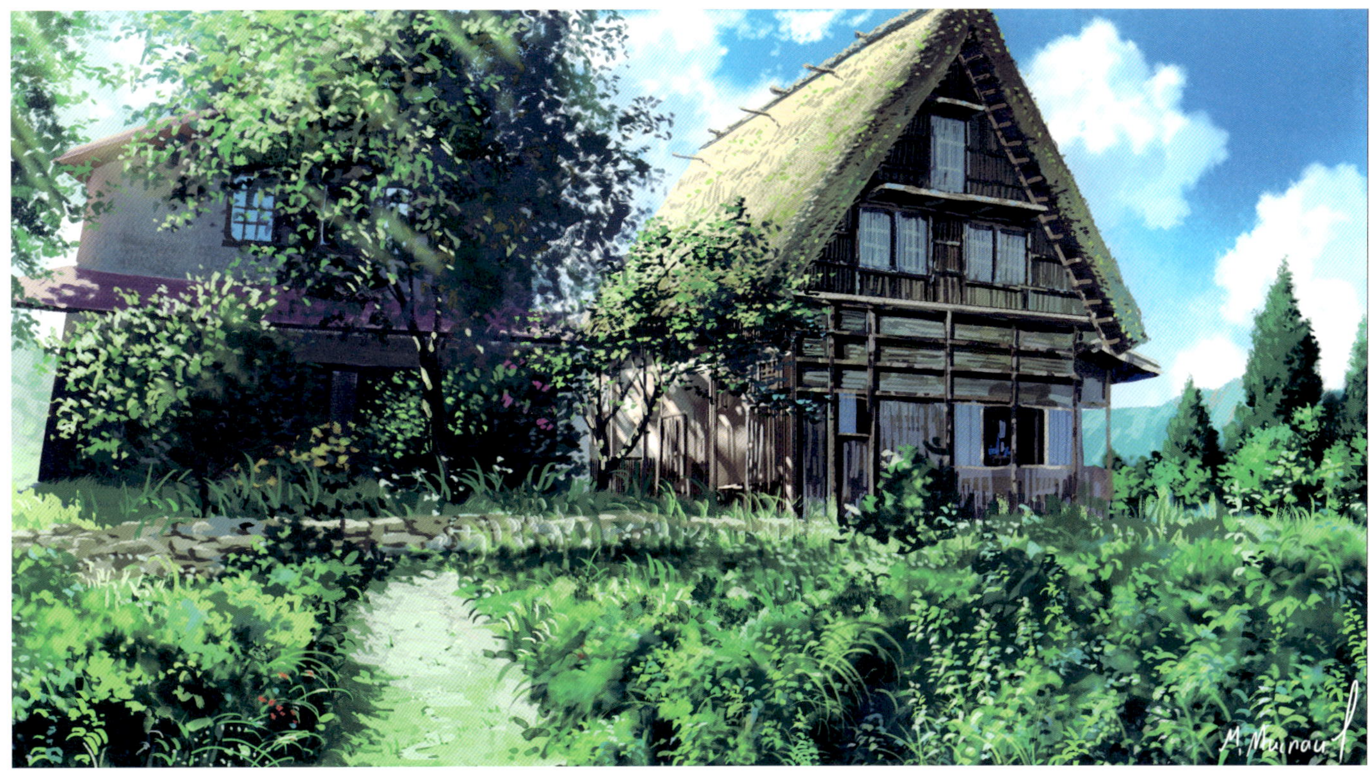

夏風 ｜ Summer Breeze

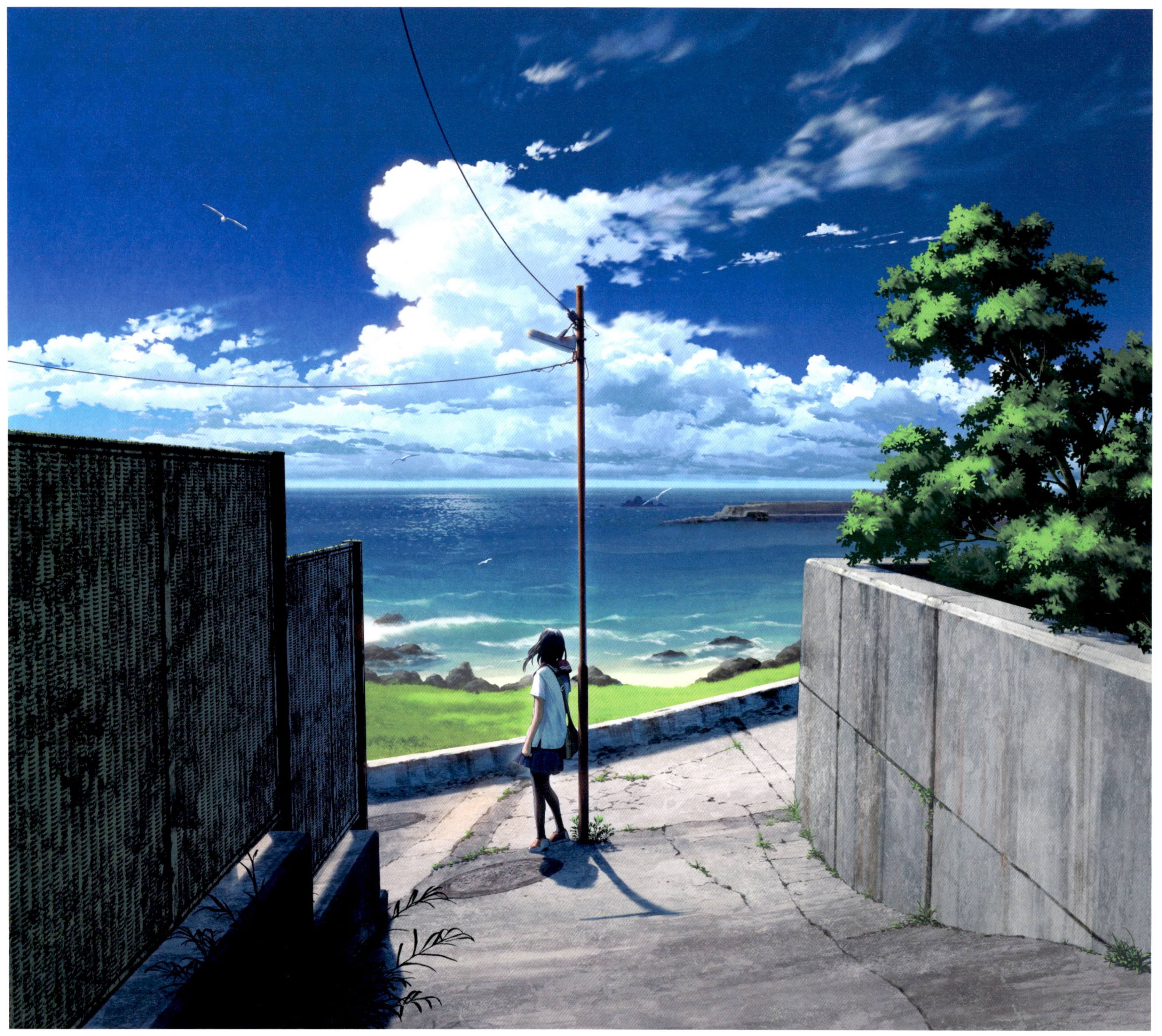

夏影『背景作画 ゼロから学ぶプロの技 神技作画シリーズ』（mocha著、KADOKAWA）描き下ろしイラスト
Summer Shadows, an illustration for *Haikei Sakuga: Zero kara Manabu Puro no Waza – Kamiwaza Sakuga Series* (written by mocha, published by Kadokawa Corporation)

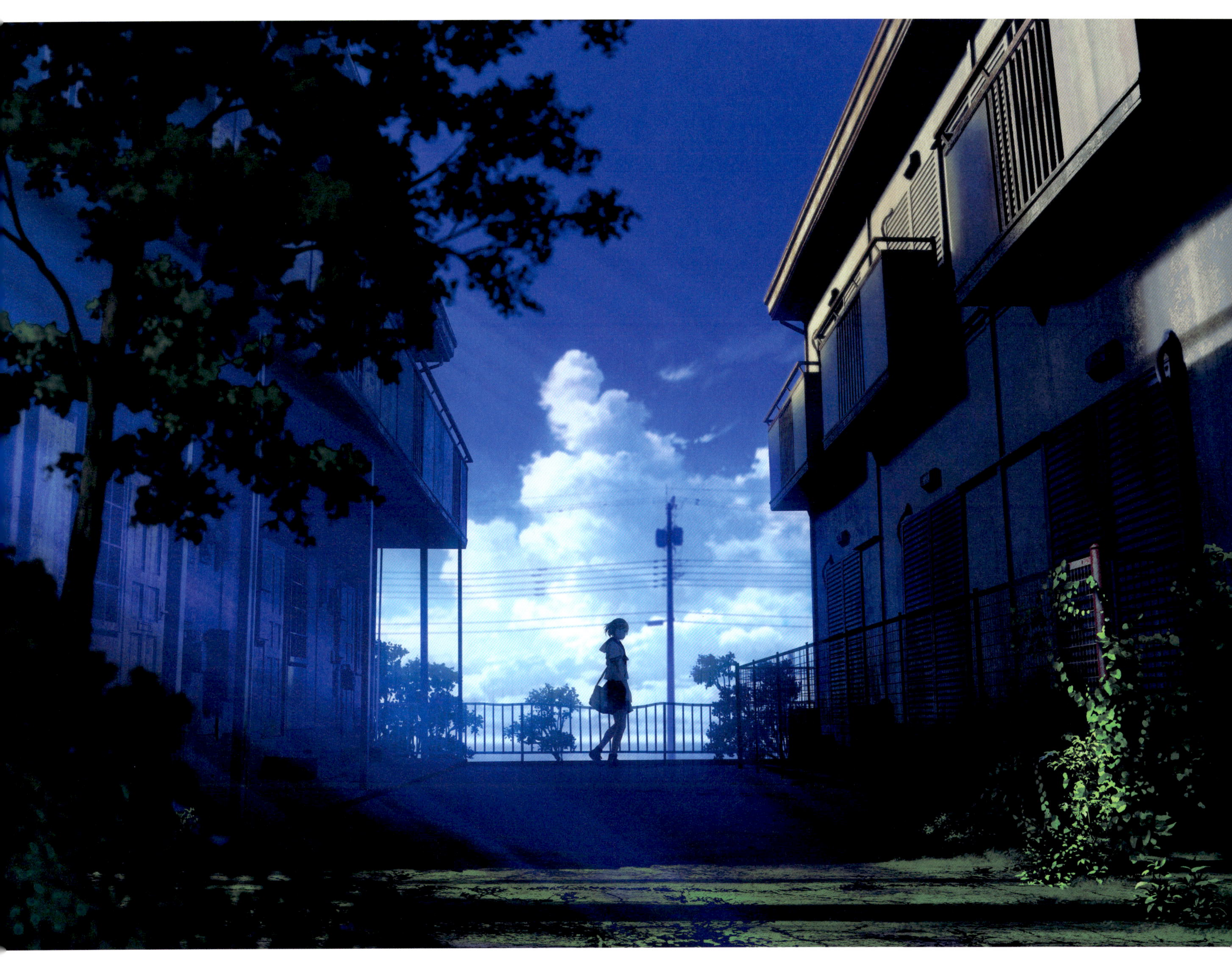

青の狭間　|　Blue Gap

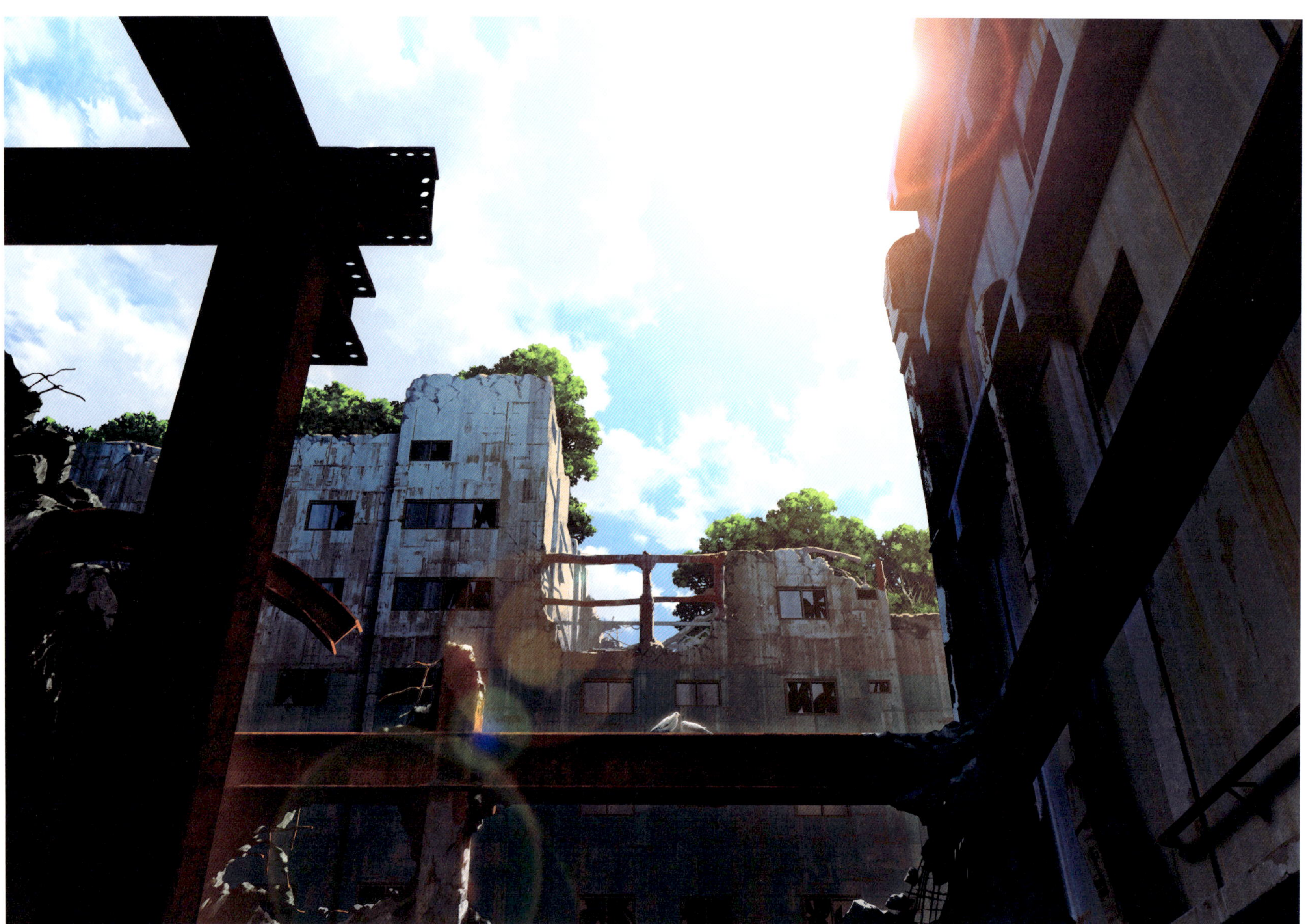

鉄骨に鳩　｜　Steel Frame and Pigeon

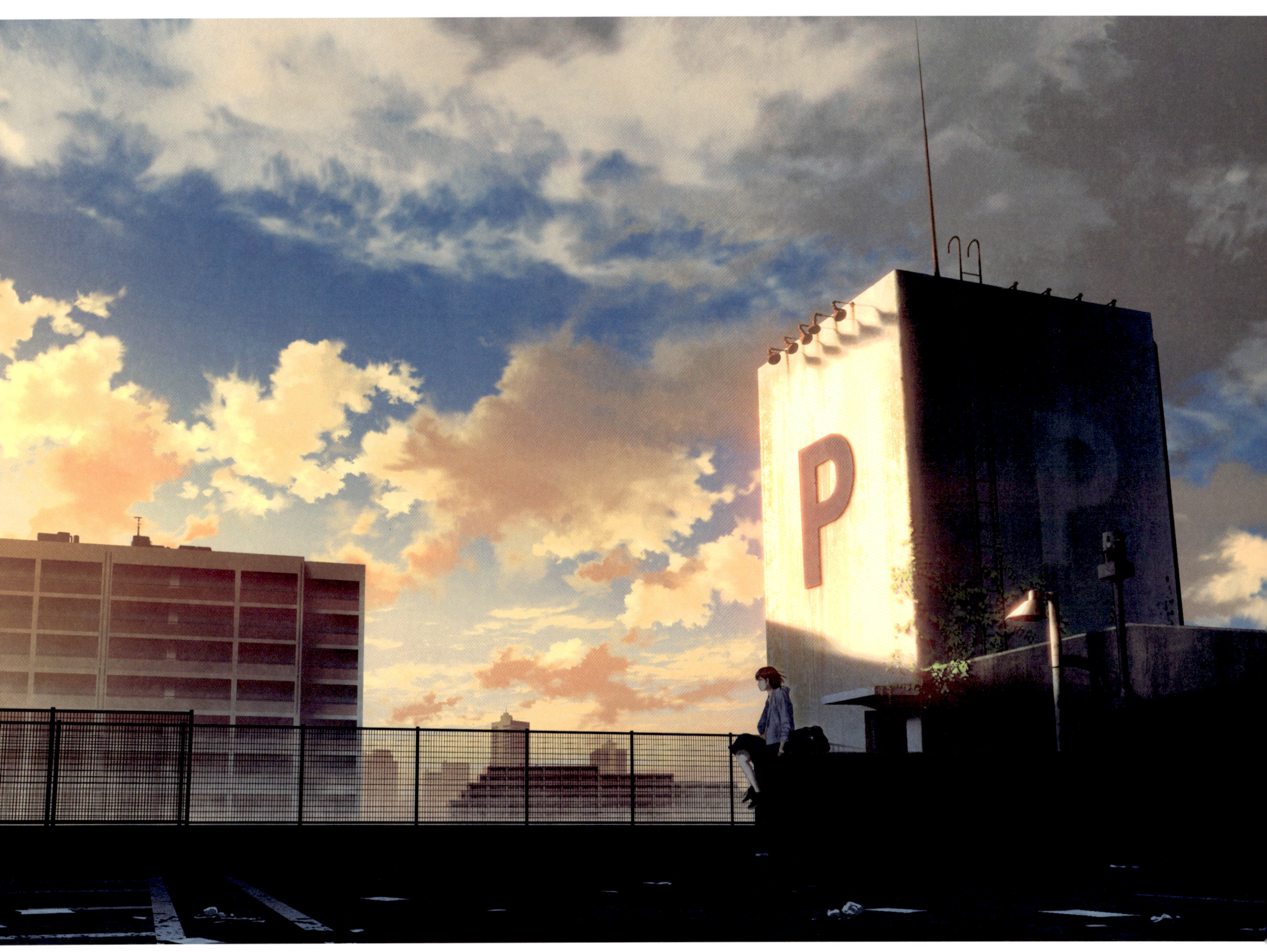

P 「Elevation」（SANOVA、Victor Entertainment）CD ジャケットイラスト ｜ P, a CD cover illustration for *Elevation* (SANOVA, Victor Entertainment)

吉田誠治　｜　YOSHIDA Seiji

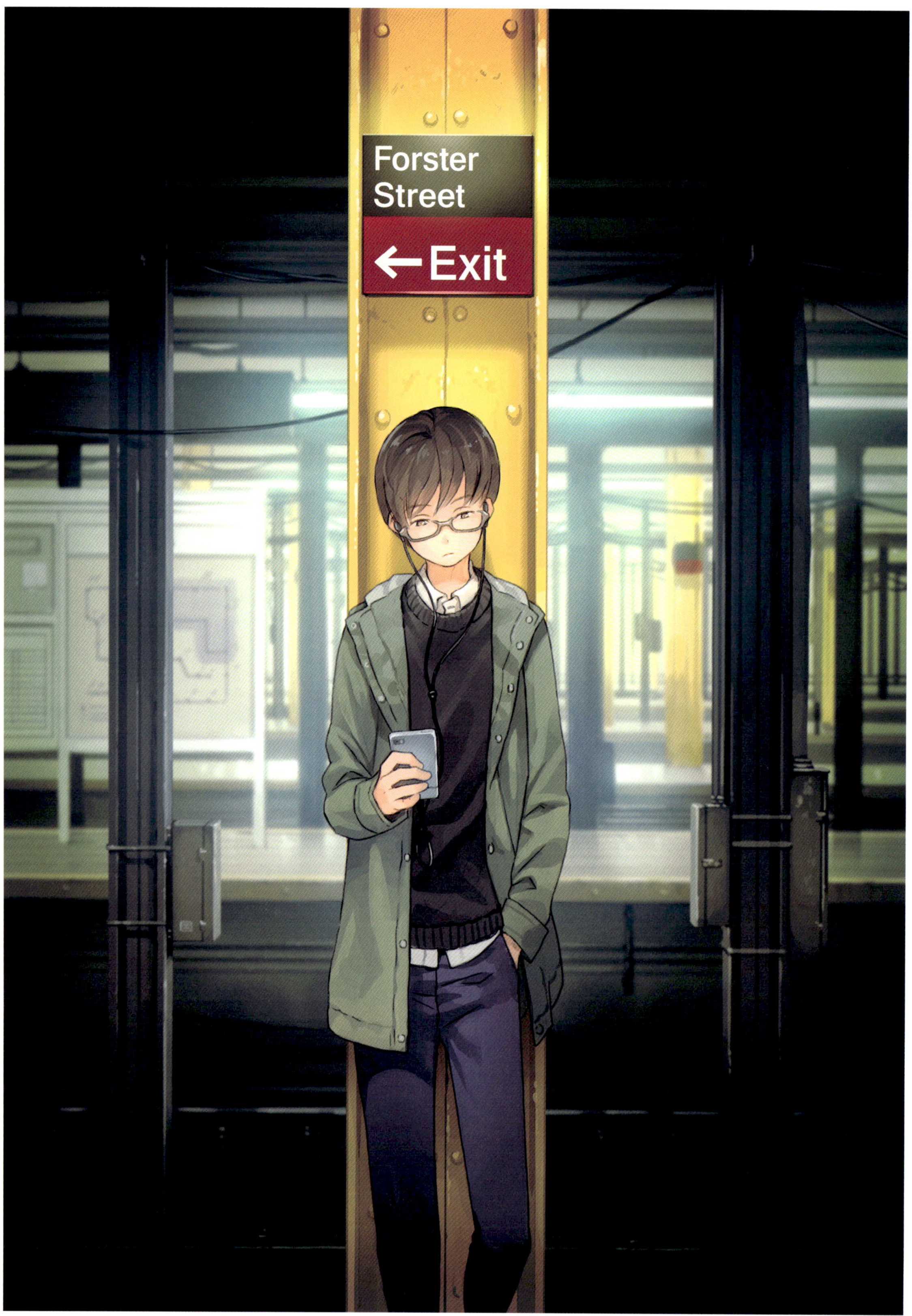

Platforms

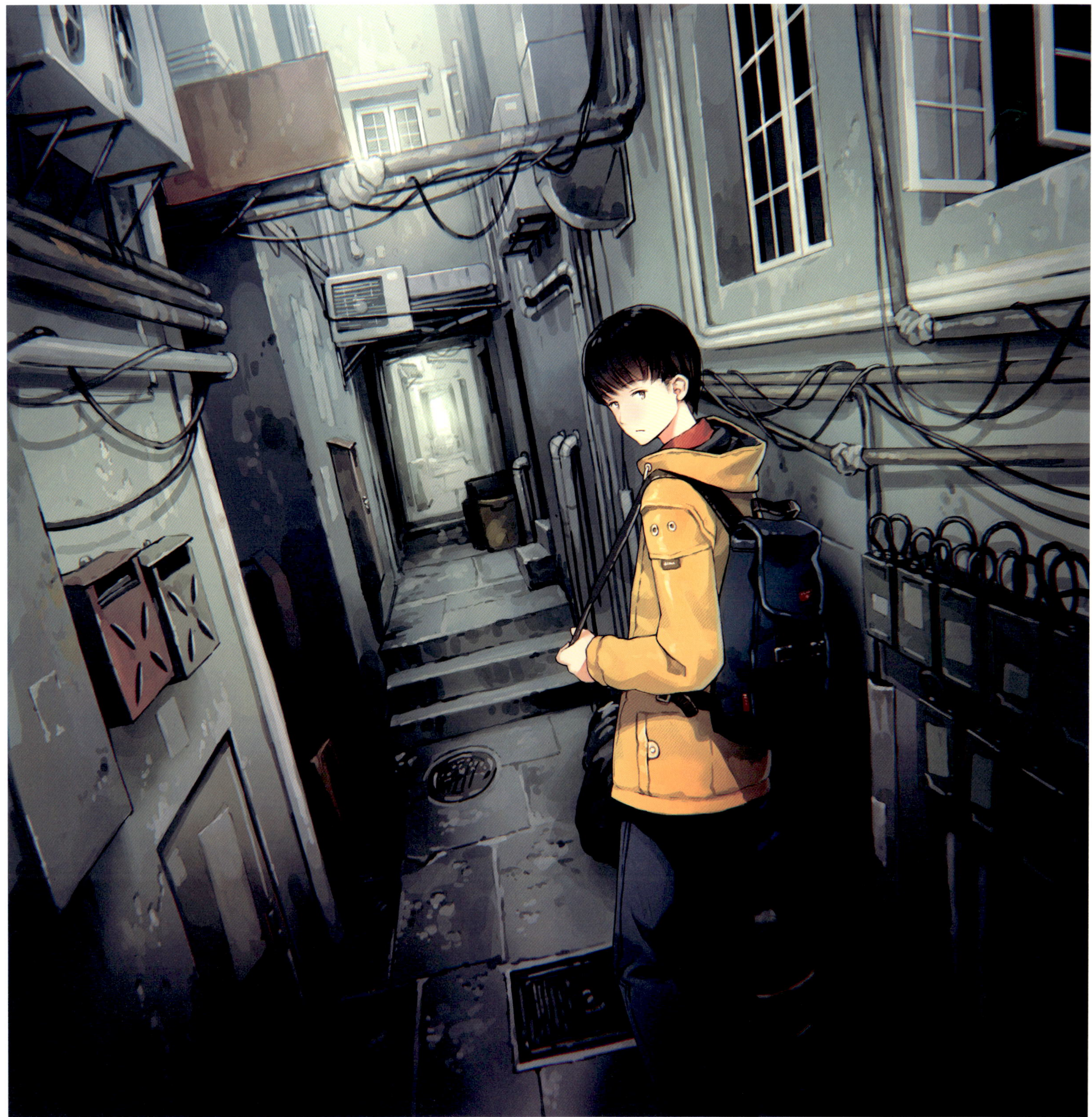

Straight

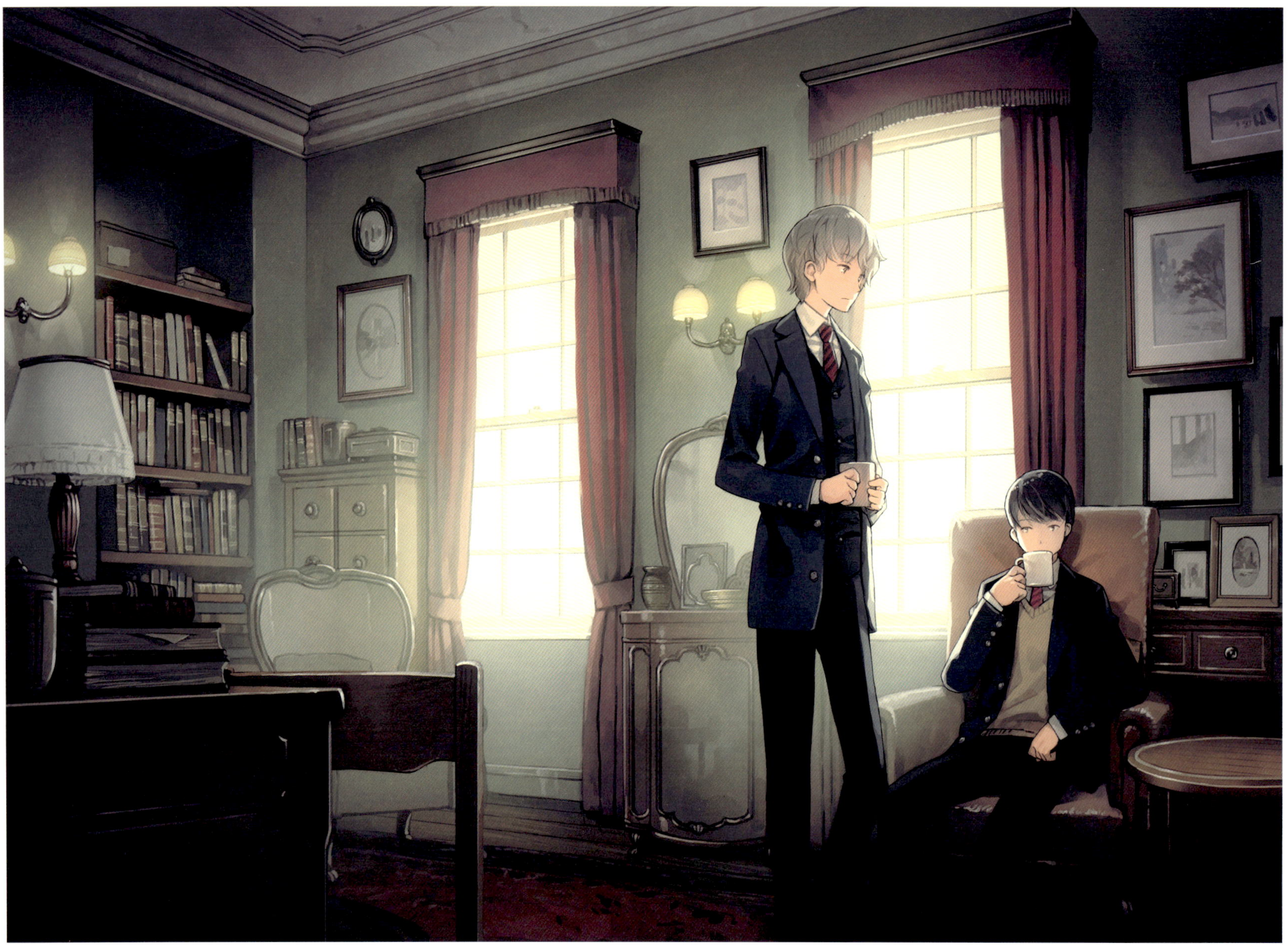

Dormitory

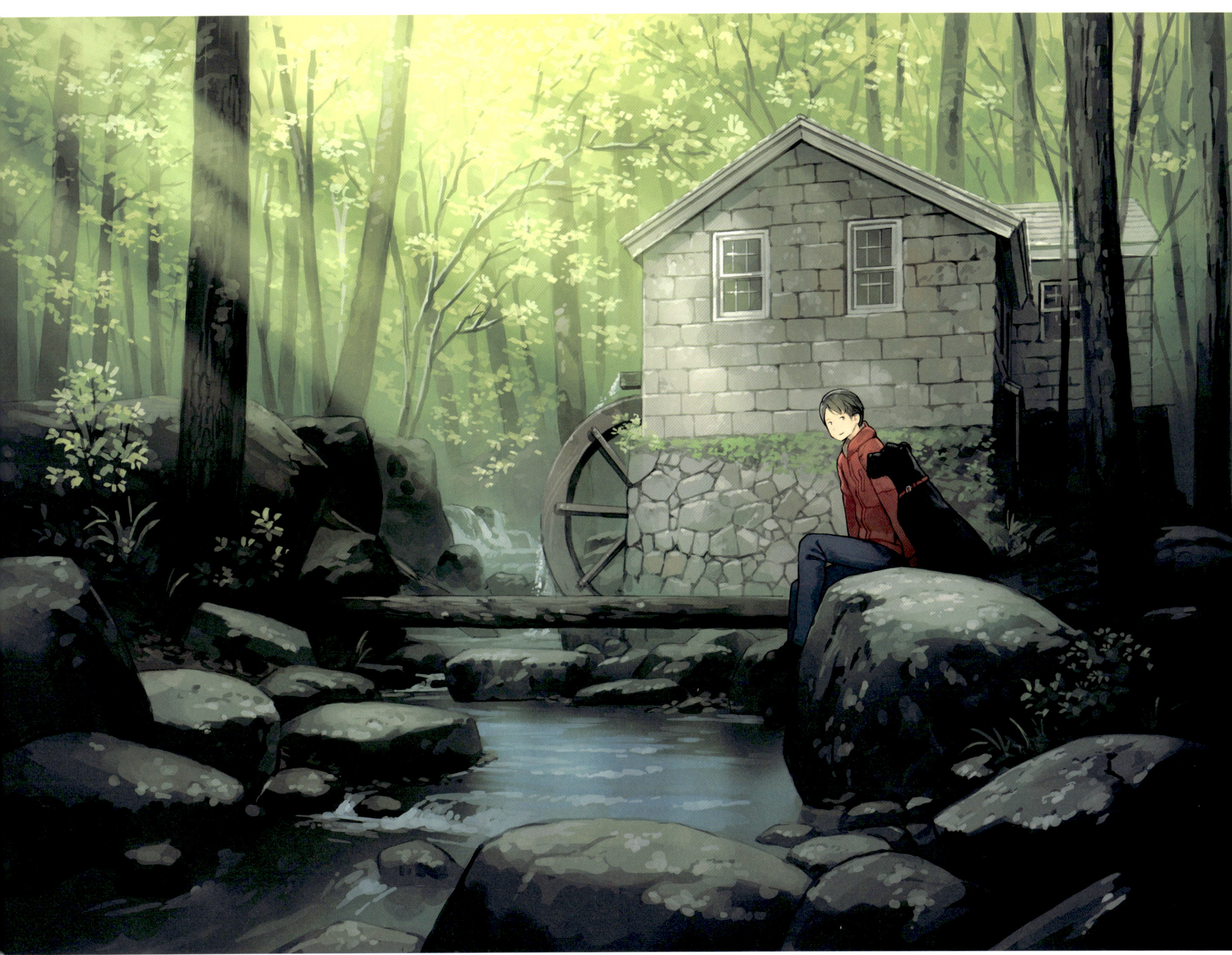

Watermill

Illustrations created for this book

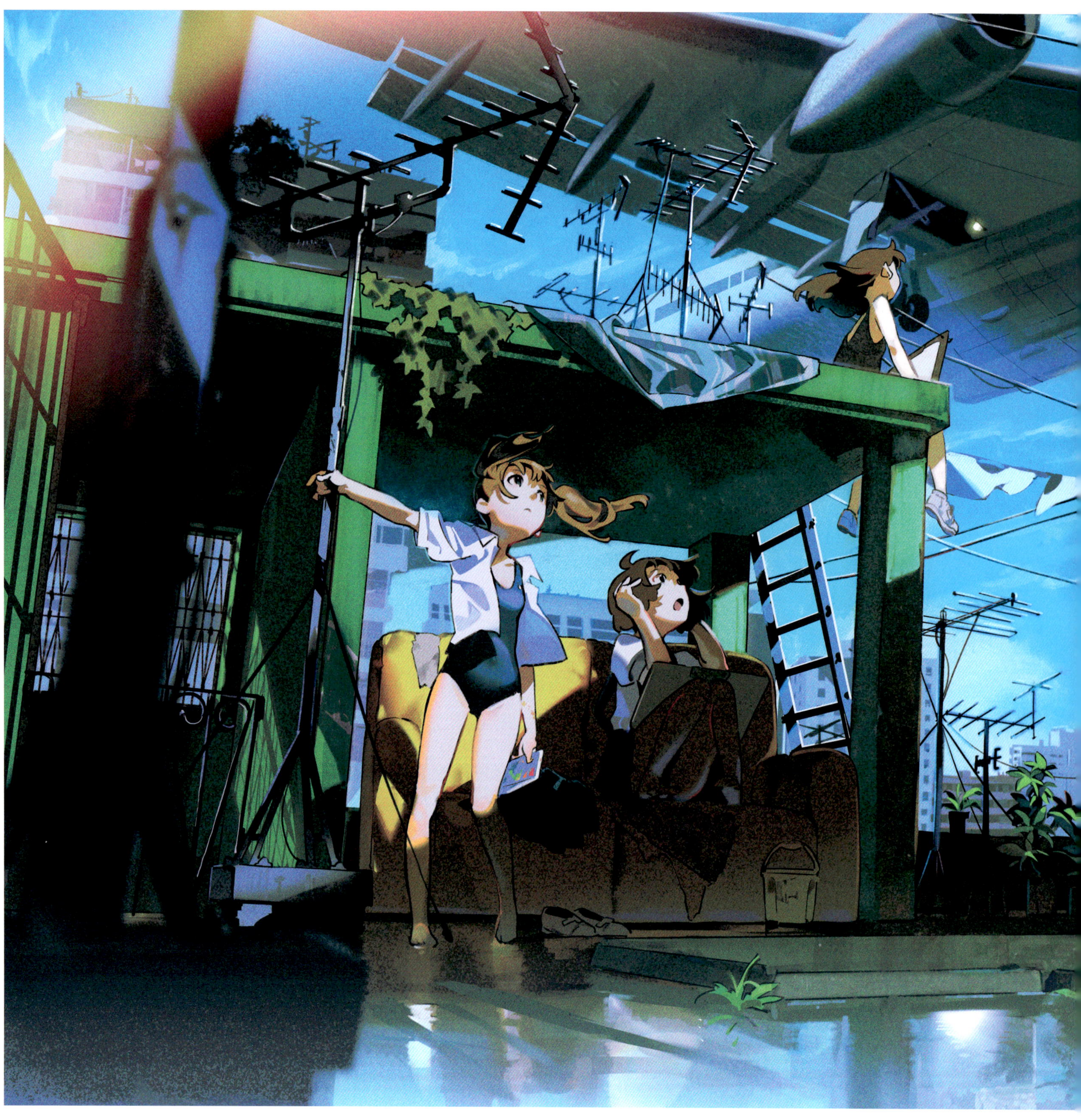

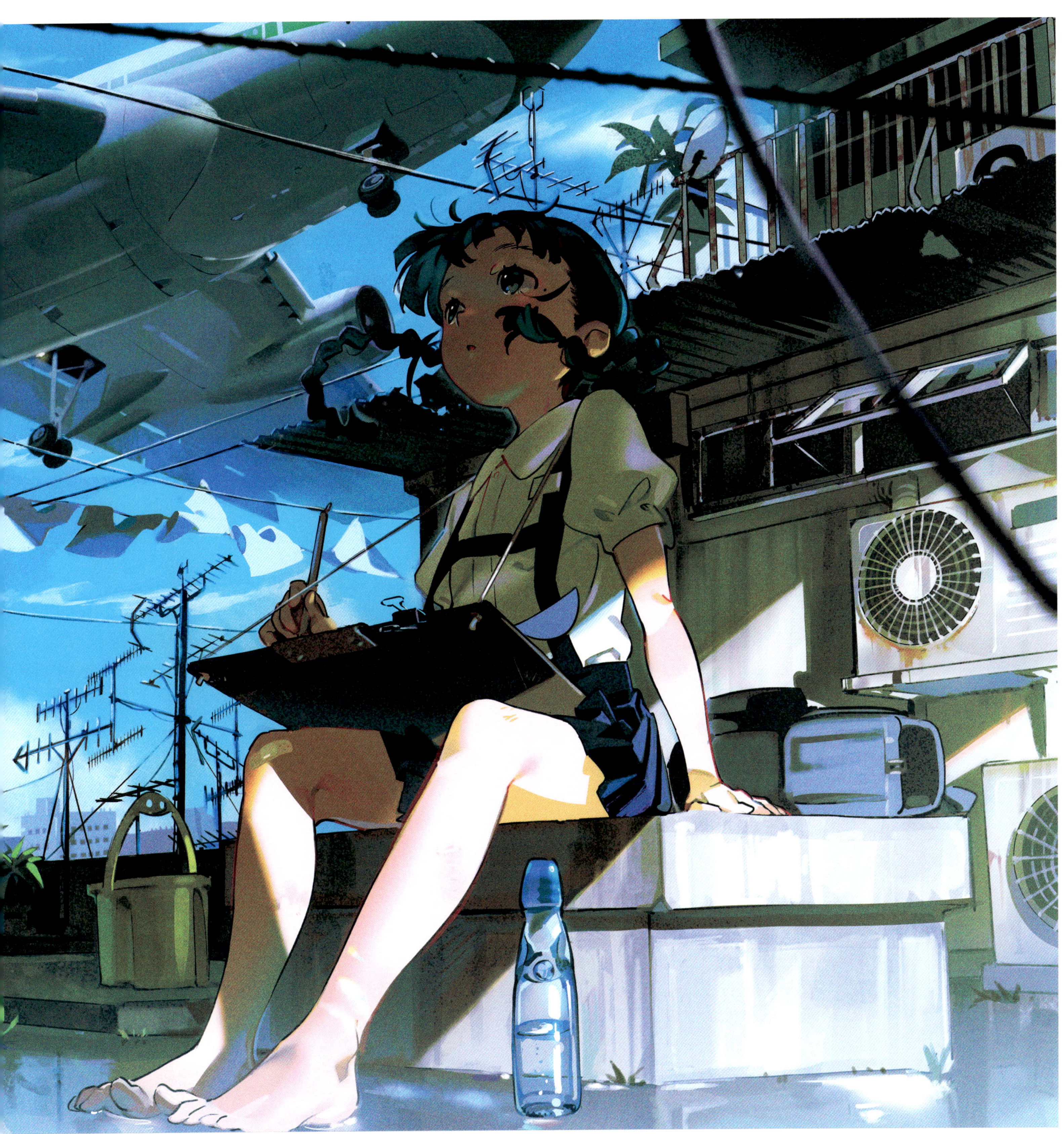

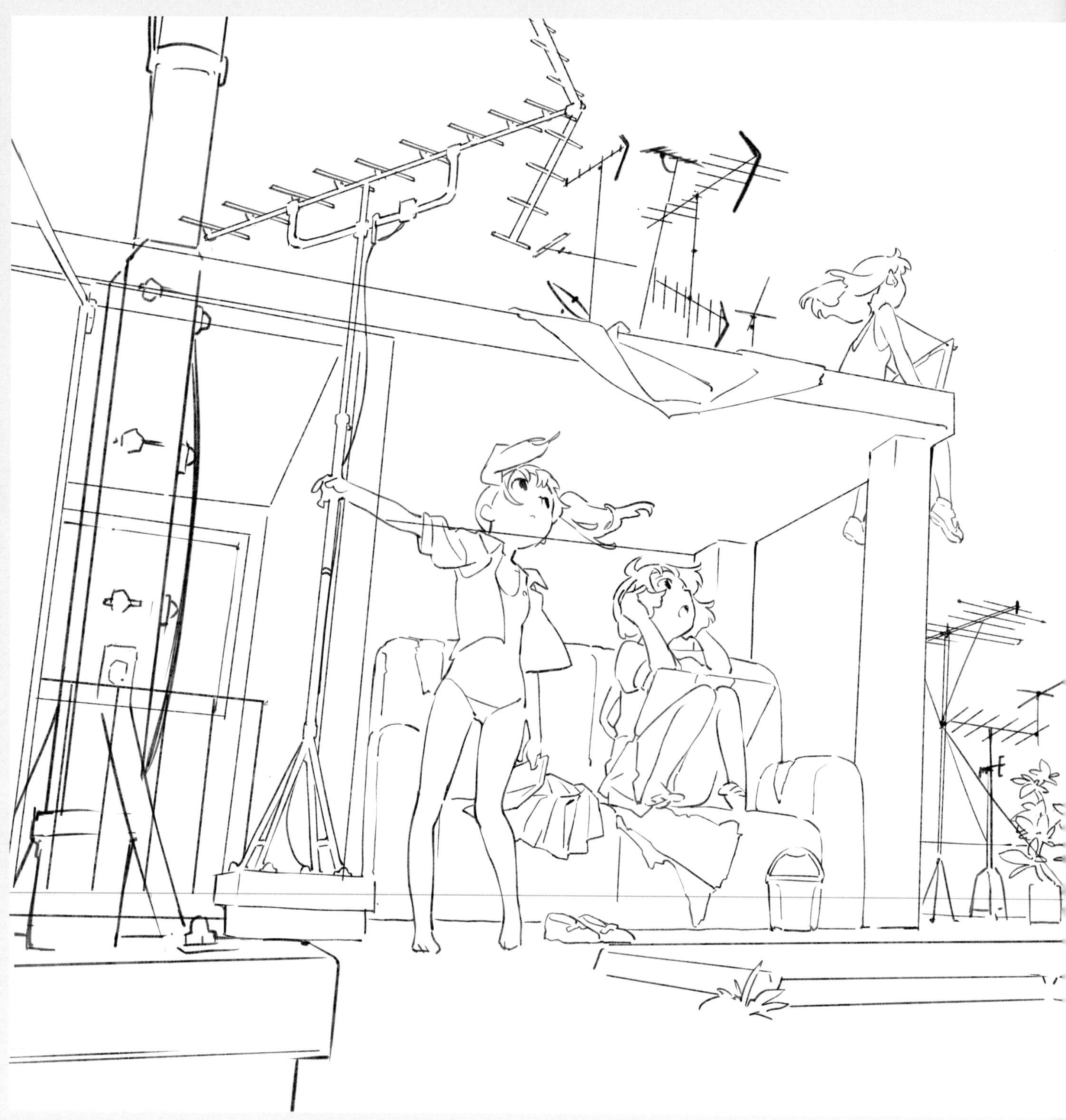

幼少期に暮らしていた台湾の集合住宅がモデルです。
小さい頃ってどこでも遊び場とか秘密基地になったなあというのと、
あの時やたらと大きく感じた飛行機とエンジン音を思い出しながら描きました。

The model for this illustration is an apartment complex I used to live in as a kid in Taiwan.
I drew this while remembering how as a kid, I could play or discover a secret hiding space wherever I went.
I also thought about how, at that time, the sounds of airplane engines sounded so loud to me.

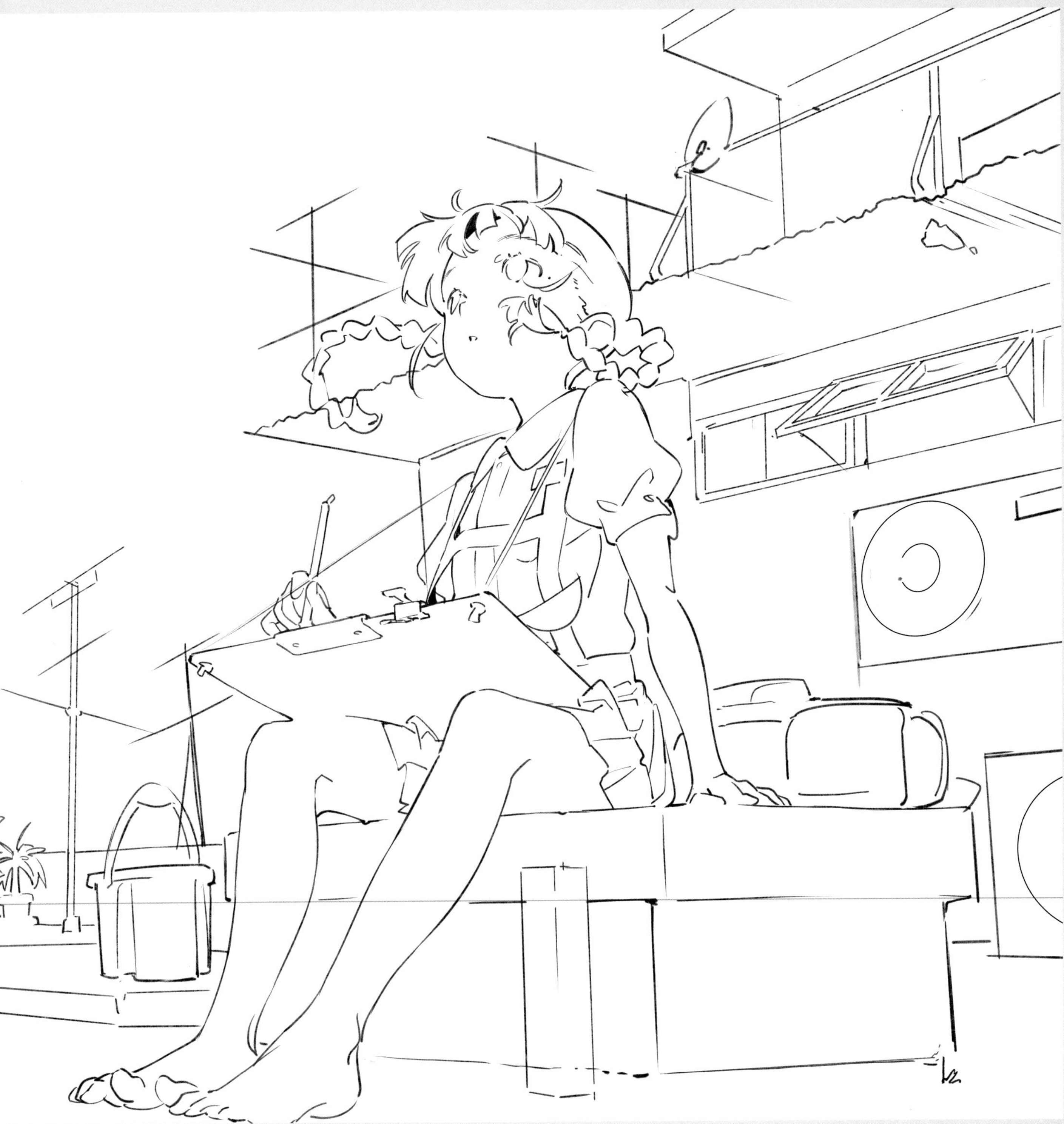

childhood（線画） ｜ childhood (Line drawing)

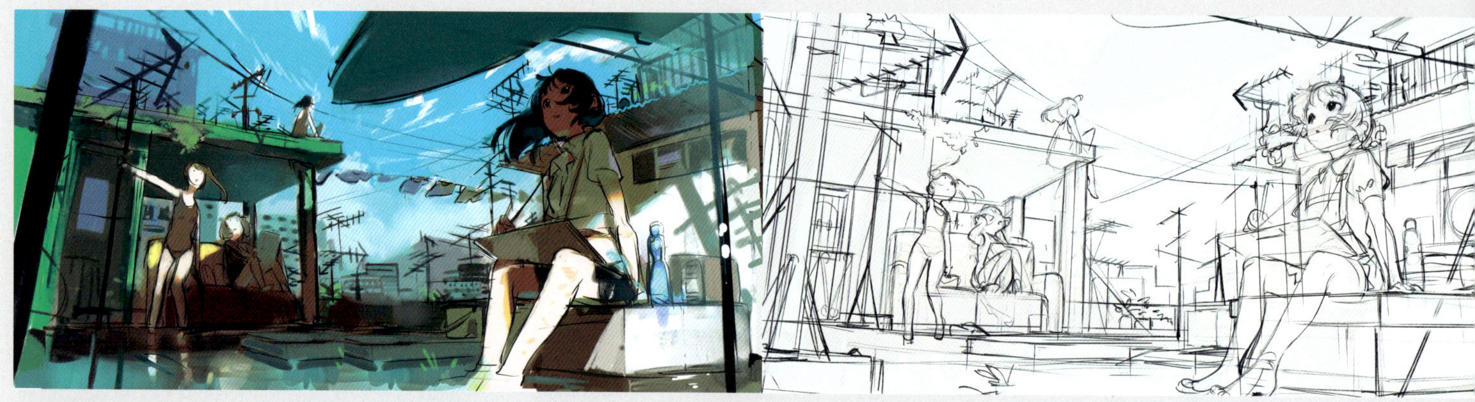

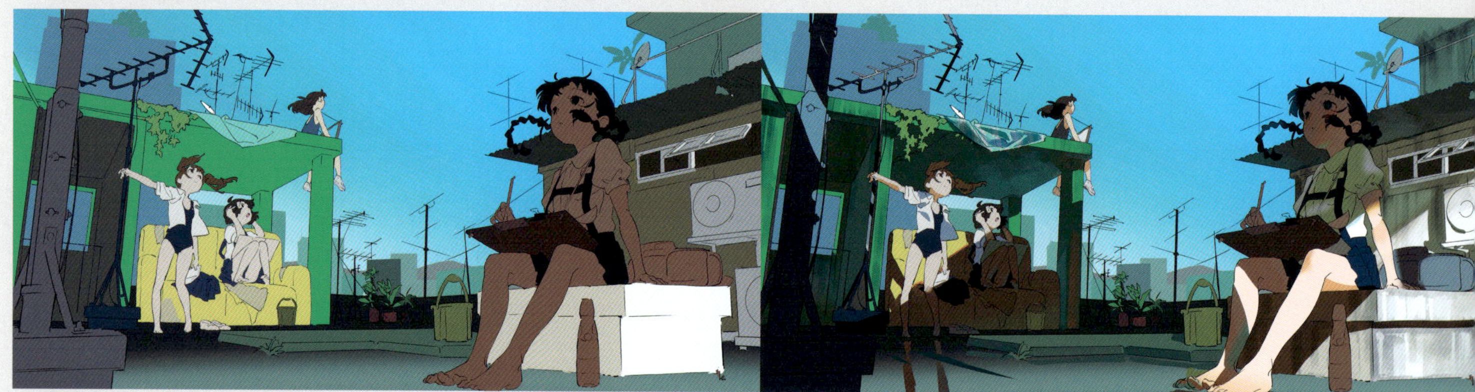

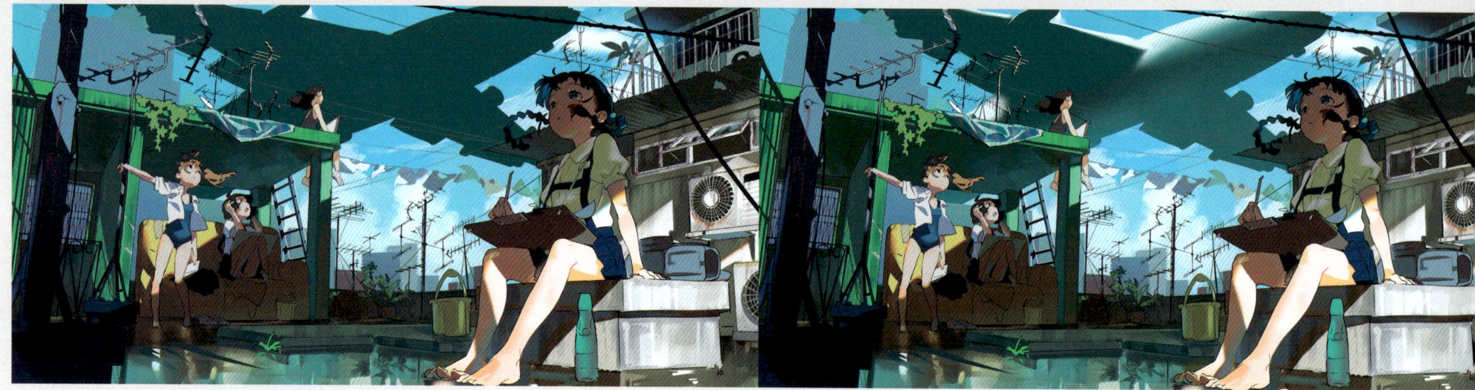

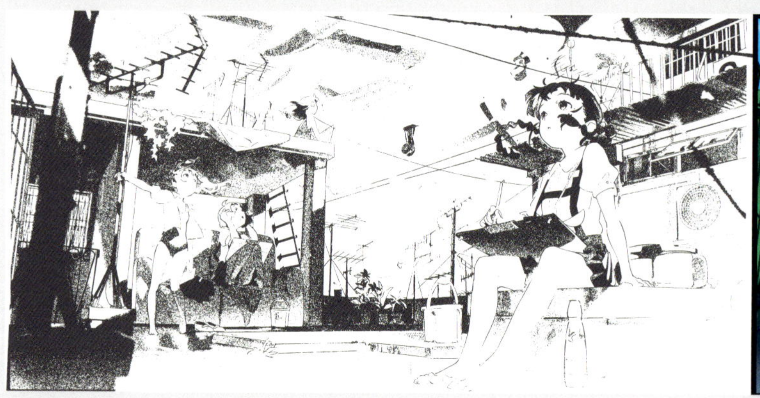

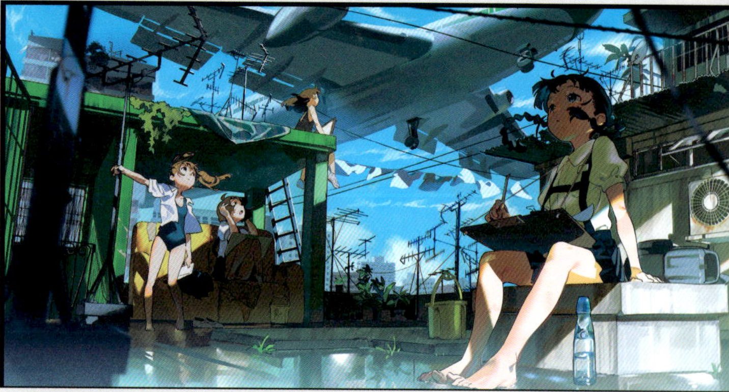

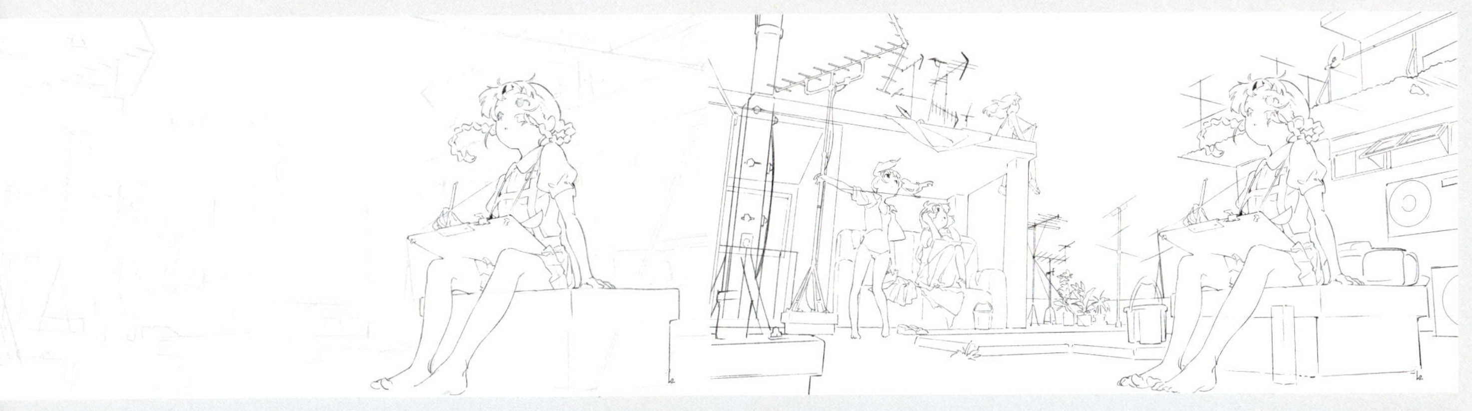
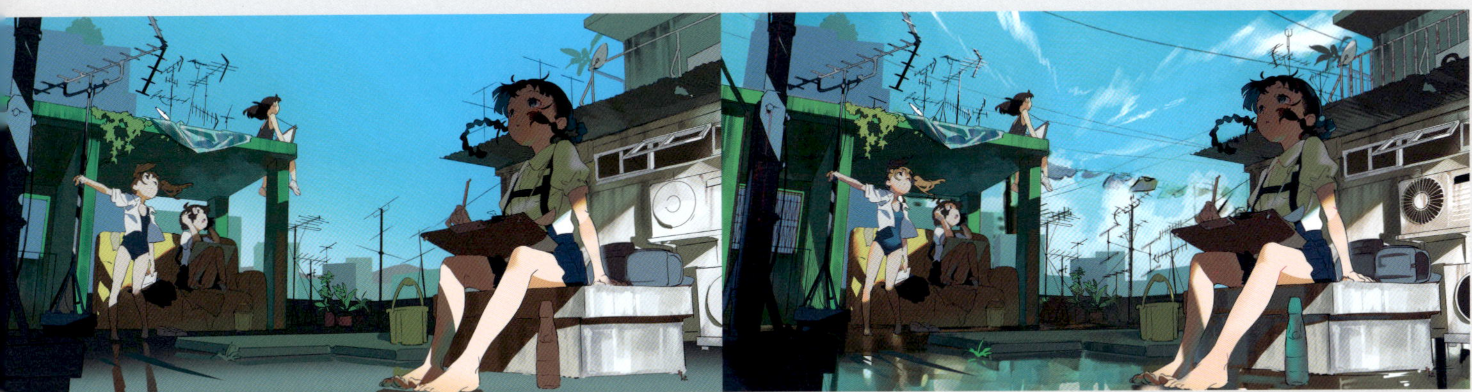
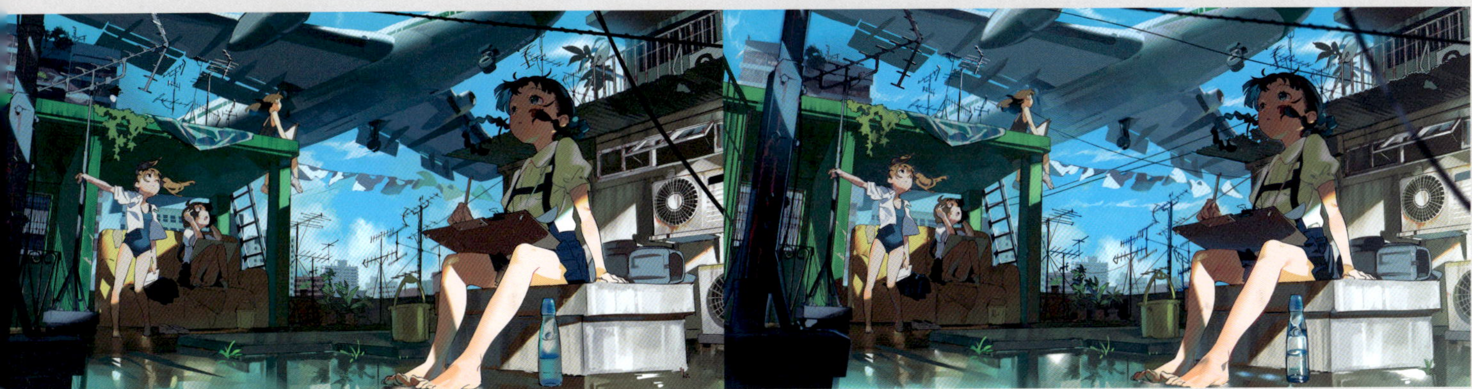
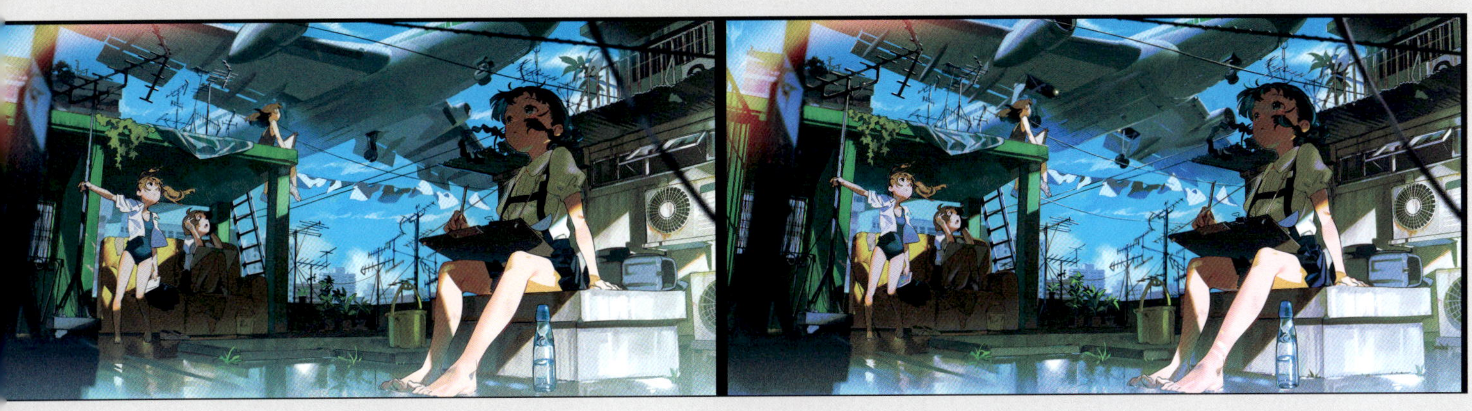

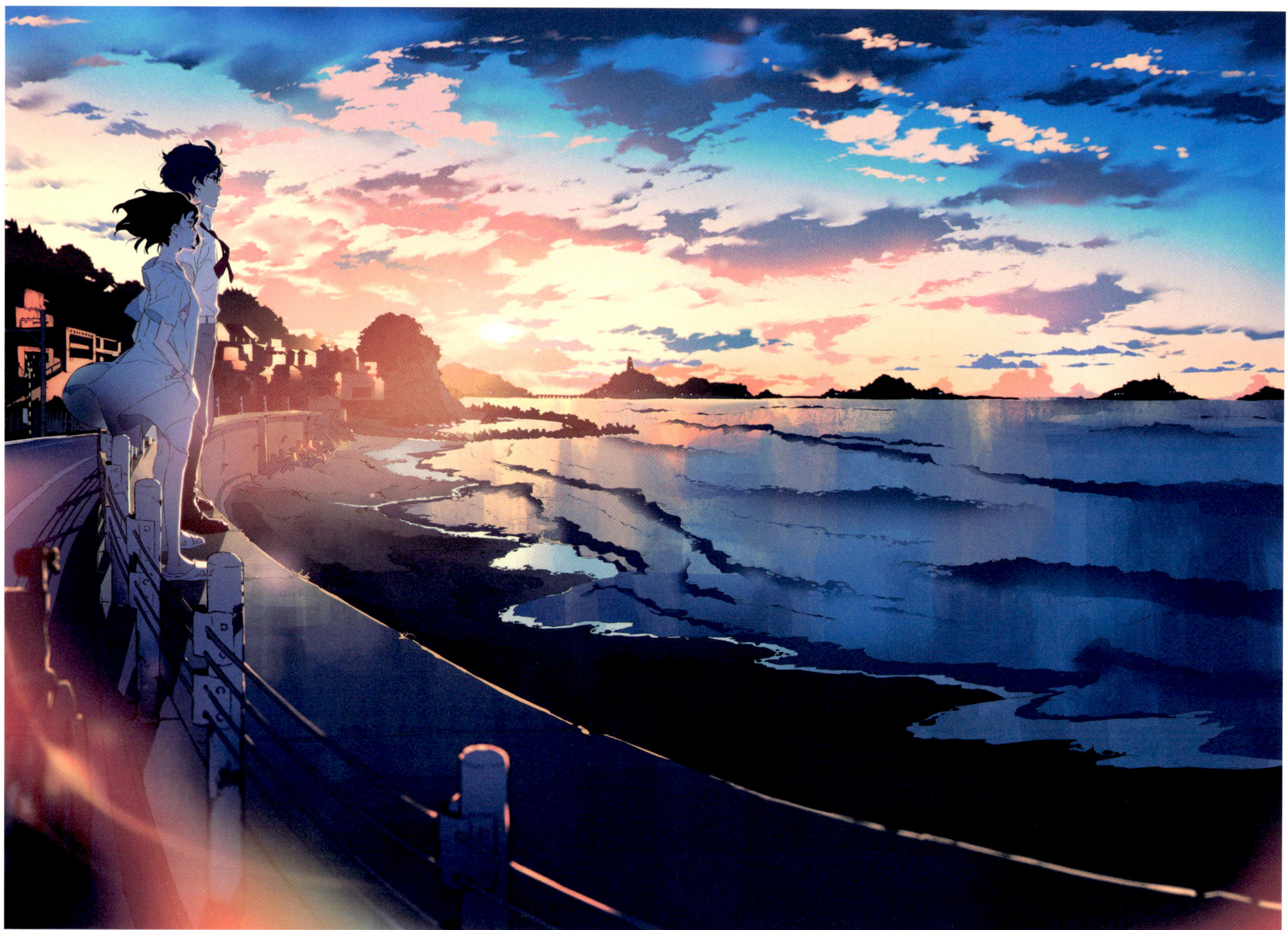

『海辺の病院で彼女と話した幾つかのこと』（石川博品 著、KADOKAWA）装画
Cover illustration for *Several things I talked to her at the beach hospital* (written by Hiroshi Ishikawa, published by Kadokawa Corporation) ©Hiroshi Ishikawa 2018

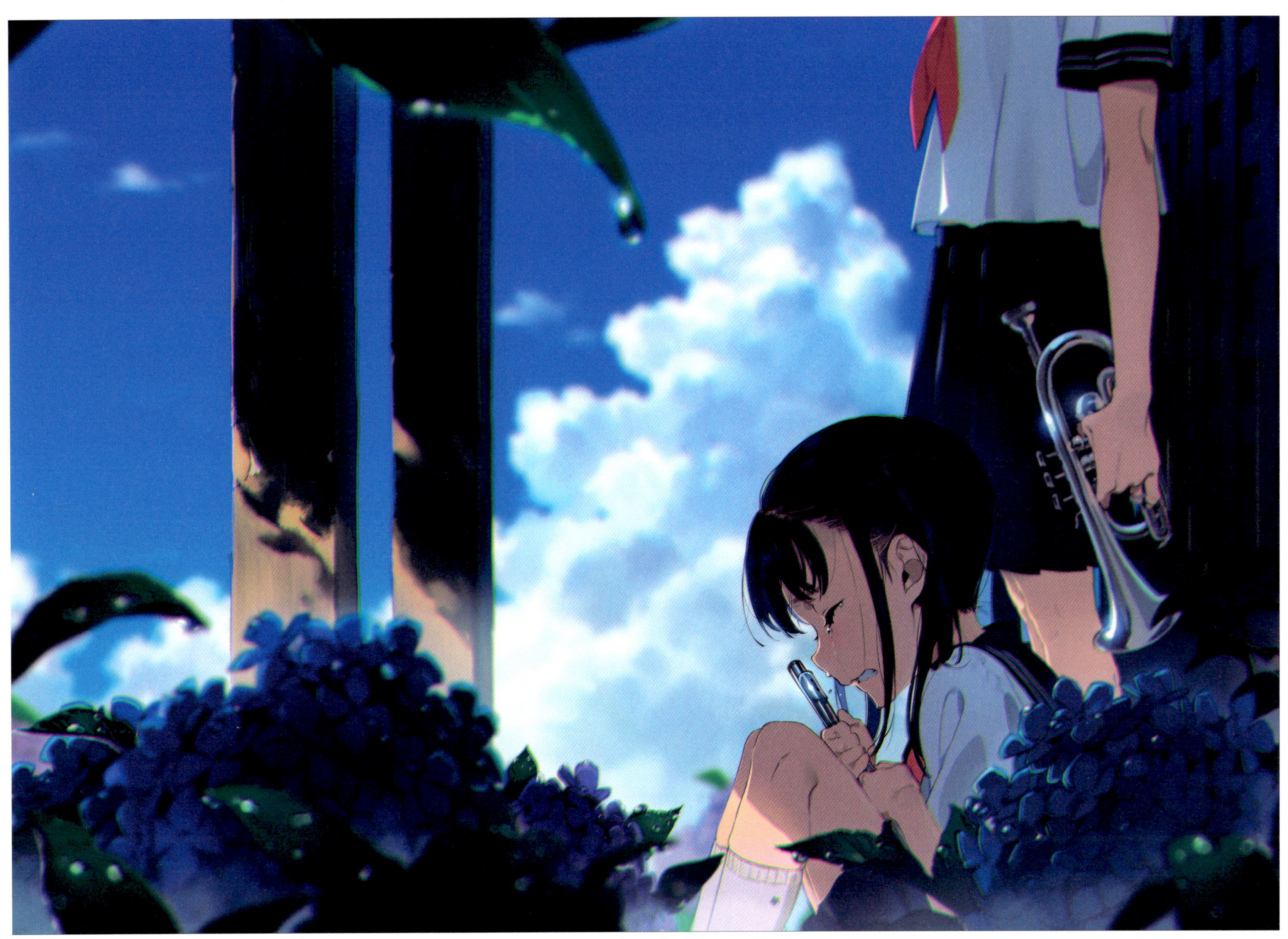

JUNE 『月刊ニュータイプ2016年4月号』付録カレンダーイラスト
JUNE, an illustration for a supplementary calendar for the April 2016 edition of *Newtype*

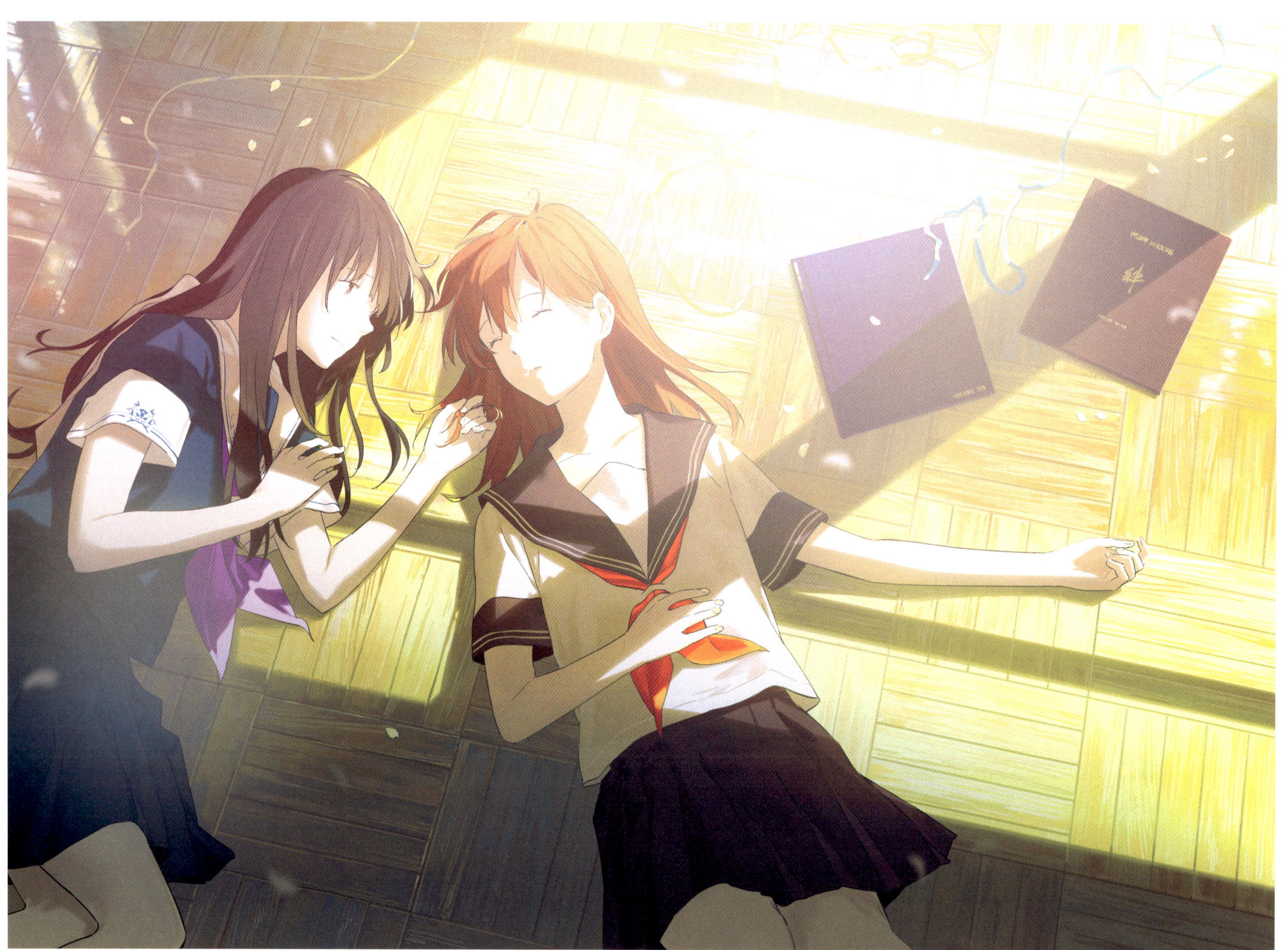

『月刊MdN2017年9月号「マンガ雑誌をMdNがつくってみた！」』スペシャル企画「loundraw×最果タヒ」(loundraw×最果タヒ 著、エムディエヌコーポレーション)コラボレーションイラスト
Collaborative illustration for the special "loundraw x Tahi Saihate" in the September 2017 edition of *MdN Design & Graphic*, entitled, *MdN Tried Their Hand at Making a Manga Magazine!*
(written by loundraw and Tahi Saihate, published by MdN Corporation)

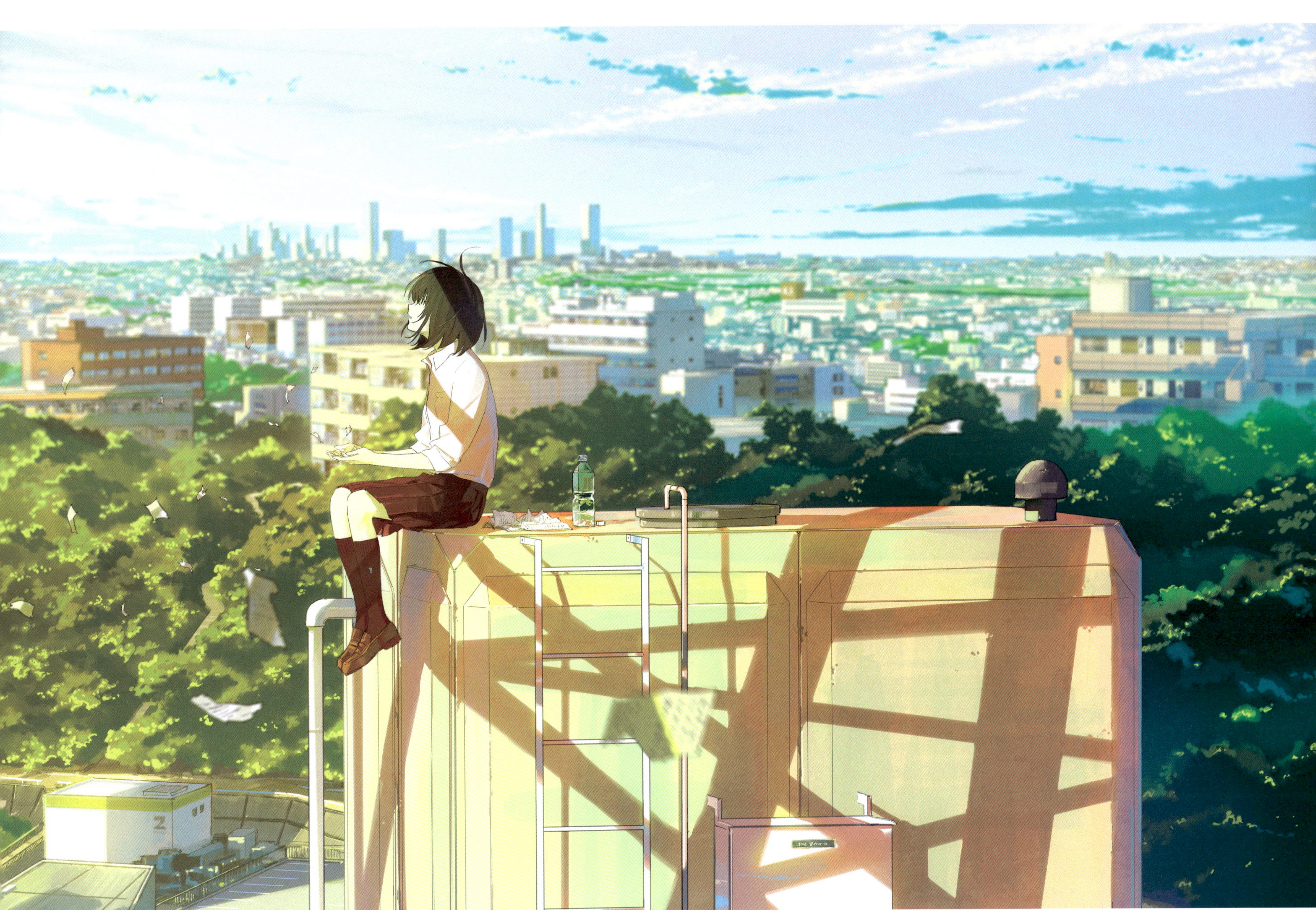

『少女は夜を綴らない』（逸木裕 著、KADOKAWA）カバーイラスト　　|　　Cover illustration for *Girl never spells the Night* (written by Yu Itsuki, published by Kadokawa Corporation)

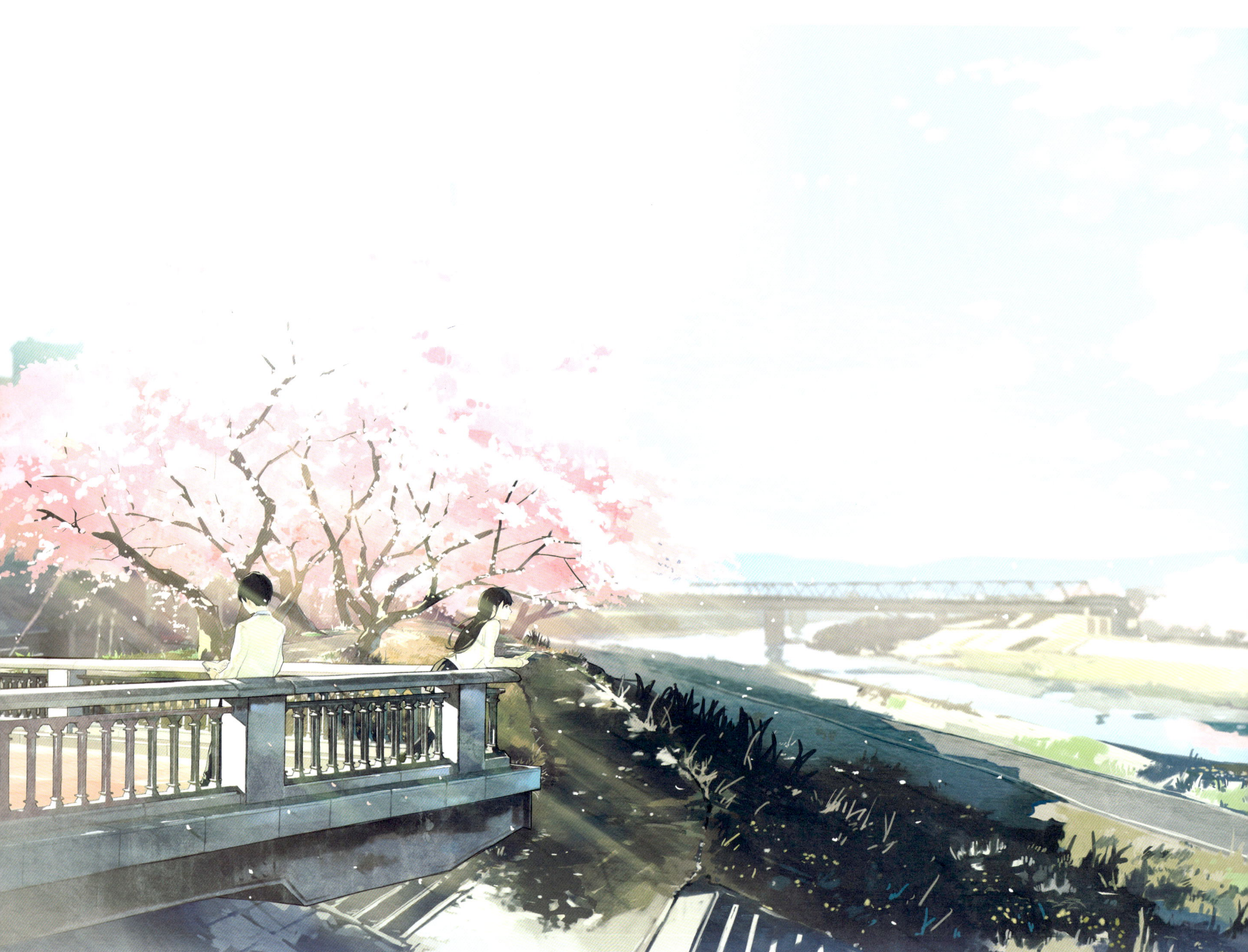

『君の膵臓をたべたい』（住野よる 著、双葉社）カバーイラスト　　|　　Cover illustration for *I Want to Eat Your Pancreas* (written by Yoru Sumino, published by Futabasha Publishers)

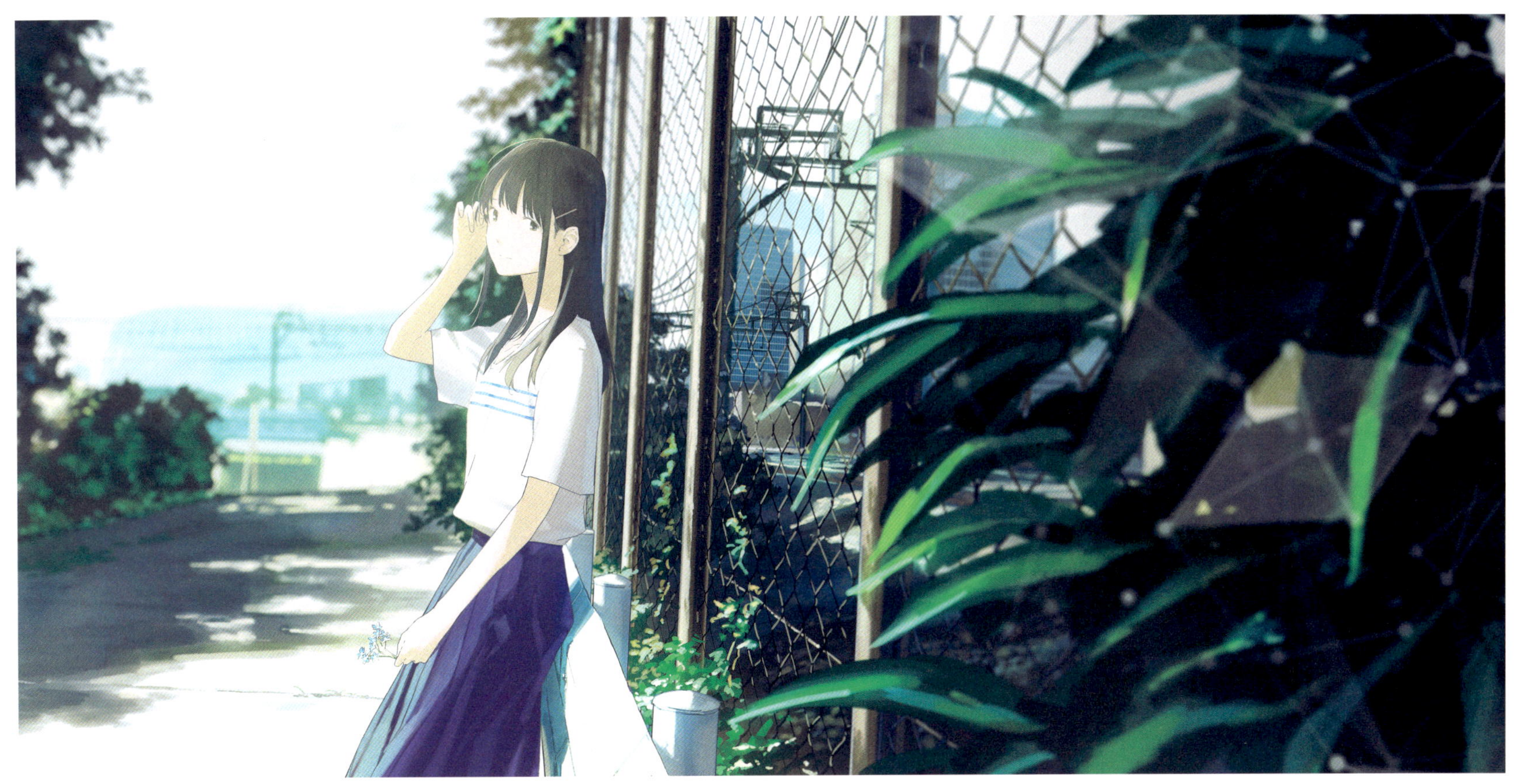

『僕はロボットごしの君に恋をする』（山田悠介 著、河出書房新社）カバーイラスト　｜　Cover illustration for *I fall in love with you through a robot* (written by Yusuke Yamada, published by Kawade Shobo Shinsha)

LAL!ROLE

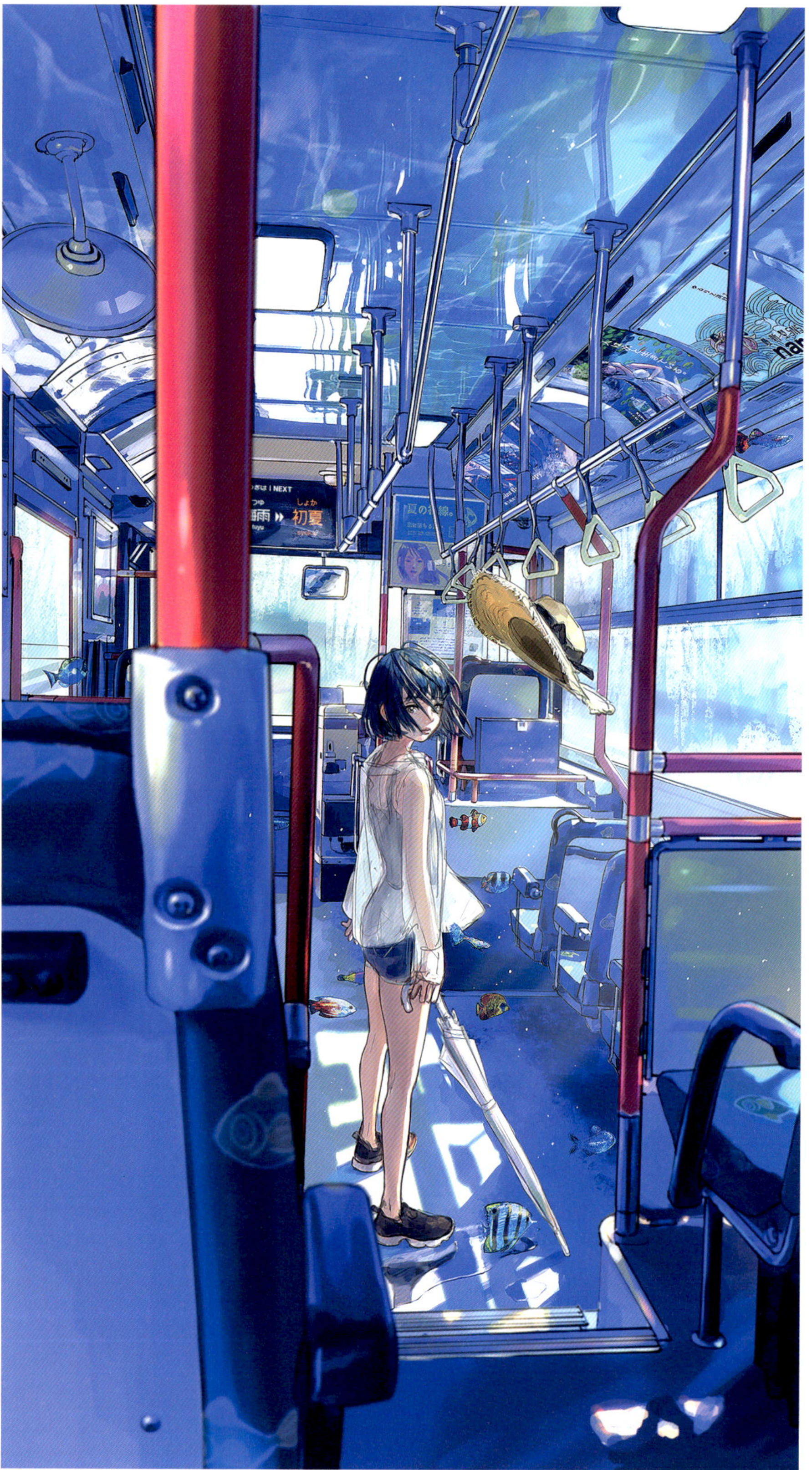

夏行きバスの白昼夢　|　Daydream of a Bus Bound for Summer

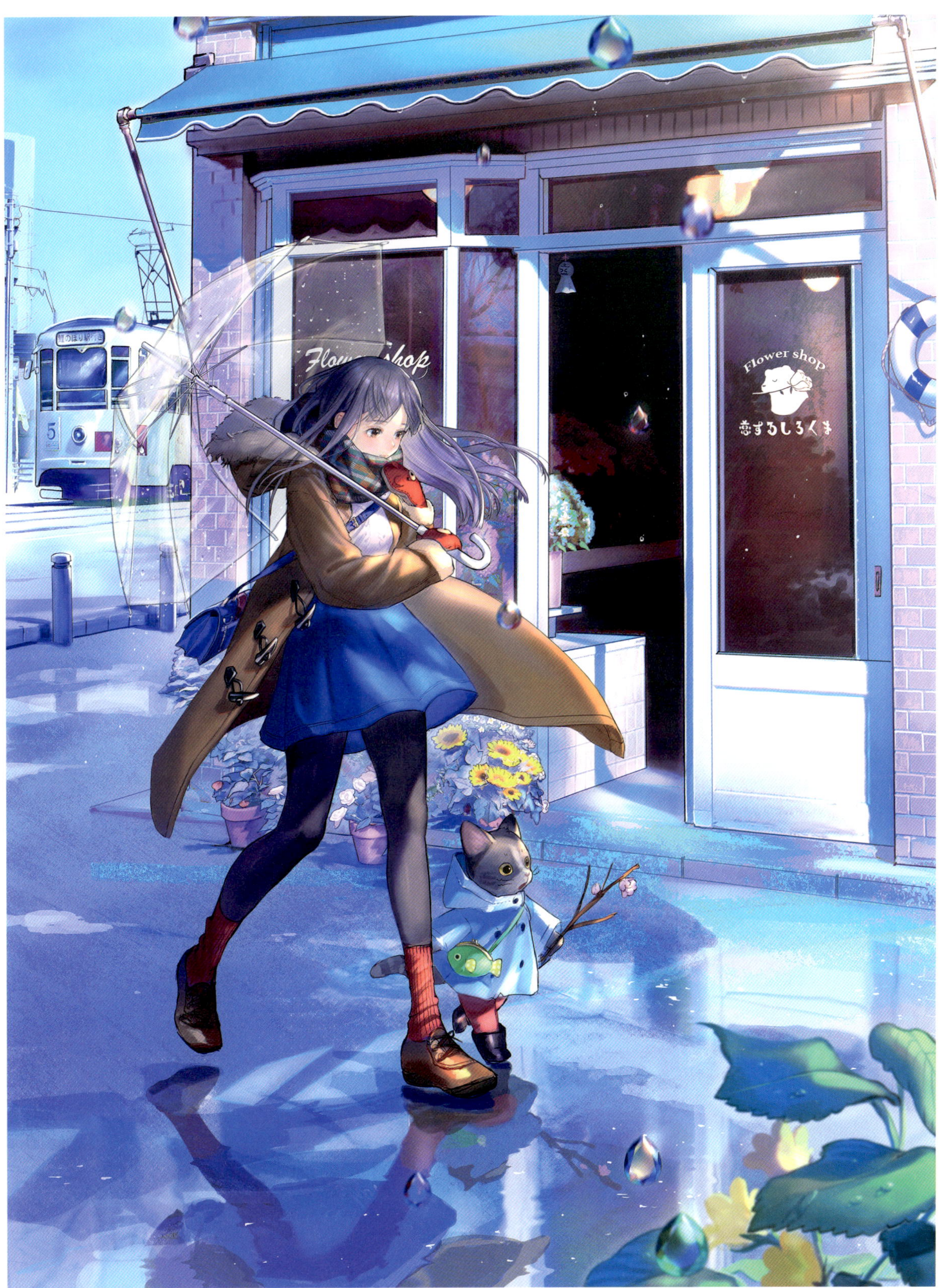

キラキラ堕ちる ｜ Glittering Defeat

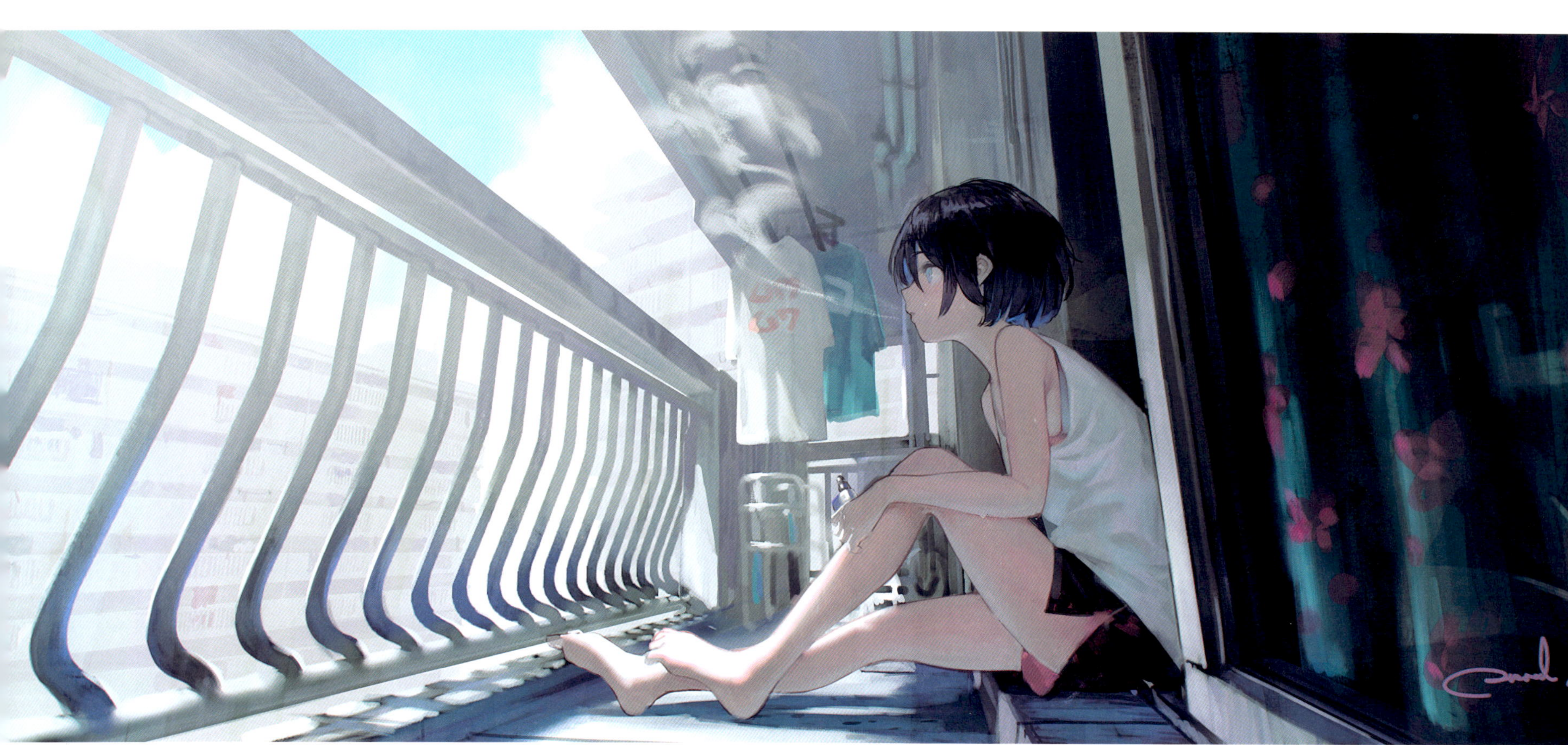

メンソール入りの夏　|　Summer with Menthols

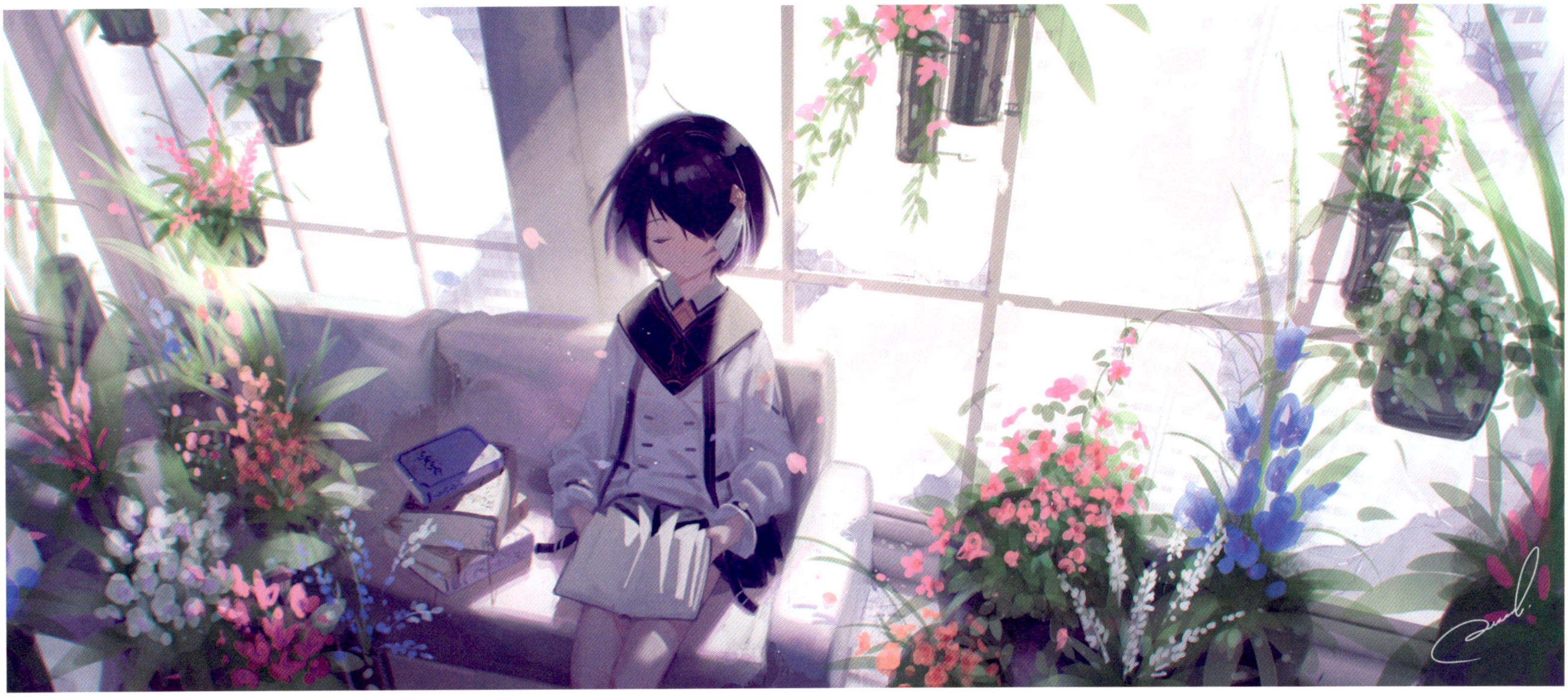

ふきさらし ｜ Windswept

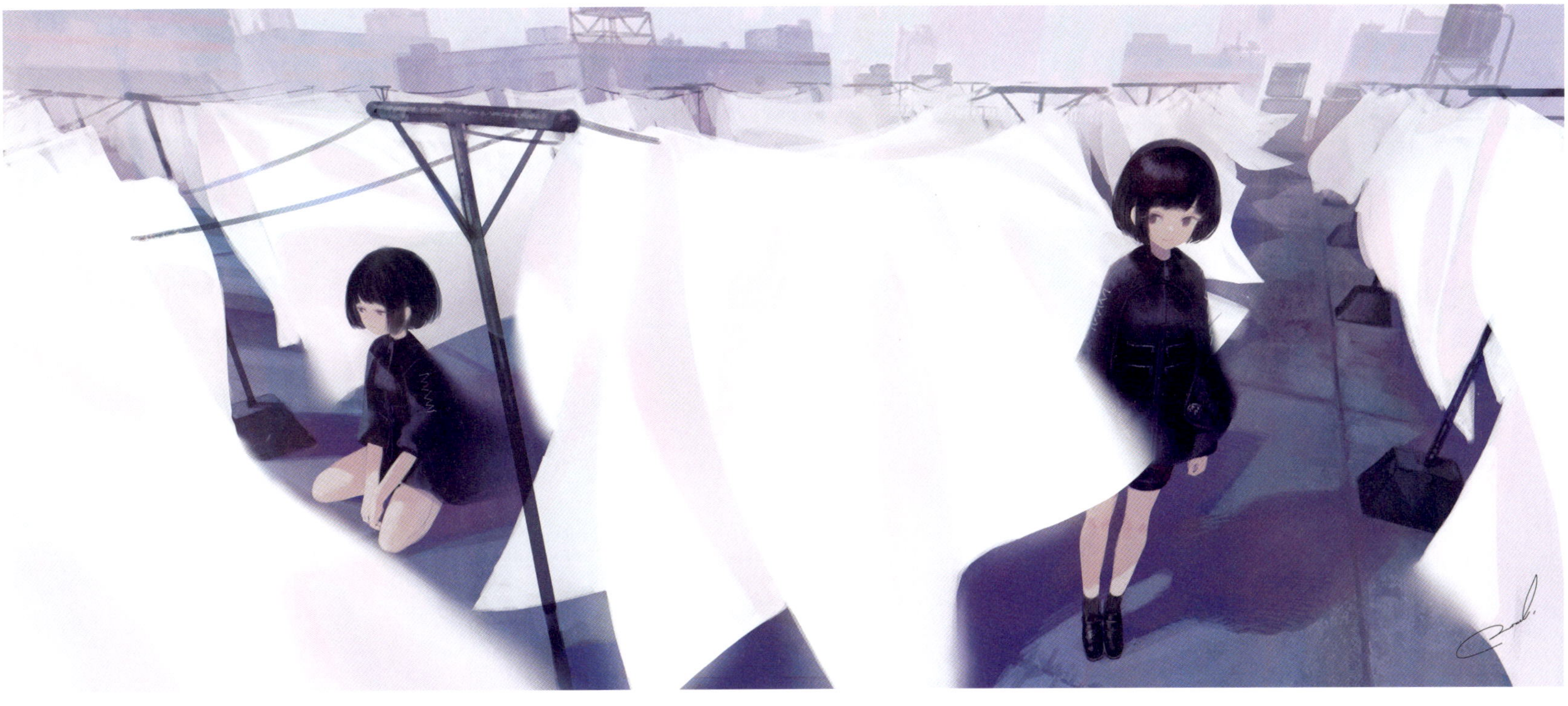

薄膜 ｜ Thin Film

カバーイラストメイキング

Showcase of the cover illustration process

物語のワンシーンのようなストーリー性と、キャラクターの心情や
空間の臨場感を印象的に描いた本書のカバーイラスト。
イラストを手がけたイラストレーターのげみさんに、
思わず引き込まれる情景イラストの描き方についてお聞きしました。

The illustration for the cover of this book incorporates the sense that the scene comes from
a story together with the emotions of the character and the presence of the space in an impressive way.
We asked Gemi about the drawing method used for this illustration,
as it seems to draw you in without even noticing.

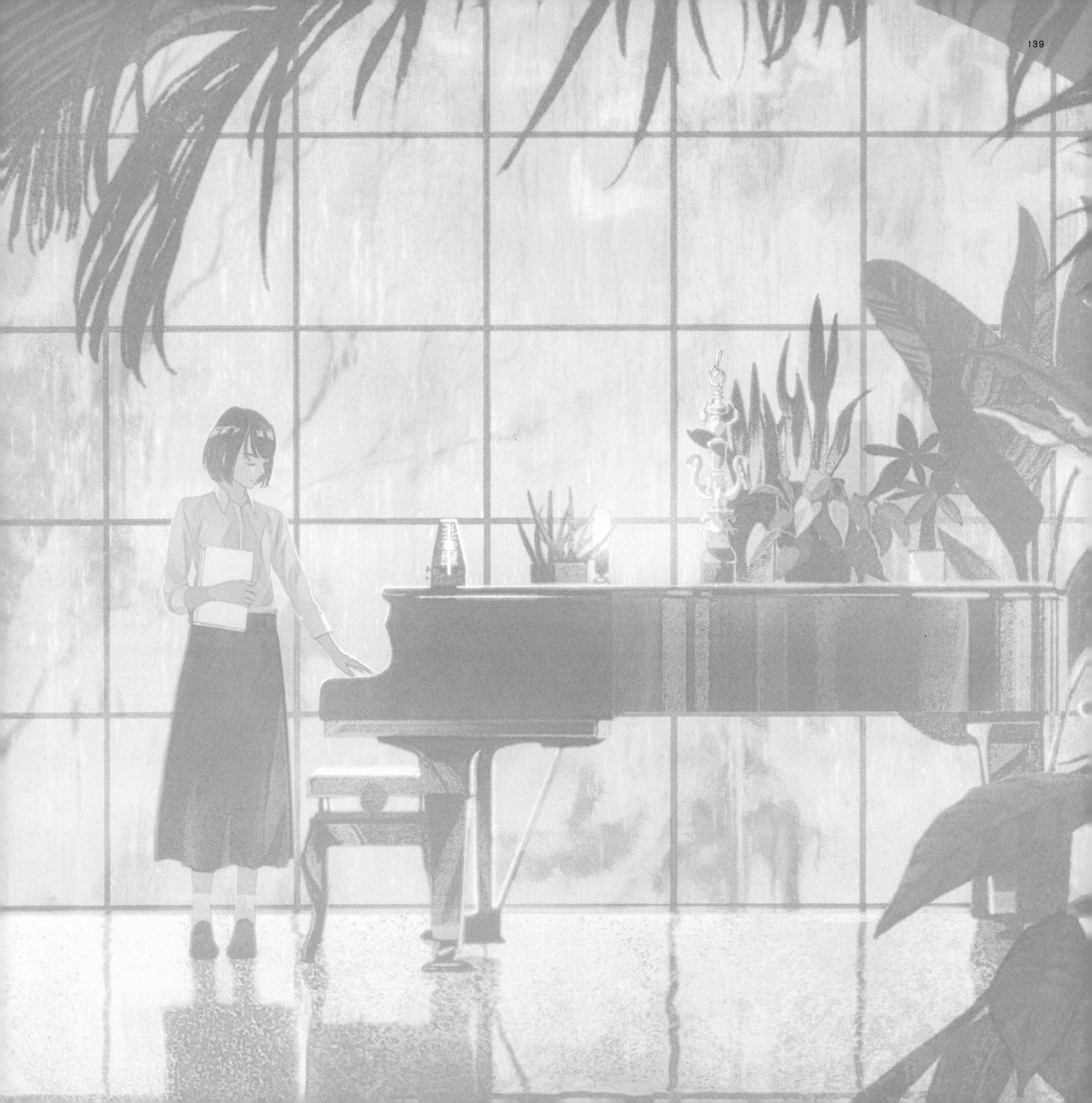

1 : [ラフを描く | Drawing the rough sketch]

依頼されたテーマが「オレンジで魅せるノスタルジックな情景」だったので、昔に描いた「べっこうあめ」という絵を懐かしむような気持ちで描こうと考えました。

I was asked to create an illustration that was to be a nostalgic scene bathed in orange, so I thought about drawing something nostalgic like what I drew before in *Hard Candy*.

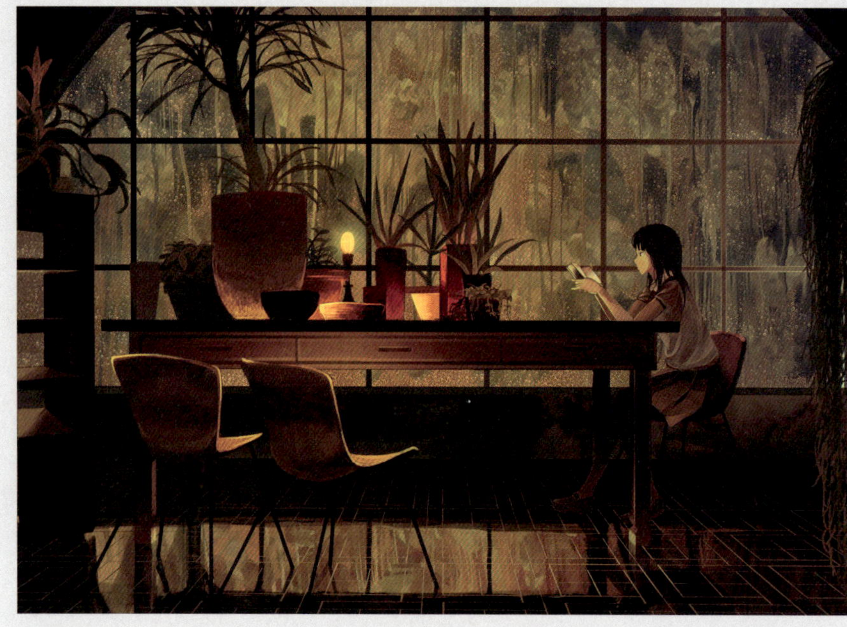

べっこうあめ | *Hard Candy*
©Gemi

絵を描く前の打ち合わせで「昔はピアノを弾いていた女性が、今は弾かなくなったピアノを見て当時を懐かしく思う」というストーリーを考えました。このストーリーを元にラフを考えていきます。洋館や古い建物の窓が好きなので、取材した写真から描きたい窓を探し、書籍のテンプレートに当てはめながらモチーフを配置します。今回は半円の大きな窓を選びました。四角い窓だと画面が固く閉鎖的に見えてしまいますし、外の景色も見づらくなります。そして、何より鑑賞者の視点も左右に広がらないので、表紙からはみ出るくらいの半円の窓を描くことにしました。

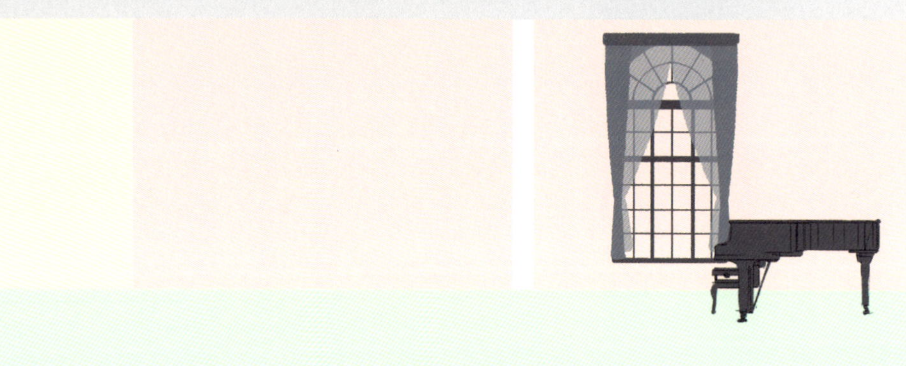

At the meeting with the client before I started drawing, I thought about a story of a girl who used to play piano but thinks fondly of that time when she looks at the piano that isn't played anymore. Using this story as my guide, I began to think about the rough sketch.
I like the windows from Western-style and old buildings, so I searched for a good window from the photos I had taken as research and arranged my motifs while adapting them to the book template. I chose a large, half-circle window for this illustration. A square window would've made the illustration very insular, and it would've made the scene outside the window hard to see. So, I chose to draw this half-circle window that protrudes from the cover so as to keep what the viewer sees from being too limited and enclosed.

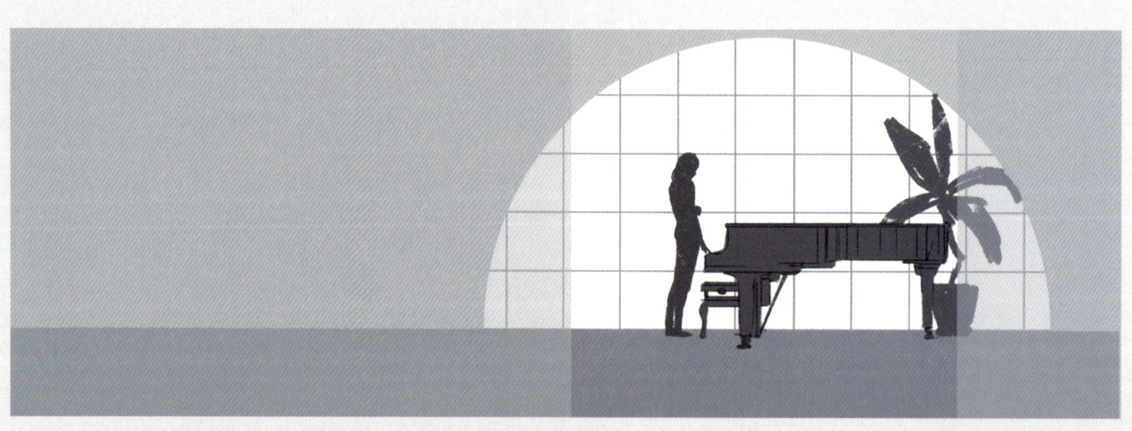

表紙映えを考えるときに重要なのが、人物と重要なモチーフをどこに配置するかです。人とピアノと窓を優先的に配置し、大きさを調整しました。
次に雰囲気を出すための観葉植物や照明、本棚など、設定したストーリーを害さないモチーフを配置します。ピアノの上に敢えてモチーフを置いたのは「長く使われていない状態」を表現するためです。
今回は平面的な構図なので、前後をわかりやすくするために白黒でモチーフを配置しました。ライティングとシルエット重視の演出で空間を表現します。

When thinking about how everything will look on the cover, I paid the most attention to where to arrange the human subjects and important motifs in the illustration. I prioritized the arrangement of the person, piano, and window over other elements, and made adjustments to the window size. Next, I arranged leafy plants, lights, a bookshelf, and other elements that wouldn't take away from the story in order to create a certain mood. I deliberately placed objects on top of the piano to show that the piano hasn't been used in a while.
This illustration had a flat construction to it, so I arranged the different motifs in black and white to easily show any changes. This allowed me to create a space with serious consideration for lighting and silhouettes.

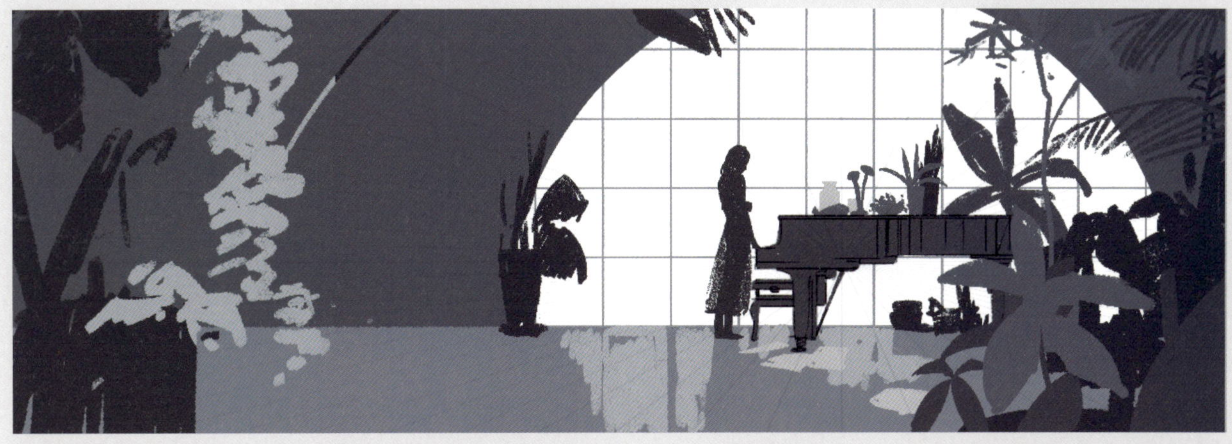

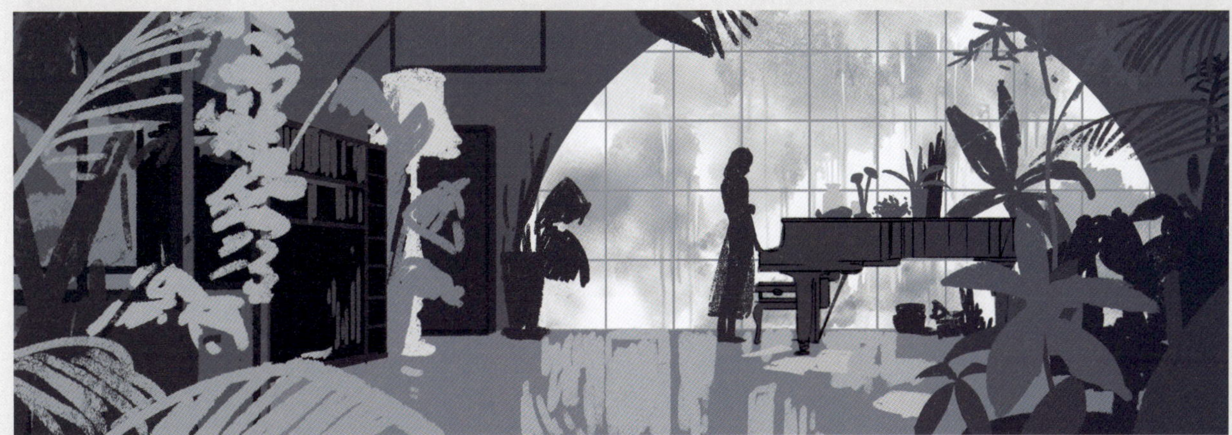

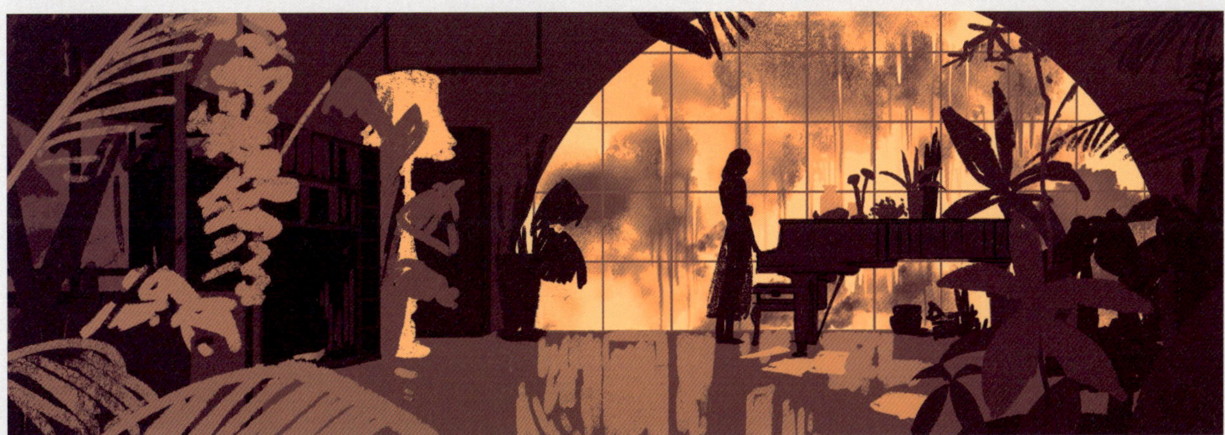

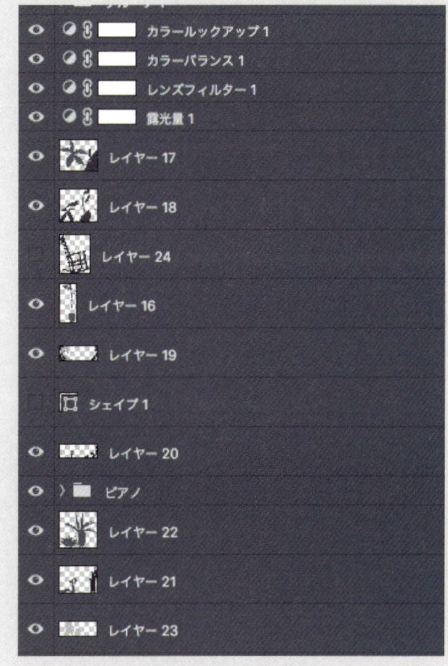

ある程度モチーフを配置したら、色調補正のレイヤーで色を足します。現在はモチーフごとにレイヤーが分かれています。

After arranging the motifs a bit, I added colors in tone correction layers. At this point, each motif is separated into a different layer.

2: [モチーフを配置する | Arranging the motifs]

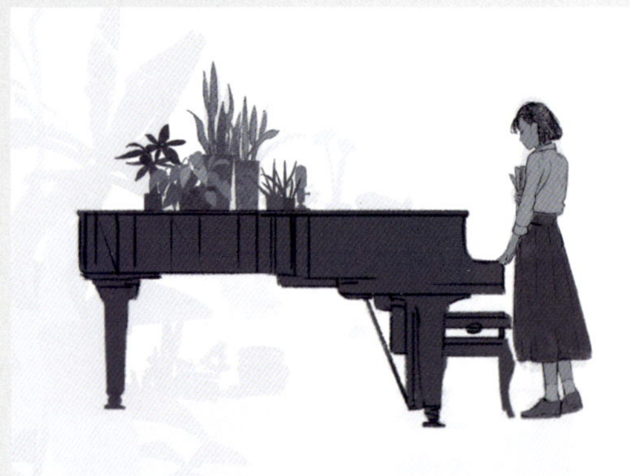
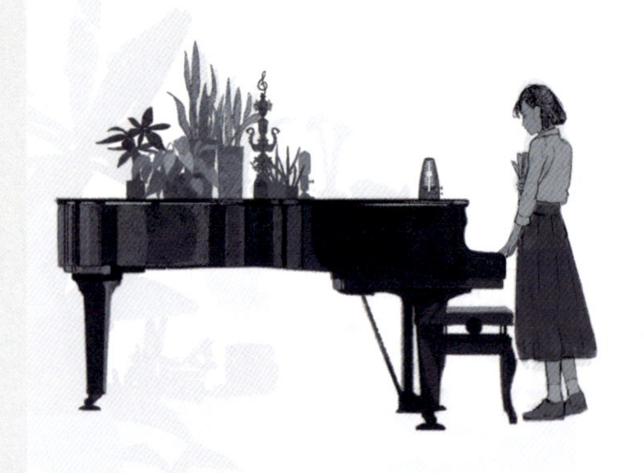
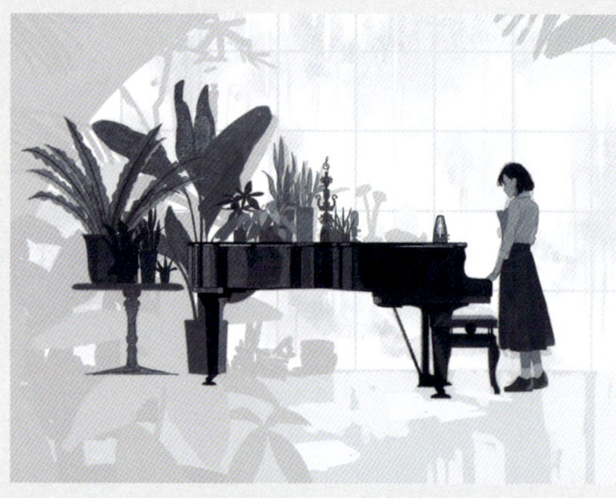

ピアノや植物をラフから新たに形を
取ったものに差し替えます。描き進
めながら左にあるモチーフや部屋の
形を何回か修正していきます。
色の調整レイヤーは表示、非表示を
切り替えながら明暗を調整しています。

I started by replacing the piano
and plants from the rough sketch
by drawing them again. I made
adjustments to the motifs on the left
and the shape of the room multiple
times while drawing.
Then I adjusted the brightness by
showing and hiding each color layer.

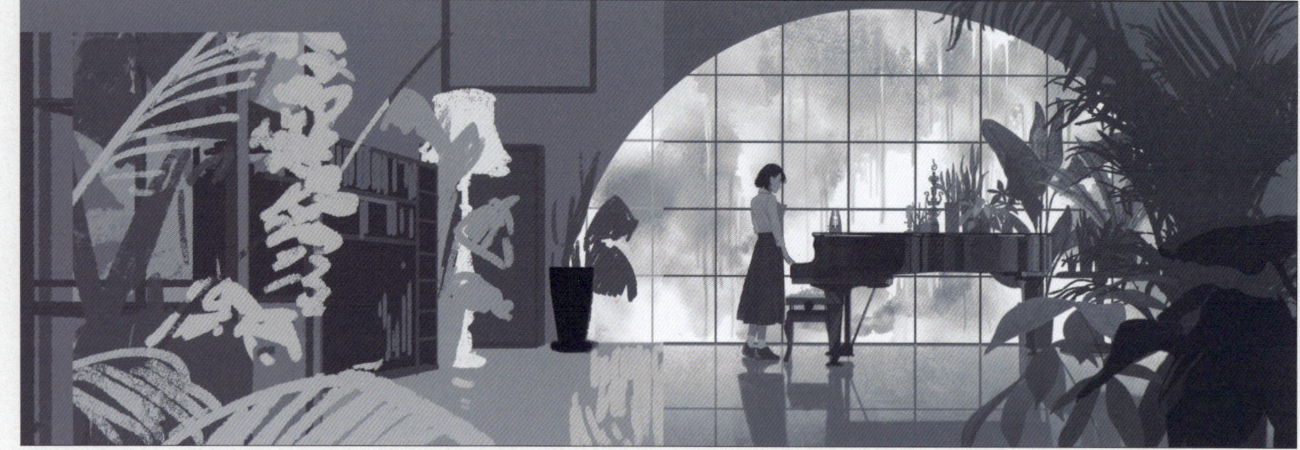

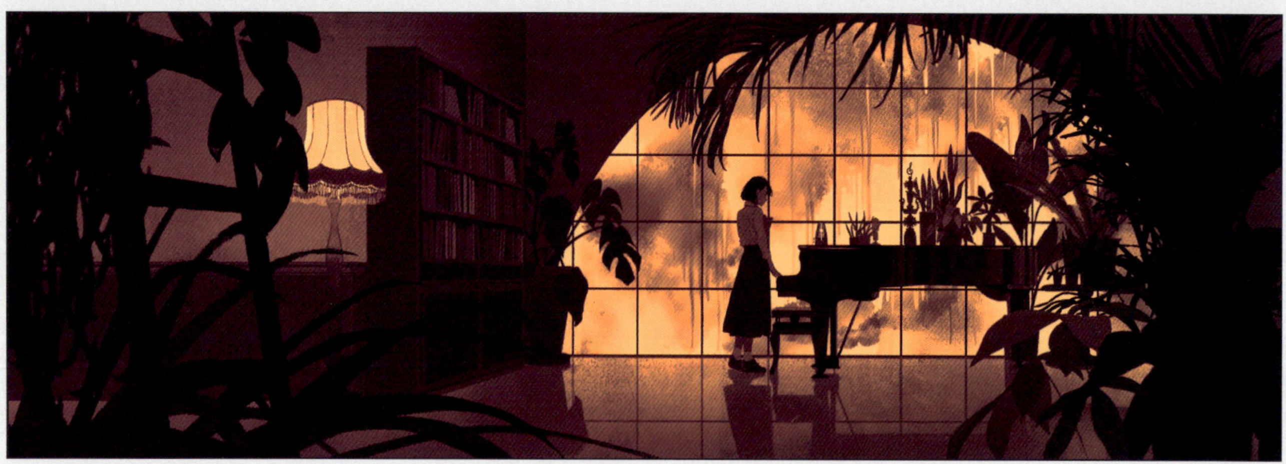

3 : [色分けをする | Making color adjustments]

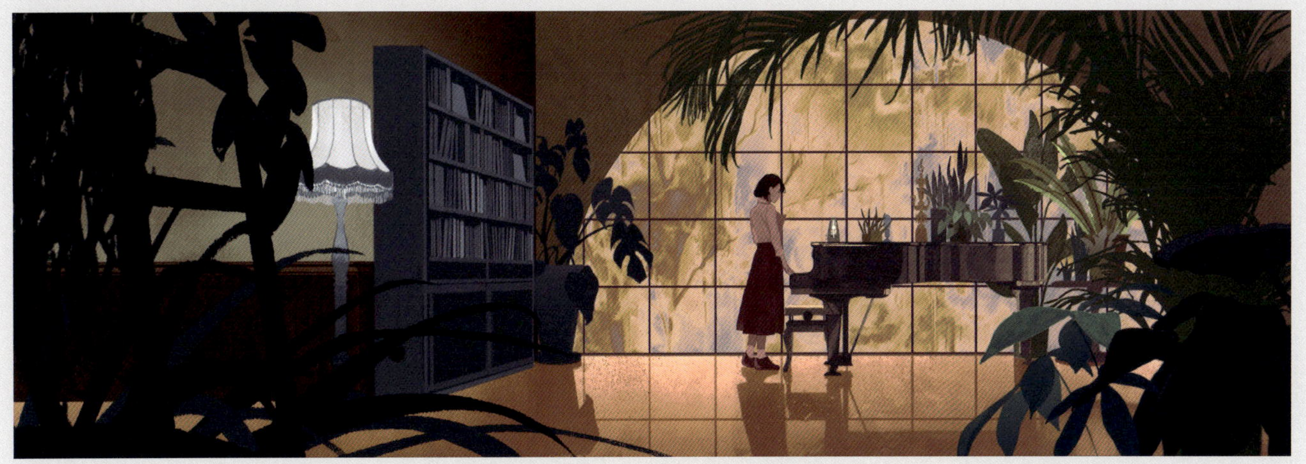

この時点でもレイヤーはまだ結合していません。個別のモチーフにカラーバランスなども調整しながら色を入れます。モチーフごとに色が違うという事実が欲しいので、色分けはあまり細かくせずに色を入れるという感覚です。モチーフごとに色を変えることで、白黒だけで調整していたときとは違い、微妙な色の変化が画面に出て、絵に深みが増します。

At this point, the layers were still not combined. I added colors to each motif individually while adjusting the color balance and other elements. I wanted a different color for each motif, so I added colors without being too detailed. By changing the colors for each motif, the illustration gains more depth as the minute color changes appear on screen – different from adjustments made to the black and white version.

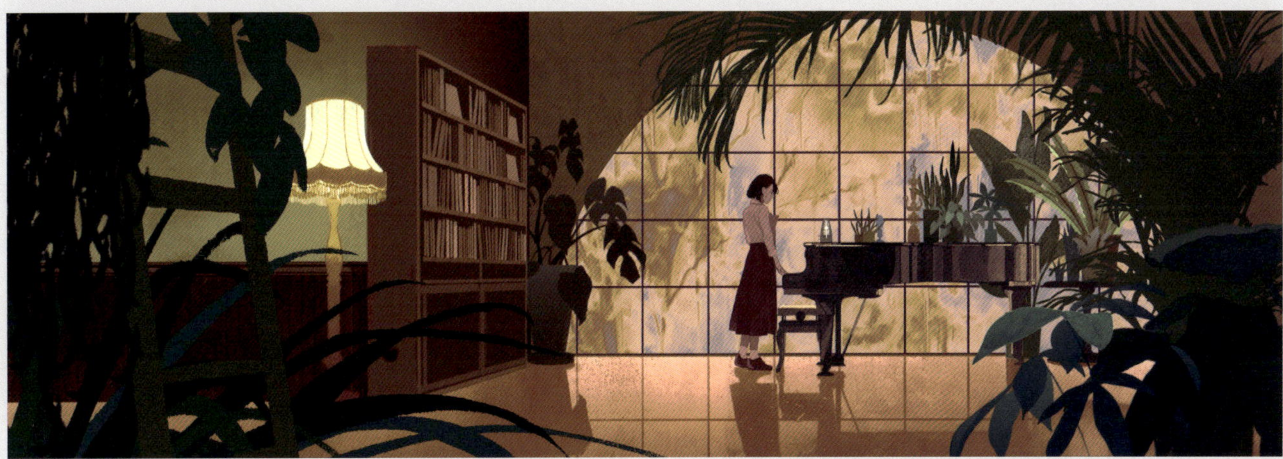

これは好みの話になりますが、私はデータ上に真っ黒と真っ白な部分があるのが嫌いなので、レイヤーの一番上に「露光量」という調整レイヤーを入れています。オフセットの数値を＋に動かすと、黒かった部分が灰色に近づきます。露光量の数値を－に動かすと絵全体が暗くなります。これで絵がかなり落ち着いた色になります。

This is my personal taste, but I don't like when there are completely black or white spaces on my illustrations, so I added an Exposure layer to the very top layer.
By adding value to the Offset value, black areas turn grayer. Removing value to the Exposure value causes the entire illustration to become darker. Tweaking these values gives the illustrations a more relaxed color scheme.

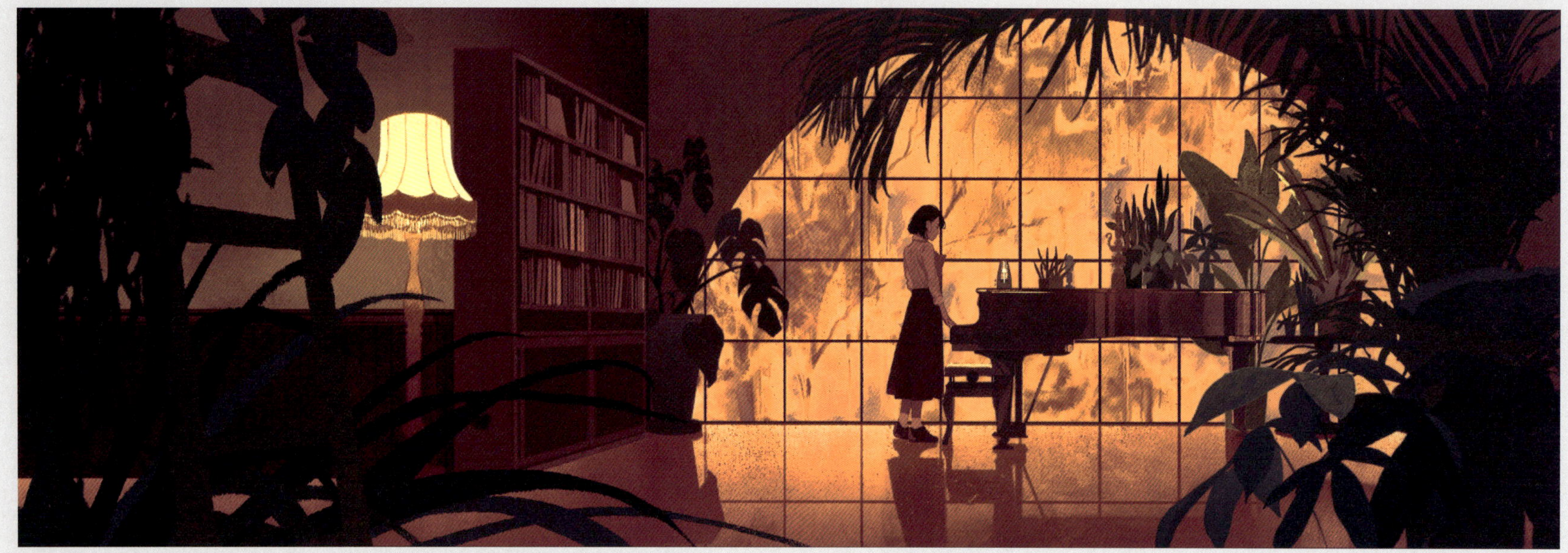

光を表現するときに白く飛ばしたりすると思いますが、画面が真っ白になってしまうとそこに情報量はなく、軽い絵になってしまいます。それを避けるために 100％白い部分は作らないようにしています。私が描く絵は装画など、絵を使ってデザインしていただく場合が多いので、白文字も入れていただけるように調整しています。

I think we tend to use white to show light, but a spot that is completely white on the screen means that there isn't any information there, which leads to an illustration with less depth. I try to stray away from creating any 100% white spaces in my illustrations to avoid this. I work on a lot of book covers and my illustrations are turned into book covers by others later on, so I adjust my illustrations so that white letters can be added.

4 : [人物を変更する │ Altering the human subjects]

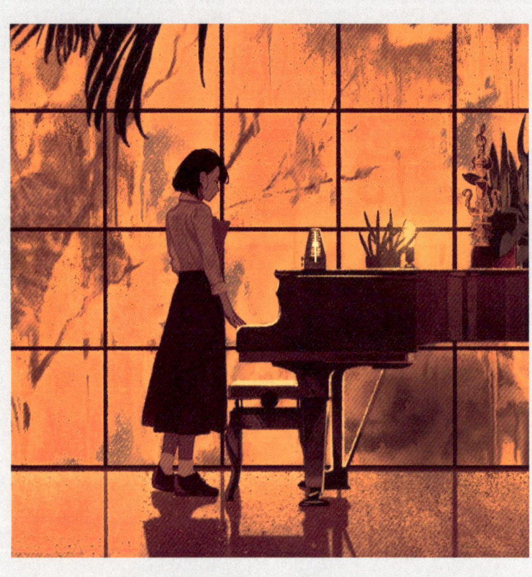
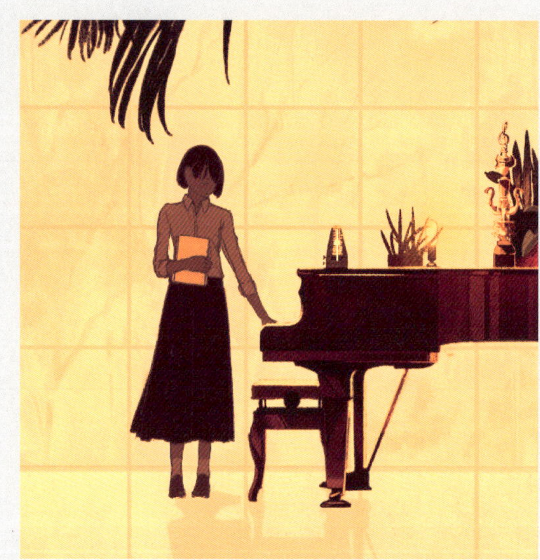
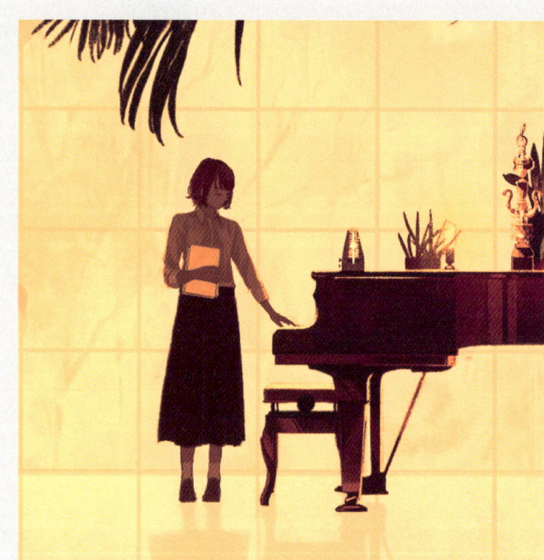

人物のポーズを変更することにしました。
理由は「後悔の念が強く見える」からです。なので、少し前向きな気持ちをプラスするように「懐かしむ」「思い出す」というイメージで描き直しました。現時点でのレイヤーは大まかに分けてあります。

I decided to change the pose of the girl in the illustration.
I did this to keep from showing her feelings of regret too much. In addition to the positive pose, I re-drew the girl as if she was feeling nostalgic and remembering times from the past. At this point, the layers were roughly separated.

5 : [描き込む | **Drawing details**]

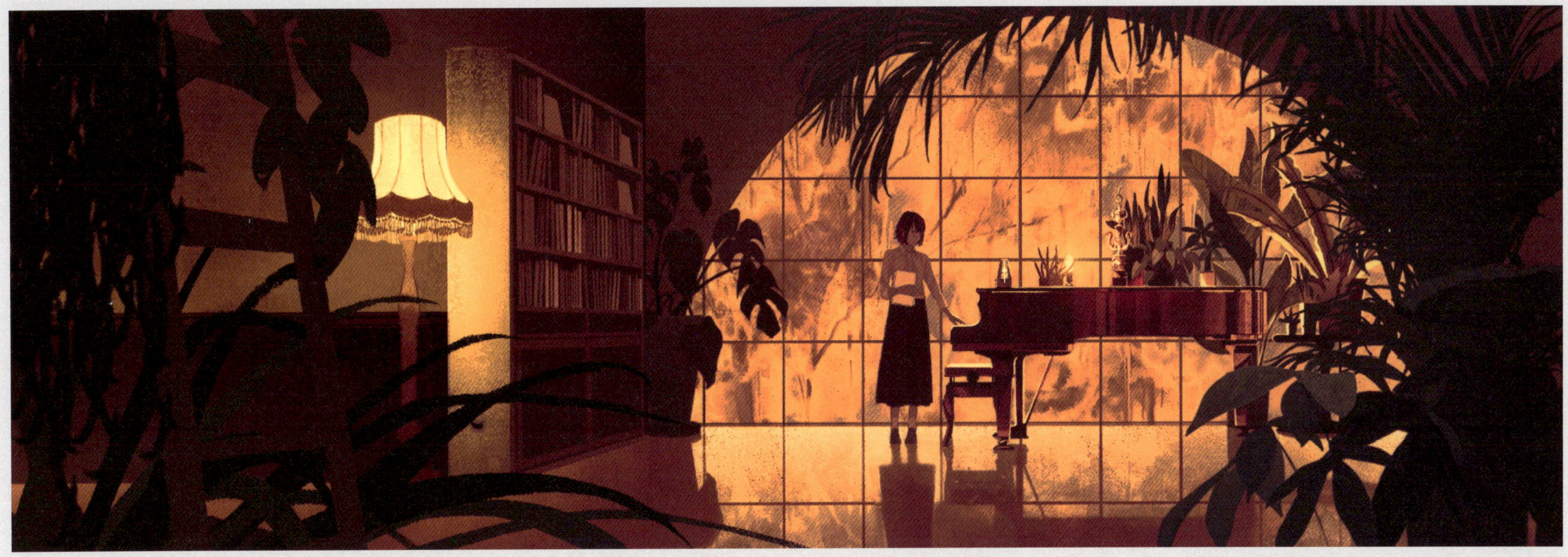

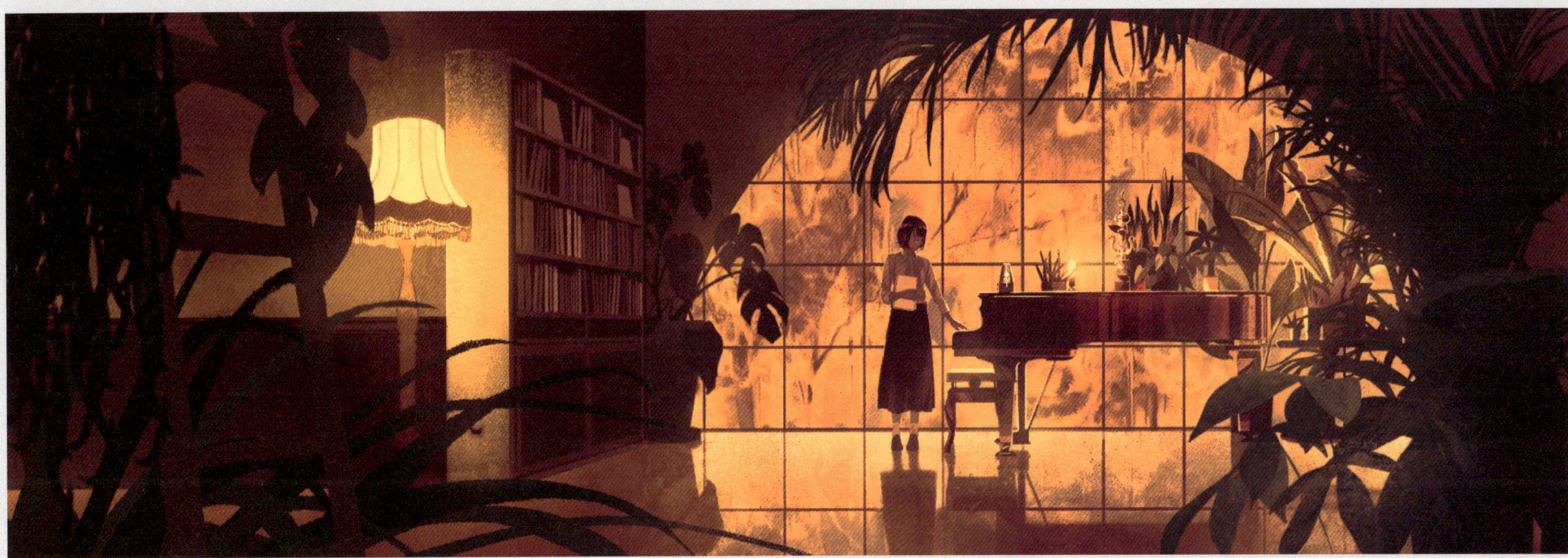

色、配置、構図、ポーズがある程度決まったので描き込んでいきます。描き込むときは「絵は平面」ということを意識しています。レイヤーで分けられたモチーフごとの質感が前後のレイヤーと違うと、どうしてもツギハギの切り絵のように見えてしまいます。そういう面白さもありますが、自分の絵では気になるので、この工程からレイヤー感を潰していきます。自分の絵は質感に気を使う場面が多いので、テクスチャを反映させた描き込みの方法を説明します。

描き込み用のレイヤーを一番上に作り、まず明るい色をスポイトで選択して、不透明度を 20 くらいに設定します。光を感じる場所にポンポンと乗せ、空気感を出します。

I move on to drawing the details, as the colors, arrangement, construction, and human subject's pose have been decided upon. I'm constantly aware of the fact that this is a flat illustration as I add details. If the texture of each motif, separated by layers, is different to other layers, the illustration ends up looking as if it was made from piecing together different illustrations. That may be an interesting idea, but it bothers me when my illustrations are that way, so during this process, I get rid of the sense that layers exist in the illustration. My illustrations are often used in situations where texture is scrutinized, so I use the following technique to reflect texture in my illustrations.

I create a new topmost layer for adding details, and select a bright color using the Eyedropper tool, and set the transparency to around 20. I add this color liberally to spots where light should be, creating a sense of space.

次は暗い色をスポイトで選択して、ブラシパネルの「反転」
にチェックを入れます。反転することで、先程描いた明るい
色のテクスチャを残しながら、暗い色で描くことができます。

Next, I select a dark color using the Eyedropper tool, and I
check the box for Invert in the Brushes panel. By inverting the
dark color, I can draw with the dark color while keeping the
texture that I just added before with the light color.

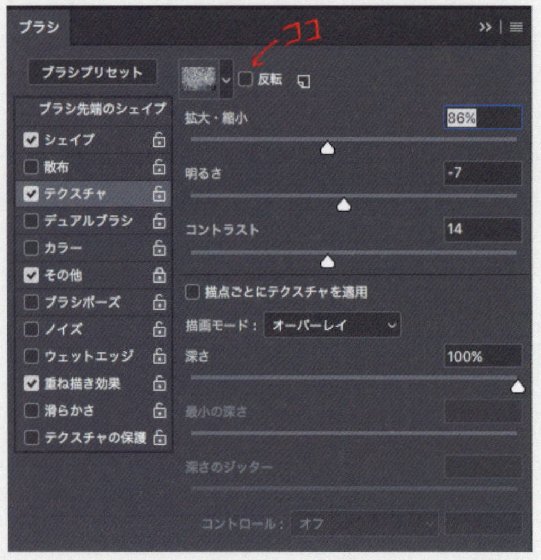
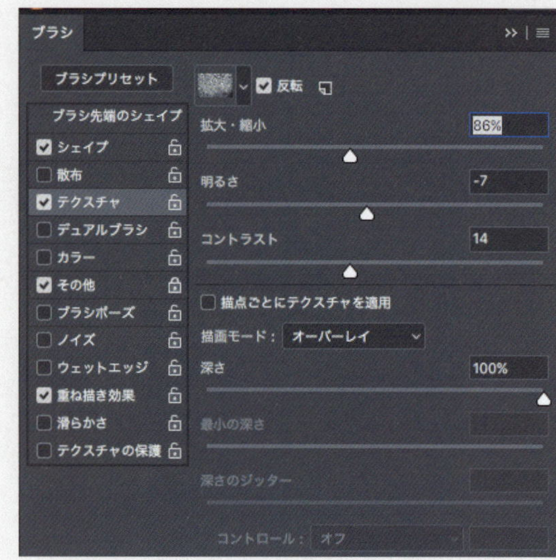

「反転」にチェックを入れずに暗い色を入れたのが右、反転
させたのが左です。反転させると、色の混ざり方が自然にな
り、さらに、最初の明るい色が潰れません。この方法で質感
を生かしながら描き込みます。

On the right is what it looks like when adding dark colors
without checking the Invert box, and on the left is with Invert
checked. Through inverting, the color is mixed more naturally,
and it doesn't replace the light colors that were there before. I
add details to my illustrations while adding texture in this way.

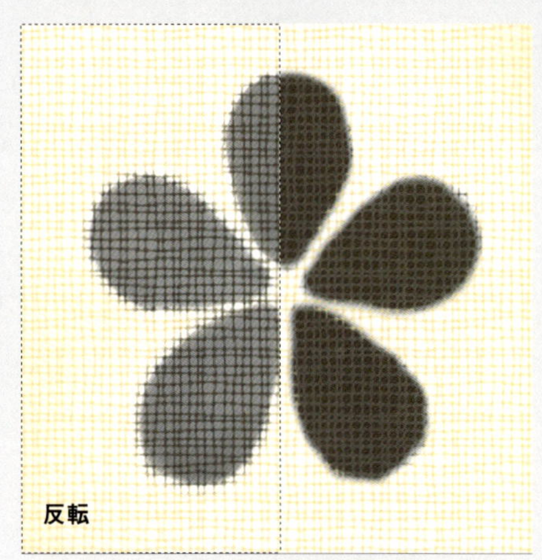

手前の植物にも陰影をつけながら、リアルになりすぎない程
度に葉脈を描いていきます。

While adding shadows to the plants in front, I add veins to the
leaves without making it too realistic.

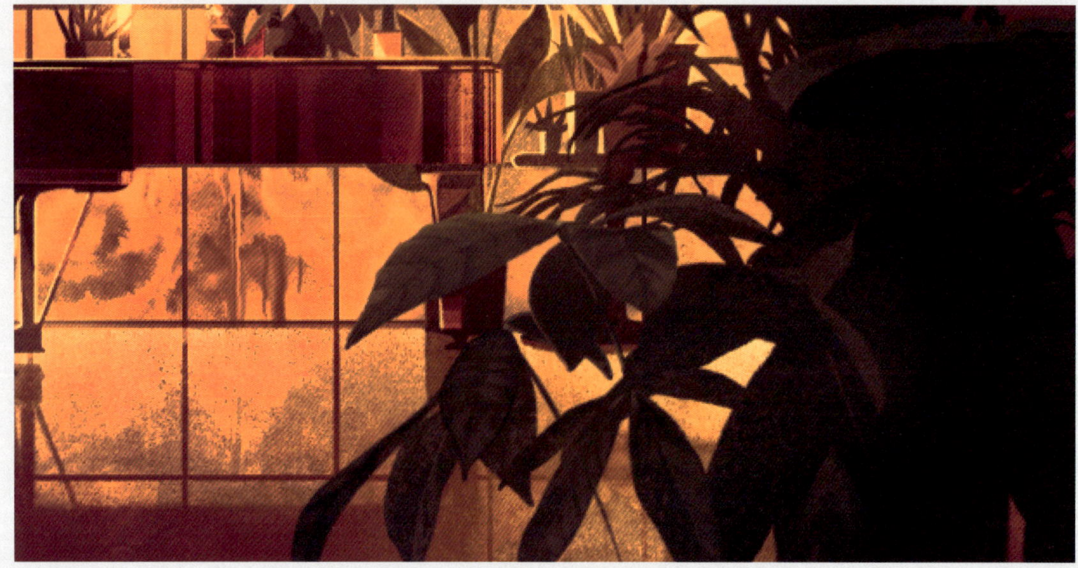

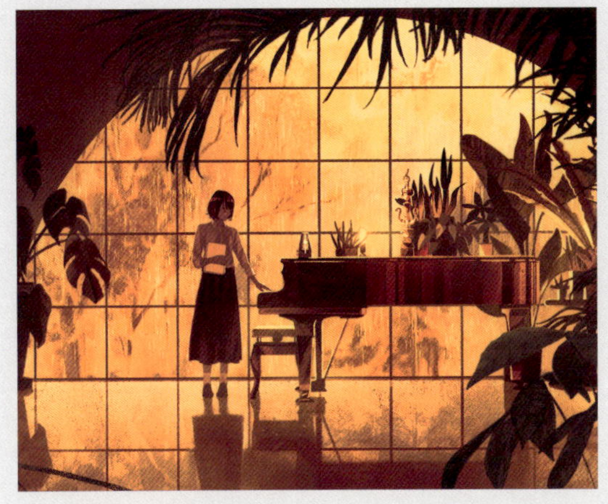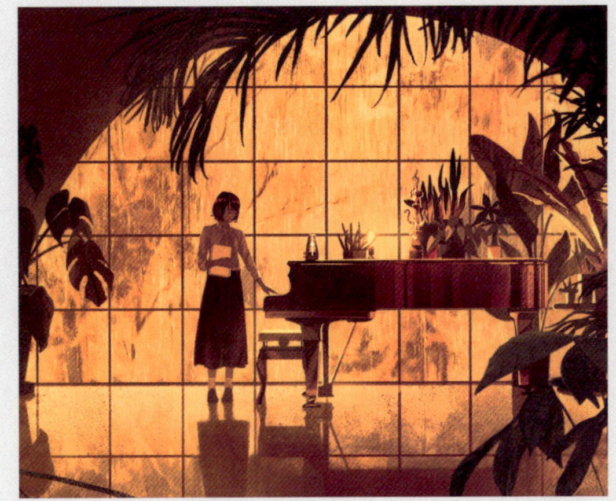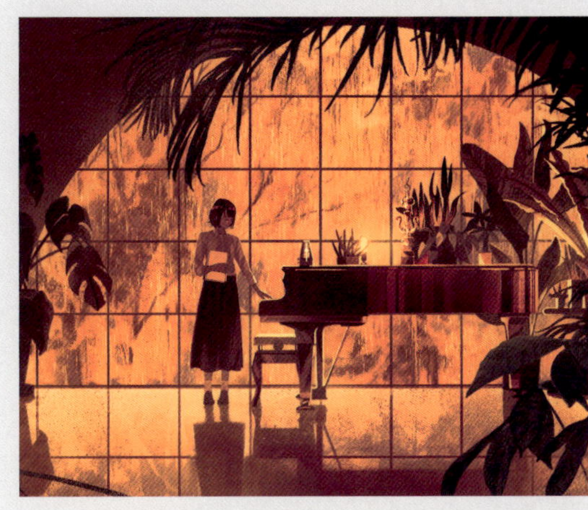

窓の外を描いていきます。窓の外は質感で遊べるので楽しい部分です。
外と中でレイヤーを分けているので、その間に「オーバーレイ」レイヤーを作って雨粒の光を入れていきます。雨粒を描き終えたら、消しゴムで明るすぎる部分を削ります。削ることで筆跡を消し、より自然なにじみを表現することができます。

Now I draw what's outside the window. The outside world is fun to draw as you get to play around with textures.
The outside and inside are separated into different layers, so I add an overlay layer between these layers to add the light from the raindrops. After drawing the raindrops, I take the eraser to get rid of any overly bright spots. Erasing gets rid of hand drawn lines, which creates a more natural blurring effect.

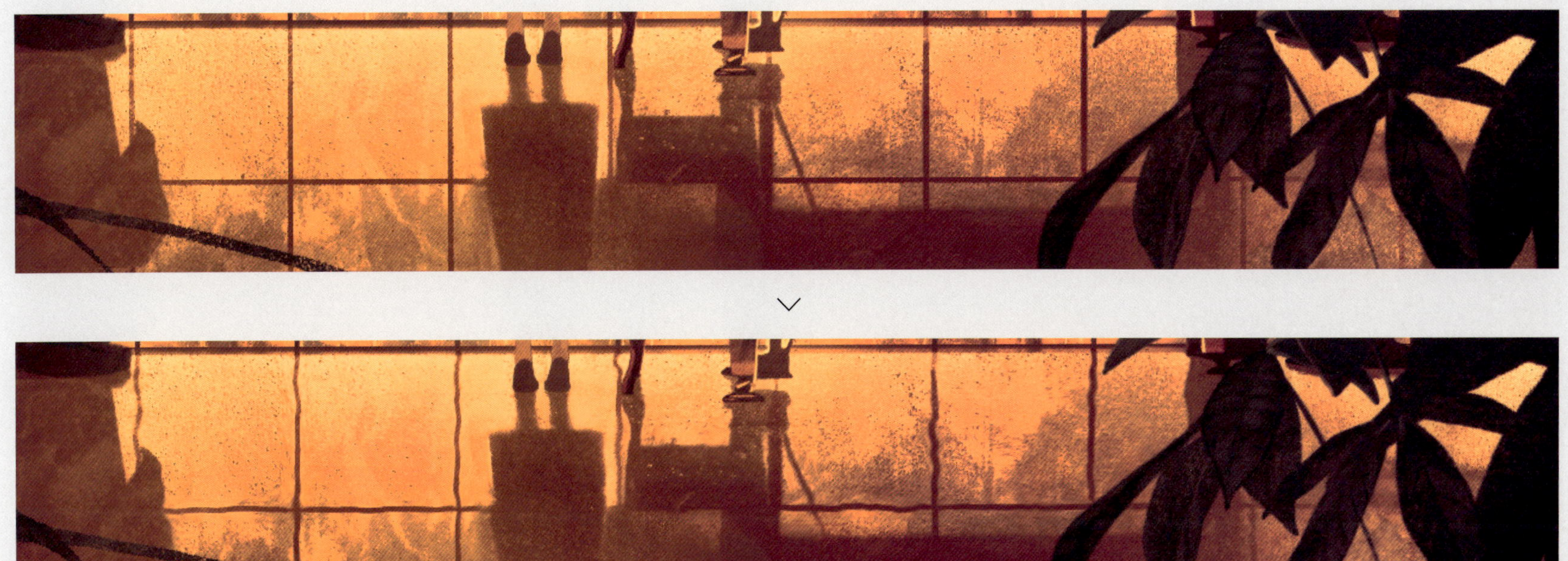

次に地面の反射を調整します。今は反射がまっすぐなので、歪みを加えます。
指先ツールで太めの筆を選んで上下左右に動かし、反射面をガタガタにします。

Next, I adjust the reflection on the floor. The reflection is currently perfectly straight, so I need to add some distortion. I select the Smudge tool and a thick brush tip and use this tool to create wobbly lines in the reflection by smudging up, down, left, and right on the reflection.

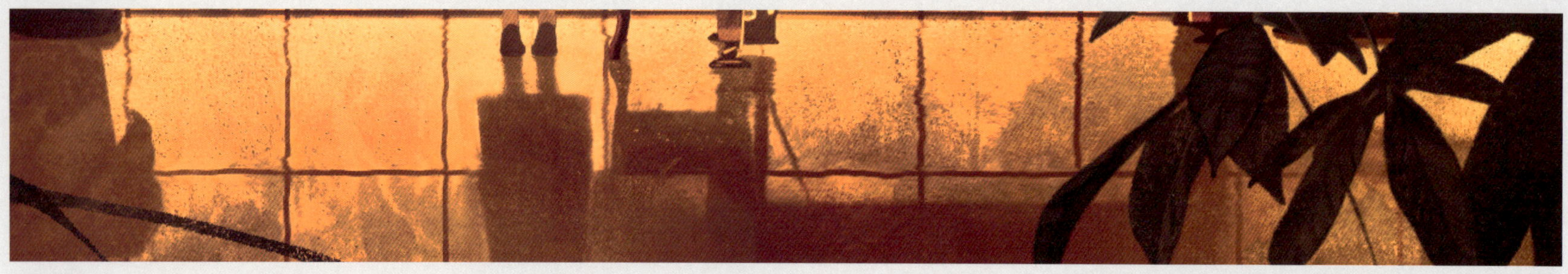

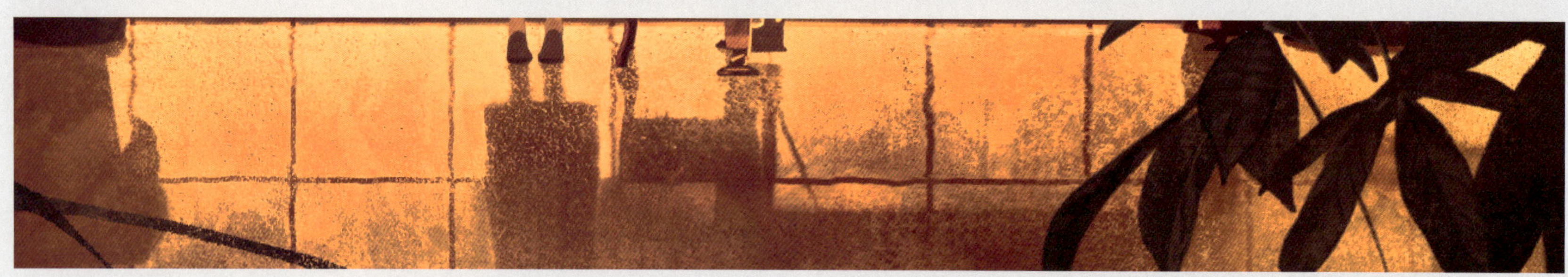

次に筆を先程より細くして、細かな歪みを足します。指先ツールを使用すると特有の変なボケ感が出てしまうので、もう一度 145〜146 ページで説明した描き込みの方法でなぞります。ボケ感が解消されました。「このツール、フィルタを使ったな」という感じが画面に出るのが嫌なので、使用した様子がわからなくなるまで描き込むことを意識しています。

Next, I select a finer brush tip, and add finer distortions. Using the Smudge tool creates a characteristic and strange dull effect, so I trace the areas I've smudged using the method again that I explained on page 145 - 146. This gets rid of the dull effect. I hate it when someone looks at my illustrations and can tell I've used a certain tool or filter, so I take great care in ensuring I add enough detail so that the tools or filters used can't be recognized.

6 : [仕上げをする | Fine tuning]

私は線画を描くのが苦手なので、普段は線画は描いたり残したりしませんが、線画のある絵は好きなので、今回は線画を作ってみます。
作り方は自己流です。まず、これまでのレイヤーすべてをコピー、結合して1枚絵のレイヤーを作ります。このレイヤーのフィルターギャラリーを開き、「塗料」でブラシサイズを調整します。絵のサイズや描き込みの細かさにもよるので、数値は適宜調整してください。

I'm not very good at line drawing, so I usually don't draw or leave line drawings in my works, but I like the way illustrations with lines look, so I tried my hand at line drawing for this illustration.
I use my own method. First, I copy all the layers I have made so far, combine them into a single layer, and create a new, combined drawing. Then I open the Filter Gallery for the layer and select Paint Daubs and adjust the brush size. Be sure to adjust the values properly, as different values are required based on the size of the illustration and level of detail used.

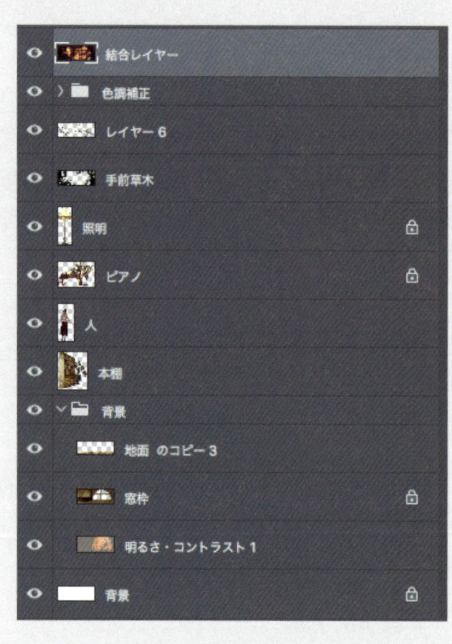

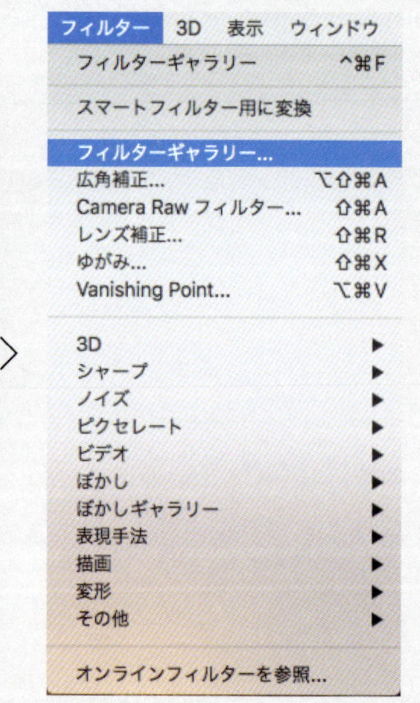

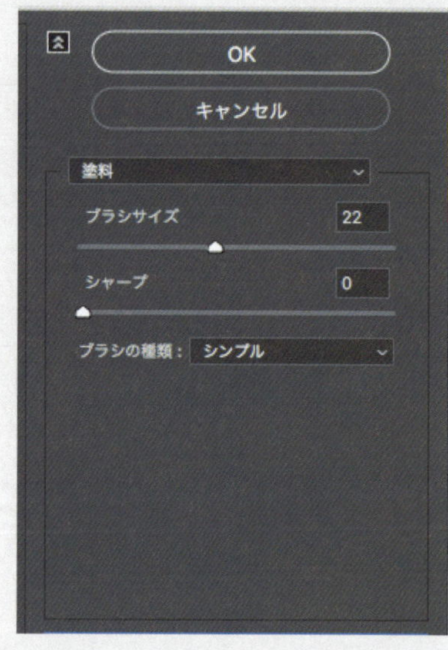

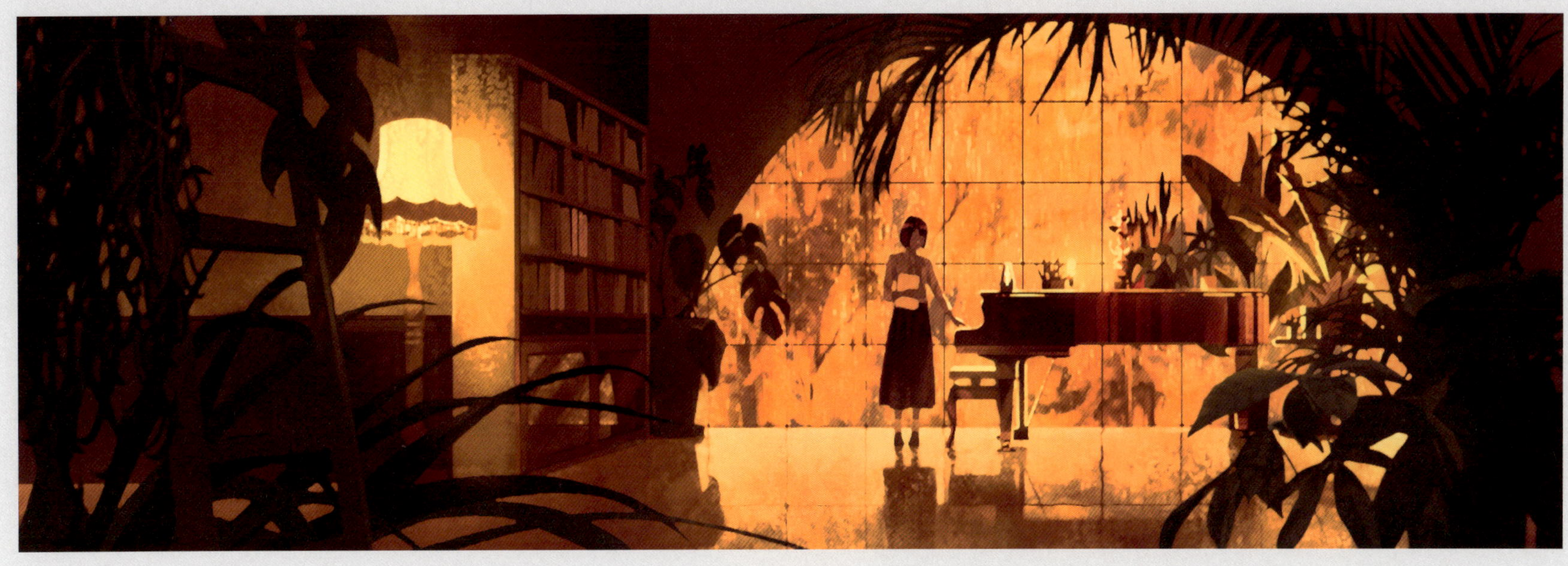

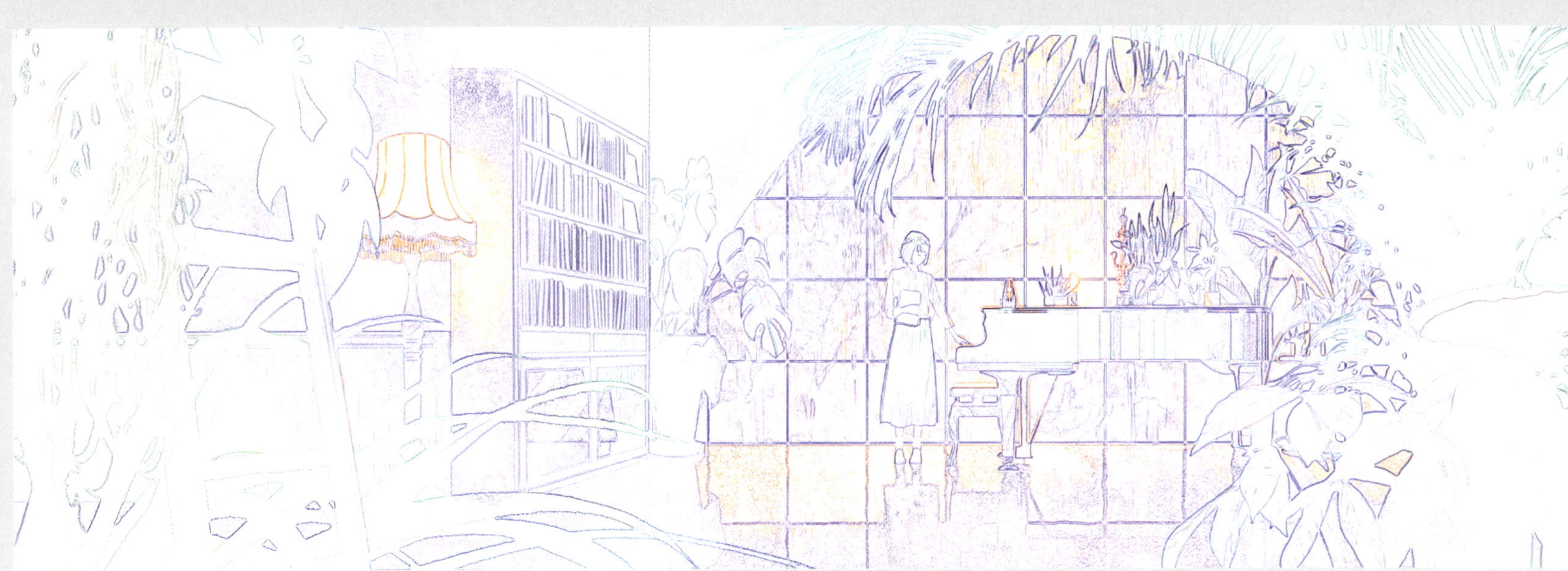

絵がにじみました。このレイヤーを「除算」で重ねます。
すると色鉛筆で描いたような線ができます。シルエットで見えなくなっていた色と色の境界線まで浮き彫りになります。この線が見える状態ですべてのレイヤーを複製、結合し、それを「乗算」で乗せます。
色と色の境界に線が入りました。現状では濃すぎるので不透明度を調整し、うっすらと見える程度にします。不要な部分は消しゴムで削ります。

The borders in the illustration have been blurred and this layer has been placed on top of the illustration using Divide.
Lines that look as if they were drawn by colored pencils appear. This creates a sense that the border between colors seems to float out of the illustration. This effect is created by the colors that now appear, with clear border lines between colors. With the lines visible, I copy all the layers, combine them, and blend them with Multiply.
Now there are lines at the borders between colors. The lines in the illustration are too thick, so I adjust the transparency so that the lines appears thinner. I erase any unnecessary parts with the eraser.

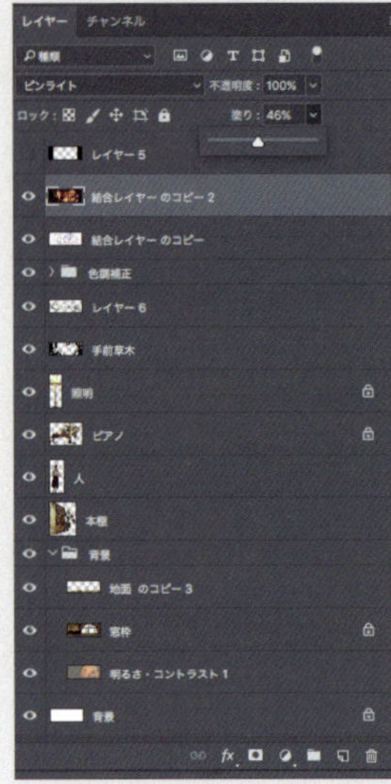

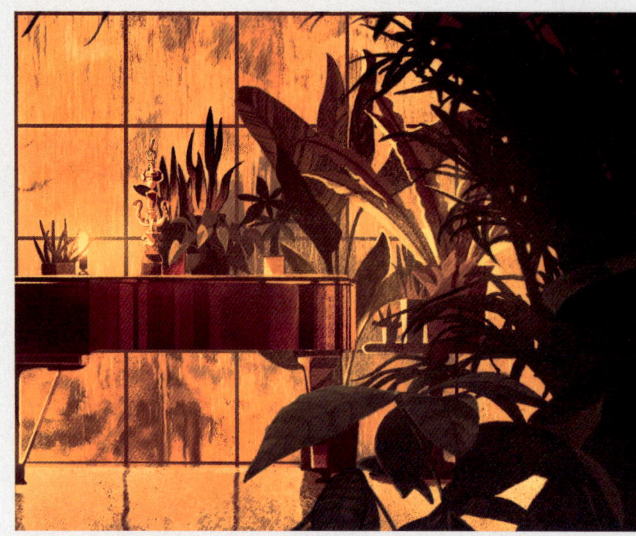

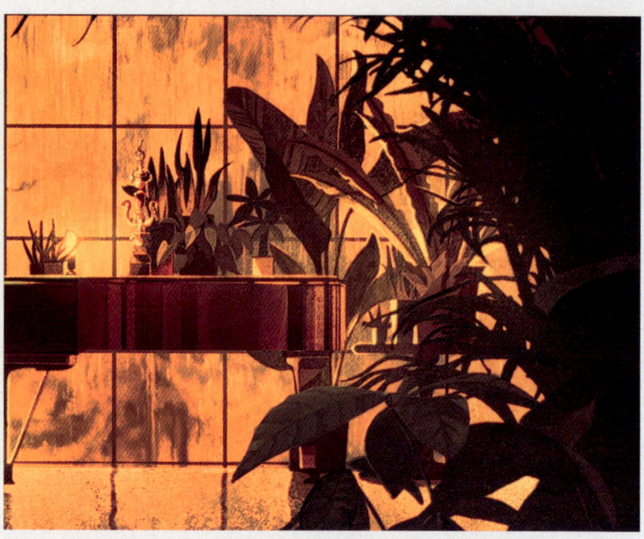

レイヤーには先程「塗料」で加工した絵が残っているので、そのレイヤーを「ピンライト」に変更し、線画レイヤーの上に乗せます。すると、画面の明るい部分の周りに赤く発光した色が乗ります。このレイヤーも不透明度を調整して、消しゴムで削りながらうっすらと残るようにします。

For the remaining layer to be processed - the illustration that was processed through Paint Daubs before - I added the Pin Light effect, layering this on top of the line drawing layer. Doing so adds a bright red color to the areas around the bright parts of the illustration. I adjust the transparency for this layer, too, using the eraser to get rid of certain areas, creating a dimmer appearance where less red is visible.

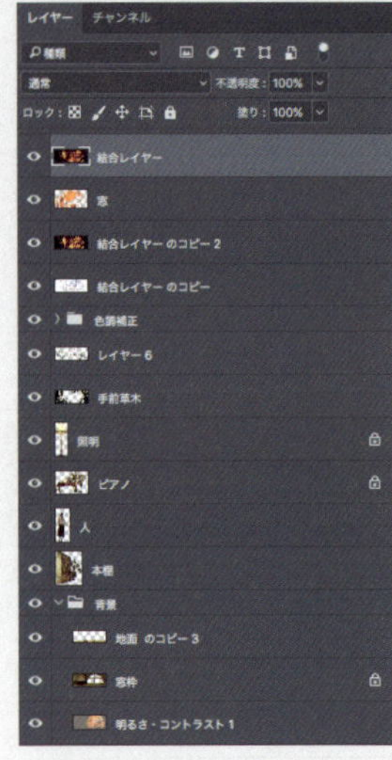

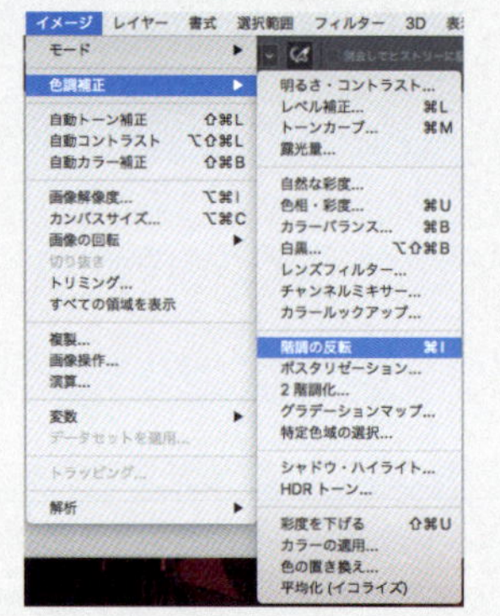

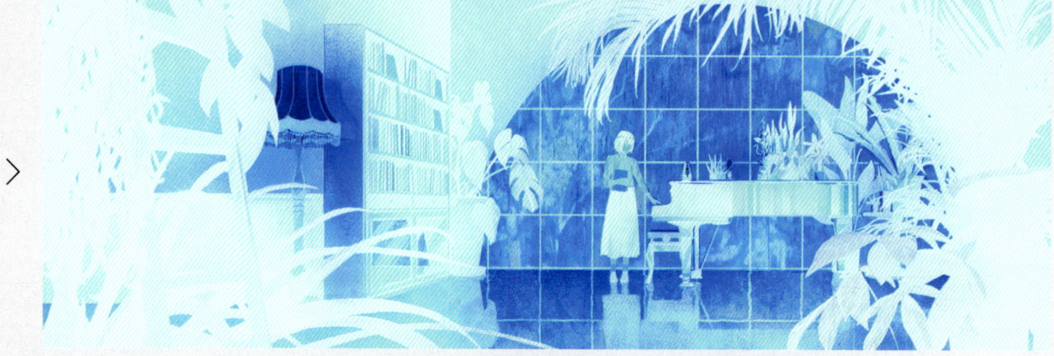

次に黒い部分に灰色を追加します。またすべてのレイヤーを複製、結合し、「階調の反転」をします。

Next, I add gray to the black areas. Then I copy all the layers, combine them, and Invert.

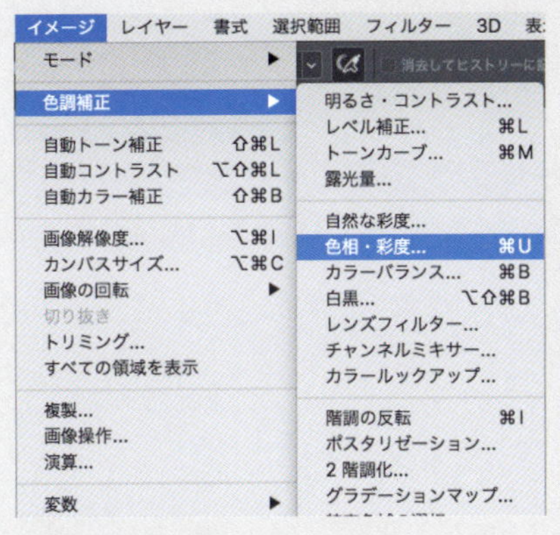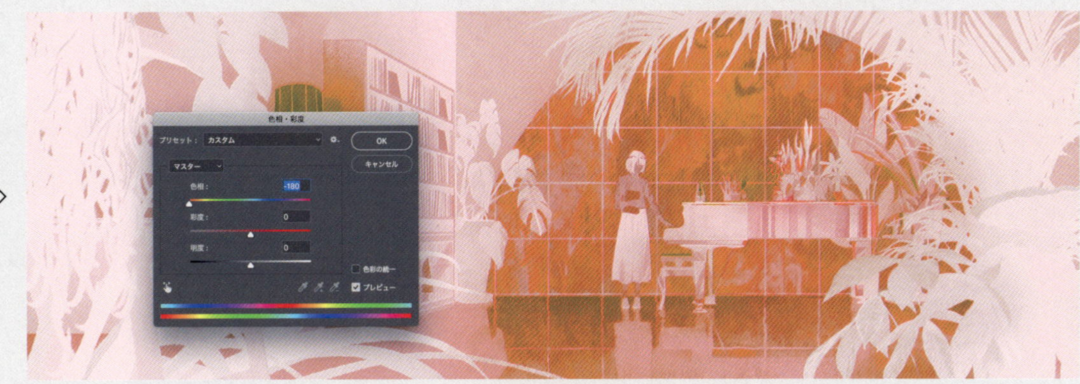

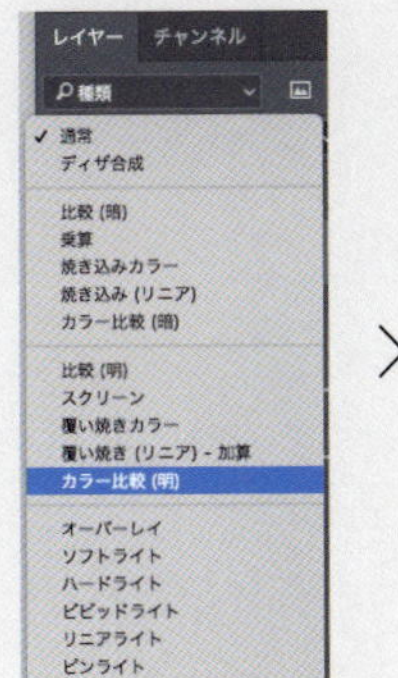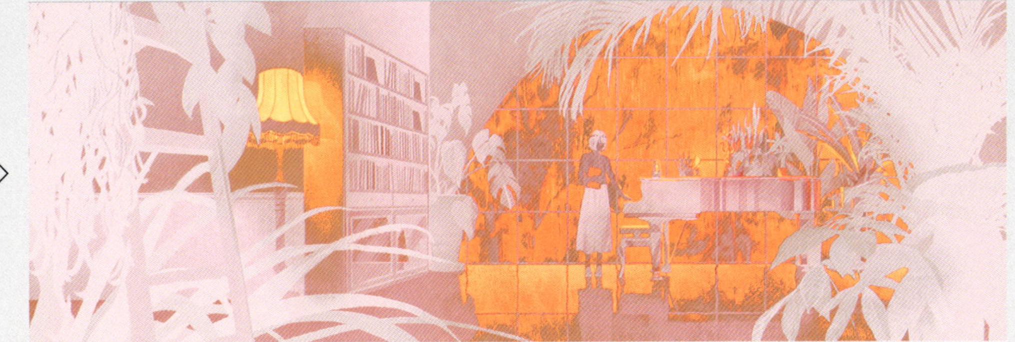

青くなってしまったので、色調補正の色相・彩度を調整して赤に戻します。さらに、レイヤーの種類を「カラー比較（明）」にし、コントラストを調整します。画面で黒かった部分が灰色になりました。

This turns the layer's elements blue, so I adjust the Hue/Saturation so that the layer returns to a red color. I then change the layer Kind to Lighter Color and adjust the contrast. The black parts become more of a gray color.

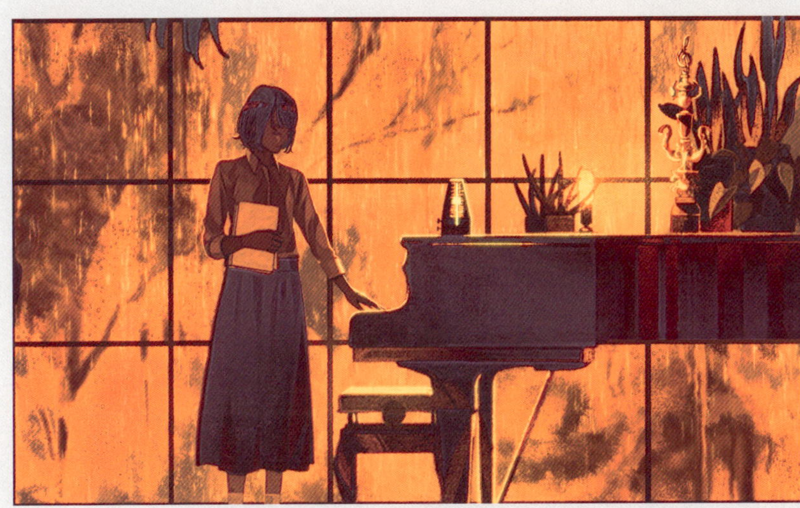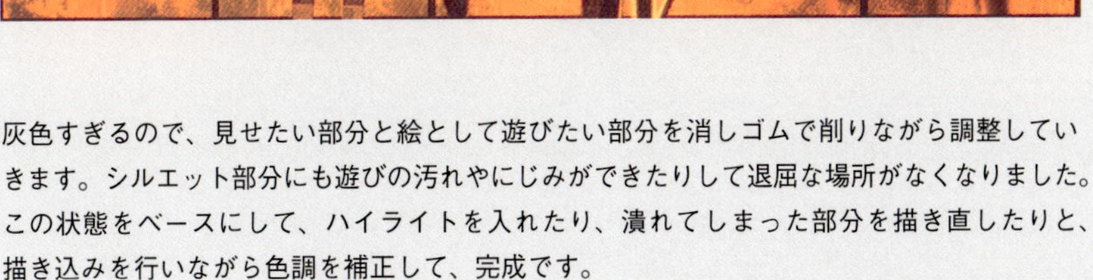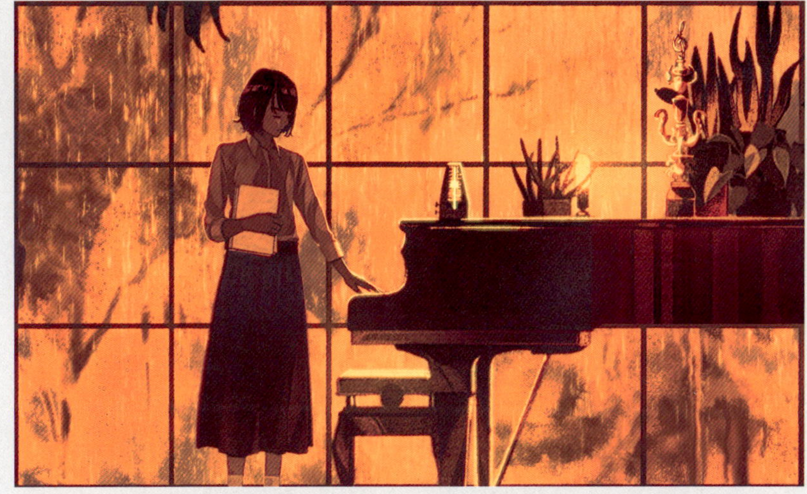

灰色すぎるので、見せたい部分と絵として遊びたい部分を消しゴムで削りながら調整していきます。シルエット部分にも遊びの汚れやにじみができたりして退屈な場所がなくなりました。この状態をベースにして、ハイライトを入れたり、潰れてしまった部分を描き直したりと、描き込みを行いながら色調を補正して、完成です。

The gray color is too strong, so I adjust the illustration by erasing the gray color from the parts I want to show and the parts I want to enjoy from an artistic point of view. I also get rid of any uninteresting areas in the silhouetted areas by adding fun impurities and distortion.
With this as my base, I add some highlights, re-draw some parts that were lost in the process, and continue adding detail while adjusting hues, and finally, the illustration is complete.

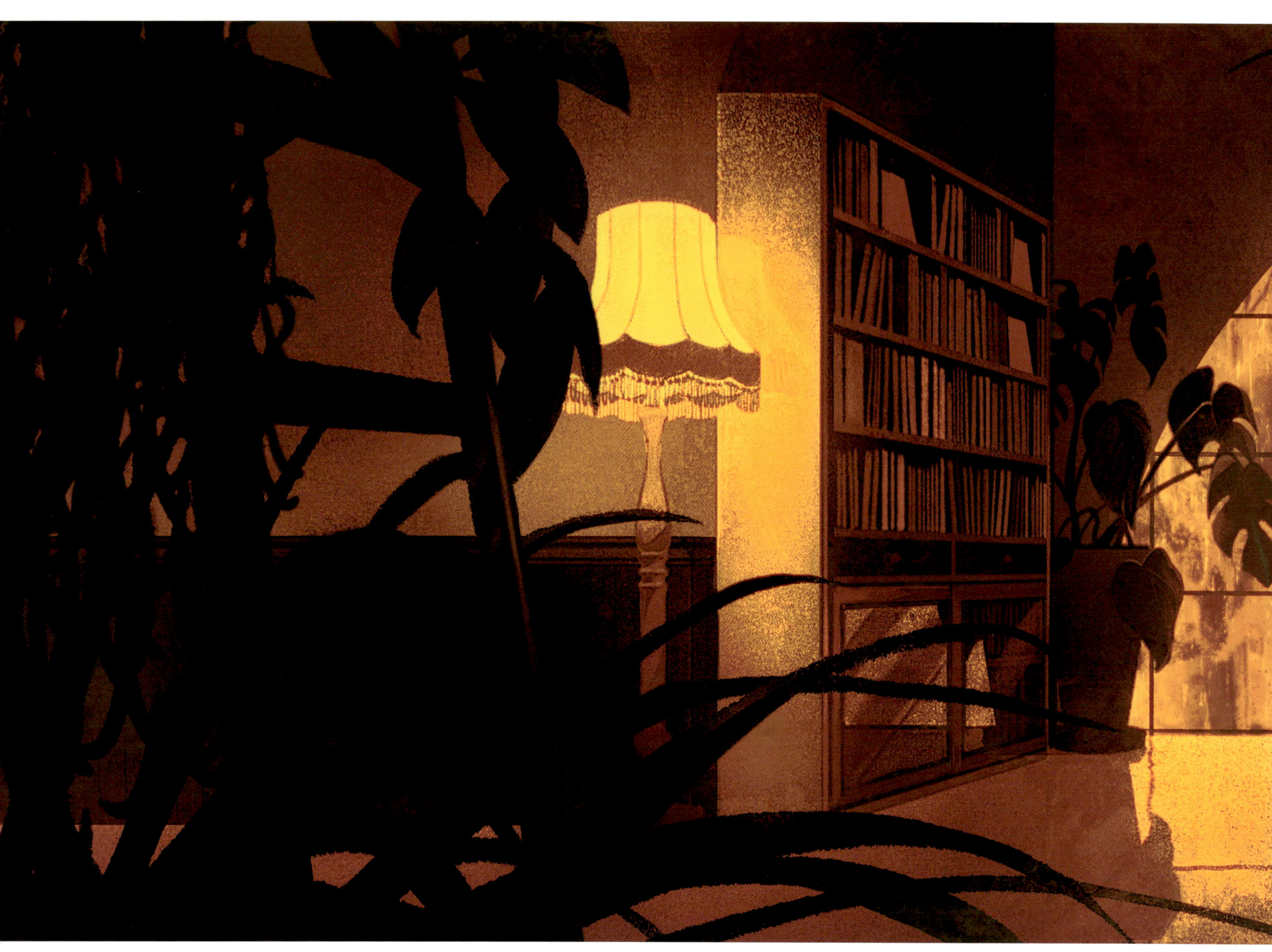

自分の作品は決して目立つ絵ではありませんが、日常のちょっとした出来事
で思い出すような、人の心の隅に残るような絵になればと思って制作してい
ます。なので、ノスタルジックというキーワードで、自分の作品を表紙に起
用していただいたのが嬉しかったです。ありがとうございました。

My illustrations are never showy or flashy. I try to create illustrations that remind the viewer of something from
their everyday life and remain in their hearts. So it is satisfying for me when my illustrations are used on book covers
because they have a sense of "nostalgia". Thank you.

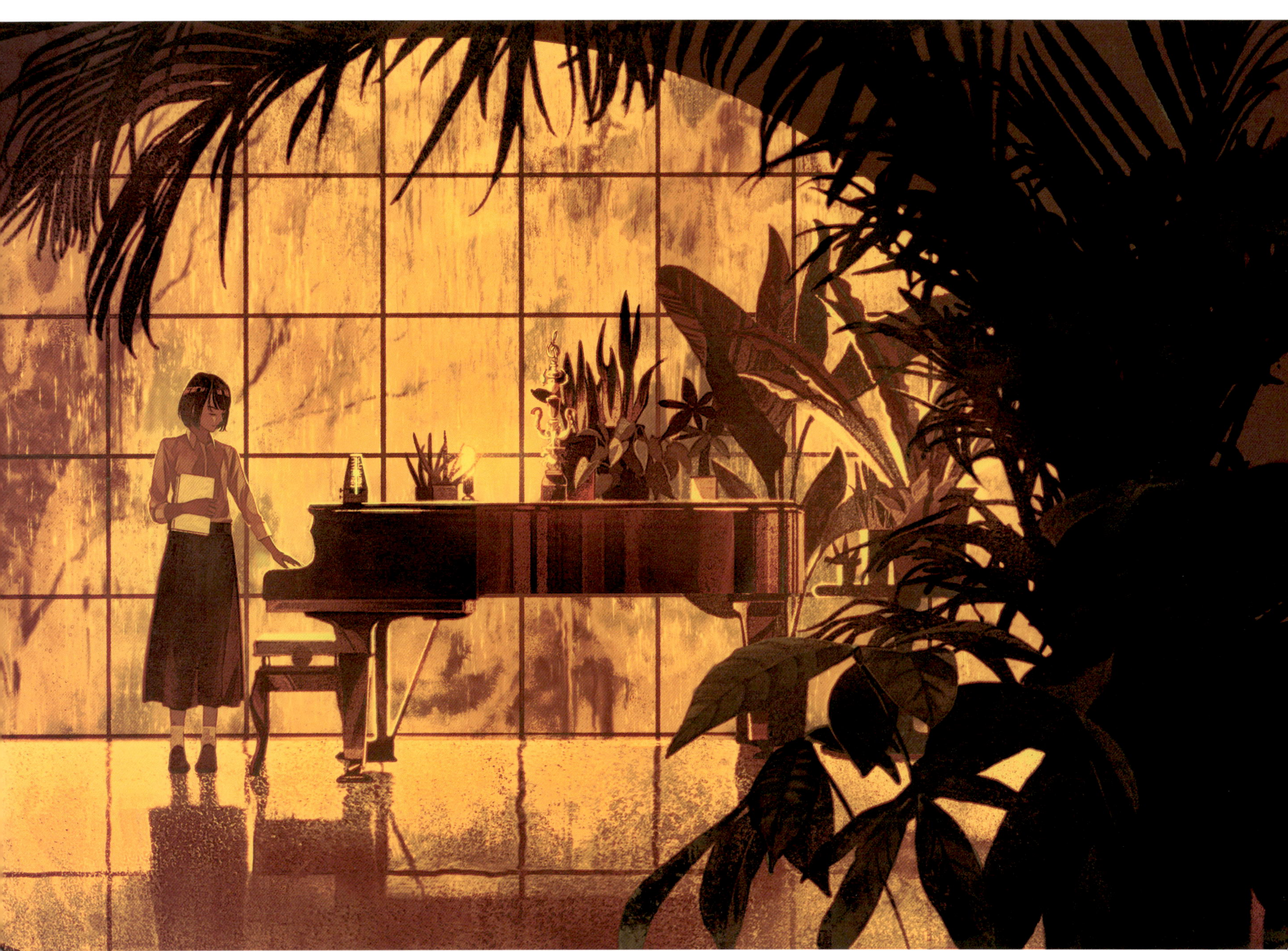

蒼川わか　｜　Waka Aokawa

W：aokawa-waka.com　**M**：wykkoo@gmail.com　**Tw**：@aokawa_waka　**Pi**：25587

P：東京都在住のイラストレーター。文房堂アートスクール講師。書籍の装画やCDのジャケットイラストの他、アナログ画材を生かしてライブペイントや個展等の活動を行う。
An illustrator residing in Tokyo, and an instructor at Bumpodo Art School. In addition to book and CD case cover illustrations, the artist also hosts live art events and private exhibitions using physical art materials.

C：日常と非日常の境目のような、不思議な感覚を抱いていただけましたら幸いです。今後はアナログとデジタルを併用した表現に取り組んでいきます。
I hope you are surrounded by a strange feeling when looking at my work, as if on the border between the ordinary and the extraordinary. I plan to experiment using physical and digital art forms to express myself.

T：透明水彩 / Photoshop CC / CLIP STUDIO PAINT / Affinity Photo
Watercolors / Photoshop CC / CLIP STUDIO PAINT / Affinity Photo

あきま　｜　akima

W：akimasaweb.3zoku.com　**M**：akimatutix@gmail.com　**Tw**：@AkimatutiX　**Pi**：19301797

P：東京生まれ、静岡育ち。コンセプトアート、背景、キャライラスト、航空イラストなどを描く。書籍装画や漫画制作で活動中。
Born in Tokyo, raised in Shizuoka, Japan. Specializes in drawing concept art, backgrounds, illustrations of fictional characters and aircraft, and more. Currently working on cover art for books and graphic novels.

C：日々の生活の周縁や自身の記憶からヒントを得て描いています。
I draw taking hints from minor moments of everyday life and from my own memory.

T：Photoshop CS5 / ミリペン / マーカー
Photoshop CS5 / Drawing pen / Marker pen

粟木こぼね　｜　Kobone Awaki

W：kobone0401.tumblr.com　**M**：awk0401@yahoo.co.jp　**Tw**：@nodonisasaru　**Pi**：28675154

P：2017年から創作絵の公開を始める。現在は主にTwitterなど、SNSでの作品公開を中心に活動している。
Began showing drawings in public in 2017. Mainly exhibits works via twitter, but also via other forms of social media.

C：作品をご覧いただきありがとうございます。これからも、自分ならではの描写を追求していきたいです。
Thank you for having a look at my illustrations. I want to continue to strive for a style that matches who I am.

T：Photoshop CS6

いつか　｜　itsuka

W：itukai.tumblr.com　**M**：ki.pa.co0728@gmail.com　**Tw**：@itukaki　**Pi**：7457683

P：イラストレーター。書籍の装画・挿絵・漫画制作・キャラクターデザインなどを手がける。単行本『いくつもの季節を、君と。いつか作品集』（KADOKAWA/2016）、『君まであともう少し』（徳間書店/2017）を刊行。
Illustrator. Works on illustrations for books and their covers, graphic novels, character design, and more. Works are published in *I want to see all seasons with you. A Collection of Works by Itsuka* (KADOKAWA, 2016) and *Itsuka Presents: Kimi Made Ato Mou Sukoshi* (Tokuma Shoten, 2017).

C：柔らかくて温かみのある、日常を切り取ったようなイラストを目指しています。
I try to create gentle, warm illustrations that portray snapshots of everyday life.

T：CLIP STUDIO PAINT EX / SAI

いとうあつき　｜　ATSUKI ITO

W：itoatsuki.tumblr.com　**M**：palpal32n@yahoo.co.jp　**Tw**：@atuki2126　**Pi**：86322

P：千葉県出身、東京都在住。文教大学教育学部卒業。「夢より素敵な現実」を描くことを大切に、女性向けの広告、書籍等を中心に活動中。
Born in Chiba, and currently residing in Tokyo. Graduated from the Faculty of Education, Bunkyo University. Mostly works on advertising, books, and more for women, focusing on drawing beautiful realities, as opposed to fictional scenes.

C：大好きな東京の街を散歩して、お気に入りの風景を探しています。悩みや迷いを主題にした絵を、明るくやさしく描くように心がけています。
I am always on the search for scenes that speak to me as I walk over the city I love - Tokyo. When an illustration features distress or bewilderment, I try to draw it in a bright and affectionate way.

T：Photoshop CS5 / 透明水彩
Photoshop CS5 / Watercolors

いもに　｜　imoni

W：gggzooo4.webnode.jp　**M**：gggzooo85@gmail.com　**Tw**：@GGGZOOO　**Pi**：15276054

P：1998年8月25日生まれ。愛知県出身。『紅魔闘伝』（tryal 原案、星崎梓 原作、L-boom）のイラストなどを手がける。
Born August 25, 1998, in Aichi, Japan. Illustrations provided for *Kurenai Matoden* (story by tryal, script by Azusa Hoshizaki, produced by L-boom) and other projects.

C：作品を見ていただきありがとうございます。近年はポルトガル、クロアチア、日本などの風景を中心にさまざまなイラストを制作し、Twitterやpixivで発信しています。今後も精力的に風景イラストの制作をして参ります。
Thank you for taking time to browse my works. Lately, I've been working on a wide variety of illustrations focusing on scenery from Portugal, Croatia, Japan, and other countries, and I've been uploading these illustrations to Twitter and pixiv. I plan to continue passionately pursuing landscape illustrations.

T：MediBang Paint Pro

イリヤ・クブシノブ　｜　Ilya Kuvshinov

Instagram：kuvshinov_ilya　**M**：kuvshinovsns@gmail.com　**Tw**：@Kuvshinov_Ilya

P：ロシア出身、日本在住のイラストレーター。モスクワの美術学院でデッサンなどを学ぶ。ゲーム会社でデジタルイラスト、モーションコミックの監督として働く。2014 年からフリーランスで活動を開始。第 8 回国際漫画賞で銅賞を受賞。2016 年に画集『MOMENTARY』（パイ インターナショナル）を発売。
An illustrator from Russia, currently living in Japan. He studied drawing at Art Lyceum in Moscow. He worked at a game company, creating digital illustrations and directing animated comics. He began working freelance in 2014. He received the Bronze Award at the 8th International MANGA Award. His artwork collection book *MOMENTARY* was released in 2016 (PIE International).

C：背景を描くのはロシアに住んでいるときから好きでしたが、日本に来てからもっと好きになりました。だって、日本の風景は日本のアニメの背景にそっくりじゃないですか。笑笑　これからも魅力的なストーリーを感じられる作品をつくりたいと思います。
I enjoyed drawing background art while living in Russia, but I have come to love doing so even more since I came to Japan. I mean, the scenery of Japan is exactly like the backgrounds from anime, right? =) I want to continue creating works that feel like they are part of an interesting story.

T：Photoshop CC / CLIP STUDIO PAINT PRO

浮雲宇一　｜　uiti

W：uiti-ukumo.tumblr.com　**M**：warauyurikago@gmail.com　**Tw**：@kumori_ufo　**Pi**：15765760

P：平成二年生まれ。趣味で絵を描きつつ、時折書籍の装画等などに関わらせていただいています。
Born in 1990. While continuing to draw as a hobby, he also occasionally works as an illustrator, creating illustrations for book covers and more.

C：ファンタジックなものと美しい青年が好きです。お楽しみいただけたなら幸いです。
I enjoy drawing fanciful things and beautiful young characters. I hope you enjoy my illustrations.

T：Photoshop CS6 / SAI 2

カタヒラシュンシ　｜　Shunshi Katahira

W：katahi0829.tumblr.com　**M**：katahira.colored.pencil@gmail.com　**Tw**：@katahi_0829　**Pi**：124191

P：色鉛筆を使って絵を描いています。
Draws pictures using colored pencils.

C：文字や言葉での説明が必要ない絵を描くことを目指しています。
I aim to draw illustrations that don't require explanations through letters or words.

T：鉛筆 / 色鉛筆 / ミリペン
Pencil / Colored pencils / Drawing pen

川野　｜　kawano

W：yuroy.rdy.jp　**M**：yyuroy@gmail.com　**Pi**：16029

P：岡山県出身、在住。
Was born in and lives in Okayama, Japan.

C：のんびり好きな絵を描いていきたいと思います。
I want to draw illustrations I like on my own time, at my own pace.

T：Photoshop CC / シャープペンシル / 丸ペン
Photoshop CC / Mechanical pencil / Mapping pen

くじょう　｜　Kujoo

W：kujyoo910.tumblr.com　muyunoyuu.wixsite.com/kujyoo　**M**：muyuno_yuu@yahoo.co.jp
Tw：@kujyoo11　**Pi**：3706126

P：関東在住のイラストレーター。同人イベント等で作品を発表しつつ、書籍の装画や企業パンフレットの挿絵などを手がける。
An illustrator living in the Kanto region of Japan. Works on cover illustrations for books, drawings for corporate pamphlets, and more, while showcasing works at fan conventions and other events.

C：『美しい情景イラストレーション』に載せていただけて嬉しいです！これからも綺麗な絵を描き続けたいです。
I'm so excited that my works are featured in this book! I want to continue drawing many beautiful illustrations.

T：Photoshop CS6

げみ　｜　Gemi

W：gemi333.com　**M**：geeeeemi509@gmail.com　**Tw**：@gemi333　**Pi**：396769

P：東京都在住のフリーランスのイラストレーター。京都造形芸術大学美術工芸学科日本画コース卒業。書籍の装画を中心に、広告イラスト、アニメーションのキャラクターデザイン等も制作。著書に『げみ作品集』（玄光社）、『檸檬』（梶井基次郎・げみ 著、立東舎）・『蜜柑』（芥川龍之介・げみ 著、立東舎）、『春の旅人』（村山早紀・げみ 著、立東舎）。その他、「わたしとリプトン」（森永乳業）キャラクターデザイン、ファミリーマートのバイト募集ポスターなど。
A freelance illustrator living in Tokyo. Graduated from the Japanese Painting Course, part of the Department of Fine and Applied Arts at Kyoto University of Art & Design. Works mainly on book cover designs, in addition to advertising illustrations and character design for animations. Authored books include *Gemi Sakuhinshu* (Genkosha), *Lemon* (by Motojiro Kajii and Gemi, published by Rittorsha), *Mikan* (by Ryunosuke Akutagawa and Gemi, published by Rittorsha) and *Travelers in Spring* (by Saki Murayama and Gemi, published by Rittorsha). Also worked on character design for the *Me and Lipton* promotion (Morinaga Milk), recruitment posters for Family Mart, and more.

C：流行に左右されない作品を目指して制作しています。シーンを切り取ったような絵から幻想的な絵など、季節感や時間、天候などを感じさせる瞬間を意識しています。物語との親和性の高いイラストレーションを追求し、幅広い場所で今後も活動していきたいです。
I create illustrations aiming to make something that doesn't bend to any trends. I'm very concerned with sensing the seasons, as well as time, weather, and other moments that are experienced in magical illustrations and those that appear to be scenes taken right out of the real world. I try to create illustrations that are compatible with stories, and I'd like to continue working in an even wider scope in the future.

T：Photoshop CC

焦茶　｜　cogecha

W：cogecha.tumblr.com　**M**：mazmazcoge@gmail.com　**Tw**：@BARD713　**Pi**：12845810

P：1995 年 7 月 13 日生まれ。埼玉県出身。2016 年より活動を開始。
Born on July 13, 1995, in Saitama, Japan. Began illustrating in 2016.

C：もっと幅広く想像もつかないイラストを描いていきたいです。今後はキャラクターデザイン、書籍の装画、楽曲のジャケット、アパレルなどに展開していきたいです。
I want to create illustrations in a wider range of genres that go beyond the imagination. I hope to be able to work on character design, book cover and CD cover illustrations, clothing design, and more.

T：CLIP STUDIO PAINT

さけハラス　｜　sakeharasu

W：koba10212110.wixsite.com/sakeharasu　**M**：koba10212110@gmail.com
Tw：@hunwaritoast　**Pi**：10958370

P：京都市在住のイラストレーター。同人活動や背景画・書籍等の商業イラスト制作を行っております。
An illustrator residing in Kyoto. Works on fan works, as well as commercial illustrations, including background art and book illustrations.

C：2 次元と 3 次元の境界をどんどん曖昧にして、よりキャラクターに実在感を持たせるというテーマで創作活動を行っています。今後はシズル感のようなものが感じられる、リアリティのある背景を追求していきたいと思います。
I've come to blur the lines between 2D and 3D, creating illustrations based on the theme of giving the subjects in the illustrations a greater sense of truly existing. I want to work towards creating realistic background scenes that have a sort of sizzling feeling, as well.

T：Photoshop CC / CLIP STUDIO PAINT

456　｜　shigoro

W：makina7.com　**M**：456@makina7.com　**Tw**：@456log　**Pi**：2327032

P：1989 年生まれ。群馬県在住。「日常と非日常の間」をコンセプトに絵を描いています。主に書籍の装画、CD ジャケット、キャラクターデザインなどを手がけています。2018 年 7 月よりフリーランスとして活動中。
Born in 1989, and currently residing in Gunma, Japan. Draws pictures that conceptualize the space between the usual and the unusual. Mainly works on illustrations for book and CD case covers, character design, etc. Has worked as a freelance illustrator since July of 2018.

C：人の心をノックできるようなイラストを描きたいです。
I hope my illustrations speak to the viewer's emotions.

T：Photoshop CC / CLIP STUDIO PAINT

しまざきジョゼ　｜　Joze Shimazaki

W：hurumi.web.fc2.com　**M**：jozephine.1123@gmail.com　**Tw**：@joze_phine_　**Pi**：762663

P：東京都在住。デザインフェスタやコミティアを中心に活動。
Currently resides in Tokyo. Mainly involved with Design Festa and Comitia events.

C：デザインに馴染みやすく、かつ物語が伝わるようなイラストを目指しています。ジャンルにとらわれず、さまざまなお仕事をしたいと考えています。
I aim for illustrations with familiar designs that tell a story. I hope to be able to work on a variety of illustrations regardless of genre.

T：Photoshop CS5

杉87　｜　sugiyama

W：liewonblog.tumblr.com　**M**：lie.won.1121@gmail.com　**Tw**：@k_su_keke1121　**Pi**：1736499

P：1995 年 11 月 21 日生まれ。静岡県出身。2017 年からイラストレーターとして活動を始め、現在はゲーム会社に勤務しながら個人でも活動中。
Born November 21, 1995, in Shizuoka, Japan. Began working as an illustrator in 2017, and now continues illustrating on his own time while working at a game company.

C：作品を見ていただきありがとうございます。その場の空気や音、光などが感じられるイラストを目指しています。
Thank you for looking at my works in this book. I aim to create illustrations that allow you to sense the air, sounds, light, and more of the place in the illustration.

T：Photoshop cc / CLIP STUDIO PAINT

染平かつ　｜　KATSU SOMEHIRA

W：somehirakatsu.com　**M**：katsu.h0703@gmail.com　**Tw**：@Katsu0073　**Pi**：2745133

P：1993 年 7 月 3 日生まれ。石川県金沢市出身。
Born July 3, 1993, in Kanazawa, Ishikawa, Japan.

C：染平かつと申します。主にネットを中心に活動。普段はキャラクターデザインや背景の仕事などの他に、趣味の絵を描かせてもらっています。少し遠くて近い世界をテーマに現代から SF、ファンタジーなどの世界観の表現を目指し、今後は自分の世界観を生かせるような仕事や活動をしていければなと思っています。
My name is Katsu Somehira. I mainly work on the internet. In addition to working on character design and background art as my job, I also draw pictures as a hobby. Aiming to express a variety of world views - from modern to science fiction and fantasy - based on a world that is near yet slightly far away, I hope to be able to create art that will allow me to make use my own world views.

T：Photoshop CC / CLIP STUDIO PAINT

田中寛崇　｜　hirotaka tanaka

W：gomnaga.org　**M**：gomnaga1021@gmail.com　**Tw**：@tanakahirotaka　**Pi**：17007

P：1986 年、新潟県生まれ。多摩美術大学情報デザイン学科卒業後、フリーランスのイラストレーターとして活動。主に書籍装画、CD アートワーク、広告や web のキービジュアル等を手掛けている。
Born in 1986, in Niigata, Japan. Began work as a freelance illustrator after graduating from the Department of Information Design at Tama Art University. He mainly works on illustrations for book covers, CD artwork, visual elements in advertising and web design, and more.

C：常に新しい目標と広い視野を持ちながら、自分の絵を描いていきたいです。
I want to draw my own illustrations with new goals and an even wider point of view.

T：Photoshop CC / CLIP STUDIO PAINT PRO

たねんぼ　｜　Tanenbo

W：tanenboworks.com　**M**：tanenboworks.00@gmail.com　**Tw**：@tanenbo_00　**Pi**：15182840

P：1999 年 8 月 6 日生まれ。新潟県出身。Twitter や pixiv などの SNS への投稿を中心に活動中。
Born on August 6, 1999, in Niigata, Japan. Mainly showcases works via social media, such as Twitter and pixiv.

C：私にとってのノスタルジーは幼少期の記憶です。いつか誰かが経験したであろう何気ない一瞬を、絵にすることで忘れずにいたいという想いで制作しています。懐かしさ、切なさ、安心感など思い思いに感じていただけたら嬉しいです。
Memories from my childhood are nostalgic to me. When creating illustrations, I think about a desire to not forget casual moments that someone, somewhere experienced. I hope you can feel the nostalgia, the yearning, and the sense of security I try to portray in your own way.

T：CLIP STUDIO PAINT PRO

Tamaki

W：ta-ma-ky.tumblr.com　**M**：tamaki3390@gmail.com　**Tw**：@ta_ma_ky　**Pi**：19029917

P：主な活動経歴に『夏の王国で目覚めない』（彩坂美月 著、ハヤカワ文庫 JA）、『僕らの空は群青色』（砂川雨路 著、スターツ出版文庫）のカバーイラスト他、『ブルバスター』舞台設定イラスト、『ILLUSTRATION 2018』（翔泳社）にイラスト掲載など。
Main works include cover illustrations for *Natsu no Okoku de Mezamenai* (written by Mitsuki Ayasaka, published by Hayakawa Publishing Corporation) and *Bokura no Sora wa Gunjoiro* (written by Amemichi Sunagawa, published by Starts Publishing Bunko), stage set illustrations for *BULLBUSTER*, and illustrations published in *ILLUSTRATION 2018* (Shoeisha).

C：平凡な風景によって引きずり出される非凡な感動を共有できたらと思って描いています。
I draw trying to share uncommon emotions drawn out from common scenes.

T：Photoshop CC

丹地陽子　｜　Yoko Tanji

W：tanji.jp　**M**：yoko@tanji.jp　**Tw**：@yokotanji

P：イラストレーター。三重県出身、東京都在住。書籍の装画を中心に仕事をしています。
Illustrator. From Mie, Japan and currently living in Tokyo. Mainly works on cover illustrations for books.

C：また作品展をやりたいです。健康に気をつけて頑張ります。
I'd like to hold another exhibition. I will continue working hard while taking care of my health.

T：Photoshop CC 2018

中村ユミ　｜　yumi nakamura

W：cdown.higoyomi.com　**M**：cd.taiyou@gmail.com　**Tw**：@uky_t　**Pi**：435284

P：鳥取県出身、東京都在住。アニメーター、イラストレーター。アニメのキャラクター、小物デザイン、作画監督の他、装画、CD ジャケット、カードイラスト等を担当。現在フリーランスで活動しています。
Born in Tottori, Japan, currently residing in Tokyo. An animator and illustrator. Designs anime characters, engages in animation direction, and works on designs for small articles, book covers, CD jackets, card illustrations, and more. Currently works as a freelance illustrator.

C：限りある物の中に生まれる美しさと切なさが好きです。絵を通して、何か共感していただけたら幸いです。
I like the beauty and pain that lives inside things with limits. I hope you can relate to something in my illustrations.

T：CLIP STUDIO PAINT

夏目ヤスム　｜　yasumu Natsume

W：natsuyasum.tumblr.com　**M**：natsuyasum@gmail.com　**Tw**：@natsuyasum　**Pi**：1419399

P：7 月 20 日生まれ、長野県出身。二級建築士。会社員。大学では建築科に在籍。4 回生の夏から本格的にイラストを描き始める。「夏休み」と言う名前でのインターネット上での作品発表が主。2015 年から商業活動を始める。
Born on July 20, in Nagano, Japan. Works at a company. Registered second-class architect who studied in the architecture department at university. Began drawing major illustrations in the summer of his 4th year in university. His artist name alludes to summer vacation ("natsu yasumi" in Japanese), and he mainly exhibits his works with this name on the internet. Began illustrating in a business in 2015.

C：作品を創る上で気をつけているのは、「途中」を描くということです。完結した動きや空間ではなく、見た人が前後を想像できるようなイラストが良いなと思っています。人を描くというよりも、木や建物や動物と同じ一つのオブジェクトとして描き、空間を描くようにしています。今後は、もっと深みのある絵が描ければと思っています。綺麗なだけでなく、どこか毒のある絵。みんなが持っているトラウマを軽くこすれるような絵が描きたいです。
I pay close attention to drawing the "in-between" while creating illustrations. Rather than drawing completed movements or spaces, I like the kinds of illustrations that allow you to imagine what was going on in the illustration before and what will happen after. When drawing people, I don't consider them people, but instead draw them as objects, such as trees, buildings, or animals, and I draw them as a part of the space. I hope to be able to draw illustrations with more depth to them. Not just beautiful scenes, but illustrations with something poisonous in them somewhere. I want to draw illustrations that lightly draw out the trauma that we all carry around with us.

T：Photoshop CS6 / シャープペンシル / A4 コピー用紙
Photoshop CS6 / Mechanical pencil / A4 size white paper

HAI

W：aorkgk.tumblr.com　　**M**：aorkgk@gmail.com　　**Tw**：@aorkgk

P：1992 年生まれ、新潟県在住。
Born in 1992, currently residing in Niigata, Japan.

C：はじめまして、イラストを見ていただきありがとうございます。ちょっぴり懐かしい雰囲気に女の子のほんのりとした色を出せたらと、好きに自由に絵を描いてます。描いた絵が見てくださった人の心に少しでも寄り添うことができましたら幸いです。
Hello, and thanks for looking at my illustrations. I draw what I like freely, hoping to show faint feminine colors in a slightly nostalgic environment. I hope that my illustrations can touch the hearts of those who view them, even if only a little.

T：CLIP STUDIO PAINT

前田ミック　｜　Mic Maeda

W：maeda-mic.tumblr.com　　**M**：m.mic.0707@gmail.com　　**Tw**：@m_mic_0707　　**Pi**：12395539

P：1990 年生まれ、埼玉県在住。大学卒業後、短い会社員生活を経て、現在は家事育児中心の生活を送りながらオリジナルイラストの制作を行っています。
Born in 1990, and currently residing in Saitama, Japan. After graduating university, she had a brief stint working in a company. She currently stays at home to care for her children, creating original illustrations while living a life of love.

C：作品を見ていただき、ありがとうございます。近未来が感じられる日常風景と女の子を描くことを得意としています。特に光や空気の表現、何となく感じる雰囲気を大事に制作しています。目に見えるものだけでなく、そこから醸し出される何かを見てくださる方それぞれに感じてもらえたら嬉しいです。今後は独自の表現を追求しながら、幅広く活動していきたいです。
Thank you for looking over my works. I'm good at drawing common scenery and girls that give a sense of the near future. I especially take great care in expressing light and air and in creating a vibe that causes an emotional reaction. I hope that each person that sees my illustrations will see not only what is physically in front of them, but also will feel a unique emotion that arises from the illustrations. I hope to continue drawing a wide variety of illustrations while continuing to search for my own unique ways of expression.

T：CLIP STUDIO PAINT

Merrill Macnaut

W：merrillmacnaut.wixsite.com/in-the-cornfield　　**M**：merrillmacnaut.job@gmail.com
Tw：@k_i0624　　**Pi**：856869

P：宮城県出身。武蔵野美術大学映像学科卒業後、アニメーションスタジオにて美術制作に従事。映像的思考から生み出される作品はどこか懐かしさを感じさせる神秘的な世界観、リアリティとドラマ性を重視した画面設計など、一枚のイラストの中に背景の物語までをも描く。
Born in Miyagi, Japan. After graduating from the Department of Imaging Arts and Sciences at Musashino Art University, Macnaut began working on art production at an animation studio. The artist's works, created in a cinematic way, each have their own background story, with a mysterious world view that inspires nostalgia, layouts that juxtapose reality with drama, and more.

C：絵を描くときはいつも、「ずっと続いてきた誰かの人生のある一瞬を抜き出す」ようなつもりでモチーフや構図を決めています。映画でいうところのスチール写真に近い感覚かもしれません。ここで何が起こっているのだろうという物語性と、絵としての美しさを兼ね備えた景色を、これからは人物にもっとフォーカスを当てて描きたいと思っています。
When drawing, I always decide on the motifs or structure by thinking about how each illustration is just one moment that keeps going from the life of someone. Perhaps it is somewhat similar to a still shot from a movie. I want to draw scenery that combines the beauty of the illustration itself with a story of what might be going on in the scene, and I also want to draw with even more attention given to the human subjects in my illustrations.

T：Photoshop CS6

mocha

W：mocha708.wixsite.com/mocha708　　**M**：mocha708@gmail.com　　**Tw**：@mocha708　　**Pi**：648285

P：背景担当代表作『Re:LieF 〜親愛なるあなたへ〜』（RASK）、『祝姫』（DMM GAMES）など。多数の TV アニメ、劇場アニメ作品に背景スタッフとして参加している他、文庫の装画、CD ジャケット用イラストなどを手がける。
Created the background art for *Re:LieF – Shinainaru Anata e –* (RASK), *Iwaihime* (DMM GAMES), and more. In addition to working as background art staff for various TV and cinematic anime productions, the artist also creates illustrations for book and CD case covers.

C：はじめまして。mocha と申します。私は普段、背景をメインに描いて活動しています。背景メインに絵を描いていますが、今後はキャラクターにも力を入れて一枚絵の完成度を上げていきたいと思っております。
Hello, I'm mocha. I mainly draw backgrounds. While I mainly work on backgrounds, I would like to spend some time drawing characters, allowing me to create a more complete illustration.

T：Photoshop CC

吉田誠治　｜　YOSHIDA Seiji

W：yoshidaseiji.jp　　**M**：ys@yoshidaseiji.jp　　**Tw**：@yoshida_seiji

P：背景グラフィッカー、イラストレーター。美少女ゲームメーカー勤務を経て 2003 年からフリーランスで活動を開始。『サクラノ詩』（枕）、『素晴らしき日々〜不連続存在〜』（ケロ Q）、『神学校 -Noli me tangere-』（PIL/SLASH）、『仏蘭西少女』（PIL）、『夏めろ』（AcaciaSoft）などの背景を担当。他の仕事に、『美しい情景イラストレーション　魅力的な風景を描くクリエイターズファイル』（パイ インターナショナル）装画、『コルヌトピア』（津久井 五月 著、早川書房）装画など。
Background graphic artist and illustrator. After working for a game company specializing in games that feature young girls, he began working as a freelance illustrator in 2003. Main background art includes *Sakura no Uta* (Makura), *Subarashiki Hibi – Furenzoku Sonzai –* (KEROQ), *Shingakko – Noli me tangere-* (PIL/SLASH), *Furansu Shojo: Une fille blanche* (PIL), *Natsu Mero* (summer melody) (AcaciaSoft), etc. He also created the cover art for *Everyday Scenes from a Parallel World: Background Illustrations and Scenes from Anime and Manga Works* (published by PIE International), *Cornutopia* (written by Itsuki Tsukui, published by Hayakawa Publishing Corporation), and more.

C：「訪れてみたくなる風景」をコンセプトに背景やイラストを制作しています。あまり難しく考えず、多くの方に楽しんでいただけるような絵を描いていきたいです。
I create background art and illustrations so that the viewer will want to go and visit the location in the illustration. I like to draw illustrations that many people can enjoy without having to think too hard.

T：Photoshop CS5

米山 舞　｜　MAI YONEYAMA

W：yoneyamai.work　　**M**：yoneyamai@hotmail.co.jp　　**Tw**：@yonema　　**Pi**：1554775

P：1988 年長野県生まれ、イラストレーター、アニメーター。主な経歴は「レーシングミク」（グッドスマイルカンパニー）2016ver. イラスト、TV アニメ『ダーリン・イン・ザ・フランキス』、『キルラキル』作画監督、『キズナイーバー』キャラクターデザインなど。
An illustrator and animator born in Nagano Prefecture in 1988. Main works include illustrations for the 2016 version of Good Smile Company's *Racing Miku* products, animation direction for *DARLING in the FRANXX* and *KILL la KILL* (anime for television), and character design for *Kiznaiver*.

C：人物の表情や心情を表す絵を得意としています。近年はイラストの仕事がメインで、キャラクターイラストやデザインをしています。それらで得た技術や表現をアニメーションや色々なジャンルに生かせればと思っています。
I'm good at creating illustrations that show human feelings, emotions, and the expression of those feelings and emotions. Lately, I've been doing a lot of illustrations, mainly working on character illustrations and designs. I hope to be able to use the techniques and expressions from this work and apply it to animation and a variety of other genres.

T：Photoshop CS5 / CLIP STUDIO PAINT

loundraw

W：loundrawblr.tumblr.com   **M**：loundraw.job@gmail.com   **Tw**：@loundraw   **Pi**：772547

P： イラストレーターとして 10 代のうちに商業デビュー。透明感、空気感のある色彩と、被写界深度を用いた緻密な空間設計を魅力とし、さまざまな作品の装画を担当する。声優・下野紘、雨宮天らが参加した卒業制作オリジナルアニメーション『夢が覚めるまで』では、監督・脚本・演出・レイアウト・原画・動画と制作のすべてを手がけた他、小説『イミテーションと極彩色のグレー』、漫画『あおぞらとくもりぞら』の執筆、アーティスト集団・CHRONICLE での音楽活動など、その活動は多岐にわたる。2017 年 9 月に自身初の個展『夜明けより前の君へ』を開催。
Debuted as a commercial illustrator while in his teens. He considers detailed spatial design that uses transparency, airy colors, and depth of field to be enticing, and he creates a wide variety of book cover illustrations. In addition to directing, producing, and creating the script, layout, illustrations, and animations for *Yume ga Sameru Made* (his thesis art project in university, an anime which also features voice actors Sora Amamiya and Hiro Shimono), he also has created a wide variety of works, including writing a novel entitled *Illumination to Gokusaishiki no Grey* and a graphic novel entitled *Aozora to Kumorizora*, musical activities for a group of artists called CHRONICLE, and more. In September of 2017, he held his first exhibition, entitled *Yoake yori Mae no Kimi e.*

C： イラストレーションを軸として、それに紐づくお仕事も幅広くさせていただいております。その中で得られたことをまたイラストに還元するように、常に皆さんを楽しませられるような作品作りに努めてゆきます。今後は他の方々の力をお借りしながら、より遠くまで届くものを作ることができればと考えています。
I mainly work on illustrations while also working in a wide variety of fields that are related to illustrating. What I draw from the other fields, I then put back into my illustrations, and in this way, I try to create works that will bring more and more enjoyment to those who view my work. I hope to be able to create something that can reach even more people by working together with others.

T： Photoshop CC / CLIP STUDIO PAINT EX / SAI / After Effect CS6

LAL!ROLE

M： lalirole@gmail.com   **Tw**：@Laxxxli   **Pi**：10537869

P： 1996 年生まれ、東京在住のイラストレーター。左手に甘いもの、右手にペンを握りしめて一生懸命奮闘中。ソーシャルゲームのイラストをメインに、トレーディングカードゲームのイラストや書籍のカバーイラストなどを手がけている。
Illustrator born in 1996, currently residing in Tokyo. Works intensely with something sweet in one hand and a pen in the other. Mainly works on illustrations for social games, but also works on illustrations for trading card games, book covers, etc.

C： 自分の描いた絵が見ていただいた方の心に 1 秒でも長く寄り添えればとっても幸せです！ 寝ながら描けるようになるのが夢です。
I hope that my illustrations touch the viewer's heart, even for just one second! My dream is to be able to draw while lying down and sleeping.

T： Photoshop CC

れ お え ん ｜ reoenl.

W： reoenl.com   **M**： reoenl@gmail.com   **Tw**：@reoenl   **Pi**：3927625

P： 1996 年生まれ、千葉県在住。ゲームが好きです。
Born in 1996, in Chiba, Japan. Likes video games.

C： 薄暗い世界観だけれど、光だけは満ち満ちている絵が好きです。誰かがひどい目に遭っていても、ボロボロの街で暮らしていても、ラスボスとの最終決戦を繰り広げていても、陽の光がそれを明るく照らす瞬間が実はあって、そういう一瞬に尊さを感じているのだと思います。
I like pictures that are full of light, despite the subdued atmosphere. Even if you are having a hard time, even if you live in a run-down town, or even when the final battle with the final boss unfolds before you, there are still moments where sunlight manages to shine brightly, and I think I feel a sense of respect for the light in those moments.

T： Photoshop CC / CLIP STUDIO PAINT

美しい情景イラストレーション
ノスタルジー編
情緒的な風景を描くクリエイターズファイル

Retrospective Scenes from a Sentimental World:
Background Illustrations and Scenes by an Up-and-Coming Creators

2018 年 11 月 15 日　初版第 1 刷発行
2020 年 12 月 10 日　　　第 2 刷発行

編著
パイ インターナショナル

カバーイラスト
げみ

装丁・本文デザイン
杉山峻輔

翻訳
Christian Traylor
ブレインウッズ株式会社

編集
杵淵恵子

協力
ETOPICA
エムディエヌコーポレーション
oldflame
学研プラス
KADOKAWA
角川文庫
河出書房新社
吉祥寺ココマルシアター
月刊ニュータイプ
光文社文庫
新潮社
徳間書店
中川祥治
Victor Entertainment
双葉社

発行人
三芳寛要

発行元
株式会社 パイ インターナショナル
〒170-0005
東京都豊島区南大塚 2-32-4
TEL 03-3944-3981
FAX 03-5395-4830
sales@pie.co.jp

印刷・製本
株式会社 廣済堂

© 2018 PIE International
ISBN978-4-7562-5126-8 C0076
Printed in Japan

Retrospective Scenes from a Sentimental World

Background Illustrations and Scenes by an Up-and-Coming Creators